SO-AZH-636

ODYSSEY

Also by Neil McAleer

THE COSMIC MIND-BOGGLING BOOK
THE BODY ALMANAC
EARTHLOVE: A SPACE FANTASY
FREEDOM STATION: A NEW WORLD IN SPACE
THE MIND-BOGGLING UNIVERSE
THE OMNI SPACE ALMANAC

ODYSSEY:

THE AUTHORISED
BIOGRAPHY OF
ARTHUR C. CLARKE

NEIL McALEER

LONDON
VICTOR GOLLANCZ LTD
1992

To Fred
for his faith,
encouragement, and friendship

First published in Great Britain 1992
by Victor Gollancz Ltd
14 Henrietta Street, London WC2E 8QJ

Copyright © Neil McAleer 1992
Foreword © Patrick Moore 1992

The right of Neil McAleer to be identified as author of
this work has been asserted by him in accordance with the
Copyright, Designs and Patents Act, 1988.

A catalogue record for this book is available
from the British Library

ISBN 0 575 05448 4

Photoset in Great Britain by
Rowland Phototypesetting Ltd, Bury St Edmunds, Suffolk
and printed in Great Britain by
Mackays of Chatham plc, Chatham, Kent

Contents

Acknowledgements

So many people helped along the way that I must first – right now – thank them all. Their names, thoughts, memories, knowledge – often their unique *voices* – are found on these pages and articulate the reason for my gratitude in concrete and real ways.

About two hundred people were interviewed during the research for this biography. Many more gave me other important resources and information. Rather than print a long list of names, I've decided to be selective and give credit to four groups: first, those who gave outstanding interviews; second, those who gave helpful and often rare print resources; third, those who provided photos and other visual resources; and fourth, those who contributed their fresh eyes and skills to this book during the publishing process.

Special thanks to the following people for enlightening, lively, informative, or otherwise unique interviews: Brian Aldiss, Isaac Asimov, Ian and Betty Ballantine, Gregory Benford, Willie Blake, Robert Bloch, Russell Bowie, Ray Bradbury, John Brunner, Roger Caras, Arthur Clarke, Fred Clarke, Michael Clarke, John Clarke, Walter Cronkite, Lester del Rey, Hugh Downs, Daniel Drachman, Olga Druce, Fred Durant, David Fowke, Bert Fowler, Tony Frewin, Leonard Hobbs, Peter Hyams, Dick Jenvey, Dot Jones, Steven Jongeward, Kathy Keeton, David Kennard, Dick Kriegel, David Kyle, Gentry Lee, Lloyd Lewan, Lee Lubbers, Ian Macauley, Marjorie May, Marilyn Mayfield, Scott Meredith, Harry Morrin, Sam Moskowitz, Julian Muller, Kerry O'Quinn, Fred Ordway, Tom Paine, Joseph Pelton, John Pierce, Bobby Pleass, Fred Pohl, Jerry Pournelle, Eric Rabkin, Gene Roddenberry, Carl Sagan, Ken Slater, Harry Stine, Eric Taylor, Joan Temple, Pat Weaver, and Sam Youd.

For various and essential print materials, special thanks to: Ian and Betty Ballantine, Roger Caras, Arthur Clarke, Fred Clarke, Val Cleaver, Brenda Corbin, Michael Craven, Fred and Pip Durant, Lloyd Eshbach, Rodney Jonklaas, Laura Kapnick, Barry King, David and Ruth Kyle, Ian Macauley, Mary Clarke Maclean, Bill MacQuitty, Scott Meredith Literary Agency, Kerry O'Quinn, John Pierce, Harold Rosen, David Samuelson, Bill Temple, and Sam Youd.

For photos, videos, and other visual resources, special thanks to: Joel Banow, Willie Blake, the British Interplanetary Society, Arthur Clarke, Fred Clarke, Michael Craven, David Doubilet, Fred Durant, Doug Faulkner, Dean Grennell, Kathy Keeton, Robert Knecht, *OMNI* magazine, Fred Ordway, Smithsonian Institution, and Frank Winter.

There have been several supportive and skilful people who also deserve my gratitude: Fred Durant, who helped get this project started; the Scott Meredith Literary Agency, especially Scott Meredith, Joshua Bilmes, and Russ Galen for their efforts on behalf of this biography over a five-year period; Tom Erickson for his assistance in printing out the thick first draft; and Anne Sweeny-Smith, Victoria Petrie-Hay, and Richard Evans for their fresh eyes, editorial expertise, and co-ordination efforts.

Finally, two special people I cannot thank enough: my wife, Connie, who cheerfully shared two lives during this period; and Fred Clarke, keeper of the Clarkives, who was always there and always a great help – a true brother to me in this effort.

Foreword

by Patrick Moore

Mention the name of Arthur C. Clarke and what comes instinctively to mind? One of two things, probably: the first idea of the communications satellites which have become so vital in the modern world, or the classic film *2001: A Space Odyssey*. The first of these shows Arthur in his role as a scientific prophet, the second in his alternative guise of a scientific prophet plus fiction writer.

In fact, Arthur is in many ways unique. He is an excellent scientist in his own right, and equally skilled as a writer, but he has been able to do more than combine the two; he has blended them together, true, but has also added something extra which marks him out from everybody else.

He has had a varied career. During the war he served with the Royal Air Force with distinction (and in this book I read wryly about his involvement with FIDO; I once brought an aircraft in in that way, and it is not something I would want to do very often, to put it mildly). It was soon after this that he made his classic contribution to *Wireless World*, which will never be forgotten, and also began that series of remarkable books which took us not only to the Moon and the boundaries of the Solar System, but further out in both space and dimension. I suppose that everyone has his (or her) 'favourite Clarke'. Dare I give my own? It is, I admit, *The Sands of Mars*, but I know quite well that Arthur has written books of much greater importance than that; I am bound to be prejudiced, as an astronomer with a special interest in the Red Planet!

Many of his predictions have come true, though when he made some of them, in his earlier days as a writer, they were regarded as far-fetched. I venture to suggest that many of his later predictions will prove to be equally close to the mark, even though we may not know for several decades yet – in which case neither Arthur nor I can hope to be around to judge. But I believe that anyone of the year, say, 2080 who reads Neil McAleer's biography will realise the wisdom of what Arthur proclaimed.

It is significant, too, that his work has had a great influence not only upon 'the general public', but also upon officialdom and even upon Governments. He has received many honours and will receive more in the years to come – and he richly deserves them, because his contribution to human progress has been so great.

I have spent many hours with him over the past half-century or so, and I have been privileged to broadcast with him, both on 'steam radio' and on television. He is above all fluent, but you always know that when he begins a sentence he has something worthwhile to say. Some may disagree with him, but nobody can suggest that he is not talking eminently sound sense.

This is Arthur's first biography, and Neil McAleer has performed his task splendidly. He has given us an accurate, readable and enthralling account of Arthur's career, and he has carried out a tremendous amount of research. Many of the other great characters of the Space Age are here, ranging from Wernher von Braun, Willy Ley and Hermann Oberth, to Neil Armstrong and Yuri Gagarin; all these have been anxious to pay tribute to him as one who has been an inspiration. I can speak with authority here, because I too know (or knew) them – though in most cases probably not as well as Arthur did. And all the way through Arthur Clarke's personality shines through; though he has never himself ventured into space, and though he has made no major scientific discovery, he will be remembered with respect and with great affection long after most of his contemporaries have been forgotten.

I am honoured to have been asked to join in this tribute to one of my most valued and long-standing friends.

Patrick Moore
June 1992

Preface

This is the first biography of Arthur C. Clarke – one of the great visionaries of the twentieth century and a man who has every expectation of celebrating the arrival of the new millennium and the twenty-first century on 1 January 2001.

After seventy-five orbits around the sun, Clarke continues to be an active and productive global resource, always involved in a dozen or more projects and championing worthwhile causes for the good of our global family. The benefit of Clarke's co-operation with his life story, and the access to interviews, letters, and other documents it afforded, far outweighs any influence his co-operation might imply or exert.

So what does 'authorised' mean with respect to this biography? The truth is that nothing was ever said to be off limits by anyone who contributed information and memories to this work. It is also true that this writer never probed too deeply into Clarke's private affairs. I no more wanted to describe intimate details of a living man's private life (assuming the information was available) than he or his contemporaries wanted to read about them. If this is the compromise of an 'authorised' life, so be it. All of us alive know about life's compromises. A written life is no exception.

Certainly this is a better book because of the co-operation of many people, including Clarke. I can't therefore uphold the humorously cynical view of one British biographer, Humphrey Carpenter, who has written '[W]hile the authorised biographer generally Knows Everything, the authorised biography usually reads like a report in Pravda.' Well, not this one.

After several requests for some stories and memories for this work, Stanley Kubrick told me that 'Arthur is not an anecdotable character.' This, as far as it goes, may be true, but people's different perspectives on the same person are often enlightening and help to form a more objective reality. If readers also sometimes hear the unique voices of the people interviewed as they read their spoken words, then this will be the ultimate compliment to all of us.

Almost a year after beginning this work, and at least fifteen hours of in-person and primarily telephone interviews with Clarke, as well as nine feet of print resources and dozens of taped interviews with others, this writer sensed that he was in danger of becoming a captive to his own research. Because of this ever-present and menacing information overwhelm, I did not despair when Clarke first mentioned his personal 'journals in their little iron box', an entirely different set from his daily working journals that have been so helpful in the research.

'I have about thirty volumes, beginning on 4 December 1938,' Clarke told me. 'Right up to now. It's the best part of four or five million words, I imagine. Minute detail. There's no way I'm going to do anything about them. And no one looks at them until fifty years after my death.'

After Clarke read a few jottings to me about his famous 1945 article, 'Extra-Terrestrial Relays', his personal journals went back into their little iron box to await the future.

Thinking of those four to five million words that probably will remain locked up until some time beyond 2050, let me now wish good luck to all the future biographers of Arthur C. Clarke.

'From the great deep to the great
deep he goes.'

'Come, my friends,
'Tis not too late to seek a newer world.
Push off, and sitting well in order smite
The sounding furrows; for my purpose holds
To sail beyond the sunset, and the baths
Of all the western stars, until I die.'

Tennyson

CHAPTER 1

New Moon over Somerset

For when the story of our age comes to be
told, we will be remembered as the first of
all men to put their sign among the stars.
                    – *The Making of a Moon*

The stars were bright over Somerset in 1917. In France, however, the skies were filled with the flares and artillery shells of World War I, and it was here that Charles Wright Clarke was fighting when his first son, Arthur, was born in Minehead on the coast of the Bristol Channel. His birth date, under a waxing new Moon, was 16 December.

Few 'space cadets' were born in the first decades of the twentieth century. They were a rare breed then, long before the deluge of cosmic images in film and television began to permeate our collective consciousness after World War II. But Arthur Charles Clarke was one of the early few who would point to the Moon and stars and show a great many of us – future astronauts, engineers, scientists and enthusiastic youth everywhere – the way. As he has described his vision of the future over the past seven decades in both his non-fiction and fiction work, he has also entertained and educated us with his imaginative cosmic plots and unique view of planet Earth.

Why has Arthur C. Clarke become one of the twentieth century's most influential writers and visionaries of the future? The answer lies in the full and purposeful life he has lived. Ever since boyhood, he has been driven by a passionate enthusiasm and energy for exploring the universe around him – its celestial and terrestrial wonders, and humankind's unending stream of ideas, desires and imaginings.

Clarke has never stopped searching – for new questions and possibilities as well as answers – for what the near and distant future holds for humanity. His imaginative extrapolations of science and technology have created many possible futures, most of them positive, that have reached millions of readers.

This quest constantly delights him. He derives great natural pleasure from what he does and who he is, and this quality comes through in his writing. All his work – books, articles, lectures, media appearances, TV series, films – is accented with a touch of personal enthusiasm, which has been an important element in attracting a global audience. An enthusiasm, optimism, and prescience about the future – rare characteristics in his chosen genre during the century of two world wars – have set Arthur Clarke worlds apart.

Minehead was a good place for an explorer to begin his life. It is located near Bristol, one of the world's great ports from which a long history of maritime adventure and commerce has been witnessed. The north coast of Somerset offers vistas of the Atlantic Ocean, which created the illusion of infinite space, and there was the regular excitement of ships leaving port and beginning voyages to distant lands.

From Minehead a person could set course and journey anywhere, and that's what Arthur C. Clarke eventually did. His birthplace provided a convenient mooring from which to cast off and see not just the world but other worlds as well: the Moon, the planets, the stars, the galaxies – and *Homo sapiens'* future adventures among them. Arthur Clarke's childhood shore helped provide him with the cosmic view of planet Earth and its place in space and time, a perspective which dominates his work and his philosophy to this day.

Mary Nora Clarke (née Willis) gave birth to her son on the morning of 16 December 1917 in her mother's house at 4 Blenheim Road, Minehead. (The address was later changed to 13 Blenheim Road because the road was extended.)

'Mother decided that her grandchild must be born at her home and told me I must arrange to come to her,' Nora wrote in her privately printed memoir in the late 1970s. 'Arthur arrived early one [Sunday] morning and mother was in seventh heaven with a lovely little grandson to cuddle.'

Minehead and the stone Victorian house in Blenheim Road, known as 'Sunnyside', remained Arthur's home for the first few years of his life. He attended kindergarten in nearby Irnham Road and later his first infant school, Llanberis School, in Blenheim Road.

After World War I ended and Charles Wright Clarke was discharged, he bought the family's first farm. Called Beetham, it was near Chard in Somerset.

Charles Clarke was the eldest son of Thomas Clarke, postmaster of the village of Bishops Lydeard. Charles had grown up around the post office his father had built; indeed, that is how he came to meet Nora Willis, whom he married on 29 July 1915. Nora had worked at various Somerset post offices, including those at Minehead, Porlock and Bishops Lydeard. After training, young Charlie had worked in the Taunton Post Office before serving in the War as a lieutenant in His Majesty's Royal Engineers.

Although his post office position had been reserved for him while he was serving in France, Charles Clarke decided against going back to it. Like many other returning soldiers, he could not settle for confining office work after the stress and action of the war. He had been injured and suffered lung damage; he wanted the outdoor life and decided to become a farmer, even though he had no experience. Nora urged caution as he searched for a farm to buy. It wasn't long before he and a partner went ahead and signed a contract for a farm. The quick decision did not include Nora – or common sense.

'The seller had used the old trick, seeing he had a pair of suckers to deal with,' Nora later wrote. If they didn't make a quick decision, the seller told them, the property would go to another interested party. The ploy worked. The two veterans signed on the dotted line.

While Nora had no great expectations, the farm was much worse than she had imagined. 'The price was far too high and the house in a bad state. There was little water on the farm and in dry spells it had to be hauled for miles.' To make matters worse, neither Charles nor his partner had enough money for the purchase and the banks declined to help. Nora had to lend the only money she had, a sum she had inherited at the age of three when her father had died. Her husband's partner, a man by the name of Donald, also had to borrow money from relatives.

The farm turned out to be a disaster. The postwar slump was beginning. Some of the twenty cows bought with the farm soon had to be sold to pay expenses. There was a bit of joy, however, during this difficult time: the birth of Frederick William Clarke on 7 April 1921. Nora travelled back to her mother's house in Minehead for the birth. The Clarkes now had two sons.

Finally, in the early 1920s, the Beetham farm had to be sold at a loss; Charles and Nora were without a home and without a job. Despite their predicament, Nora was thankful that they had at least avoided bankruptcy.

The Clarkes were not down on their luck for long. Nora heard of a suitable farm from her mother-in-law, Elizabeth Mary Clarke, the postmistress at Bishops Lydeard. 'The name was Ballifants, and I knew nothing of it,' recalled Nora, 'for it was away from all roads.'

It came from the breakup in 1913 of the Lethbridge family estate known as the Sandhill Park Estate. Much of the land became the villages of Ash Priors, Bishops Lydeard and Combe Florey, and the fields were parcelled into lots. The fields and their buildings became the so-called smallholdings which were offered to veterans and their families.

Ballifants was one such smallholding. It consisted of a five-hundred-year-old turreted farmhouse built of Somerset sandstone, as well as cow sheds, barns, an apple orchard, a pond, two grass fields in front of the farmhouse, a large arable field for crops behind it and two adjoining fields a mile away that could be reached via a winding road.

Charles and Nora applied at once. To strengthen their position, they also asked and received the support of Sir Dennis Bowles, MP, of Watts House, Bishops Lydeard. Good luck was with them and the property became theirs. The family moved to Ballifants in 1924, the same year that Hermann Oberth's classic, *The Rocket into Interplanetary Space*, was published in Germany.

The farm was inland, but the coast always beckoned and Arthur spent some of his early years at his grandmother's house under the care of his Aunt Nellie. As his mother got better control of running the farm and making a living at it, Arthur and his younger brother Fred lived at Ballifants, but spent school holidays and weekends in Minehead. His birthplace remained his second home while he was growing up.

The beach, no more than a quarter of a mile away from his grandmother's house, became Arthur's favourite haunt. There he built battlements of sand and explored the tidewater pools among the rocks.

'I was always digging trenches and moats, then breaching them and letting the water flow in. When the tide came in, of course, the whole lot would go.' Even today Clarke admits that the only place he ever feels completely relaxed is by the edge of the sea, 'or better still, hovering weightless beneath it, over the populous and polychromatic landscape of my favourite reef.' And while his active scuba-diving days are now over, Arthur still loves to swim. His home in Colombo, Sri Lanka, is on the Indian Ocean.

The Somerset coast was Arthur's dream beach where his body and imagination played, creating ideas for his future work and prophetic visions of what life would be like – on and off the planet.

The short story, 'Transience', written in the late 1940s and first published in *Startling Stories*, drew many of its descriptive scenes from his boyhood memories. 'Underfoot, the sand was coarse and mixed with myriads of broken shells. Here and there the retreating tide had left long streamers of weed trailed across the beach . . .' The story describes the same beach at three different times in geological history, each through the eyes of a child playing there. The beach and coastline in the story change over millions of years.

'Beyond the sea wall and the promenade, the little town was sleeping through the golden summer day. Here and there along the beach, people lay at rest, drowsy with heat and lulled by the murmur of the waves.'

This second beach is no doubt Arthur's childhood shore. Finally, in the last far-future scene, planet Earth is abandoned as the solar system encounters an immense Dark Nebula that will eventually make the planet uninhabitable. On that distant future beach the boy is alone, guarded by a machine, 'but he was a solitary child and did not greatly care. Lost in his own dreams, he was content to be left alone.' These few words describing the boy named Bran also tell us more about Arthur C. Clarke than many of his interviews.

'Transience' also has the added distinction of being the only Clarke short story to be set to music. David Bedford, the British composer, created the piece, and the late Sir Peter Pears, who commissioned the work, sang it.

Arthur Clarke's landlocked school days may have been less influential than his return visits to the coast and the variety of experiences he had there, including time spent with his Minehead neighbours, the Kille family, who lived 'about three doors along at the end of the road'.

Mr and Mrs Kille had three sons and a daughter, Nellie Kille, who married a man by the name of Arthur Cornish. 'He was an archaeologist and a very nice guy who definitely influenced my scientific interest. He gave me quite a lot of stuff, including fossils and a mammoth's tooth.' Fossils became Arthur's earliest hobby before he began building his own telescopes when he was in his teens.

One of the sons, Larry Kille, read science fiction magazines and provided Arthur with his first glance at the kind of publication which would captivate and exert such a tremendous influence on him a few years later. Larry Kille was the first of thousands of science fiction fans whom Arthur would encounter over the next seven decades.

The first science fiction magazine Arthur ever saw was the November 1928 issue of *Amazing Stories* at Larry Kille's house. He was eleven years old at the time and was visiting his grandmother in Minehead during one of his school holidays. The cover, painted by space artist Frank R. Paul, depicted the giant planet Jupiter dominating the sky of one of its moons, with a tropical moonscape and a cylindrical-shaped spaceship in the foreground. From the spaceship earthlings disembarked.

Larry Kille's grandmother, known to everyone as 'Old' Mrs Kille, left an even stronger impression on young Arthur. Clarke remembers a small room in the Kille house which was filled with the most advanced knitting machines of the day. With foot power alone, she produced yards of stockings and sweaters. Sometimes Arthur was allowed to provide the pedal power.

'I can still hear the clicking of the hundreds of needles and the whirr of the well-oiled gearwheels,' recalls Arthur. 'My own interest in science owes much to the fascinating hardware that Mrs Kille operated with effortless skill.' She also loaned books to the youngster and stimulated his curiosity and imagination in other ways. One such book was Ignatius Donnelly's *Atlantis: The Antediluvian World*, which Arthur naively accepted as truth when he first read it.

The Kille family helped to expand the boy's horizons beyond provincial Minehead; he was already beginning to form the global and cosmic perspectives that are consistently found throughout his work.

In the early 1930s, when Arthur was about fourteen, his second home in Minehead was put on the market. The move was a short distance away, 'only about four hundred yards', brother Fred Clarke recalls, to another house up the road on North Hill. It was named Woodcote. Arthur improved the grounds by planting an acorn which became a tree.

Though Arthur was not yet seven years old when his parents moved to Ballifants, he vividly recalls riding with his father on the pony trap. On the common of Bishops Lydeard, Charles Clarke handed his son a series of picture cards depicting prehistoric animals. The cards came from the packets of cigarettes he'd just purchased. Says Arthur, 'The first card I examined had a picture of a weird beast on it – a stegosaur.'

This casual gift became an instant treasure and created one of the lasting memories Arthur has of his father, who died six years later. The picture on the card evoked an interest in palaeontology, and Arthur began collecting fossils.

Maud Hanks, Arthur's schoolmistress at Bishops Lydeard Elementary, encouraged his natural storytelling abilities. And the dinosaur cards, which Arthur had begun collecting after his father had started him off, were used as visual aids to help illustrate the tales of giant creatures he told to his classmates.

In about 1927 Arthur took to the air and experienced his first flight. One day, probably in the summer before his tenth birthday, his mother took him flying in an aircraft owned by the Cornwall Aviation Co. Ltd. of St Austell. It was a British Avro 504 biplane, with its cross-wired wings and three-axis control. The passengers strapped themselves in with leather lap-belts, and they heard the high-pitched singing of cross-wired wing rigging at times during the flight.

'It was a very famous type, with a skid under the two bicycle-type wheels,' says Arthur. 'Mum was sitting behind me, and the lady in front of me looked a bit like Aunt Floss, but she was a stranger.'

From then on Arthur was hooked; he's been flying around the planet ever since.

Before World War I, Charles Wright Clarke had worked as a post office engineer – the early equivalent to today's telecommunications engineer. 'He was concerned with telephone and telegraph circuits,' says Arthur. 'Compared to what it is now, it was very simple in those days.'

There was no telephone when the family moved to Ballifants in the mid-twenties and it would be a few more years, around 1930, before a service arrived at the Clarke farm. (Electricity would have to wait until after World War II.)

'My father got the contract for putting up the poles to take the telephone to us, which paid for the phone for quite a few years,' says Arthur. 'And he had to install quite a few telephone poles to get there.'

Because the history of communications is so relevant to the career of Arthur C. Clarke, it is not surprising that several family members, including Arthur, worked for the post office at one time or another. 'We were all,' he says, 'a post office family.' His mother, Nora, had worked as a telegraphist and her mother-in-law, Elizabeth Mary, was postmistress of Bishops Lydeard. Nora learned Morse code from her and accumulated some valuable experience on the two common telegraphic instruments: the single needle and the so-called sounder which superseded it. Ernest Clarke, Arthur's paternal uncle, was a post office telegraphist, and for many years his paternal Aunt Zebah was the postmistress at Bishops Lydeard. She married a Grimstone who also had a career as an electrical engineer, although he too helped out around the post office. So while the telephone may have come late to the Clarke farm, the post never did.

Arthur remembers his first experience with global communication when he worked at the Bishops Lydeard post office in his teens.

'I was night operator for quite a long time at Bishops Lydeard, and one night there was a call from New York – an international call. It was very rare in those days. The call came by radio, of course; it was long before there was any telephonic cable. Apparently I was listening in on the call. The operator in Taunton must have detected me, and told me to unplug. I was probably weakening the signal.'

Communications – post, telegraph or telephone – was a common career speciality for the Clarkes, but no one (with the possible exception of Arthur himself) could have foreseen how he would carry the family tradition into the future.

Lieutenant Charles Clarke had suffered several injuries while fighting in France, and his lungs had been severely damaged by inhaling poisonous gas and by living under the horrible conditions of trench warfare. He began having violent attacks of pain soon after the family moved to Ballifants. In less than a year he was an invalid, unable to do any work on the farm. Like so many veterans of the war he had signed a release, one of the many papers requiring his signature before he could be discharged. Unfortunately, by signing the document, he lost any right to a pension.

Nora took up the full burden of providing for the family. 'I was able to deal with the small stock we had, so did not need extra labour. I continued as far as I could with my paying guests, and their pay provided our feed.' Some of these guests became Arthur's earliest good friends.

As Charles' physical condition worsened, Nora needed and expected more help from her older children, Arthur and Fred. Siblings Mary and Michael were too young to do much work.

There were cows to be milked, eggs to be collected, clotted cream to be delivered, apples to be picked and pressed, and an assortment of animals – horses, cows, lambs, pigs, chickens, turkeys, geese and dogs – to be fed and cared for. The beloved Cairn terriers alone, sometimes more than a dozen around the farm at any one time, regularly ate substantial piles of food. But they were pedigree and always sold for good prices. The horses were used for riding lessons.

Both Arthur and Fred remember seeing their father in bed during his long illness. They would take up his medication or a hot water bottle. 'I had to walk a mile,' recalls Fred, 'through fields and woods, in the dark, three times a week to get his medicine. It was probably morphine, issued only in small doses.'

Charles Wright Clarke died in hospital in Bristol in May 1931, under the ministrations of a doctor who was experimenting with mercury injections. He was forty-three years old. His son Arthur was thirteen.

The loss was buried deep in young Arthur. It was a critical time in his life, as he began his teens. Most boys turn to their fathers for self-definition, but Arthur Clarke was alone. As the eldest son he assumed the role and responsibilities of the male head of household.

'It was a very hard time in the thirties,' says Michael Clarke, Nora's youngest child who became the farmer of the family and the one to run Ballifants, which is now a dairy farm. 'Even the good farmers couldn't make a living then.'

Nora did just about everything to bring in extra income. 'She used to knit gloves, string gloves I seem to remember,' says Michael, 'and sell them for a very small amount.'

'We all had our work on the farm,' recalls Fred, 'because our father was ill and died early. If anybody wasn't doing their share, mother used to say, "Don't let it ever be said your mother bred a jibber." A jibber is a horse which won't do what you tell it to do – won't jump over a fence, but swings to one side instead. Or won't haul a heavy load, but puts its head down and refuses to move.'

After a hard day's work, Nora's great pleasure was to have her long dark hair brushed. 'She'd sit before the fire every night, and one or another of us would brush her hair, which went down over her shoulders,' says Fred.

As it turned out, Nora bred no jibbers. All the Clarke children were taught to work hard, even if they did occasionally try to avoid particularly gruelling or unpleasant tasks. Arthur, of course, later worked very hard at a hobby which became a vocation. The example at Ballifants no doubt influenced his prolific literary production in future years.

Arthur C. Clarke's personal odyssey has been motivated in part by a need to seek what he had lost in his youth. As his fiction illustrates, there are no heights (or depths) to which he won't climb to seek and find the missing element. His writing represents, on a biographical level, a search for his missing father and his own identity.

'More than his father had been buried today; the falling earth had covered his childhood,' Arthur later wrote in his novel, *Glide Path*, when Alan Bishop, the young RAF officer, attended his father's funeral. 'He could never escape from its influence, for it had shaped his character irrevocably . . .'

CHAPTER 2

Adventures at Ballifants

> He remembered his first glimpse of the *Sinus Iridium*, through the little homemade telescope he had built when he was a boy . . . [It] had given him more pleasure than the giant instruments of which he was now the master.
>
> – *Earthlight*

From an early age, Arthur's dreams of space travel gave him a keen interest in observing the night sky. When the family moved to Ballifants in 1924, the only instrument they possessed was a small field telescope that had been used in the Boer War. While it could spot rabbits or other game, it was not designed to observe the Moon, planets or other celestial wonders.

When Arthur was in his early teens, he constructed the first of 'four or five' refractor telescopes which he aimed mainly at the Moon to explore its mountains, craters and the immense and smooth waterless seas, the maria.

'I used to collect lenses, put them in cardboard tubes (the kind used for holding maps and pictures that were about three inches in diameter and perhaps three feet long), and try different lens assemblies. I used whatever long-focus lenses I could find such as old magic lantern lenses, and then any magnifying glass for the short-focus eyepiece.'

'His first telescope,' remembers his sister Mary, 'was mounted on an old bicycle embedded upside down in an earth mound. He sat on a milking stool and used the wheel to move it around.'

A few years later, Arthur received a Meccano set for Christmas. After building every possible construction offered in the Meccano instruction booklet, plus a few designs of his own, he designed and assembled a tripod for his refractor that would last for the rest of his amateur astronomy days.

He enjoyed sharing his enthusiasm with friends. 'It came as a great surprise to my friends that, with a telescope that could be made for a few pennies, craters on the Moon could be observed.'

During his mid-teen years Arthur observed most nights when the skies were clear. Because his homemade telescopes were limited to twenty to thirty power at best, his observations were mostly of the Moon.

'It wasn't good enough for the planets,' he says, 'so I concentrated on the Moon. I had sketchbooks full of drawings of the lunar craters.' More than once Arthur has written that he knew his way around the Moon much better than he did around his native Somerset.

One of several secondhand astronomy books young Arthur bought was Robert Ball's well-known, nineteenth-century *Story of the Heavens*. 'I remember copying out and tracing all the star maps on tissue paper.'

Clarke saw the moons of Jupiter, aligned specks of light, with one of his early telescopes, but it was not until 1941 that he finally saw Saturn's beautiful rings through an old Navy telescope he bought in Wales just before he joined the Royal Air Force. 'This old Navy telescope was the sort that Nelson put to his eye. I took out the internal optics and put in a very short-focus eyepiece. Then, for the very first time, I could just glimpse the rings of Saturn. That was quite a revelation.'

In the early 1930s, Arthur also constructed several homemade rockets. He joined the British Interplanetary Society in the summer of 1934.

'Please could you send me particulars about your Society, as I should very much like to join it,' Arthur wrote to Les Johnson, the Society's secretary, after learning about the group in a magazine. 'I am extremely interested in the whole subject of interplanetary communications, and have made some experiments with rockets. I am sixteen, have an extensive knowledge of physics and chemistry and possess a small laboratory and apparatus with which I can do some experiments in this line.'

After joining, Arthur often wrote enthusiastic letters to Les Johnson. '[He] became one of my liveliest correspondents, describing amongst other things how he had fitted dart-like wings to penny rockets and launched them off a roof.'

Unknown to the Society or its members at the time, 1934 was the same year that Wernher von Braun developed a liquid-fuel rocket in Germany which reached an altitude of 1.5 miles (2.4 kilometres). Arthur Clarke's rocketry was on a much smaller scale.

'He used to spend his spare pocket money in woofing up home-made rockets on his mother's farm,' says Bobby Pleass, his physics teacher at Huish's Grammar School in Taunton.

His rocket experiments evolved from first making fireworks, which, once perfected, he'd set off to entertain his mother and her friends who watched from a safe distance. The gunpowder was made by following the recipe in his chemistry textbook, combining sulphur, saltpetre and charcoal and mixing them with the kitchen's pestle and mortar, which his mother used to grind icing sugar for cakes.

'My hair stands on end now, thinking about it,' says Arthur, 'but I sometimes used to grind up gunpowder in a metal tin for fuel. I was very lucky to get away with it – well, almost. One day I was mixing the gunpowder inside the house, and it caught fire! It happened in the downstairs sitting room which was my study. I don't think it caught fire to anything outside the container. I threw it out of the window before any damage could be done. It certainly gave me a fright and taught me a lesson.'

After some experimentation, the powder mix was right and Arthur decided to prepare for the next Guy Fawkes Day with homemade fireworks. By wrapping a sheet of notepaper around a pencil and glueing it down, he formed a small tube into which he packed the gunpowder. Into the gunpowder were mixed iron filings that brother Fred made in the workshop. These became sparklers.

Larger tubes, formed in the same manner over a broom handle, became fiery and colourful fountains, some of which shot into the air and sometimes emitted explosive bangs to the delight of Arthur's siblings Fred, Michael and Mary. After the fireworks, Arthur knew it was time to graduate to rockets.

'They were simple powder rockets,' he says, 'foot-long or less cardboard tubes, probably toilet paper cylinders – nothing really sophisticated. I'd go outside, put them in a bottle, light a match and launch them. But they never flew very far. I do remember trying to make a rocket glider, but it didn't work. I probably had the centre of gravity in the wrong place.'

As his model rockets got bigger, Arthur began to add payloads. 'First there were balsa wood wings which helped them glide back to earth,' Fred recalls, 'and I was sent to the far end of the field to retrieve them. Later came heavier and heavier payloads until the rocket could barely leave the ground, and burst asunder at face level.'

One friend of Arthur's, Jimmy Dulborough, was devoted to

making sophisticated and beautiful model airplanes, some of which would take him months to build. Jimmy would often come over to the farm and fly his splendid models in the Clarke's open fields.

After Jimmy flew his latest model plane one afternoon, Arthur had an idea and persuaded Jimmy to lend his model for a worthwhile experiment – the basic piggyback approach to rocketry. By attaching one of his rockets to the bottom of Jimmy's model plane, Arthur argued, it would be carried to a much higher altitude and would therefore fly a considerably greater distance.

Jimmy Dulborough was protective of his pride and joy at first, but Arthur eventually prevailed after discussing the technical aspects of his proposal. The mating of rocket and airplane was accomplished and the countdown began.

'As the rocket rose from the ground,' Fred Clarke recalls, 'the flames licking out behind it enveloped the tail of the plane, and the balsa wood and lacquered masterpiece crashed like an exploding fire-ball in front of Dulborough's agonised eyes. We did not see him again for many months.'

In the mid-1930s, when Arthur was about seventeen, he constructed his most memorable early project – 'the thing I'm proudest of making' – a light-beam transmitter, which used light to transmit sound.

'My uncle, George Grimstone [his father's brother-in-law], gave me a broken photocell which came from the "Talkie" equipment at the place he worked. He was chief engineer for all the electrical equipment at a place called Cotford, a big lunatic asylum about two miles from our farm, Ballifants. (He was not an inmate in the asylum as some people had deduced.)

'I took an ordinary bicycle lamp, a carbon microphone to modulate the light beam, a couple of batteries, put them in series, and then it worked. When you talked into the microphone, the light flickered. And I aimed it at the photocell detector, the amplifier, a few dozen feet away. It worked quite well.'

'When the light was shone on the photoelectric cell,' recalls brother Fred, 'every word could be heard in the earphones. Arthur was soon transmitting speech across the room and later across the field.'

Arthur frequently enlisted his siblings' assistance. 'He used to drag me in to help him,' Michael recalls. 'I had to hold the transmitter, aim it at him and speak into the microphone. I can remember the apparatus was a cigar box, and a convex lense was held in the aperture by what we used to call butterfly tape.'

Uncle George Grimstone was an important source of free communication supplies which helped advance Arthur's early experiments. After George installed a new telephone system in the mental institution, Arthur became the lucky recipient of obsolete telephone sets, plenty of wire, batteries and switch gear. He utilised whatever he could from all the passed-along parts and began improving the communications at the farm. First he installed an intercom system between the kitchen and his study so that he could be told when his tea was ready. Next he wired his bedroom for wake-up calls. Finally, using the fencing wires around Ballifants, he wired the entire perimeter to determine how far a message would travel, but because the sheep kept breaking through the fence this was not a permanent circuit.

Wireless crystal sets were also part of Arthur's early experiments in communications, and Uncle George taught him how to build them. A single shilling would buy the necessary components – the crystal, the holder and the coiled wire known as a 'cat's-whisker'. Once these parts were mounted on a wood base and connected to an aerial, all that was needed to hear live music in Somerset over the BBC was a pair of earphones. Arthur earned pocket money by building these sets for a shilling and then selling them for half a crown.

Listening was all well and good, but Arthur soon wanted to transmit as well. From one of the salvaged telephones he took the carbon mouthpiece and built a microphone.

Brother Fred recalls one innovative way Arthur used his wireless equipment. 'I remember listening to music on the wireless one evening when the programme was interrupted with a "newsflash" of such horror that our visitors nearly fainted. Luckily mother recognised the Somerset accent, which would have been inconceivable on the BBC in those days, and slipped out to Arthur's den. The resulting howl came over clearly before the concert was resumed.'

During her husband's long illness and after his premature death in 1931, Nora depended even more on her riding pupils and paying guests to supplement the farm produce income and keep Ballifants going. An advertisement in the local *Holiday Haunts* read: 'Riding Lessons,/also/Board Residence,/with or without riding./NORA CLARKE,/Ballifants Farm,/Bishops Lydeard.' Some of the guests from London and elsewhere who took their holidays at Ballifants became friends with the Clarkes and remained so over the years.

One such good friend was Dick Jenvey, who met Arthur at the farm in about 1934 when he and a chum took a holiday there.

'My first impression on meeting Arthur on our first day at Balli-fants was that he was a studious individual, ahead of his years so far as his intellectual capabilities were concerned. He showed us his book-lined study with masses of books, novels of space travel with lurid covers of strange craft and film-like figures with ray guns spit-ting all over the place. Then he would inveigle us into long and learned discussions on space travel for the future, which left us with open mouths and trying to say something sensible into the bargain.

'He wanted a willing ear,' Jenvey continues. 'I always used to feel with Arthur it became a one-track obsession. He was so involved, so enthusiastic about his subject. But Arthur, bless his heart, had a lovely sense of fun and would never "bore us to tears", as he used to say.

'His sense of fun was there when he persuaded me to mount a horse in the paddock for the first time. I had never been on a horse before. But according to Arthur, all I had to do was hold on to the reins and Bobby Sunshine would do the rest. So I was told.

'Well, Arthur's smack on Bobby's rump may have had something to do with it, but Bobby took off heading toward the nearest fence with me hanging on for dear life. How I managed to land on the other side still attached to his back confounds me. Those who watched said there was a lot of daylight between my backside and the saddle. Old Arthur, he was a real card. I just don't know how we really did click, but we did. All of us feel those early days really meant something to him, that a bond of friendship formed. And we never forgot it.

'But the real classic has to do with the nickname we gave Arthur. It stuck and has been accepted by him with much affection over the years. I refer to our naming him "Scientific Sid". This was based on his original, insatiable love of science fiction, which became part and parcel of him from those early days.

'I never cease to be amazed that even now his letters and endorse-ments of his novels to us are always signed "Sid". His affection toward us has always included that particular name because he knows it means a lot to us.

'And for all his tremendous enthusiasm for his interests, he always knew where my interest lay. I was studying architecture, and when I qualified Arthur sent me a book, *The Autobiography of Frank Lloyd Wright*. On the flyleaf he wrote:

'"To old Dick, against the day when I ask you to build me an airtight, meteor-proof house, with a bay window looking towards Earth. Sid. Easter 1946."'

15

CHAPTER 3

Huish's Grammar School

He'd spend his time doodling, and many
wonderful things were produced, things
that would fly in the air and go over the sea
and go under the sea – all in one vehicle.
— Bobby Pleass, Teacher

Arthur and his brother Fred both attended the church school at
Bishops Lydeard. One of Fred's enduring memories is of being caned
by the schoolmaster, Mr Tipper, for being late. Arthur's memory of
his schoolmistress, Maud Hanks, is more uplifting and positive. He
remembers her with great affection.

Miss Hanks (later to become Mrs Quelch) encouraged Arthur to
tell stories to the class, which he often did. His imagination was
tapped to create tales of adventure. Little did Maud Hanks know that
her pupil would become one of the world's great cosmic storytellers,
no doubt in part because of her encouragement and faith in his talents.
Eventually she did find out – Arthur's favourite schoolmistress lived
to the grand old age of ninety-nine and he kept in touch with her all
those years.

After leaving the elementary school in Bishops Lydeard Arthur
began his secondary education at Huish's Grammar School, five miles
away in Taunton, a few months before his tenth birthday in 1927.
He was able to attend under a foundation scholarship from the village
school.

An all-boy school of about 250 before World War II when Arthur
attended, Huish's pupil population doubled when London schools
were evacuated during the war. It is now known as Richard Huish
College.

The boy who dreamed of rockets travelling to the Moon and
beyond had to pedal an old postman's bicycle ten miles a day to and
from Huish's Grammar School.

'It was made of cast iron and felt like it weighed about three hundred pounds,' Arthur recalls. The Moon would often rise up from

the rolling Quantock Hills of Somerset as young Arthur Clarke bicycled back and forth. During the winter months he cycled home in the dark, with the stars and Moon illuminating his route in clear weather. Such starry evenings influenced Arthur's budding cosmic consciousness. The silent night sky above him stirred his imagination and brought forth images of the future. Men would walk on the Moon someday, he knew, and later they would leave their bootprints on the red sands of Mars. Even the gulf between our sun and other stars would be bridged eventually, and their planets explored by the descendants of our species. Young Clarke was convinced that the exploration of space was inevitable and just a matter of time.

Arthur's morning bicycle trek to Huish's was not his first activity each day.

'That was after I delivered the post,' he says. 'I was night operator at the same time. I slept in the post office, greeted the postmen when they came in about four o'clock in the morning, sorted the mail, delivered it, which meant riding three or four miles, and then went to school. And I managed to read about two books a day. There was no TV then; that made all the difference.'

His mother almost always put his studies first, recalls sister Mary.

'When any major catastrophe occurred, such as animals breaking out through the Heath Robinson fences, which was frequent, Mamma would hastily call up her troops to round them up. Never Arthur, though – he must not be disturbed in his studies. How clever the rest of us might have been had the fences been better!'

Fred Clarke remembers that Arthur did not always escape the chores: 'When he got caught he had to muck out the stables with the rest of us.'

Bobby Pleass was Arthur's physics and mathematics teacher at Huish's in the early 1930s. 'I recall Archie very well,' says Pleass. 'He came into the sixth form where I had him for physics and maths.' Pleass called the boy 'Arthur C.' which later merged into Archie.

Arthur liked mathematics very much, but for some reason he had trouble with passing his Oxford School Certificate in it and failed three times before passing it. What makes this even more puzzling is that soon after, when he took the Civil Service examination, he scored extremely highly – in the top two per cent of 1,500 applicants.

Why he had trouble with the maths exam at Huish's is anybody's guess, but perhaps he was spending too much of his time designing spaceships and dreaming about rocketing to the planets. After all, a curriculum for rockets and space travel was not available in the 1930s.

Bobby Pleass remembers Clarke as a teenager. 'Now Archie was a loner. Don't get the impression that he wasn't a friendly type; he was friendly. But he didn't make real personal friends. He was out in his own world a lot of the time, out in the clouds, although he was still a sound member of the community, especially with his writing articles for the school magazine.'

To many of his schoolmates Arthur had the smell of the farmyard, which he carried to school on the big farm boots he wore. 'Some of the kids used to complain about this,' says Pleass. And that wasn't the only way young Arthur stood out. 'He was made to wear short trousers by his mother, and the other boys had long trousers. Archie didn't like that.

'I wish,' said Pleass, 'I'd preserved some of what we call "scrib-blers" – you know, the rough book. He'd spend his time doodling, and many wonderful things were produced, things that would fly in the air and go under the sea – all in one vehicle.

'I used to fight battles for Archie,' Pleass recalled. 'The rest of the staff would say, "What the hell can we do with this lazy so and so Clarke? He doesn't attend, and this and that and the other." But the thing was, you see, he was way ahead of them. He was always ahead of the teachers. They classified him as a nitwit, but he wasn't any such thing. I used to fight on his behalf in the staff room, discussing reports and things. I said, "That boy's got something; you wait."

'I taught the old–style physics,' Pleass continues, 'which was based on experimentation. The boys had to experiment and find out things.'

Usually. But sometimes things happened too fast for experimenta-tion. Once a unique form of natural energy appeared before Arthur and Bobby Pleass at the school. They were preparing test tubes in a small room known as the 'Dungeon', where the sixth-formers would go for private study. It was located partly below ground level under the physics lecture room. Across the ceiling of the Dungeon ran the heating pipes which came from the nearby boiler house.

'I saw this glowing globe in the air in front of us, between Bobby and me,' says Arthur. No mini–UFO this, but a ball of fire hanging from a joint in the heating pipes. It was a ball of lightning, resulting from a thunderbolt which hit the tall boiler chimney, splitting it from top to bottom. Student and teacher both ran from the Dungeon, thinking that it could blow up in their faces at any time.

Huish's Dungeon became a significant place for Arthur's introduc-tion and commitment to science fiction. It was here that he found, read and totally absorbed the March 1930 issue of *Astounding Stories of Super-Science*. Unlike the mild interest he had shown in his neighbour's 1928 copy of *Amazing Stories*, this was exciting stuff; he couldn't get enough. The time was right. His cosmic sails were set.

'I read that March 1930 *Astounding* from cover to cover, doubtless when I should have been doing geometry or algebra or (ugh) Latin, then returned it to the literary debris of the Dungeon.' The cover depicted a spaceship, looking 'like a cross between a submarine and a glass-domed conservatory', travelling toward a celestial body that was *supposed* to be the Moon. It did not convince Arthur, however, who had had so much telescope time observing our satellite in detail.

The cover copy displayed the featured story by the American writer of pulp adventure fiction, Ray Cummings: 'Brigands of the Moon – A Thrilling Interplanetary Novel of Intrigue and Adventure'.

A few days later, when he saw that no one had claimed it, Arthur decided he would be the person to best care for this prize – this physical manifestation of his youthful fantasy life. This began his serious collection of science fiction magazines that would grow and remain intact until he entered the Royal Air Force during World War II.

Every day Arthur would devote some of his school lunchtime to searching for science fiction magazines on the shelves of Taunton's Woolworth's. 'I'd save up all my spare coppers to buy issues. I was insatiable. I couldn't bear to miss one. I used to make lists of all the copies there ever had been, so I could plug the gaps and get a complete file.'

They were not easy to find, however, but were randomly scattered throughout the piles of other pulp magazines – the westerns, confessions and detectives – that were shipped over from the United States. It was catch as catch can. Some issues, Arthur came to suspect, probably never even reached the United Kingdom, let alone Somerset towns like Taunton and Minehead.

The overseas distribution of these American pulp magazines was apparently rather haphazard, and it was commonly said that the unsold copies in the United States, the so-called surplus, reached the United Kingdom as ballast in returning cargo ships.

David Kyle, co-partner of Gnome Press, Arthur's first American publisher, is well versed in the early history of science fiction.

'The early American science fiction magazines – *Amazing Stories*, and then the Gernsback *Wonder Stories* and *Air Wonder Stories*, even the early *Astounding Stories* – were quite common in the secondhand bookstores in England,' says Kyle. 'They were not sold on the newsstands because they were secondhand copies stamped with some kind of mark, often a big purple star, to show they were secondhand. These magazines were sent over to England because they were being taken off the market in America. They were the only source of science fiction for the young English fans then.

'I don't think they were actually just used as ballast in ships, but they were tantamount to ballast because they represented such a little bit of money. The space in the hold wasn't wasted and the shipping companies got some return for it. Probably the magazines were just bundled up and thrown on a ship. When they got to England some dealers would bid on the lot, and sort them out. What was usable was usable; what wasn't was thrown away.'

This is probably why young Arthur Clarke had such a frustrating time obtaining a full sequence.

'There were heart-breaking gaps in my collection,' he says. 'Sometimes it took me years to assemble all the instalments of a serial.' On his lucky days, when he discovered a new issue he didn't have, he would buy it for what was then threepence.

Arthur's devotion to his collection also led him to come into contact with other science fiction fans through the correspondence columns, which proved to be a good forum for buying or swapping missing issues. During his Huish's Grammar School days, when he worked at the post office before lessons, he once received an entire box of magazines he'd purchased from another fan. Another time he obtained a full set of covers from a fan who was binding his copies.

Two years before Arthur left Somerset for London and a Civil Service job in 1936, he ingeniously rigged up flash lighting for his camera and took several self-portraits in his study at Ballifants.

'I had a candle and a stand with a bit of magnesium ribbon, and a bit of string. I pulled the magnesium ribbon into the candle and waited for it to ignite.' In the background his shelves were filled with his treasured magazines, but it would be five or six years later, when World War II broke out in 1939, before Arthur acquired a complete run of *Amazing Stories* and *Astounding Stories* totalling several hundred copies. This was when his collection reached its maximum extent, before it got dispersed during the war.

As much as Clarke loved the pulp science fiction magazines, he had no illusions about any high and consistent literary standards. But he was objective and sophisticated enough to see the merits of the best in the genre.

The stories brimmed with ideas, and amply evoked that sense of wonder which is (or should be) one of the goals of the best fiction. No less a critic than C. S. Lewis has described the ravenous addiction that these magazines inspired; the same phenomenon has led me to call science fiction the only genuine consciousness-expanding drug.

In July 1930, six months before Arthur became a teenager, a literary work was published which would have a profound influence on his future writing. The book was W. Olaf Stapledon's *Last and First Men*, which Arthur found at the Minehead Public Library during his summer holidays. Clarke can vividly remember the details of his Stapledon discovery and can even visualise where he found it on the library shelf: slightly below knee level. With its timescale of some five billion years, the book did nothing less than change Arthur Clarke's perception of the world and universe around him, giving him a cosmic scale of time and space, a grand and majestic set on which to place humanity's evolution and future extra-terrestrial adventures.

'No book before or since ever had such an impact on my imagination,' Clarke wrote in a short autobiographical piece, 'Of Sand and Stars', which appeared in the *New York Times Book Review* in 1983. Twelve-year-old Arthur was not the only one who raved about Stapledon's book. Winston Churchill, temporarily a failed politician in 1930, praised it, and Arnold Bennett applauded Stapledon's 'tremendous and beautiful imagination'.

When Arthur was living in London eight years later he heard Stapledon lecture on the subject of 'Literature and the People'.

'He was very good, in fact the sincerest speaker of the lot,' Arthur wrote to a friend. 'Other speakers were Elmer Rice, Rose Macaulay, John Strachey and Victor Gollancz.'

Last and First Men was unique and wholly original, although more than one critic has noted the influence on Stapledon of another Clarke literary mentor, J. B. S. Haldane, and his essay 'The Last Judgment' published in 1927. Arthur has readily acknowledged his debt to Stapledon many times, and there is no doubt that *Last and First Men* influenced Arthur's first novel, *Against the Fall of Night*, which he began during his Huish Grammar School days and eventually published in its first version in *Startling Stories* in November 1948.

Just as Stapledon's book covered immense expanses of time, often tens and hundreds of millions of years, so too Arthur's first novel spoke of past and future events on an immense timescale of hundreds of millions of years: 'Nothing had changed: the mountains resumed their watch over the sleeping land. But a turning-point in history had come and gone, and the human race was moving towards a strange new future.'

After the war, in 1948, Arthur served the first of two terms as chairman of the British Interplanetary Society. In this capacity he asked Stapledon to give a lecture at one of the BIS meetings in London. The address was entitled 'Interplanetary Man'. Clarke was already fictionalising some of Stapledon's themes in work that would become known in the 1950s and launch his career in the prosperous US market.

'Perhaps the final result of the cosmical process is the attainment of full cosmical consciousness,' Stapledon said, 'and yet (in some very queer way) what is attained in the end is also, from another point of view, the origin of all things. So to speak, God, who created all things in the beginning, is himself created by all things in the end.'

Besides Arthur's early excitement and enthusiasm for Stapledon's work and for science fiction magazines, he also read the classic works of Jules Verne and H. G. Wells. But it was another new book that captured his imagination, and Clarke remembers it well.

Arthur was visiting his Aunt Nellie and his grandmother in Minehead during the summer holidays in 1931, just weeks after his father died. While peering in the bookshop window of W. H. Smith near the house where he was born, Arthur found another treasure. The book was *The Conquest of Space* by David Lasser. A young American editor in his late twenties, Lasser edited and nurtured two of Hugo Gernsback's early magazines, *Science Wonder Stories* and *Air Wonder Stories*, from their inception in 1929. Lasser is also known as the founder of the American Interplanetary Society (1930), the name of which was later changed to the American Rocket Society because 'interplanetary' was considered too far out by the leadership. The ARS, in turn, eventually became the prestigious American Institute of Aeronautics and Astronautics.

The Conquest of Space was one of the great finds of Arthur's youth. 'Only a few hundred copies of the British edition were sold,' wrote Arthur, 'but chance brought one of them to a bookshop a few yards from my birthplace. I saw it in the window, knew instinctively that I *had* to read it and persuaded my good-natured Aunt Nellie – who was looking after me while Mother struggled to run the farm and raise my three siblings – to buy it on the spot. And so I learned for the first time that space travel was not merely delightful fiction. *One day it could really happen*. Soon afterward I discovered the existence of the British Interplanetary Society, and my fate was sealed.'

Today *The Conquest of Space* is considered a classic of space literature. Upon its publication in 1931, it became the first book in the English language to review the dreams and work of the early rocket pioneers and to discuss the possibility of interplanetary space flight. In contrast to Stapledon's immense and immeasurable cosmic realm, Lasser's book focused on the more practical, immediate and accessible side of rocketry and space travel. These two books, plus the fiction of the pulp magazines, are the major print influences that helped launch Arthur C. Clarke on his writing career.

The English master at Huish's Grammar School, E. B. Mitford, was another strong influence on Arthur Clarke. Mitford, an enthusiastic and fiery Welshman, whose physical appearance Arthur compares to the actors John Mills or Alec Guinness, oversaw the school literary effort, the *Huish Magazine*, as one of his many additional duties. Under the leadership of Arnold Goodliffe, who was headmaster during the first four decades of this century (1903 to 1941), the school magazine was issued once every term instead of once every year.

Mitford was a veteran of World War I, 'a short-haired man who had won the Military Cross', Arthur recalls. Although Mitford held the rank of captain, he was known as 'Mr Mitford' at school. That was his preference. Because he was not a regular army officer, but was instead called up, he was not comfortable using his military title.

'Mitty', as the boys called him among themselves, would gather his young editorial staff around a table about once every week to work on the school magazine. If Arthur or any of the other boys came up with a bright idea that especially pleased their English master, they would be rewarded with a toffee from a large bag of assorted favourites on the table before them. Arthur does not remember the 'heavy metre ruler' ever being used during these editorial sessions, although it was swung occasionally during regular classes to dispense some down-to-earth discipline.

It was in the *Huish Magazine* that some of Clarke's earliest work first saw print in the autumn of 1932. It appeared, however, without his byline, under the pseudonym, 'One-Time Sixth-Former' – a fictitious old boy of the school. This was only one of several pseudonyms Arthur used for the work appearing in the school magazine, a practice he continued for several years when he began publishing in the amateur and commercial science fiction magazines. While at Huish's, Arthur's pen names included 'Clericus', 'A. Munchhausen', 'De Profoundus', and 'Court'. Besides the fun of choosing the pen names, there was also a practical reason for their use. There were many articles to write and only a few boys to write them.

The first piece, 'Correspondence', was an imaginative, two-page letter describing the difficulties of working in an extreme environment. Two more pieces on the same theme, also bylined by the fictive old boy, appeared in the magazine in 1933.

In Clarke's autobiographical essay 'Of Sand and Stars', he admits that the locale for these letters, described to Huish readers as 'a torrid and high-altitude Outpost of Empire (Vrying Pan, British Malaria)' – note that the playful humour was there from the beginning – was actually the Moon of his imagination.

'Our houses are built on the principle of the Dewar vacuum flask, to keep out the heat, and the outsides are silvered to reflect the sunlight . . .'

By the age of fifteen, then, Clarke was already a devoted 'space cadet', his imagination blending with the science he knew to describe his visions of other worlds. And E. B. Mitford was the first editor among many in Arthur's prolific writing career. Almost four decades later, in 1967, Arthur dedicated his volume of short stories *The Nine Billion Names of God* to his teacher.

> To 'Mitty' (Captain E. B. Mitford),
> who encouraged my initial scribblings
> at Huish's Grammar School, 1930–36
> and became my first editor

Besides his work on the school's literary magazine, Arthur was a founding member and elected secretary of the Huish Film Club in February 1936. He helped arrange film shows.

'*Metropolis* was one film that I arranged to show, and I can remember screening it,' Arthur recalls. 'I can still remember cycling back through the dark after seeing *Frankenstein* starring Boris Karloff.'

Both print and film would continue to play a significant role in Arthur's life while sports and the playing field, so important to many of his classmates, would not hold much interest for him. Later in his career, however, he would write some imaginative pieces about possible sports that could be played in the zero gravity of space, including a unique zero gravity swimming pool with the water in a complete circle. (Think of water on the inner surface of a large open-ended cylinder.)

In the spring of 1936, before leaving Huish's Grammar School, Arthur travelled to London and took a Civil Service examination – the entrance exam for 'executive grade'. It was Arnold Goodliffe, the headmaster himself, who directed Arthur to take the exam. Goodliffe was proud of young Clarke and groomed him for the Civil Service.

'I found myself scribbling away in what is now the Museum of Mankind, just off Piccadilly,' Arthur recalls. He did extremely well, and was placed twenty-sixth of the 1,500 who took the exam. This allowed him to choose the branch of the Civil Service he preferred. Because he had scored a hundred per cent in arithmetic, it was recommended that he join the exchequer and audit department.

It was a year after Penguin Books introduced the first paperbacks which would later become so important to his writing career.

CHAPTER 4

London Life

I think that Interplanetary is run – and
always has been run – by visionaries, poets
if you like, who also happen to be scientists.
Sometimes the disguise isn't very good.
    – *Prelude to Space*

Arthur was a few months short of nineteen when he boarded the
Great Western train at Taunton Station in the summer of 1936
and left for his new government job and digs in Paddington in
London.

His younger brother, Michael, then seven years old, remembers
the day he left. 'I was standing on the porch and thought of him as
being so grown up,' he says. 'He would have been a father figure to
me, you see. I sensed an atmosphere of portent. A sense of occasion
was impressed upon me, a feeling that this was something big in our
family.'

Arthur was excited. He especially looked forward to spending
more time with his fellow science fiction fans and members of the
British Interplanetary Society who shared his enthusiasm for the
promise of space.

'I rarely made friends at the farm, so I was looking forward to
seeing the whole gang of science fiction and space nuts in London
who shared my interests. That is why I was so anxious to get there.
Really, the Taunton–Minehead axis was the whole of my existence
before I left for London in 1936.' The only exception had come two
years before in 1934, when his Aunt Zebah took him on a brief visit
to the capital.

Arthur had already met a few of these space cadets when they
visited the family farm, Ballifants, but many were friends through
correspondence. Walter H. Gillings was one such early pen friend.
He won Arthur's gratitude by supplying him with some hard-to-get
science fiction magazines – and by giving him his first typewriter. A
year after Arthur arrived in London, he began a correspondence with

Sam Youd (whose later pseudonym was John Christopher) which continued into the 1990s.

Some of these letters were published in the early science fiction magazines, when readers would enthusiastically exchange their ideas and visions about manned rockets travelling to the Moon and planets, and how space travel would become reality in the future.

When Arthur arrived at Paddington Station in London, he had a nearby address to go to: a small hotel at 21 Norfolk Square in Paddington, where his father's youngest sister, Aunt Molly, was staying.

'She was an unsuccessful, but I thought quite good actress,' Arthur recalls. 'Always resting between jobs. Very talented. She was a good artist, too, and a fashion designer. I remember seeing a lot of sketches.'

Aunt Molly was the close-at-hand family member for young Arthur if he ever ran into trouble. But years later Aunt Molly was the one in trouble. She became anorexic and eventually died of malnutrition in her sister's garage at Bishops Lydeard. 'Very sad,' says Arthur. 'She became very eccentric. Still, she was helpful and friendly when I was in London, and I have fond memories of her.'

During Arthur's first months in London his only difficulty was adjusting to his newly acquired digs – a tiny 'bedsit' in a house in Norfolk Square which was just large enough for a bed, a sink and a cupboard. Without a single chair, Arthur could only offer guests a seat on the bed or the windowsill.

The modest quarters were the subject of many jokes in the fledgling science fiction community during Arthur's almost two years at the address. His science fiction friend, writer and future roommate in larger digs, William F. Temple, wrote the most famous joke in one of his many humorous sketches, 'The British Fan in his Natural Haunts', which appeared in the June 1938 issue of the fanzine *Novae Terrae*.

'There is a tale that Arthur once wore a double-breasted suit for the first time and got wedged between the walls for three days.' Temple went on to describe, in his role as the jester scribe for the London science fiction fans, his first visit to the Norfolk Square room:

'For there was hardly room for the two of us, and A[rthur]'s Ego had to be left outside on the landing. A. himself generously opened the window and sat himself half outside it to allow me to look around freely.'

Throughout Temple's sketch several allusions were made to Arthur's 'Ego', a label which stuck to Arthur among friends and fans and one he sometimes took up himself and used as a pen name a few years later. While there has been a mild controversy from time to time as to how Arthur became known as 'Ego' Clarke in the early London days, Bill Temple, with good reason, claims credit as originator.

'The appellation was born in that *Novae Terrae* interview published in June 1938,' says Temple. 'I realised *that* early, that Arthur was a dual personality: one, the boaster: "I'm the greatest!" Two, the quiet humorous, generous soul. Arthur *had* to prove he was a winner, to come out on top. He was born competitive.'

In his playful piece, Temple mentioned several books Arthur possessed about the Moon, and then continued:

'You BIS Moonatic,' I said, 'haven't you anything else less technical?'

A. replied: 'My library is at Taunton, my home town. It contains complete sets of *Wonder, Astounding*, about a hundred science fiction novels and more than a hundred books of pure science.'

'Darned if I'm going to Taunton (if there is such a place) to check up on it,' I said. 'So I'll have to take your word for it.'

Here A.'s conscience smote him. 'Well, to tell you the truth, my *Astounding* collection is two short,' he mumbled.

The Ego thrust its head into the room at this, and gave A. such a look of utter contempt that the poor fellow blushed.

'A fine chance to boost yourself without being detected – and you throw it away you weak twirp!' it remarked bitterly and withdrew.

To this day 'Ego' remains intact as an affectionate appellation used by his friends, fans and himself. In the 1980s Arthur initiated an 'Egogram', a newsy, word-processed page he sometimes sends to friends to bring them up to date on his activities.

David Kyle, Arthur's first American publisher and friend going back to the early 1950s, believes he can put the 'Ego Clarke business' into its true context.

'Arthur is an enthusiast because he is interested in what he is doing,' says Kyle. 'But many of his acquaintances felt that Arthur talked so much because he was interested in himself, that he was into self-aggrandisement. But that is not Arthur. At any opportunity, whether he was with somebody important or whether it was just a teenage fan, Arthur would whip out his photographs and discuss something he was interested in at the time.

'Some of the other professionals, those who perhaps feel they have outgrown talking to fans, kept this label pinned on him as being an egotistical person, so "Ego" was a derogatory term to them: Old Ego Clarke, showing off his photographs again. Yet it has sometimes been used affectionately by his friends.

'If you want to capture the spirit and essence of Arthur Clarke, you must look to his roots and relationship to fandom to understand his enthusiasm. He still has the enthusiasm of youth. Some people, regretfully, have misinterpreted this enthusiasm for blatant egotism.'

In Bill Temple's humorous 1938 sketch, he described Arthur C. Clarke for the rather small readership of *Novae Terrae*.

> I beheld a tallish, rather clever-looking fellow (appearances are deceptive) whose eyes glinted at me through hornrims with a condescending expression. He looks as if he hopes he looks like a scientist, does A. His hair cannot make up its mind whether it is dark or fair, is perfectly dry and sticks up like a wire brush . . . He's somewhat impatient and highly-strung, and says he's not, and is given to sudden violent explosions of mirth (mostly at his own jokes).

One of Arthur's old Civil Service friends, Leonard Hobbs, adds, 'Arthur was pretty thin and tall in those days. He always wore glasses, and he had all his hair then – lots of wavy, light brown hair. Even today when he speaks he's got a little bit of a West Country burr; it's rather nice actually. Just a little trace of it.'

When Arthur wasn't working as an auditor at Whitehall, he got together with his science fiction or British Interplanetary Society friends. Not surprisingly, it was his passion for science fiction and his dreams of space travel that motivated him and gave him pleasure, not his Civil Servant duties.

Arthur kept in touch with all those who shared his enthusiasms, and much of his spare time was spent writing letters – often dozens each week. It was in the summer of 1937 that he began writing to Sam Youd and shared many of his opinions and self-evaluations with him. Their letters often mentioned their favourite authors, short stories, music and poetry.

In an early letter Arthur made it clear that he strongly favoured stories with a scientific basis, although he still admired Lovecraft and C. A. Smith. In the late thirties, however, he was ambivalent about his own writing.

'I have four short stories,' he wrote Sam in October 1937, 'and although I swore never to do any more story writing as it took up so much time, I fear that I shall be at it again in a very short time. I am best at short humorous stories, though what I consider my best stories have been "straight".'

In January 1938 he told Sam what he was reading, and again tried to define for himself where writing fitted into his life.

At the moment I am reading Esnault-Pelterie's monumental tome *L'Astronautique* which is lousy with differential equations. It takes me about a day to read a page, as every other line I run up against something that I can't integrate. Last Sunday I went out to Walter's [Walter Gillings] and he gave me a long harangue on what a wicked waste it is for me to spend my time on stuff like this when I could be setting the sf world by the ears – perhaps! But I shall do as I jolly well please, and there is more chance of fame in astronautics than sf, I'll tell the Universe! That is, if one wants fame, and modesty was never one of my vices. But Walt can't understand my attitude and cannot see the 'keen, unpassioned beauty' of mathematics, the queen of the sciences, that attracts me, nor does he realise that the man who holds the equations of astro-dynamics in his head will one day be worth his weight in radium. Not that I ever will, but maybe I can make it look like it.

Less than two weeks later the subject of fame and writing came up again in another letter to Sam.

I don't want writing fame, and can see no reason to believe that I have any great literary ability. I can turn out an amusing story at times, and if I spent enough time in perfecting my style I believe that I could do better than most of the 'pulp' writers – I aim no higher than that! As I haven't the time to devote to writing seriously, I shall just put pen to paper when the mood seizes me, and no oftener. It takes such a tremendous time to write a *serious* story that I sincerely hope I don't often get the urge. At the moment, owing to the malign influence of Lord Dunsany, I am in imminent danger of starting on a rather weird scientific play. It will be a play in form only, and could never be put on the stage, as there will be directions like this:
    'The sunlight shining through the window slowly fades over a period of about a thousand million years.'

The intensive effort and time necessary to write good stories came across loud and clear in Arthur's letters, and he knew from experience that it was easier to criticise and tear down a piece of writing than it was to create and construct it.

'I maintain that no one should criticise stories severely until they have tried to write them themselves,' he told Sam. 'So until you produce a wad of dog-eared MSS from your little bottom drawer I shall not regard you as a qualified critic. Shucks!'

Arthur's first Civil Service job was helping to audit accounts for the Board of Education. His office was located in King Charles Street, next to Downing Street.

As a junior auditor, Arthur's initial salary amounted to three pounds a week. While he doesn't recall ever being short of money, he admits there were some things he wished he could afford – especially a room larger than ten by six feet.

Arthur's job at the Board of Education consisted of checking teachers' pensions, for which he needed nothing more than simple arithmetic to multiply a teacher's last five years' earnings by a certain factor. This he accomplished in a few seconds.

> I quickly realised that an auditor didn't have to get figures *exactly* right; that was the job of a mere accountant, probably cranking the handle of a mechanical calculator (though I don't remember seeing even one of those extinct monsters during my five years in the Civil Service). The auditor's job – as *I* defined it – was to see that the figures were approximately right – say to within one per cent, or tuppence in the pound . . .
>
> I prided myself on having the fastest slide-rule in Whitehall, so I was usually able to do all my work in an hour or so, and devote the rest of the day to more important business.

This included leisurely lunch hours and pleasant walks around Green Park and St James's Park. Arthur also had plenty of time to think about the business of the British Interplanetary Society: spaceships and voyages to the Moon and beyond.

The British Interplanetary Society was founded in Liverpool in October 1933 by Phillip E. Cleator, an astronautical expert, and a few other dreamers with their feet on the ground. There were only fifteen members at first and the Society's prewar annual income was never more than one hundred pounds. Today it has a worldwide membership of four thousand and has had a profound impact by anticipating and preparing for the Space Age that began with the 1957 launch of Sputnik and that will continue for as long as *Homo sapiens* survives and explores.

At weekends Arthur sometimes walked across Kensington Gardens to the Science Museum, which soon became one of his favourite places. He liked to spend time in the room with mathematical machines and was impressed with the uncompleted Babbage Machine.

'Today, of course, it is famous as the premature herald of the Computer Age; but in 1936 only a few specialists had ever heard of it.'

During his years as a Civil Servant Arthur learned how to play table tennis, a game which has brought him much pleasure and which he has continued to enjoy well into his seventies.

'We were both very keen on table tennis,' says Leonard Hobbs, a Civil Service colleague who still keeps in touch with Arthur. 'We used to play at lunchtime and whenever else we could – that's how we got to know each other. He was a ferocious table tennis player. I tell you, he was very determined to win.'

For a variety of reasons, but mostly because of his involvement with fellow space enthusiasts, the prewar London years represented the good life to Arthur.

'I can thank science fiction for that, because it was through the magazines that I got in touch with London "fandom" and, most important of all, the fledgling British Interplanetary Society. (There was about an eighty per cent overlap between the two groups.)'

Of course a move away from the Paddington 'broom-closet' into a spacious flat made Arthur Clarke's good life even better. His imagination knew no bounds when it came to dreaming about space travel and manned rockets to the Moon, but he desperately needed more room on Earth.

In May 1938 Bill Temple was hunting for a place to live and decided to visit his friend Arthur Clarke at his room in Norfolk Square. It was, according to Temple, 'the world's tiniest bed-sitter', and he playfully suggested that Arthur's love of space travel may have been boosted by his feeling of claustrophobia.

Both young men were members of the British Interplanetary Society and the Science Fiction Association. Both enjoyed music and aspired to being professional writers. After some discussion, they decided to pool their resources and look for a spacious flat together.

They finally found one at 88 Gray's Inn Road, Bloomsbury. It was a few blocks east of the British Museum and just around the corner from where Virginia Woolf lived, although no one realised it at the time. After signing a three-year lease, Arthur and Bill moved into the flat in July 1938. It consisted of four rooms on two upper floors

– plenty of space for books, friends and meetings. The floors below the flat housed a foot clinic, a socialist press and the International Writers' Club.

'We have plenty of space here,' Arthur wrote Sam. 'And it is central, so no doubt many SFA and BIS meetings will gravitate here eventually.'

The two space cadets – Clarke and Temple – soon settled in. Arthur lived on the top floor (the 'attic' to him), which had a kitchen and dining area, a bathroom and a small bedroom. The sitting room was on the floor below. Bookshelves ran along one entire wall, but there wasn't much other furniture – a few chairs, but not enough to seat everyone at the meetings. Bill provided a table, which was in the dining area upstairs. Although it wasn't large enough, he and Arthur attempted to play table tennis on it.

'The huge Moon photo dominated our study wall,' Bill Temple wrote years later, 'as the Moon itself dominated our thoughts. Number Eighty-eight became the headquarters of the British Interplanetary Society, which gathered there to discuss ways and means of reaching those lunar maria.'

The British Interplanetary Society had been founded in Liverpool in 1933 by Phillip E. Cleator and a few other dreamers. In March 1937, its headquarters was moved from Liverpool to London . . . to 88 Gray's Inn Road. At about the same time Professor A. M. Low, one-time editor of *Armchair Science*, became the Society's first chairman. He was chosen to bring some prestige to the BIS.

'He was,' says Arthur, 'quite a well-known popular science writer – in fact, the best known one of his time. A lot of people, however, had some doubts about the legitimacy of his professorship because he had been affiliated with some minor institute at one time. Anyway, he was very interested in the future. Low graciously resigned later, when he thought his name was not all that good for us.'

Arthur became treasurer and Bill Temple replaced Ted Carnell (who was also editing the BIS *Journal*) as publicity director in 1938. The promotional hat was worn by everyone, of course, including Arthur, who wrote Society brochures (without bylines) to educate the public, generate press coverage and bring in new members. One such brochure began:

The British Interplanetary Society is a Society devoted to the study of Astronautics – the science of Space Travel. Since its foundation in 1933 it has done everything in its power to convince the public of the possibility of interplanetary communication, for it believes that the conquest of space could be accomplished *today* by means of the rocket motor and known chemical fuels. The scientific grounds for this belief are indicated at the end of this leaflet, and are the results of research extending over a number of years.

Further on in the same brochure young Arthur Clarke waxed eloquent about the Society's vision of interplanetary flight.

> Go out beneath the stars on a clear winter night, and look up at the Milky Way spanning the heavens like a bridge of glowing mist. Up there, ranged one beyond the other to the end of the Universe, suns without number burn in the loneliness of space. Down to the south hang the brilliant, unwinking lanterns of other worlds – the electric blue of Jupiter, the glowing ember of Mars. Across the zenith, a meteor leaves a trail of fading incandescence, and a tiny voyager of space has come to a flaming end.
>
> Looking out across immensity to the great suns and circling planets, to worlds of infinite mystery and promise, can you believe that man is to spend all his days cooped and crawling on the surface of this tiny Earth – this moist pebble with its clinging film of air? Or do you, on the other hand, believe that his destiny is indeed among the stars, and that one day our descendants will bridge the seas of space?

This was heady stuff for 1938, a year before World War II broke out. It is easy to understand why the visionary British Interplanetary Society was not taken too seriously by many people and by institutions who held more established and conservative views. Indeed, its goals of building a spaceship and sending a manned expedition to the Moon were often ridiculed. Members were considered cranks by many people. The same attitude that considered rocket pioneer Robert Goddard a lunatic in the late 1920s was working against the goals of the British Interplanetary Society in the late 1930s. World War II and Germany's V-2 rocket would put that attitude to rest for good.

Another space enthusiast, Maurice Hanson, was invited to join Arthur and Bill at the flat, and he moved in after a few months. At the time Hanson was editing what many consider to be Britain's first science fiction 'fanzine', *Novae Terrae*. Its initial issue appeared in March 1936, just months before Arthur said goodbye to his Somerset youth and went to live in London. The October 1937 issue was the first under the joint editorship of Hanson, E. J. Carnell and Clarke. Twenty-seven more issues were produced, the last being the January 1939 edition.

'Maurice came,' Temple recalls, 'carrying his typewriter . . . [and] so Number Eighty-eight became the editorial offices of *Novae Terrae*, too, with Arthur and me as assistant editors. Often in the small hours the three of us would be fighting a temperamental duplicator to produce *Novae Terrae* or the BIS *Bulletin*. Or getting out copy for the BIS *Journal*, which depicted detailed plans of our proposed moonship, so similar in the event to the *Apollo* vehicle. (A proud moment when my own tatty copies of the *Journal* were shown on TV that momentous week when the "giant leap" was made.)'

Besides Clarke, Temple and Hanson, the regular members who often met at the flat or the nearby Red Bull pub included Ralph A. Smith, whose pioneering space art illustrated some of Arthur's earlier space books including his very first, *Interplanetary Flight*; Val Cleaver, who was one of Arthur's best friends and would later become Chief Engineer of the Rolls-Royce Rocket Division and in charge of Britain's Blue Streak rocket; Jack Edwards, Technical Director of the BIS research effort in designing a spaceship and some of its instruments, including a 'space speedometer'; and Walter Gillings, journalist, 'fanzine' publisher (*Scientifiction*), and early devotee of science fiction.

The meetings of the British Interplanetary Society were held every other Thursday, usually alternating with Thursday-night gatherings of science fiction fans (most of whom, not surprisingly, were also BIS members).

'We were a group of English eccentrics,' says Bill Temple, 'trying to keep alive the flickering flame of space-travel research for its own sake – not for war applications, as had happened to the German Interplanetary Society now that the Gestapo had taken it over.' Temple also recalls that the Germans sent a member over to investigate the work of the British Interplanetary Society, which, despite appearances, was serious.

This Nazi journalist interviewed Arthur and Bill at the flat just before the war. They were both convinced he was a spy. Bill remembers how this 'tall fellow with the quiet voice and the restless hazel eyes looked through our cuttings book, and appeared very *unin*terested in those dealing with war rockets'.

'I think we succeeded in giving the impression that we were only a bunch of fools and could be ignored,' Temple recalled.

Certainly the British Foreign Office and the Air Ministry didn't take the Society too seriously, although they did sometimes respond to BIS letters. One such government response to a BIS letter about jet engines was received shortly before World War II broke out.

The letter read in part, 'We note your remarks. However, we cannot seriously envisage Mr Frank Whittle's jet engine replacing the piston engine.'

'Unbelievable?' asks Temple. 'I've seen the original letter in the BIS files. The military mind, whether British or German, is always unimaginative.'

This could hardly be said of the Society members who were seriously thinking about how to design a manned spaceship that would fly a round trip to the Moon and who were also promoting the feasibility of the idea to all who would listen.

'The meetings were often quite crazy, lots of fun and [full of] laughter,' Temple recollects. 'Sometimes they got side-tracked altogether. Once Ego set up his three-inch refractor telescope on its tall tripod beneath the wide skylight which covered our upper landing (and could be uncovered). It was a cloudless night with a full Moon. And Ego focused the telescope on the Moon and let us in turn examine the lunar territory which was our goal.'

With the Red Bull pub next door, some of the meetings split into two factions: the teetotaller group, headed by Arthur and Maurice, who remained at the flat for the meeting; and the drinkers including Walter Gillings, Bill Temple and others who believed that the discussion improved with a few drinks.

Temple tells how the drinkers rejoined the teetotallers at the flat for supper and talk until several members caught the last trains home.

'One night we returning revellers found the stairs to the flat barred by a heavy table and other flat furniture, with Arthur and Company armed with mops and brooms prepared to keep the drunks out. We stormed the barricade. Thanks to some smart rapier play by [John] Carnell and his rolled umbrella, we broke through. After all, the flat was *ours* too – it was everybody's.

'We staged revenge. We sent Arthur out for the fish and chips, and fixed a booby trap over the door. When he entered a large tin tea-tray fell on his head. He didn't turn a hair – and in those days he *had* hair.

'The fish and chip suppers were a ritual. Even the elegant John Wyndham (then John Beynon Harris) would eat them with us out of newspaper.'

*

Besides the general meetings of the British Interplanetary Society every other Thursday, Experimental Committee meetings were also held on the fourth Tuesday of each month. The technically inclined and gifted members, about twelve in number, worked on the general spaceship designs and decided what, if any, system components could actually be designed, built and tested within the modest budgetary limits of the Society. It was this group that designed the BIS spaceship (and some guidance components) which got a fair amount of attention in 1939, thanks to the efforts of several BIS members.

Temple, in charge of publicity at the time, gave some good news to the membership in the March 1939 issue of the BIS *Bulletin*. Their spaceship design was receiving some great publicity from large circulation magazines such as *Time* and *Practical Mechanics*.

> The cover of the March *Practical Mechanics* depicts in glorious colour the BIS spaceship roaring down towards the Moon, intent, apparently, upon landing on it upside down. Wisps wrapped around it show clearly how it is revolving, and lines streaming away from the nose show how it is cutting through the air in airless interplanetary space. The main article of the issue is a reprint from the *Journal*, H. E. Ross's description of the ship.

It was the BIS *Journal*, published quarterly and printed on glossy paper, which presented the Society's serious work. The *Bulletin*, in contrast, published the lighter, less scientific articles in the typed and mimeographed, do-it-yourself publishing format of the day. Technical papers and designs were produced by various specialised committees.

One such Experimental Committee meeting, held at the home of Ralph Smith in the East London suburb of Chingford, was written up by Bill Temple for the BIS *Bulletin* of September 1938. Known for his humour, Temple claimed that his description of the meeting, some of which is reprinted here, was only slightly a 'humorous exaggeration'.

> I fell to examining an intriguing but only partially completed model of a spaceship altimeter on the table, a heavy disc of aluminium which spun smoothly on its bearings in a framework, and soon other members came trickling in: Messrs Edwards, Ross, Bein, Day, Bramhill, Cowper-Essex and Janser. A general discussion began, which ranged from the

composition of a new steel, which could withstand thermite, to the composition of a dog's dinner. Mr Smith, who knows only too well how these meetings persist in wandering miles from the point, called for order, and the meeting proper began. First on the agenda was the question of whether to buy four small magnets for the altimeter and alter them, or continue a so far unsuccessful search for a suitably large one. It was decided to get the four small ones if their jaws could be widened by cutting.

This inertia-governed altimeter (space speedometer, if you will) was going to be tested on the Chancery Lane Underground escalators. It never got that far, however.

At a Technical Committee meeting in January 1939, Edwards reported that the space altimeter wasn't behaving as it should. (Edwards was, according to Clarke, an eccentric genius and 'the nearest thing to a mad scientist I have ever met outside fiction'.)

'Sometimes when it was supposed to indicate the exact height to which it had been lifted,' wrote Temple in the *Bulletin*, 'the indicator shot back past zero and pretended the thing was buried in the ground. Mr. E. pointed out how embarrassing this would be if it happened at a public demonstration. "We could always tell them that that proves space is curved," rapped out Clarke smartly, and everyone guffawed.'

Clarke later wrote in a *Holiday* magazine feature: 'The theory of the device was perfectly sound, and something similar steers every satellite into orbit today. But the engineering precision demanded was utterly beyond our means, and Mrs Edwards put her foot down on hearing of our intention to cast lead weights in her best saucepan.'

A topic on the agenda for the September 1938 meeting was a discussion of an efficient, lightweight battery to heat the spaceship. Temple wrote:

Here Messrs Edwards and Janser started an argument on such a highly technical plane that I just sat there between them agape, and the stream of words passed over my head like a beautiful rainbow. I gathered it was something about conductivity values. Arthur Clarke made occasional interjections, which might or might not have been to the point, but at any rate showed us that Arthur grasped what was going on. Which was what Arthur wanted to show us, anyway. It all ended with Mr Janser promising to hunt through his books (all two thousand of them) to find certain tables, and perhaps consult the National Physical

Laboratory on this important subject. (Wish I knew *what* subject.)

Another piece of hardware designed, built and tested – this time successfully – by the BIS in the late 1930s was an instrument called the coelostat. With this optical device a commander and crew of a spinning spaceship could observe the Earth, Moon, stars, or another spaceship, as a fixed image that was not spinning – a necessity for navigational purposes.

The coelostat depended on four mirrors to stop the local solar system from twirling. Two were stationary and two were spinning. Arthur donated the spring motor of his phonograph to the project, which was begun at the Experimental Committee meeting in September 1938. First Jack Edwards made a cardboard model of the coelostat. Then, wanting to demonstrate its fundamental principles, he sent everyone searching for mirrors. The Smiths donated their compact and shaving mirrors. Wall mirrors and dressing-table mirrors were also brought forth by others.

After some experimentation, Edwards took the small mirror from Mrs Smith's compact, which he wanted to use as the viewing mirror, and placed it carefully on the piano. He then asked everyone to take up a position and hold mirrors at various angles. 'Soon,' reported Temple, 'the room was full of living statuary, standing in graceful and artistic poses, holding mirrors above their heads.' Finally, after many contortions and no convincing demonstration, it was decided to build a working model of the coelostat. The meeting then broke up.'

Eventually the coelostat was built and worked well. A public demonstration at the South Kensington Science Museum in 1939 was a success in every way, and generated good publicity for the Society. Perhaps these 'crackpots' were producing valuable scientific results after all. The original Wright biplane, on display next to the demonstration room, gave this rather modest scientific event a boost in significance.

Attendees saw a spinning disc, with its affixed blurred lettering on it, on one side of the room. At the other end of the room was the coelostat, a foot-square wooden box, 'looking rather like the result of a misalliance between a periscope and an alarm clock', Arthur wrote after the event.

By looking through the coelostat at the spinning disc across the room, the blurred lettering became distinct and readable: the inscription, not surprisingly, was the acronym for the British Interplanetary

Society – 'BIS'. If the viewer looked at the rest of the room, however, it would be spinning. In a spinning spaceship, the coelostat could stop the twirling stars and allow the navigator to get a fix on its position.

Now all the Society needed was a real spaceship, not just drawing board blueprints, in which to put the coelostat and the space speedometer. But with only membership brain power and practically no assets, BIS would have to settle for a detailed on-paper design. The result was the 'cellular' spaceship design published in the BIS *Journal* in 1939, just months before Germany invaded Poland and Britain and its allies declared war on Germany. Out of World War II would come the fundamental rocket hardware that would eventually evolve into the sophisticated machinery that would take men to the Moon for the first time in human history.

Armed with youthful enthusiasm (most BIS members were in their twenties) and imagination, a realistic spaceship design emerged in 1939. Cylindrical in shape, with its crew quarters housed in the nose, the single-stage Moon rocket was designed to take three astronauts to the Moon and back. The propulsion system contained main and auxiliary rockets in a honeycomb structure. These were solid propellant rockets, and the number fired would determine the acceleration. As the individual rocket tubes were fired they would be jettisoned.

Various types of flight scenarios, rendezvous techniques and refuelling procedures for a Moon journey were seriously discussed. Just as NASA would do in the 1960s to a much greater degree, the journey was broken down into several stages so that specific problems could be identified and solutions found. One scenario called for a mother ship to remain in lunar orbit and a smaller ferry craft to actually land on the Moon. This anticipated the fundamental approach of the historic *Apollo* voyages by some thirty years.

Drawings were made of the BIS spaceship, and they were published in the *Journal* in 1939. Arthur tells a good story of how two Scotland Yard investigators stopped him on the street as he returned to 88 Gray's Inn Road from his Greek printer's shop in Theobalds Road. He was carrying two parcels filled with freshly printed copies of the *Journal* – the entire edition, as a matter of fact.

'Excuse me, sir,' one of them said politely, 'but we're from Scotland Yard. Could we see what you have in those packets?' Considering the Irish bombings of post offices and the gathering storm in Europe, this was a reasonable request from two well-spoken men in mackintoshes.

'To the considerable disappointment of the detectives,' Arthur later wrote, 'I was not even carrying *Tropic of Capricorn* [the banned book by American expatriate Henry Miller], but when I presented them with copies of the *Journal* they very gamely offered to pay. Tempting though it was to acquire a genuine subscriber (the cash box held about fifteen shillings at the time), I refused the contribution; but I got them to carry the parcels the rest of the way for me.'

The Society's spaceship design in the *Journal* gained a fair amount of attention, even from the prestigious publication *Nature*, which made the valid point that until practical experiments were performed that supported the theories produced by the BIS the Society could not be taken *too* seriously. This prompted the membership to launch a fund-raising effort for experiments. This is how the modest funds for the spaceship's navigational components were solicited.

Arthur's immersion in BIS affairs during the late 1930s would serve his writing well in the decades to follow. All the ideas generated among Society members, many of whom brought different perspectives, knowledge and skills to the space flight cause, were put through the rigours of friendly debate. Arthur C. Clarke would use many of them in his future fiction and non-fiction writing. In fact, Arthur was writing fairly regularly during these London years. Besides the promotional brochures for the Society and non-fiction articles for the BIS *Journal*, he was doing pieces for various science fiction 'fanzines', including some for *Novae Terrae* which he was helping to publish from the flat with Temple and Hanson.

In 1937 a fanzine piece titled 'Travel by Wire!' appeared in *Amateur Science Stories*, and two more tales ('How we went to Mars' and 'Retreat from Earth') were published in the same fanzine in 1938. He began using his nickname 'Ego' as a pseudonym – sometimes with slight variations: 'Ego', 'Arthur Ego Clarke' and E. G. O'Brien. But he was writing much more non-fiction than fiction during these prewar years. This was primarily because he was producing so many words for the regular and special one-off publications of the BIS. And he placed his writing wherever he could at this time of his career. With all his avocational activities, it is easy to forget that Arthur Clarke was still a full-time auditor for the Civil Service. He even found a non-fiction market with his employer. 'Into Space' was published in the Exchequer and Audit Department Association's publication *Chequer-Board* in October 1937.

In the piece Arthur outlines the next hundred years of space ventures.

With present-day materials and known fuels, it is possible to build a machine to leave the Earth, go around the Moon and return to Earth. With rather more trouble, and with the experience gained on the first flight, it will be possible to build a ship to land on the Moon and return. Once we have reached the Moon, going to the planets is merely a longer job, requiring practically the same amount of fuel. Out in space, distance makes little difference, for once a body has started moving it will go on for ever unless it is stopped again, as Sir Isaac Newton observed . . .

Looked at logically, the conquest of space is only a matter of time, experiment – and money. It may take fifty years, it may take a hundred, it may take much less.

It took less. Arthur's forecasting came true. Some thirty-two years later the first manned landing on the Moon took place.

The days at the flat in Gray's Inn Road were 'merry days', reflects Bill Temple, 'but there was a shadow over them.'

The storm broke on 3 September 1939 when Britain and her allies declared war on Germany. Everyone's life changed. Nobody knew how soon they would be called up.

Maurice Hanson was the first to be conscripted into the army (he was already doing national service), and John Carnell took over the editorship of *Novae Terrae* which he renamed *New Worlds*.

On 16 September 1939 Bill Temple married his fiancée, Joan Streeton. For a wedding gift Arthur gave them a print of Sir Francis Drake's ship, the *Golden Hind*. The Temples' fifty-year nuptial voyage together had begun.

'I married in haste but have never repented at leisure,' Temple wrote later. 'We lived at the flat. Arthur ignored the war and began writing his first novel, called *Raymond*. He'd burn the midnight oil working at it, then burst into our bedroom in the small hours to declaim to us some passage of pure genius he'd just penned.' It was a story he had begun in Somerset before coming to London.

'I still know exactly how it all began,' Arthur said later in an introduction to the work. 'The opening scene flashed mysteriously into my mind, and was pinned down on paper, around 1935. It was an isolated incident, unrelated to any plot I had been trying to develop.'

The work became *Against the Fall of Night*. From its beginnings at the family farm to the time an early version of it first appeared in

Startling Stories in November 1948, this work went through as many as six versions, its word count climbing over time. But that was not the end of it; Arthur couldn't let it go and it was eventually published as a novel by Gnome Press in 1953. Next Arthur undertook a major revision, and *The City and the Stars* was published in 1956. Twenty years had passed since Arthur had visualised the opening scene when he was in his late teens. Some critics believe that this marathon write was worth it. Frederik Pohl, for one, considers it to be Arthur's finest novel.

Bill and Joan Temple remember more about the time Arthur was beginning the first draft. 'We used to, the three of us, go out to supper together,' Bill recalls, 'which required a short underground journey. Coming home, Joan and I would, being normal, take the UP escalator. More often than not, we'd become aware of Ego racing us to the top exit via the DOWN escalator. And he'd win. Maybe he taps into cosmic energy. I call that cheating. Joan suspected that Ego sublimated his sexual energy through ceaseless writing.'

Arthur was pleased about the woman's touch at the flat, even if it was to be for only a few months. 'I could hardly boil water at the time,' says Joan, 'although Arthur says that the domestic and house-keeping [arrangements] improved when I moved in, which I was surprised to hear. As long as it was possible, they still held their meetings on Thursdays. I dished out sausage rolls and things I bought at the delicatessen around the corner.

'When my husband and Arthur first moved in they had given keys to various friends, so that whenever they were in London and they needed somewhere to go they could go to the flat. And when I moved in I found it all quite amusing and sometimes quite embarrassing because I would be happily getting on with things and suddenly somebody I didn't know would come in with the door key. I never felt I knew quite who was going to turn up.'

Because of his Civil Service job, a reserved occupation, Arthur was deferred. Bill Temple was still working at the Stock Exchange and thought he'd be called up in early 1940. Everyone expected that London would be bombed, and the flat was in the city centre. It was time to go.

Joan, Bill and Arthur left the flat in late December 1939, and went their separate ways. None of them would see it again the way they left it.

'When I was demobilised after the war,' says Temple, 'I returned to the scene. The flat had been in the centre of a terrace. Its inner walls had become outer walls. Everything adjacent had been bombed

43

out of existence, including the Red Bull pub and the fish and chip shop, which were completely destroyed.'

Arthur also went back in the 1970s. 'It still stands at 88 Gray's Inn Road, though a Luftwaffe bomb has neatly excised the pub where we entertained so many of our friends.'

Some fans have even tried to establish when the bombs hit, and their research points to April 1941.

There's a certain historic justice in the fact that it was Luftwaffe bombs that fell on to Gray's Inn Road, home of the British Interplanetary Society and its visionary rocketeers, and not V-2 rockets that began raining down upon London in September 1944.

When Arthur's friend, Leonard Hobbs, knew he was looking for new digs he thought he could help because his two older brothers were already off to the war.

Says Hobbs, 'I asked my mother, "Can Arthur stay with us?" She said "Sure" and so he settled in. My mother was Swiss and she liked cooking. She looked at Arthur, who was thin and tall, and decided to fatten him up a little bit.'

By March 1940 Len Hobbs had left his job in the Ministry of Works, where he had been ordering fire pumps for the expected Blitz, and joined the Royal Air Force. Not long afterward Arthur's duties as a Civil Servant also changed, when officials decided that the tea of the British Empire should be protected during the war.

'Early in 1940,' says Arthur, 'some genius at the Ministry of Food realised this, and all the tea chests in the London docks were dispersed throughout the land. I spent my last civilian summer battling with innumerable bills of lading, trying to find exactly where the stuff had gone.'

The Ministry of Food was evacuated from London in September 1940 and Arthur found himself in the safety of North Wales for the last few months of the year.

'Here I sat out the Blitz,' he recalls, 'peacefully checking the accounts of the Ministry of Food, until I exchanged civilian clothes for RAF blue.' The Ministry of Food had early punched-card sorters called Holleriths that produced ration cards, and Arthur worked with them. This would be the closest he got to computers until long after the war.

'It was a very pleasant time in Colwyn Bay,' says Arthur, who was billeted at 12 Erw Wen Road. 'I did a lot of cycling and sightseeing in North Wales, and got to know quite a lot of people. There was a naval school there, and I fell in with a local group of young merchant marine cadets (most of whom probably didn't survive the war). Along with my Civil Service friends, we went all over the place, including one seventy-mile trip to Conway Castle.

'We were billeted with local landladies. Generally two or three of us would be billeted with a landlady, and she would make our meals, although we had our midday meals in the canteen.'

It was from one of the naval cadets that Arthur bought his first telescope, and he also bought a new Remington Noiseless Portable and named it after the Athenian general and politician, Alcibiades.

'He really is a beauty,' Arthur wrote Sam Youd in September 1940. 'When I came down here I intended to do slabs of writing, but alas, apart from one spell in the train back from Somerset, I am afraid my output has been nil. It's a pity, as I have three stories unfinished and I don't lack ideas. The trouble is that I am an extrovert and after being here about a week, I made some dozen friends whom I haven't left since. In addition, the average digs are hardly suitable for any creative work. I am doing this, for instance, on a table that shakes like an aspen in a very bad light.'

The new typewriter no doubt renewed his incentive because he got back to work on *Against the Fall of Night* in the autumn of 1940.

'I did a lot of writing on the early draft of this novel and finished the first draft at Colwyn Bay in late 1940, just before I volunteered in early 1941 for the RAF.'

It would be some time before Arthur Clarke again wrote regularly.

CHAPTER 5

The Royal Air Force and WW II

There were great sheets of fire roaring on
either side [of the runway], clouds of steam
rising into the mist, and a heat like that from
an open furnace beating into our faces, for
we were only a hundred feet from the nearest burners.

– Glide Path

Auditing and trying to locate Britain's tea as an executive officer in
His Majesty's Exchequer and Audit Department was not, Arthur
realised, how he wanted to be serving his country in wartime. And
even though he was deferred for the time being because of his reserved
occupation, he knew that sooner or later he'd be called up. In early
1941 he decided to join the Royal Air Force.

'I determined to go where *I* wanted to go – not where the random
processes of the draft decided.'

Because of his interest in astronomy, Arthur wanted to learn
celestial navigation and put it to use for the Royal Air Force.

'I bought books on the subject by Francis Chichester (later famous
as a single-handed round-the-world sailor) and studied them avidly.
I then went behind the back of the Civil Service while in Wales
and enlisted clandestinely,' he says. 'Without telling my superiors, I
sneaked away from the Civil Service and just registered. That was it.
I don't even remember where the recruiting office was, but it must
have been somewhere not very far from Colwyn Bay. Then I waited
for the call-up. My papers arrived a few weeks later.'

After having his RAF medical examination in nearby Chester in
early March, Arthur enlisted at the No. 3 Recruit Centre on 18 March
1941. He entered the Royal Air Force as an Aircrafthand Radio Wireless Mechanic/Aircraftman Class 2. His service number was 1097727.

Arthur displayed some last-minute civilian independence during
his enlistment. If an inductee had no formal religious affiliation, the
RAF policy was to put 'Church of England' on his identity disc.

'I was annoyed about this,' says Arthur. 'I got the man who was

46

handling the paperwork, and made them change it to "pantheist".'

The annoyance was justified. First and foremost, the Church of England label was inaccurate – Arthur had no such affiliation. It was a demand for truth that prompted his response rather than any desire to defy bureaucratic authority. His devotion was to science and science fiction, both of which depend on a rigorous intellectual scepticism. The scientific method and the science fiction quest are antithetical to religious faith. But at least *pantheism*, by equating God with the forces and laws of the Universe, was true to his value system – and his strong individualism.

Clarke's consistent aversion to organised religion over the last fifty years is based on the fact that any religious dogma, by definition, claims it has found the ultimate truth, an idea that Arthur finds absurd. From the perspective of science, there's a tremendous amount we still don't know about our vast and mysterious Universe. Any such premature claim of ultimate knowledge has to be based on faith, not the scientific method, and Arthur has never been willing to replace knowledge with faith.

On 27 March Arthur reported to the Initial Wing No. 4 Recruit Centre for basic training. Very basic, indeed, according to Arthur, who summed up the common experience with just a few well-known words: 'If it moves, salute it. If it doesn't, paint it.'

After basic training, where he and thirty others had been taught 'how to behave without disgracing the Royal Air Force', Arthur was ordered to London for technical training with the Air Ministry Unit. It was the summer of 1941. He was one of several hundred other Aircraftsmen 2 ('the lowest form of animal life in the RAF') who were receiving training in electronics. They were billeted in a partly bombed-out infant school building in London's East End.

'It was near Aldgate Underground Station. The ruins were still smoking, and *that* was all I ever saw of the Blitz.'

No one knew it then, but the last major air attack on London – the heaviest and deadliest raid of the war – had taken place a few days before the young recruits were sent to the city on 16 May 1941. The devastation was everywhere. Westminster Abbey, the House of Commons, the British Museum and other historic buildings were hit by the primitive iron bombs. It was during this time that Clarke started to imagine what '*real* war would be like' and wrote some material which, after revision, would eventually become chapter seventeen of his novel, *Earthlight*, describing a full-scale space battle.

During this period of technical training in London, Arthur was singled out from the other troops.

'One day we were lined up on parade and inspected by the senior Warrant Officer, who selected me, of all people, to be his batman. As life on the farm had bred in me a complete indifference to tidiness and even to general hygiene, the WO's choice has always struck me as somewhat astonishing; perhaps I merely looked less moronic than the rest of the recruits.'

By keeping this Warrant Officer's quarters clean, and polishing his boots and brass, Aircraftsman 2 Clarke avoided peeling potatoes or cleaning latrines. Another great break for Arthur. He did his chores quickly and used his spare time to study differential equations.

'When he discovered what I was doing,' recalls Clarke, 'my kindly *padrone* let me use his quarters as a study while he was bawling out squads on the parade ground.'

After the technical training in electronics, Clarke was selected for training in what the Royal Air Force called Radio Direction Finding or RDF. This appeared to be Arthur's first experience in military bad luck because his hope of being posted to a flight school and learning celestial navigation was not going to happen. 'It wasn't exactly what I wanted, but it certainly sounded a lot better than the medical corps,' he later admitted.

What Radio Direction Finding really was was radar, but the word and the technology were classified as secret during the war. Arthur would learn some of its secrets in the early 1940s at the Number Two and Number Nine Radio Schools in Wiltshire, on the plains not far from Stonehenge. He was posted there in late September 1941.

'Arthur was sent as a trainee to the Radar School at RAF Yatesbury when I was lecturing there,' recalls Barry R. King. 'He appeared in a class of about twenty-four men, which was put under my care and tutorage for the duration of the course – fourteen weeks or so.'

Everyone knew that Arthur's eyes were cast upward toward the stars, that he was a member of the British Interplanetary Society and was obsessed with rockets and space travel. This earned him the nickname 'Spaceship' when he was at Yatesbury. Barry King also recalls that Clarke was an apt pupil who outshone his classmates.

'I suspect that the periods of time spent in getting his colleagues to understand were spent by Arthur in space calculations,' reflects King.

After the fourteen-week training course (consisting of a general electronics course and then a more specialised course on radar), Arthur became an instructor on the staff. He enjoyed teaching and eventually earned the rank of corporal in that capacity.

'I spent the next couple of years in the bleak and windswept –

yet to me wildly exciting – world of Number Nine Radio School, Yatesbury,' he says.

Yatesbury was a large camp, with four wings. The fourth wing was Number Nine Radio School, which was in a compound about a quarter of a mile outside the main camp and was surrounded with the usual barbed wire and military police. The camp barracks were wooden huts, each one accommodating about twenty-four men, with a storeroom area and an NCO's room at the end. For heat they had a coal stove.

Harry Morrin, one of Arthur's students, arrived in Yatesbury in the summer of 1942. 'We were introduced to the mysteries of radar by Corporal Clarke,' he says, 'on the evening shift – from about five p.m. to midnight. He was a good lecturer. He took us through the theory of radar and all the theory of circuitry which was used in the ground radar sets at the time.

'We had him for two or three nights, and then one day in the canteen we got to talking with some of the boys who had been there longer. They said, "Who's your lecturer?" We said, "Corporal Clarke," and they replied, "Oh you're lucky. Get him talking about spaceships. Say that rockets won't work in a vacuum or something like that."

'Sure enough, a few nights later in class someone actually got the conversation around to it. It was about ten p.m. Before long Arthur was giving us all the facts about how to get to the Moon – about multi-stage rockets and lunar orbiters. He went on for half an hour or so, and he had all sorts of diagrams on the board.

'Somebody asked how big the rocket was going to be, with the fuel and the rest of it. And Arthur's answer was, "Well, somewhere about the height of St Paul's Cathedral." This turned out to be remarkably prophetic because the height of the *Saturn* rocket for the first *Apollo* mission to the Moon was within a few feet of the height of St Paul's Cathedral!

'Arthur set up a telescope in the storeroom at the end of the barracks, and I often remember being treated to a mini-lecture on the moons of Jupiter or the rings of Saturn.'

During this period Arthur became good friends with John Burns Maxwell. 'Johnnie Maxwell was a Royal Canadian Air Force Radar Sergeant (or Flight Sergeant) on the Yatesbury staff. He was a very bright radio ham type, and became my closest friend. We spent holidays together until he left for Canada, and I later met him and his family, staying with them in Toronto.'

Johnnie, along with Val Cleaver, another good friend, encouraged and advised Arthur to attend university upon his release from the RAF.

During his free hours at Yatesbury, Arthur took advantage of the good library on the base and read technical literature on such specialised subjects as electrical circuit theory. This individual study eventually led him to write several technical pieces, one of which, 'More Television Waveforms', was published in *Electronic Engineering* in November 1942. The article passed the scrutiny of the wartime censors because the mathematical formulas were presented in the context of television, not radar, the technology of which was actually derived from television.

A few weeks later, on 2 December 1942, one of the great scientific breakthroughs of the twentieth century took place: Enrico Fermi and his colleagues at the University of Chicago started their famous nuclear reaction that would change the world.

During the war years Clarke produced more non-fiction than fiction, which is understandable in view of his technical training and the fact that he had much less access to the community of science fiction fans. The only year from 1940 to the present when nothing was published – neither fiction nor non-fiction – was in 1943. This is certainly no mystery in view of the fact that the previous year, 1942, was Clarke's first full year in the RAF. Saluting his superiors and other duties at Yatesbury no doubt took most of his time.

Publication of the technical 'Waveforms' article, Arthur contends, helped him obtain his commission as a technical officer. Not long after publication Arthur was called into Group Headquarters and questioned at length by Wing Commander Edward Fennessey (who would later become Managing Director of Post Office Telecommunications). Young Clarke obviously made the grade because soon thereafter, in early 1943, he was sent to a radar installation.

'The ten-centimetre CHL [Chain Home Low] Station I worked on was in Lincolnshire, near the coast. This is where I was immediately before I joined GCA [Ground Control Approach] at Davidstow Moor, their second home.'

Davidstow Moor was not far from King Arthur's legendary castle at Tintagel. It was August 1943 when Arthur met up with a team of American scientists there. He found himself 'on an airfield in Cornwall with a bunch of wild young scientists and engineers from the Radiation Laboratory of the Massachusetts Institute of Technology. They were demonstrating a brand-new radar system called GCA [Ground Control Approach], designed, for a change, to do something

Lieutenant Charles Wright Clarke, circa 1917.

Below Wanderlust at an early age. A two-year-old Arthur C. Clarke begins his travels.

Below The Clarke family in the late 1920s, when father was ailing from war wounds. *Clockwise from top*: Arthur, mother Nora, baby Michael, Mary and brother Fred.

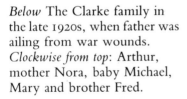

Top Arthur's first flight in 1926, when he was eight years old. Nora Clarke is in the rear.

Teenaged Arthur in his study circa 1936 with (*above left*) his crystal set and experimental equipment and (*above right*) his beloved collection of science fiction magazines on the shelves behind him.

Left Arthur peers through his first telescope at his 'Dunghill Observatory', Ballifants.

constructive. It could *talk* aircraft down, rather than shoot them down.'

The new orders would prove a boon to Clarke's future. For the first time in his life he was working with trained scientists, and the project involved state-of-the-art secret technology as well.

Arthur arrived at Davidstow Moor the same month that 571 allied bombers flew a night-time raid against Peenemünde, hitting Germany's V-bomb experimental bases with more than 1,900 tons of bombs.

Luis W. Alvarez, the Nobel Prize-winning physicist, led the scientific team which developed the prototype Ground Control Approach radar system at MIT's Radiation Laboratory in 1942. The British brass, knowing how important such a blind-approach radar system could be for the war effort, arranged for Alvarez and his American team to bring the prototype Mark I system over to England for advanced testing.

'Luis' brainchild,' Arthur said in a speech given at MIT in 1976, 'provided me with a peaceful environment, totally insulated from the hard things going on elsewhere – invasions and bombings and so forth – that allowed me to work out the principles of communication satellites back in 1945.'

Before Arthur met the team at Davidstow Moor, the formal trials of the GCA radar system had been run at the RAF bomber base at Elsham Wolds in north-east England. Alvarez, his four-man Rad Lab team and their equipment arrived in July 1943. The testing programme had the blessing of the station commander – as long as it did not interfere with his bombing missions to Germany.

The GCA equipment was mobile and was contained in two trucks weighing some twenty tons. One truck held the power plant and transmitter antennas, housed in odd-shaped structures jutting out, and had no room for personnel. The other truck was the manned control van, with the radar screens and other controls, where the actual talking down was done. Eventually the production Mark II models would be contained in only one truck.

Once the prototype system hardware was reassembled and checked out, the GCA tests began and lasted for six weeks. Each day the GCA trucks drove to the operating site near the runway. The diesel power plant was then started up, and it took about thirty minutes to warm up the vacuum tubes and align the circuits.

Glide Path, Arthur Clarke's novel about this radar work in England during World War II, was published some twenty years after the fact, in July 1963. Often described as Clarke's only non-science-fiction novel, much of it is autobiographical material from his Royal Air Force days. One passage from the novel gives a general description of how the Ground Control Approach radar works. The words are those of Flight Lieutenant Deveraux to the protagonist, Flying Officer Alan Bishop.

> The idea's extremely simple, even if the equipment isn't. What we have is a very precise radar set, capable of tracking an aircraft to within a few feet. A controller on the ground has the information presented to him, and he talks to the pilot over the radio, telling him what course to fly in order to keep on the glide path. If the pilot obeys orders, and everything's working OK, he'll find himself over the end of the runway. The Americans call it a 'talk-down' system, which is a good way of describing it.

Air Chief Marshal Sir Ludlow-Hewitt visited and observed the operational testing in August 1943. He was impressed with how the system successfully landed a variety of RAF planes returning from missions in zero visibility. The GCA team was always on alert when the Lancaster bombers were flying during bad weather, but as much as the Ground Control Approach radar tests went well (the Air Ministry decreed that the formal trials at Elsham Wolds had been successful) the decision was made that such a blind-approach radar system should be further tested at a bad-weather base. The MIT Rad Lab team and its support group would also train the RAF group in its operation and maintenance before leaving British soil.

It didn't take long for everyone to agree that Davidstow Moor in Cornwall had the worst weather of anywhere they had ever been. This was the RAF's Coastal Command, which flew bombers over the Atlantic on anti-submarine patrols.

After Alvarez passed his leadership duties on to his colleague George Comstock and flew back to the United States to join the still-secret Manhattan project team, the four members of the MIT group headed for Davidstow Moor in late August 1943.

It was in the fog, rain and mist that the MIT group met the RAF team, including Arthur C. Clarke, who would eventually take over the Mark I GCA radar set and maintain it for the British. The Americans, including Bert Fowler and Neal Jolley whom Arthur got to know, were also responsible for training the RAF personnel in operation and repair.

Because of the miserable weather, the RAF base at Davidstow Moor had been closed for seventy-five per cent of the time – that, of course, was why the GCA unit was sent there. At least everyone had the same thing to complain about, and it wasn't ducking bullets. Bert Fowler of the MIT team recalls that it rained twenty-one out of the twenty-three days they were there.

At Davidstow Moor Technical Officer Clarke 'found the American scientists amplifying their already excellent vocabularies over expiring transformers, and complaining bitterly that their equipment wasn't built for underwater operation. At night, when the apparatus closed down and cooled off, the all-pervading mist would creep gleefully into every cranny, depositing moisture in high-voltage circuits so that brief but spectacular firework displays would ensue in the morning.' To help solve the moisture problem, electric heaters were positioned in the equipment and turned on at night.

It was also a good thing that the Americans had brought along a large supply of spare vacuum tubes because at least one was lost every day in the system, including those in the various radio sets.

'I can still remember my amazement,' Clarke says, 'at the number of vacuum tubes in the GCA Mark I. It came to the incredible total of almost a thousand. I'd have laughed scornfully if some crazy science fiction writer had predicted that one day every engineer would have carried in his hip pocket, not a Colt .45 but an HP-45 calculator – this mere handful a dozen times as complex as our Mark I. The explosion in complexity and implosion in size are two of the main parameters determining future communication technology.'

Clarke and the others were billeted in a black-painted steel Nissen hut heated with two coke-fired stoves. Several of these veterans vividly recall many enthusiastic discussions taking place there about mankind's future in space.

'I do remember,' says Arthur's long-time friend, Bert Fowler, 'talking about what it took in the way of thrust to get weight into orbit, and about the plans and designs for a colony on the Moon and spacesuits which would provide oxygen and protect you against the vacuum. Most of us, I think, were just fascinated that somebody had not only thought about these things, but had actually put numbers into them and done some engineering thinking about the problems of manned space flight. None of us had ever been exposed before to someone who actually thought in technical terms of getting to the Moon and what it would take to live there.' This was, after all, twenty-five years before Neil Armstrong and Buzz Aldrin landed *Eagle* on the Sea of Tranquillity.

Neal Jolley was claiming his bunk and unpacking when Pilot Officer Clarke put his bag on the next bunk and introduced himself.

'I soon decided he must be some kind of screwball,' says Jolley.

'He talked of belonging to the British Interplanetary Society, and took for granted rocket-launched satellites that could appear to be stationary over Earth. We all knew that was impossible in the foreseeable future and not even worth wasting time thinking about.'

Jolley's scepticism was not uncommon on either side of the Atlantic, and he was hardly the first to refer to space enthusiasts as 'screwballs'. In fact, 'crackpots' was probably the more common phrase in the 1940s. Had this attitude prevailed after the war, however, planet Earth still might be waiting for a chosen few of its inhabitants to walk on the Moon's surface.

During off-duty hours the clack of table-tennis balls echoed in the cramped quarters. Arthur was at it again, challenging everyone to his favourite sport which, through persistent practice, he had all but mastered.

'The most memorable thing about Arthur's game,' says Bert Fowler, 'was that his feet were rarely on the floor. We used to kid him that the reason he won most of the time wasn't because of his talent but rather because of the way he would demoralise the opposition by hitting the ball with both his feet off the floor.'

After a few September weeks of getting waterlogged at Davidstow, spending what seemed like more time maintaining the equipment than operating it, the unit moved to St Evals, about thirty miles to the south-west.

Quarters at St Evals were considerably improved from the cold and damp temporary huts at Davidstow Moor. There were private rooms in permanent prewar buildings. More importantly, the rooms were steam-heated. The unit's mission at St Evals was to set up a school for training RAF crews – the controllers, mechanics and operators – who would use the production units, the Mark IIs, which would start to arrive a year or so later. The Mark I also continued to be a demonstration model to convince the top RAF brass that this was what their aircraft and pilots needed.

The last of the Americans were soon gone. Fowler returned to the States in early October 1943 and Jolley left later in the month. At about this time in Europe, the Russians swept west and Italy declared war on Germany.

Arthur and his RAF comrades were sorry to see the Americans go. 'They were a grand crowd,' Arthur reflects. 'Our discussions were by no means devoted entirely to waveguides, magnetrons and pulse techniques. We also taught them some interesting songs.' These were the bawdy songs and dirty limericks for which the RAF was so well known. When the GCA team had their reunion outside Boston in October 1971, guess who won the dirty limerick contest? None other than the space cadet from Somerset, Arthur C. Clarke.

Clarke now had full responsibility for the one-of-a-kind Mark I. 'We were very much on our own and could no longer run to the experts when anything went wrong – as it frequently did. It had never been intended that the laboratory-built Mark I should be used continuously, month after month, for training and for innumerable demonstrations, in a foreign country and run by people who hadn't watched it grow up from a blueprint.'

Still, the RAF team always managed to get it up and working when the top brass dropped in for a look. They were finally impressed enough to approve the system for the Royal Air Force, although the road to acceptance was long and arduous.

In the beginning the pilots were against the system and they remained sceptical for quite some time. Their attitude was understandable. The pilots, after all, were being asked to relinquish control of their aircraft and give it over to the GCA radar technicians on the ground. But the hard fact that the RAF was losing more planes to the nasty English weather than to the German Luftwaffe made the GCA radar system a top priority. As the system proved itself and its reliability was demonstrated hundreds of times during the testing programme, the pilots slowly, cautiously, began to trust and appreciate it.

In early 1944 another classified project came to St Evals airfield on the Cornish coast. It was called FIDO (an acronym for Fog, Intensive, Dispersal of), but it was more analogous to a fire-breathing dragon than a domesticated canine. By generating tremendous amounts of controlled fire and heat, FIDO was designed to burn off the fog and mist on runways and give an extra margin of safety with approach and touchdown visibility to pilots. The system was meant to change, with fire and fuel and fury, local bad weather into better weather for RAF airfields.

By positioning fire-producing pipes vertically in rows for three miles along the runway and feeding them, through connecting fuel lines, with immense amounts of fuel (a hundred thousand gallons each hour), a colossal heater was created to burn off the bad weather with what was estimated to be ten million horsepower of heat. If FIDO did what it was designed to do, pilots could then make visual landings during the last few seconds before touchdown. In theory, by combining this system with Ground Control Approach radar, any aircraft could land with complete safety in otherwise impossible weather conditions.

No one ever forgot the experience when FIDO was lit. 'The scene might have come from Dante's *Inferno*,' Clarke wrote in 1949. 'There were great sheets of fire roaring on either side, clouds of steam rising into the mist and a heat like that from an open furnace beating into our faces, for we were only a hundred feet from the nearest burners.' And in his World War II novel, *Glide Path*, Clarke has his protagonist, Alan Bishop, walk on to the runway and experience FIDO's full heat and fury up close.

> The hissing roar rose to a crescendo; the heat from the blazing jets battered for a moment with terrifying violence against his exposed skin. Then he was through, and the fire and fury subsided behind him. The open runway was ahead . . . And there they fell silent, beholding a miracle.
>
> Like most miracles, it was a very simple one. Overhead, the stars were shining.

A combined test of the Ground Control Approach radar and the fog-eating FIDO was conducted at St Evals in early 1944. Miserable weather and zero visibility was necessary for the test. Finally, after a stretch of good weather, drizzling fog settled in.

One fogged-in midnight all was ready: FIDO was lit, the GCA technicians were monitoring their radar screens in the control truck and the pilot and station's commanding officer were on board preparing for takeoff. Then came trouble. The Search radar, which presented the big, 360-degree picture like any air traffic control system, broke down. Only the narrow, thirty-degree glide-path radar system still functioned. While there was some additional risk, it was decided that the test could go ahead with only the narrow sector of radar tracking.

FIDO roared its fire and the aircraft took off, but it soon became lost outside the narrow active radar sector. After instructing the pilot to do a 180-degree turn, GCA soon picked up the plane again and lined it up for its landing.

'The pilot was unable to land on this run: he found himself at the edge of the runway, but visibility was so bad that he could only see a single line of FIDO burners and didn't know which side of the runway he was! So the manoeuvre had to be repeated, and luckily the second approach was successful despite the attempts of the FIDO-induced gale to push the aircraft off course.'

These were the worst weather conditions under which the GCA

Mark I was ever operated. Arthur remembers how technicians stood on the running boards of the two radar trucks and shouted out instructions to the drivers who slowly made their way back to the hangar. This test was the prototype's last hurrah, and the fire-breathing FIDO was subdued and eventually put to rest for ever by a rapidly improving radar technology.

The Mark I was soon dismantled, never to be reassembled. It had, with the help of tender and loving overhauls, worked exceptionally well right up to tear-down day. Soon the operational Mark IIs, under production in the United States, would arrive and join the GCA group in late 1944 and early 1945 at its newly assigned airfield in Honiley, a few miles outside Stratford-upon-Avon.

'Many years after the war,' says Arthur, 'with my sadly missed friend Val Cleaver, we tried to find the old *circa* Stratford Airport. We found the hangars, but that was about all that was recognisable. It was like the opening of *Twelve O'clock High!*'

The Mark II GCA units arrived too late for extensive use in the European war effort, but the new technology made the Berlin airlift a success during 1948 and 1949, with more than 270,000 flights, and it was also available and used extensively in the Pacific.

It seemed appropriate that Arthur's last duty station was near Shakespeare's birthplace, and that his first professional sale and payment for a short story happened there. The RAF's Ground Control Approach radar team was now training in operation and maintenance of the new Mark II. The end of the war in Europe appeared certain, and it was probably this fact rather than a lively Avon muse that had Arthur C. Clarke writing.

During the GCA radar days Clarke wrote almost two dozen pieces, most of which were non-fiction. There were some notable exceptions, however. The short story 'Rescue Party', with its optimistic view of humanity's future among the stars and its effective punch-line ending, was written at the Honiley airfield in March 1945, although it didn't appear in *Astounding Science Fiction* until May 1946. This was the first story Arthur sold professionally. *Astounding* editor John W. Campbell sent a cheque for the then significant amount of $180.

It was 1945 – Arthur's last full year in the Royal Air Force – and he wrote whenever he could. The fact that the German High Command surrendered unconditionally on 7 May 1945 allowed everyone to begin considering the future.

Gradually Arthur started thinking more about rockets and space travel and less about his wartime concerns of microwaves and radar.

He and about a dozen other loyal members of the British Inter-planetary Society corresponded with one another again, and began making plans. The Society's public relations efforts would be much easier after the war, Arthur realised, thanks (ironically) to Germany's rocket development. No longer could people *easily* dismiss the BIS members as screwballs, nuts and crackpots. The war proved that large rockets could be built and flown; Germany had built thousands of them. And so while the credibility of BIS members and their goals was less of a problem, there still was no single, motivating reason to build very expensive rockets.

The question that Arthur and his fellow space cadets were focusing on when the war ended was: how can rockets make money? Once rockets could deliver profits plenty of money would become available to build them. Many crazy schemes were proposed, although the mail-carrying rocket schemes of the 1930s were no longer seriously considered. Then Arthur came up with a promising idea which he developed in more detail and subsequently published.

'Some time in the winter of 1944–5 I thought of one which seemed a little less crazy than the others.' It was a system of geostationary satellites that could provide global communications.

The following summer Arthur further refined and elaborated his concept during his off-duty time while stationed at Honiley, and in July 1945 he wrote his seminal piece 'Extra-Terrestrial Relays', which was published the following October. His personal journal records the event:

'1945. July 2 to 6. Started typing out my thesis on the space station, which I'm calling "The Future of World Communications". I'll send it to *Wireless World* first, I think. Handed it in for censorship on the 6th. It runs to 3,000 words and four drawings.'

It was Clarke's unique combination of interests during 1945, his wartime specialities of microwaves and radar and a renewed concen-tration on rockets and space travel, which proved essential to the genesis of his most famous non-fiction article. But 'Extra-Terrestrial Relays' did not become well known until long after its initial publi-cation.

Little did Arthur know that this single article (and a relevant letter to the editor of *Wireless World* he had written earlier in the year) would eventually establish his name in the science history books as the 'father of satellite communications' and the visionary who foresaw the revol-ution in global communications. He had no idea that this somewhat technical piece, quietly published in a specialised British journal shortly after the end of World War II, would bring him numerous awards and honours over the years.

During a June 1982 address at The Hague, where Arthur had come to accept the Eighth Marconi International Fellowship Award, he said with uncharacteristic modesty: 'If I had not proposed the idea of geostationary relays in my *Wireless World* letter of February 1945, and developed it in more detail the following October, half a dozen other people would have quickly done so. I suspect that my early disclosure may have advanced the cause of space communications by approximately fifteen minutes.'

This humble statement deflects possible criticism from those in the scientific community who believe that a good amount of the credit should go to the men and women who did the advanced and detailed design work and who built the hardware. It's like Neil Armstrong and Buzz Aldrin constantly reminding the American public after their historic Moon flight that the true heroes of the *Apollo* programme were the thousands of men and women who built the systems their lives depended on when they landed and walked on the Moon in July 1969. All well and good and reasonable, but heroes still don't come in large groups.

Clarke has also been careful to point out possible influences and to correct false claims. He dismisses as 'ridiculous' the idea that he is somehow responsible for discovering the actual geostationary orbit itself, noting that the concept goes way back to Kepler and Newton. If many in the aerospace community today refer to geosynchronous orbits as 'Clarke' orbits, so be it – just as long as it is made clear that he in no way 'invented' such orbits. When John R. Pierce, friend and satellite pioneer of the *Echo* and *Telstar* satellites, reminded Arthur that a series of science fiction stories by George O. Smith might have influenced him, he acknowledged that possibility.

The Smith stories, published in *Astounding Science Fiction* in thirteen instalments over a period of three years beginning in late 1942, became known as the *Venus Equilateral* series. The stories took place far away from Earth orbit, on a manned radio relay station in outer space. The radio station was 'sixty degrees ahead of Venus, positioned there to maintain communications between Earth and Venus when the sun blocked the direct path between the two planets'. The way to visualise the system is think of an equilateral triangle with Earth at one vertex, Venus at another and the radio space station at the third. All three bodies, of course, are in orbit around the sun.

When Ballantine Books reprinted Smith's stories in *The Complete Venus Equilateral* in 1976 Arthur provided the introduction, in which he wrote: 'It is therefore quite possible that these stories influenced me subconsciously when, at Stratford-upon-Avon during the closing months of the war, I worked out the principles of synchronous communications satellites now embodied in the global Intelsat system.'

Whatever the possible influences (and even minor ones have been brought forth in various essays) Arthur C. Clarke's 'Extra-Terrestrial Relays' is original and historically significant. The fact that Arthur also wrote two other earlier pieces – one published and one privately circulated – that present the concept only boosts the legitimate claim of 'father of satellite communications' that he often downplays. (He prefers to be 'merely the *god*father'.)

The letter Clarke had written to *Wireless World* in February 1945 was printed under the title, 'V-2 for Ionospheric Research?', and it pointed out that the German V-2 rocket could be utilised as an important research rocket after the war and that if it were outfitted with a second stage it could reach orbital velocity.

> I would like to close by mentioning a possibility of the more remote future – perhaps half a century ahead. [Arthur's guesstimate of 1995 was twenty years too late.] An 'artificial satellite' at the correct distance from the Earth would make one revolution every twenty-four hours; i.e., it would remain stationary above the same spot and would be within optical range of nearly half the Earth's surface. Three repeater stations, 120 degrees apart in the correct orbit, could give television and microwave coverage to the entire planet.

A second typescript was written in late May 1945, although it didn't see print until 1968 – a year before *Apollo 11*'s *Eagle* landed on the Moon with its crew of two. Arthur typed up six copies of 'The Space-Station: Its Radio Applications' with its nineteen neatly numbered paragraphs on his Remington Noiseless Portable and then circulated it privately to a few friends in the British Interplanetary Society. Over the years, one of these original copies found its way to the Smithsonian Institution.

After discussing the obstacles to global communications using traditional technologies, Arthur suggests that they can be overcome with space stations.

> All these problems [for example, how to link television systems around the planet] can be solved by the use of a chain of space stations with an orbital period of twenty-four hours, which would require them to be at a distance of 42,000 km from the

centre of the Earth . . . The stations would lie in the Earth's equatorial plane and would thus always remain fixed in the same spots in the sky, from the point of view of terrestrial observers.

In late June Clarke used this 'memorandum', as he calls it, as the basis for his now famous piece. He submitted it under the title 'The Future of World Communications', which the editor changed to 'Extra-Terrestrial Relays'. Scholars who often wait for more than a year to have their papers reviewed and possibly printed would be amazed to learn that the Royal Air Force censors approved it in a month, and it was then accepted by *Wireless World* on 1 September for publication in the October issue. Its subtitle was a question: 'Can Rocket Stations Give World-wide Radio Coverage?'

The answer, of course, is yes. Clarke explains how the various problems can be solved: the rockets, the frequencies, the power requirements and the number of 'rocket stations'.

> A single station could only provide coverage to half the globe, and for a world service three would be required, though more could be readily utilised . . . The stations would be arranged approximately equidistantly around the Earth, and the following longitudes appear to be suitable:
>
> > 30 E – Africa and Europe
> > 150 E – China and Oceana
> > 90 W – The Americas
>
> The stations in the chain would be linked by radio or optical beams, and thus any conceivable beam or broadcast service could be provided.

In August 1945, a few days after the *Enola Gay* had dropped the atomic bomb on Hiroshima, Arthur received the proofs of his article to read. The bombing induced him to add a short epilogue on atomic power and its probable impact on rocket design and performance. He believed it would bring 'space travel half a century nearer'. Years later, however, he admitted that he had been over-enthusiastic about the influence nuclear energy would have on rocketry by 1965.

Wireless World was hardly *Life* magazine, and Clarke would have to wait until the 1950s for his non-fiction and fiction work to reach larger audiences. When the satellite pioneer, John R. Pierce, asked his friend to write the introduction to his 1968 book *The Beginnings of Satellite Communications* Arthur obliged. It was here that Arthur told of how the 1945 publication of 'Extra-Terrestrial Relays' was received with 'monumental indifference'. He could remember no response whatsoever, neither positive nor negative, to its appearance.

'Once I had got the idea down on paper, I more or less lost interest in it myself. There seemed nothing more that could be said until technical developments had validated (or invalidated) the basic concept.'

Years later Arthur learned that 'Extra-Terrestrial Relays' had in fact generated interest in some quarters. One was the US Navy Department, which had initiated a study on the future uses of rockets and space flight in 1944. Robert P. Haviland was conducting the study, and he read Clarke's article. Improved communications were vitally important to the Navy, and Arthur's article was a valuable resource. In fact, a formal programme was begun as a result and experts believe that this programme was a major reason for the acceptance and development of artificial Earth satellites in the 1960s.

Someone connected with the US Navy study or with an early RAND Corporation report gave a copy of Clarke's article to the *Los Angeles Times*, and this resulted in a science piece on the subject for a lay audience. Written by William S. Barton and published on 3 February 1946, the headline read, 'Tiny "Moons" Circling Earth Proposed as Long Distance Broadcasting Aid'. While Arthur was incorrectly identified as a 'Scientist Who Fought V-2 Rockets' in the subheading, the concept itself was explained accurately.

'A scientist's plan,' read the first paragraph, 'to solve television, wireless telephone and telegraph long distance broadcasting problems by establishing, with the aid of rockets, manned radio relay stations that would forever circle the earth like tiny moons, is receiving serious consideration.'

The newspaper stated that scientists in the Los Angeles area were taking the proposal seriously and considered it a real possibility for the future.

'Extra-Terrestrial Relays' has managed to withstand the test of time. That Arthur C. Clarke envisioned the relay stations as large and manned as opposed to small and unmanned is understandable in light of the fact that transistors and the entire microelectronics revolution were not foreseen in the 1940s. So while Clarke's estimate of satellite size was considerably off, all the fundamental principles presented in 'Extra-Terrestrial Relays' were valid.

Wireless World paid Arthur fifteen pounds to publish his 'Extra-Terrestrial Relays' – gravy cash to add to his regular Royal Air Force pay. Though he has never complained about the amount, he has had a lot of fun speculating in print and on lecture tours about the monetary value of his comsat concept (how many billion?) had he been able to patent it. He began thinking about this in the early 1960s during some financial difficulties.

After the fact, Arthur has asked himself, his readers and his audiences if he should have published such an important paper in the open press. Many people over the years have asked him why he made no attempt to patent his concept of global communications. The idea of doing so, he admits, never occurred to him, and he blames his own lack of imagination. He has no regrets about the matter, however, 'for in my heart of hearts, I believe that I've received everything that is due to me in terms of recognition from the people who really matter'. He adds that while others like scientists John R. Pierce and Harold Rosen have had the tough challenges and responsibilities of transforming a paper idea into real and complicated hardware systems, he has had all the fun. And having fun has always been an important part of Arthur's life and work.

During the summer of 1945, Arthur learned about an essay contest sponsored by the *Royal Air Force Quarterly*. The essay topic, 'The Rocket and the Future of Warfare', was right up his alley and he decided to give it a shot. He won. Written in November 1945, Arthur's essay was published the following March.

Some forty years later, in the 1980s, science writer T. A. Heppenheimer pointed out for the first time that the essential concept of Mutual Assured Destruction was contained in Clarke's essay long before it became the policy of the United States.

The essay put more cash into Arthur's pocket. More important was the win itself. His writing had been judged superior and this gave him further incentive to continue his word-smithing. The winning essay would also prove vitally important in opening up the academic doors to King's College, London.

CHAPTER 6

King's College and the Postwar Years

> The first great technological aid to education
> was the book. You don't have to clone
> teachers to multiply them. The printing
> press did just that and the mightiest of all
> educational machines is – the library.
> — 'Electronics and Education'

Arthur's five years in the Royal Air Force were, all things considered, a positive experience. He came out knowing a lot more about many things, including radar, than he'd known when he enlisted. The discipline hadn't hurt either. He had worked on the edge of a new technology, and several of his colleagues were well-respected scientists. This was much more stimulating and exciting than auditing various government accounts, and it dovetailed well with his outside interests. He soon realised that the life of a Civil Servant was not the one he wanted to live.

'I was still technically in the Civil Service until well after the war,' says Arthur, 'and they in fact made up my service pay.'

Before he was demobilised on 21 June 1946, Arthur Clarke began thinking about how he would make a living once he resigned from His Majesty's Exchequer & Audit Department. His writing had brought in a small income, and it wasn't unreasonable to think that such an income could be increased. Still, he knew it was risky. He also knew he had the farm to fall back on if all else failed. Then two friends persuaded him to enrol in a university and pursue an education in science.

One of these, Val Cleaver, was a fellow member of the British Interplanetary Society and was, along with Arthur, one of the most loyal and dedicated members who worked to revive and reorganise the Society after the war. He and Arthur would both serve terms as chairmen during the postwar years. They shared the same interests and were the best of friends. Cleaver's wartime work involved propeller development for the de Havilland Engine Company. In 1946 he was invited to start a rocket division for the company, and he later became the chief engineer for the rocket division of Rolls-Royce.

The other friend and adviser was Flight-Sergeant Johnnie Maxwell of the Royal Canadian Air Force. He was on the Yatesbury staff and became another good friend of Arthur's. They spent several leaves and holidays together before Maxwell returned to Canada.

Their advice to Arthur was straightforward: because of his considerable talents he should pursue a scientific education after the war rather than continue his Civil Service work.

This advice was gladly taken, and Arthur applied for a grant from the British government. These grants were established specifically for students whose studies were interrupted by military service, however, and he was not eligible.

'I was swiftly rejected on very reasonable grounds, and I do not recall being unduly depressed by this verdict,' he says. Clarke knew what he wanted, and he was only beginning to go after it. Indeed, one of the benefits of being a novice writer is that one soon becomes immune to rejections from publishers, and they no longer have any negative psychological impact. He knew he'd shortly be accepted and enrolled in a college course of his choice; all that was required was a sustained and focused effort.

When the new Labour government got into power after the war, a young Member of Parliament had come to prominence. His name was Captain Raymond Blackburn, and he had a distinguished army career. Even better, he knew something about rockets and made several references to them in his speeches and had actually written about them. Arthur sent Blackburn his award-winning paper 'The Rocket and the Future of Warfare', which had appeared in the *Royal Air Force Quarterly* in the spring of 1946. As a result, the two men became friends, and Clarke received an invitation to the House and met the War Minister.

When Arthur's university grant request was turned down, he told Blackburn about it and asked if there was any way he could help. 'In a very short time, my grant was approved and I applied for admission to King's College, London.'

Arthur went home to Ballifants for the summer of 1946 and spent his time relaxing, writing, catching up on correspondence and planning for King's College.

Housing was a real problem in London after the war, but Arthur arranged for room and board at the home of Eric Taylor and his family in 72 All Souls Avenue in north-west London. Eric, an artist and teacher, had been stationed near Ballifants during the war and had got to know the Clarke family.

'He lived with us for about two years,' Eric recalled. 'He had the small spare bedroom, and it was a bit cramped, but he seemed to fit in with anything that was going on.

'Arthur was utterly and entirely immersed in his own work, incessantly pounding on his old typewriter when he was not at lectures. It seemed a sort of fanatical drive to put down what was developing in his mind. He did not seem to indulge in any university fun and games in his absolute concentration on his work, and it appeared almost as if it was a race against time.

'Arthur introduced us to the then-new invention – a portable radio, very small for the time, which he carried wherever he went. He was very fond of classical music, which was his other main interest.'

On 7 October 1946 Arthur enrolled at King's College. King's is built around a large quadrangle with the main entrance on the Strand. The classrooms and laboratories are on the far side of the quadrangle on a large terrace above the Thames embankment. There was some bomb damage from the war, but it was not extensive.

Astronomy had been Arthur's first choice of subject; it was only offered at University College, which had no room. Instead, Arthur pursued a Bachelor of Science General Degree in physics, pure mathematics and applied mathematics.

George McVittie, a famous cosmologist and astronomer, was, according to Arthur, the most memorable professor he had at King's College. 'He taught me applied maths and I taught him about rockets,' Arthur says with genuine pleasure. 'He once referred to me as one of his ablest students.'

The compliment was returned in 1956 when the collection of short stories, *Reach for Tomorrow*, was published. In the preface Arthur says that the story 'Jupiter Five', written in June 1951, required twenty or thirty pages of orbital calculations and should be dedicated to McVittie, who taught him how to do them.

'He was a very kind-hearted and nice guy,' says Arthur, 'even if he was a little austere and remote. Eventually he went to America and helped build up the radio astronomy department at the University of Illinois. The applied mathematics McVittie taught consisted of dynamics, statics, orbital mechanics – those are the ones I remember best – and perturbation theory. Of course, I've used that in many of my stories.'

David Fowke, a fellow old boy of Huish's, was undertaking the same course of study as Arthur, but they were on different schedules.

Whenever they had the opportunity they would meet and talk.

'I was allowed to take the course in three years,' says Fowke, 'coming straight from school, whereas Arthur did it in two. In spite of this I was only able to get a second class degree whereas Arthur, taking only two years of it, sailed away with a first. He had a much quicker brain than I had. Often I would go to him and say, "What the hell does this mean?", and he would help me sort out some of the difficulties I was having. This would have been primarily in physics, which became his main interest. Although our course covered all aspects of maths as well as physics, I think Arthur saw the maths as something that was useful – a useful tool in developing his interest in physical things.'

David Fowke was encouraged to join the British Interplanetary Society by Arthur, who began his duties as chairman during his first year at university. Another recruit was the great playwright George Bernard Shaw.

Arthur delivered a paper to the BIS called 'The Challenge of the Spaceship', which was later published in the Society's *Journal* and subsequently revised, updated and reprinted several times. Soon after giving the speech Arthur read Shaw's *Back to Methuselah* and was moved by a closing speech which spoke of 'starry mansions' and the great cosmic domain of life.

'This, I thought, showed a considerable sympathy with the ideals of astronautics,' says Arthur, 'so I sent Shaw a copy of the British Interplanetary Society's *Journal* containing my lecture – not in the least expecting a reply.'

But a reply he got, in the form of one of Shaw's famous pink postcards, dated 25 January 1947.

'Many thanks for the very interesting lecture to the BIS. How does one become a member, or at least subscribe to the *Journal*?' Shaw asked. In subsequent correspondence Shaw presented his theory on what caused the fatal air crash of Geoffrey de Havilland in his experimental jet plane in September 1946. De Havilland was Shaw's neighbour.

Arthur was perplexed and didn't quite know how to reply. The fact was that Shaw's main point, that de Havilland's jet aircraft 'reached the speed at which the air resistance balanced the engine power and brought him to a standstill' was, said Arthur, 'complete nonsense'. Arthur patiently pointed out the flawed thinking in two letters, points that Shaw took well with little argument.

More importantly, George Bernard Shaw joined the BIS when he was ninety-one years old and continued to be an active member until his death. He was one of dozens of new members Clarke recruited during his first chairmanship of the Society.

'I attended some of the meetings,' says David Fowke, 'but the hours I was working made it difficult for me to follow up. But I do recall that everybody wanted to talk to Arthur. Even in those days he was recognised as an expert, an authority in that field, and everybody wanted to put ideas to him, sound him out, or just ask him for explanations of particular problems or aspects of interplanetary flight. People would queue up to talk to Arthur before or after he spoke. They were always keen to have him as a speaker.'

While the war years made rocketry and the prospect of space travel legitimate concerns in the eyes of the public, there were still many people who remained sceptical and a few who were outright antagonistic. As chairman of the BIS, Arthur was always persuading people to take the goals of the Society seriously and was often called upon to defend those goals.

Such skills of persuasion did not seem to make a convert of C. S. Lewis, however, the well-known author of *Out of the Silent Planet* (1938) and *Perelandra* (1943). Arthur first wrote to Lewis in December 1943 while he was in the RAF, and began writing again when he became chairman of the BIS.

In some of his novels Lewis attacked scientific humanism in general, and scientists and astronauts in particular, and praised traditional Christian values. In *Perelandra* Lewis refers to the 'little rocket societies' bent on exporting the crimes of mankind to other planets.

This was enough to make Arthur see red. He wrote to Lewis, his powers of rational persuasion dominating over his sense of injustice and anger – for the most part. The long letter condemned Lewis's cynical views of science fiction and interplanetary flight. This began a correspondence with Lewis, lasting for several years, in which Arthur defended the work of the Society and his own dreams for the future of space travel and what he hoped would be the future cosmic adventures of *Homo sapiens*. He was always seeking speakers for BIS meetings, and more than once he asked Lewis to give a lecture.

'It would only be fair to point out that your position might be somewhat analogous to that of a Christian martyr in the arena,' Arthur wrote, adding that many members admired his writings even if they did not always see eye to eye with them.

Lewis, of course, declined: 'I hope I should not be deterred by the dangers! The fatal objection is that I should be covering ground that I have already covered in print and on which I have nothing to add.'

Finally a face-to-face meeting was arranged between Arthur C.

Clarke and C. S. Lewis. It took place in Oxford at the well-known pub, the Eastgate. Accompanying Arthur was his good friend and fellow Society member, Val Cleaver. C. S. Lewis brought along none other than Professor J. R. R. Tolkien, whose trilogy *The Lord of the Rings* was to become world famous.

'Val and I stayed at the Mitre, which is a wonderful non-Euclidean building with no right angles in it, no two rooms the same. We met Lewis at the Eastgate, and this little man, whose name I didn't catch, was in the background. Then I found out his name was Tolkien.

'Needless to say, neither side converted the other, and we refused to abandon our diabolical schemes of interplanetary conquest. But a fine time was had by all, and when, some hours later, we emerged a little unsteadily from the Eastgate, Dr Lewis' parting words were "I'm sure you're very wicked people – but how dull it would be if everyone was good."'

Arthur's accelerated two-year programme at King's College ran from October 1946 to June 1948. His academic workload, as heavy as it was, did not preclude him from writing. Several of his classic short stories – 'The Fires Within', 'Inheritance' and 'Critical Mass', for example – with their Clarkean twists and surprise endings, were written and published during this time. So too were a variety of non-fiction articles, many of which appeared in the *Journal* and the *Bulletin* of the British Interplanetary Society.

Immediately after completing his first-year exams, Arthur committed himself to an intensive writing schedule for the month of July 1947. He wrote a novel, *Prelude to Space*, in twenty days. Never since has he written anything so fast. The reason: most of it was in his head before he began. He'd made notes for more than a year before actually putting pen to paper. In between typewriters at the time, Arthur handwrote the entire manuscript on school exercise books that were issued by the Royal Air Force during the war.

As any writer knows, often through frustration and disappointment, there's no connection between how a book is written and how it is published. Although the writing process was exceptionally quick for *Prelude*, publication came slowly. It first appeared in 1951, four years after Clarke wrote it, in a magazine format, Galaxy Novel Number Three (World Editions). It was not published in book form until Sidgwick & Jackson issued it in Britain in 1953. The next year Gnome Press issued a limited US hardcover edition and Ballantine followed with a paperback edition later in the same year.

Prelude to Space was Arthur Clarke's first space book. He was twenty-nine years old when he wrote it. Because the novel was primarily a vehicle to present Arthur's ideas and convictions about the promise of space, its writing was driven by the enthusiasm of his youth. There are many autobiographical titbits throughout the novel, and the dedication itself points to its major influence: 'To my friends in the British Interplanetary Society – who by sharing this dream, helped to make it come true.'

In a 1975 preface, Arthur places his early novel in the tradition of several space pioneers such as Tsiolkovsky, Oberth and von Braun who wrote space fiction as a means of conveying their ideas to the general public.

'I must confess,' he wrote, 'that I had similar propagandistic ideas in mind when planning this book.'

So be it. Many of Clarke's early visions in *Prelude to Space* have proven correct or nearly correct. Like the *Apollo* missions, there were three crew members aboard the novel's moonship. Although the novel's first manned Moon landing didn't take place until 1977 (Clarke was eight years off in his estimate), its predicted date of when an unmanned rocket would hit the Moon's surface was correct: 1959. And more than once Arthur presented his concept of a system of communication satellites. From the then-future perspective of 1977, one protagonist gave an overview of space history: 'The great radio and telegraph companies *had* to get out into space – it was the only way they could broadcast television over the whole world and provide a universal communication service.'

Prelude to Space also serves as an introduction to many Clarke themes which the author continued to develop in his later novels and non-fiction essays. A major theme is the importance of international co-operation for large-scale space expeditions, a concept central to *2010: Odyssey Two*. Another is the Stapledonian perspective in which millions of years pass before us, as in the famous opening sequence of *2001: A Space Odyssey*.

During Arthur's college years, two of his short stories appeared in *King's College Review*. 'Nightfall', better known as 'The Curse' when it was first reprinted in *Reach for Tomorrow* in 1956, was initially published in the *Review* in December 1947. It is a powerful story about nuclear war, filled with haunting images, the last of which is Shakespeare's gravestone and its carved epitaph sinking beneath the deadly glow of the River Avon:

> Good frend for Iesvs sake forbeare,
> To digg the dvst encloased heare

Blest be ye man spares thes stones,
And cvrst be he yt moves my bones.

Arthur wrote it while still in the Royal Air Force, stationed at the airbase in Shakespeare country where he wrote 'Extra-Terrestrial Relays'.

In December 1948 the *Review* published 'The Forgotten Enemy' (the advancing enemy from the north is not living but a force of nature), which was eventually reprinted at least a dozen times in various collections of stories, including *Reach for Tomorrow*.

Fantasy: The Magazine of Science Fiction published his story 'The Fires Within' in August 1947, but for some reason Arthur used one of his pen names – E. G. O'Brien. The story concerned a dense form of life dwelling in the Earth's subterranean depths, and it may have been influenced by the 1936 discovery and proof of the Earth's inner core by observing diffracted P waves.

Arthur graduated from King's College in the summer of 1948 with first-class honours and decided to continue with the year of post-graduate studies to which he was entitled under his programme. He enrolled in University College.

'I decided to devote my time to astronomy in my final year,' says Clarke, 'but to my disappointment found it extremely dull. I fell into the hands of an elderly professor whose main interest was instrumental defects. He spent his entire lecture time deriving long equations showing how all the possible errors in azimuth, right ascension, elevation, declination, latitude and longitude were related and how one could correct for them.'

The boring postgraduate course may have been a blessing in disguise because Arthur continued to find excitement in writing short stories and non-fiction pieces during this period. In the summer of 1948 he wrote 'Breaking Strain', a story about two men on a disabled spaceship with only enough resources for one of them to survive. Later in the year he wrote one of his most famous stories, 'The Sentinel', which has often been referred to as the 'seed' for *2001: A Space Odyssey* which appeared two decades later in 1968.

'Unlike most of my short stories, this one was aimed at a specific target – which it missed completely. The BBC had just announced a short story competition; I submitted "The Sentinel" hot from the typewriter, and got it back a month later. Somehow I've never had much luck with such contests.'

Clarke has often complained about the misleading idea, presented in print on numerous occasions, that it is the story upon which *2001* was based. In fact, ideas from several other stories were folded into the creative mix.

Even the story's extra-terrestrial artifact discovered on the Moon was very different from the black monolith of the film and novel: it was 'a glittering, roughly pyramidal structure'.

While Arthur's writing efforts continued to stimulate him, his studies in astronomy did not.

'Luckily I escaped after a single term. Before terminal boredom set in, the Dean called me to his office and said he'd heard of a job that would suit me perfectly. I applied and got it; and he was right.'

Arthur was hired as Assistant Editor of the journal *Physics Abstracts*, which had been published by the Institution of Electrical Engineers since 1900. It was considered one of the primary abstracting journals in the sciences. The editor and Arthur's boss was Dr Bernard Crowther, who had studied under Sir Ernest Rutherford, the Nobel Prize-winning British physicist.

After World War II there was a tremendous backlog of abstracting work to be done, and Arthur Clarke became one of the needed reinforcements for the task of classifying and indexing everything published (in all languages) in the physical sciences.

'My job was to go through mountains of journals (we had cup-boards-full of German and Japanese publications that had not yet been opened), and to see that everything of value was abstracted so it would be readily available to the world's scientific community.'

There were about a hundred abstracters in all, including some multilinguists who could tackle any subject in any language without having knowledge of it beforehand.

Arthur enjoyed his labours. He found that his colleagues were intelligent and the work was fascinating. The bulky arrears of scientific journals (many of which were wartime runs from enemy nations), and the exploding amount of new postwar materials produced as veterans returned to work in the civilian labs, gave Arthur the kind of challenge he enjoyed taking on.

'I probably had a bird's-eye view of research in physics unmatched by anyone else on Earth during this period,' he says, 'since *every* important journal, in *every* language, passed across my desk. And the abstracts were edited there, on the way to the printer.'

When the subject held a personal interest for Arthur, he occasionally would write the abstracts himself. He also contributed the heading ASTRONAUTICS to the index system while he was at *Physics*

Abstracts – no surprise to anyone who knew how fluent and knowledgeable he was in the subject.

His hours away from the Institution of Electrical Engineers were as busy as those on the job. He wrote constantly and continued his active involvement in the British Interplanetary Society and the London science fiction community.

It was also during the late 1940s that Arthur and his fellow space cadets found a pub to replace their prewar meeting place, the Red Bull, which had been destroyed by German bombs. It was at the White Horse, conveniently located in Fetter Lane, just off Fleet Street, where the gang of about fifty enthusiasts met every Thursday evening to exchange ideas and discuss books and stories they had read. The White Horse pub would become the fictional location for Arthur C. Clarke's humorous tall tales of science fiction written during the early 1950s and first published as *Tales from the White Hart* in 1957.

Arthur met Mike Wilson for the first time at the White Horse one Thursday night in 1950. Wilson was an energetic young man with plenty of ideas and things he wanted to do. He was working in a London hotel as a wine waiter at the time, but he had been at sea in the merchant marine. Wilson also enjoyed science fiction, and got on well with the White Horse gang. Clarke and Wilson hit it off immediately, and the friendship began to evolve.

He told Clarke about his skin-diving experiences in the Far East during one of his voyages. Clarke became enthusiastic and decided to take skin-diving lessons, first practising in local swimming pools and later hiring an aqualung and diving in the English Channel. This was the beginning of their globe-trotting adventures throughout the 1950s and 1960s, their eventual business partnership, and a long-term friendship.

After completing his first full year at *Physics Abstracts* Arthur realised that his earnings were steadily increasing from his writing and his radio appearances. Also during 1949 he received a contract from the British publisher, Temple Press, to write *Interplanetary Flight*, a non-fiction work on space flight.

'My job was interfering with earning a living. Had this not happened, I might have spent the rest of my life quite happily surveying the advance of physics from my Olympian height.'

Interplanetary Flight evolved from a two-part article, 'Principles of Rocket Flight', which was published in the British journal *The Aeroplane* in January 1947. 'The article attracted the attention of Jim Reynolds, a senior editor at Temple Press, who was then planning a series of booklets under the general title "Technical Trends",' says Arthur. 'The book was written between July and September 1949, when I was moonlighting from my job. When *Interplanetary Flight* appeared in May 1950, it was not only surprisingly successful but was quickly followed by an American edition. That gave me the necessary encouragement to step off the IEE escalator on to the freelance writer one, which seemed to be ascending more rapidly. I do not recall any particular trauma; it was as easy as that.'

Clarke's *Interplanetary Flight* was unique. It was the first book in the English language to present the basic theory of space flight with any technical detail, and general readers were not intimidated by equations because all the mathematics were put into the appendix. One teenage reader who has since acknowledged its influence on his future was Carl Sagan.

'When I was in high school,' says Carl, 'I knew that I was interested in the other planets and I knew that rockets had something to do with getting there. But I had not the foggiest notion about how rockets worked or how their trajectories were determined. Then I came upon an advertisement for a book called *Interplanetary Flight* by one Arthur C. Clarke. You must remember that at this time there was hardly any respectable non-fiction literature on the subject. I sent away my money and breathlessly awaited the arrival of *Interplanetary Flight*.

'It was a modest-looking book, beautifully written, its stirring last two paragraphs still of great relevance today. But the part about it that was most striking for me was the discussion of the gravitational potential wells of planets and the appendices which used differential and integral calculus to discuss propulsion mechanisms and staging and interplanetary trajectories. The calculus, it slowly dawned on me, was actually useful for something important, and not just to intimidate high school algebra students.

'As I look back on it, *Interplanetary Flight* was a turning point in my scientific development,' says Sagan.

Arthur has admitted that he regards his first book with 'particular affection'.

'Never in my wildest dreams,' he says, 'could I have imagined, when I began writing the book in July 1949, that exactly twenty years later I would be standing at Cape Kennedy, since renamed Canaveral, watching the first men leave for the Moon.'

The American edition of *Interplanetary Flight* was published by Harper and Brothers in 1951. Clarke's editor at Harper, George Jones, had been a colonel in the US Air Force during the war and was enthusiastic about Arthur's subjects. George would remain Arthur's editor for almost twenty years. He and his counterpart in England, Jim Reynolds, later encouraged Arthur to write an even more popular book about space, *The Exploration of Space*. It was this book that put Clarke's name and work before tens of thousands of readers for the first time.

Cut off from the steady income of his *Physics Abstracts* editorship, Arthur wrote fast and furious, both fiction and non-fiction. The modest advance of fifty pounds he'd received for writing *Interplanetary Flight* would hardly finance his new career. He was offered a number of miscellaneous assignments and contributed his expertise, for example, to the space comic strip 'Dan Dare' in *The Eagle*. Arthur was science and plot adviser.

During this time he bought a home in north London at 88 Nightingale Road, where he would live and work for several years, sharing the house with his brother Fred and his sister-in-law Dot. Fred oversaw several months of repair and renovation of the semi-detached Victorian brick dwelling, and Arthur, Fred and Dot moved into it on 2 July 1950.

Soon after the publication of his first book, Arthur began appearing on television to promote science, his work and the goals of the British Interplanetary Society. The studios were conveniently located at Alexandra Palace, within walking distance of the Clarkes' home, and the tall antenna masts could be seen from the house. Such close proximity to the media would prove a real advantage to his budding career. He soon felt comfortable on the infant medium that was fast changing the world.

His first appearance came about at quick notice. One afternoon in 1950 Arthur was being given an informal tour of the studios by a staff member, and he met the host of a science programme. They had an animated discussion and before long Arthur was invited to appear on the show. The subject was 'The Fourth Dimension'.

'He appeared on the screen for twenty minutes,' reported the *Somerset County Herald*, 'and his talk made television history by being the longest to be televised without any interpolations – in other words, the speaker alone had to hold interest the entire time. This Mr Clarke did despite the abstruse nature of the subject.'

Arthur used the concept of Flatland and its shadowy inhabitants to describe the fourth dimension, and he illustrated his presentation with blackboard drawings and conventional models.

'As an educational experiment,' wrote the editor of *The Times Educational Supplement*, 'the broadcast was a welcome contribution.

One lesson to be learnt is that for such specialisation more time is essential.'

In those days faces had to be plastered with a green pancake make-up so they wouldn't appear pasty white on the television screen. Fred Clarke remembers Arthur coming home after the broadcast with his face painted green.

'After terrifying my wife and the children, he went upstairs to clean it off and returned half an hour later with a well scrubbed, glowing but clean face. The towels were not so lucky. After four repeated launderings my wife threw them away.'

In the autumn of 1950, Arthur came up with what he considers one of his most important ideas. His technical piece, 'Electromagnetic Launching as a Major Contribution to Space Flight', appeared in the November issue of the British Interplanetary Society's *Journal*. It described how an electromagnetic launch system could be built and applied to great benefit in the low gravity of the Moon. Such an accelerator was also described several times in his fiction of the 1950s. The heroes of his young adult novel *Islands in the Sky* are saved by such a launcher on the Moon's surface; his short story 'Maelstrom II' has a launcher central to its plot; and a similar device is used as a weapons launcher in his 1955 novel, *Earthlight*.

'It is also widely recognised,' he wrote in the BIS *Journal*, 'that interplanetary travel will not be practicable on the large scale until propellants can be obtained on the Moon, with its very low gravitational potential . . . A possible long-term solution to the space-flight problem may be found in the use of electromagnetic accelerators on the Moon, launching the fuel mined there into suitable orbits round our satellite.' He backed up his Moon-based launch system with plenty of numbers and equations.

This basic system was adopted by Gerard O'Neill and fellow space-colony enthusiasts in the 1970s when they planned their large-scale space habitats during workshops and study groups. It was called a 'mass driver' during this period. 'A nice name,' says Arthur, 'until one tries to think of a propulsion system to which it *can't* be applied.' O'Neill and his colleagues worked out many of the engineering specifics and built and tested some models of the electromagnetic mass driver. It became a major element in some of their space-industrialisation scenarios in the late seventies. And most experts agree that some version of Clarke's electromagnetic launcher will be an essential component of any Moon base built in the twenty-first century.

In August 1951 Arthur's short story 'Superiority' was published in the *Magazine of Fantasy and Science Fiction*. Says the narrator, who was on the losing side of an interstellar war: 'We were defeated by one thing only – by the inferior science of our enemies. I repeat – by the *inferior* science of our enemies.'

The lesson learned by the once-superior race was that too much innovation in R & D can ultimately deplete resources and gradually transform superiority into inferiority.

Reprinted almost a dozen times, the story was also made required reading for some classes at the Massachusetts Institute of Technology, a fact which made Arthur extremely proud and which no doubt later influenced him to accept speaking engagements at MIT.

The late summer of 1951 was hectic. Arthur was again waging one of his in-print battles against someone who was spreading falsehoods about space and rocketry – and he was enjoying every minute of it! On 9 August 1951 the *Picture Post* had published an article on space travel written by their 'scientist', Derek Wragge Morley.

'It was utter nonsense,' says Arthur. 'He was an entomologist – an expert on ants! – not even an authority on space travel. And I wrote a letter [as Chairman of the British Interplanetary Society] pointing out all his errors, and the idiot flatly said we didn't know what we were talking about.

'I remember one phrase he used – that step rockets had no relevance to space travel! I wrote to a number of people, including Wernher von Braun, who wrote back enthusiastically as one space cadet to another. It was a Dear Mr Clarke letter, the first that Wernher ever wrote me.'

Von Braun's reply to Arthur began, 'You called on me as a brother-in-arms in your war with the *Picture Post* and I can only hope that I shall not disappoint you. I scanned all available American press releases on rocket firings in this country, as well as our old (meanwhile declassified) reports and files from Peenemünde, in order to supply you with reliable ammunition.'

Wernher did himself proud, and went on to present detailed factual information (three single-spaced pages' worth) that refuted Morley's statements. Arthur incorporated much of this material in his letter to the *Picture Post*, which was published as 'Space Travel: We Are Attacked', along with Morley's arrogant response '. . . And Our Scientist Replies.'

It appeared that Arthur had won the battle when the *Picture Post* gave considerable space to a review of the Temple Press edition of Clarke's book *The Exploration of Space*. It was a positive notice, and unusual in that it was written by two reviewers: Derek Wragge

Morley *and* Kenneth Allsop. The *Picture Post*, it seemed, was putting a check on Morley.

In September Arthur chaired the Second International Congress on Astronautics, which was put on in London by the British Interplanetary Society. The official subject of the meeting was the 'Earth-satellite Vehicle', but the discussions covered the entire solar system and beyond. It was attended by sixty-three delegates from ten countries. Press coverage emphasised that, for the participants, space flight was a practical goal for the next few decades, not a wild-eyed dream.

Said Chairman Clarke: 'Space flight is likely to be the next major technical achievement of our species.'

It was at this congress that Arthur met Frederick C. Durant III for the first time, and they soon formed a lifelong friendship.

'All the delegates met on a Sunday evening for an informal social,' recalls Durant. 'And that's when I first met Arthur. I knew of him because of his work with the BIS and his papers. In those days you could read everything written about space flight. I was a member of the BIS, having joined in 1948, and had great respect for the Society. They had taken their name two years after the founding of the American Interplanetary Society. The AIS had lost some of the courage of its conviction and changed its name to the American Rocket Society. [The word *Interplanetary* was too far out for industrial support.] The BIS stuck by their guns, and I've always lauded them for their courage.

'I became a little more prominent at the meeting because I presented a paper by von Braun, the opening paper, "The Importance of Satellite Vehicles to Interplanetary Flight". Wernher had just become a US citizen, but he couldn't leave the country. I was a naval aviator and a lieutenant commander then,' says Durant, 'and much of London was still boarded up after wartime bombing. So because of the paper, I did attract a bit more interest. I even appeared on the BBC radio show, "*In Town Tonight*".'

The von Braun paper that Fred Durant read outlined a voyage to Mars. This would require, of course, a Herculean effort. Just to build and supply the 'satellite station' he proposed as the above-Earth launching base required forty-six three-stage rocket ships to make some 950 trips to orbit! Von Braun's scenario was ambitious, to say the least, and it was expanded and incorporated in his book *The Mars Project*, published in 1952.

Hermann Oberth, one of the three great space pioneers (along with Robert Goddard and Konstantin Tsiolkovsky), also attended. 'I had him as my house guest,' says Arthur. 'He stayed with us at 88 Nightingale Road during the congress, but his English wasn't very good and my German was even worse.'

While Arthur was completing his juvenile book, *Islands in the Sky*, *The Sands of Mars* (written in the late 1940s) was published by Sidgwick & Jackson. This was Arthur C. Clarke's first novel to be published in book form, and he worked out much of the plot while going for walks around Ash Priors during a visit home to Bishops Lydeard.

Like many later novels, *The Sands of Mars* has a father–son relationship as a significant element in the plot. Martin Gibson, a well-known writer, is a passenger on the first spaceliner to the early Mars colony. On the voyage he meets Jimmy Spencer, a young postgraduate student. It is only later in the novel that Gibson realises Jimmy is his son from a college love affair:

'All these weeks in total ignorance and believing himself secure against all the shocks of time and chance, he had been steering a collision course with Fate . . . he was face to face once more with the ghosts of his own forgotten past.'

Martin Gibson and his son Jimmy had been separated for twenty years. They were the first of many fathers and sons separated in time and space – often for ever – in the fiction of Arthur C. Clarke.

Considering all the scientific revelations about Mars in the last forty years, the novel's science holds up quite well. Arthur has not missed the opportunity to point this out, first in a preface written in the mid-1960s and later in an introduction to the 1987 edition.

'I am agreeably surprised to find how little it has been dated by the explosive developments of the Space Age,' he wrote when *2001: A Space Odyssey* was being filmed in 1966. And he was equally pleased that this was the first novel to leave the traditional Martian fantasies behind and attempt to depict the Red Planet with scientific realism.

After the *Mariner 4* flyby of Mars in July 1965 and the *Viking* landings of July 1976, Arthur did draw attention to one major error in his first published novel. The robots from planet Earth discovered that 'the old image of a flat and geologically uninteresting Mars' was false. In his 1987 introduction, he quotes the novel's statement, 'There are no mountains on Mars', and admits that the discovery of Mons Olympus (almost three times as high as Mount Everest) has left him 'seriously embarrassed'. Still, time has been kind to *The Sands of Mars*. It remains important in the literature as the first novel to incorporate and extrapolate what science knew about the planet in the late forties and early fifties.

Things were going well, but they got even better when Arthur heard from his American literary agent, Scott Meredith, that the book club rights to *The Exploration of Space* had been sold for a substantial amount of money. With this good news, he immediately began planning a trip abroad for early 1952. This would be Arthur C. Clarke's debut in the United States – the country where he would find his first million readers. The first of many.

CHAPTER 7

New Shores

All explorers are seeking something they
have lost . . .
                        – *The City and the Stars*

The spirit of curiosity and wonder is the
driving force behind all Man's achievements. If it ever fails, the story of our race
will be coming to an end.
                        – *The Exploration of the Moon*

On 20 April 1952 Arthur boarded the *Queen Mary* at Southampton
and sailed to New York. He was thirty-four years old and, with the
exception of a short trip to Paris in 1950 to attend the First International Astronautical Congress as a British delegate, Arthur had only
travelled long distances in his interplanetary and interstellar fiction.

Life on board the *Queen Mary* during its April Atlantic crossing
was, unlike the spaceship adventures in his early novels, rather
uneventful. Arthur's lasting impressions of that voyage are few, but
he does remember the abundance and variety of good food. 'It was
wonderful to eat real food after years of rationing,' he says.

He spent many enjoyable hours playing table tennis with his fellow
passengers. As always, he was a serious competitor, out to win games
as well as new friendships. He was hard to beat – so hard, in fact,
that he won a ship's cup for his table tennis wins.

More exciting than the good food and recreation, however, was
the anticipation about what New York City, the mecca of American
book publishing, had in store for this relatively unknown British
author. Two of Arthur's books, a novel and a non-fiction science
book, were scheduled for US publication in the first half of 1952.
The novel was *The Sands of Mars*, which had been published by
London's Sidgwick & Jackson the previous year. It was issued by the
small US publisher, Gnome Press, in April – the same month that
Arthur sailed to New York.

What happened to the non-fiction book, *The Exploration of Space*, in the US had a significant impact on Arthur's future career. Essential to its tremendous success was Arthur's literary agent, Scott Meredith, who was himself at the beginning of his own career, having started his agency in June 1946. It was Meredith, along with Gnome Press's Marty Greenberg, who met Arthur when the *Queen Mary* docked in New York.

Arthur's initial contact with Scott Meredith went back to 1947 when he began sending stories to the American agent.

'Arthur had a very modest sales record at that time,' recalls Scott Meredith, 'but in those days we took on as a client anybody who had made any sales at all. He would send us everything he wrote, and we began to sell these small stories for him.

'The first story Arthur sent to us in November 1947 was "Inheritance", which we sold to John Campbell at *Astounding Stories* for seventy dollars. The second sale was "History Lesson", which went for forty dollars. It wasn't that Arthur went down; this was a shorter story than the previous one.

'The real breakthrough was the sale of *The Exploration of Space* to the Book-of-the-Month Club for a June 1952 Club Selection. My recollection is that these rights were sold for around fifty thousand dollars. I am virtually certain it was no less than that. The sale was a major advance for Arthur, and even though he only got fifty per cent (the other half going to Harper & Brothers), it was still a lot of money.'

When Scott telephoned Arthur in London with the wonderful news, Arthur was pleased but not quite sure what it all meant. 'That's marvellous,' he said. Then there was a pause. 'But what is the Book-of-the-Month Club?' This became a favourite story of both agent and client and has been repeated many times over the years.

One of the important players in BOMC's decision to make *The Exploration of Space* a selection was a Club editor by the name of Basil Davenport. He convinced the Club's judges that this was an important work that should be presented to the members. Clifton Fadiman was one of the judges. *The Exploration of Space*, he lightheartedly recalls, was chosen 'in a moment of wild escapism . . . and sent out to a large, earthbound and possibly baffled audience'. No question: it was a breakthrough popular science book. Nothing like it had ever been offered before to Book-of-the-Month Club subscribers. But despite this handicap, it was subscribed very heavily and the BOMC connection was the first big step toward making Arthur famous.

Promoting his first published novel, *The Sands of Mars*, at a science fiction convention in London, May 1951.

Below Robert A. Heinlein, Colorado Springs, 1952.

Below Executive council of the International Astronautical Federation Congress, London, 1951. *Left to right*: Hermann Oberth, Eugen Sänger, Arthur C. Clarke and Val Cleaver (*Courtesy Smithsonian Institution*)

Above Newlyweds Arthur and Marilyn
leaving the United States for England,
June 1953.

Below Early years in Ceylon, exploring for underwater wrecks
off the coast with Mike Wilson and Rodney Jonklaas.

A few years later Arthur had cocktails with Clifton Fadiman at the Plaza Hotel.

'The Oak Room is a rather worldly rendezvous,' wrote Fadiman. 'Mr Clarke is not worldly; he is other-worldly. He spoke of space satellites, lunar voyages, interplanetary cruises as other men would discuss the market or the weather. As he explained how within a decade three space stations whirling in an orbit about the equator will make possible (indeed one fears inevitable) simultaneous world-wide television broadcasting, our righthand neighbour (a vice-president of CBS) went into a kind of catalepsy . . .

'To understand a mind like Mr Clarke's we must realise that during the last fifty years, more especially the last twenty-five years, virtually a new mental species has emerged among us. They are the men who in a real sense live in the future, men for whom the present is merely a convenient springboard.'

The Book-of-the-Month Club selection marked a major turning point in Arthur's career. It allowed him to travel to the United States and meet for the first time his American agent, publishers and editors, as well as fellow writers, fans and new friends. As he travelled throughout the States, he promoted his book whenever possible. While in New York, he appeared on 'The Mary Margaret McBride Show' and the new early morning programme, 'The Today Show'.

Pat 'Sylvester' Weaver (father of actress Sigourney Weaver) was the creator of 'The Today Show'. 'I was a great admirer of Arthur's fiction,' he says. 'I had also joined the British Interplanetary Society and he was chairman. Maybe that's how we first connected. We talked about our mutual interest in satellites and the interplanetary stuff. The outer space stuff was the cement. Arthur went on the show and explained his invention of the satellite service [his comsat concept]. This was very helpful to me because it meant I could foresee so many of the developments that would be coming – the hardware side of the business – telecommunications and computerisation and miniaturisation and all the other things coming up in the new, post-war world. It was fascinating.'

The US edition of *The Exploration of Space* got front-page reviews in such prestigious newspapers as the *New York Times* and the *New York Herald Tribune*. The reviews were all good. The *Tribune* called the book 'the most important yet published in its field'. Reviewer Roy Gibbons wrote in the *Chicago Sunday Tribune*: 'What gives the book such charm and magnetism is Clarke's ability to reduce complex subjects to simple language', an attribute also praised by an *Atlantic Monthly* review.

Unlike the highly visible and successful launch of Arthur's non-fiction space book, the American edition of his science fiction novel, *Sands of Mars*, was much slower off the pad. It eventually had three printings for a total of eight thousand copies. The novel's modest beginning surprised nobody who knew the book business in the 1950s, least of all Arthur's agent and business adviser, Scott Meredith. Fiction has always been a tough sell, and it was even worse for science fiction in those days.

'In this period none of the major publishing companies, none of the *real* publishing companies, major or minor, were doing science fiction,' says Meredith. 'So several basement operations, cottage industries like Gnome Press and Fantasy Press, had sprung up and they were started by fans of science fiction. These small presses were the only markets for science fiction novels in the early 1950s. This is really astonishing when you think about the fact that so many major houses today are publishing science fiction in large numbers. But in those days if you wanted to sell a book it was to someone like Gnome's Marty Greenberg for tiny little sums you had great difficulty collecting.'

One of the people Arthur met through Scott Meredith was Olga Druce, producer of the 'Captain Video' TV show. 'He was on the set a lot,' Olga recalls. 'The studio was in the old Wannamaker's building on Ninth Street and Broadway. I didn't know a damn thing about science fiction, but I had just taken over the show for General Foods. We did five live half-hour shows a week for 6,500 dollars. Can you imagine?

'Arthur was always having fun and making fun of me in a kind way. But he also inspired me. He was appreciative of what we were trying to do for the youngsters. And these five and six-year-olds would come down to the studio, talking the space lingo of asteroids and galaxies which I never did learn, even as the show's producer. These young kids used to come down and look around the studio. They'd seem a bit confused. Then they'd ask, "Where's all the space?"

'Arthur knew some of the writers such as Jack Vance, Damon Knight, and Walter Miller.

'He helped me a lot. For example, he advised me when I wanted to have a spaceship built and nobody wanted to pay for it. He told me what to ask for, which was a big help because I had to deal with all the unions, and I had to save up enough money from my budget to pay for it. Well, we actually built the spaceship and did the first special effects for space on the air. We were also the first programme to use a teleprompter.

'I had two painters building these special effects, and Arthur advised them. And you know what? When Arthur did *2001* years later, he contacted these guys. I don't think Kubrick gave them a job, but Arthur remembered and contacted them and sent their names into Kubrick. That's the kind of guy Arthur is. It's a rare gift he has, a wonderful gift of friendship.'

At least one short story came out of his friendship with Olga and this early connection with the 'Captain Video' show. It was 'Security Check', first published in June 1957 and reprinted the following year in his collection, *The Other Side of the Sky*:

> His hand had gone out to the switch: the screen had filled with moving shapes – and, like millions of men before him, Hans was lost. He entered a world he had not known existed – a world of battling spaceships, of exotic planets and strange races – the world, in fact, of Captain Zipp, Commander of the Space Legion.

Arthur Clarke has always been a natural and enthusiastic promoter of the many ideas that excite him. This includes his optimism about the promise of space. Whenever he had an opportunity to speak before a group and talk about the subjects he loved, he did so with relish.

The Eastern Science Fiction Association invited him to be a featured speaker at their monthly meeting. On 4 May 1952 he travelled to Newark, New Jersey, and spoke before a group of about thirty at the local Polish Club. Sam Moskowitz, editor and historian of science fiction, was his host. He remembers that Arthur spoke at a number of small New York meetings in the 1950s.

'If he was around,' says Moskowitz, 'he would talk. He was a very good extemporaneous speaker, and he had a strong speaking voice. It was never hard to get Arthur to talk. He really knew his subjects. If he was talking about science, he could defend himself. And if he was talking about science fiction, he could also defend himself. So if somebody in the audience challenged him, and the guy was not right, then the person was in more trouble than he bargained for.

'One thing that impressed me about Clarke – and I had met a number of other British authors and fans – was that he was the first one to ever offer treating you to lunch or dinner. He's a very warm and friendly person. He's likeable, and he's never got over being an avid science fiction fan.'

A few weeks later Arthur joined American science fiction at the 1952 Midwestcon in Bellefontaine, Ohio. The conference was held at a small resort hotel, Beatley's-on-the-Bayou, on Indian Lake.

The Midwestcon, the first of which was held in 1950, was an informal gathering of fans and friends. It was kept simple and was purposely not publicised. About a hundred or so people attended. Everyone agreed that there should be no programmes, no scheduled speakers and no guests of honour. There was nothing commercial about the meeting. What people wanted was an enjoyable and relaxed weekend on Indian Lake talking about what they loved. This was one of the in-conventions, with the contacts made through fandom and the fan magazines, and Arthur was pleased to be invited. He drove from New York with Marty Greenberg whose Gnome Press had just published *The Sands of Mars*. They had a few fresh-from-the-press copies to spread around. Arthur gave an informal talk and slide show on space flight, based on *The Exploration of Space*.

'Arthur was accepted as one of the in-group,' says David Kyle, co-founder of the Gnome Press. 'This is where he became acquainted personally with so many people he had known about in America.' Many well-knowns and soon-to-be well-knowns were present: Robert Bloch, creator of 'Psycho'; E. E. 'Doc' Smith, one of the early masters; Harlan Ellison when he was just a kid of eighteen, and others.

It was at this Midwestcon that Arthur met Ian Macauley, a young fan and admirer from Atlanta, Georgia, who soon became his good friend.

'Ian said I should come and see the South. I was a gentleman of leisure then, and I said OK.'

Shortly after returning to New York from the Midwestcon in mid-May, he planned his trip south to Washington, DC, and Atlanta. He also wrote his first television play. 'All the Time in the World' was adapted from his story of the same name, which was published in *Startling Stories* in July 1952. He wrote the television script adaptation in one day, and the ABC Television Network aired the programme on 13 June before the story appeared. It was part of their *Tales of Tomorrow* series.

In a rare fanzine article for this stage of his career, entitled '"Ego" Visits America', Arthur wrote up some of his American experiences. He tells of 'watching the performance of my first TV play and showing unbelievable restraint when the credits didn't materialise (it later transpired that the commercial had crowded them out)'.

★

Washington, DC, was sweltering in early June of 1952. The thermometer read 102 degrees on the day Arthur arrived at Fred and Pip Durant's home in Centreville, Virginia. This would be the first of many visits to his American friends over the years.

Arthur Clarke and Fred Durant had met at the Second International Congress on Astronautics held in London the previous year. Afterwards Arthur had sent an inscribed copy of *Interplanetary Flight* to Fred, and they exchanged correspondence. Fred extended an invitation to Arthur, and that's what led to the June visit.

'Pip and I had been married almost five years and had an eight-month-old baby when Arthur arrived at our house in the country. Because of the temperature, Pip had poached a salmon and served it cold. Well, Arthur wouldn't eat anything cold. He was a real fuss-budget. We ensconced him in a large second floor bedroom. He really did live out of a suitcase with things flung everywhere. It was a mess. And of course we did his laundry.

'Pip was busy with our baby, and about the second or third time Arthur said, "Pip, would you get me a glass of water?", my wife replied, "Arthur, now you come with me. Here is where we keep the glasses, here's where you turn this thing and water comes out." And Arthur said, "Oh, yes, sure. I'll do it myself." He was laughing and everything. "That would be easier for you, wouldn't it?" It wasn't arrogance. It was the way he was brought up. Women took care of everything in the kitchen.'

Fred drove Arthur around the Washington sites, including a visit to the Smithsonian. One evening he spoke before the Washington–Baltimore section of the American Rocket Society in Baltimore.

'There are no fundamental problems of space travel that can't be solved,' he told his audience in 1952, almost ten years before Yuri Gagarin became the first human to orbit the Earth. 'How quickly science solves them depends upon the amount of money that is spent on research.'

The Durants had Arthur as their guest for about five days, and after filling up on warm food only Arthur headed south.

Atlanta, Georgia, was also hot when Arthur arrived on 10 June and met Ian Macauley at the airport. But the heat didn't stop him from keeping busy and taking in as much as possible during his six-day stay.

'He attended the Science Fiction Club,' says Macauley, 'of which I was president at the time. He met the Atlanta fans and saw all the sights, including Stone Mountain. One night I took him to the local

87

astronomy club. He also gave a couple of talks when he was visiting, and the *Atlanta Journal* interviewed him.'

Arthur returned to New York City in mid-June and on 25 June flew to Colorado Springs to visit Robert Heinlein and his wife, Ginny. There was a lot of shop talk about science and science fiction.

'We spoke about everything under the sun,' recalls Arthur, but especially the film *Destination Moon* which was based on Bob's novel *Rocketship Galileo*, although it was a very long way from it. We both felt very strongly about the production. It was the first attempt to show space travel realistically. A landmark film. Even now, four decades later, some of it stands up quite well, although portions of it are obviously naive. Bob and I were both crazy about it.'

Released in 1950 by George Pal Productions, the script was written by Heinlein and Rip Van Ronkel, produced by Pal and directed by Irving Pichel. Chesley Bonestell created a two-foot-high, twenty-foot-long lunar panorama for the film that took a hundred men about two months to build. The film had a realistic, documentary approach in contrast to the earlier space opera films like *Flash Gordon*, and for this reason it was an important film for the genre. The special effects won an Oscar in 1950.

The Heinleins were gracious hosts in their modern home on Mesa Avenue. On one trip, Arthur and Bob climbed Pike's Peak; on another they travelled in the opposite direction by taking a bucket down to the bottom of a Colorado gold mine. It was, according to Arthur, a 'wonderful visit'.

Arthur's next stop at White Sands Proving Grounds in New Mexico was arranged by Heinlein, who'd set up a visit for Arthur with fellow writer and friend, G. Harry Stine. Harry Stine met Arthur at the dusty airport in Las Cruces. He had just graduated from college and got married, and was working on rockets at White Sands Proving Ground. Naturally Arthur wanted to visit the facility.

'There was no way I was officially going to get him in White Sands because he was a foreign national,' says Stine. 'So I took the bit in my teeth and went out and got him a visitor's pass. He spoke English and looked like an American, and I didn't take him anywhere where he could see anything that might possibly be classified. Still, if I knew then what I know now about security, I probably wouldn't have done it because I was really putting myself way out on a limb.

'We were at White Sands for only a very short time. We remained in the headquarters area, the so-called containment area, and did not go to the launch sites. I didn't want to take that chance. We visited a telescope station which contained one of the rocket-tracking telescopes.

'At that time they were firing three or four Honest John missiles a day. The Honest John was a technical battlefield missile. Arthur and I saw one launched. It was launched off at an angle, and there was a lot of noise and smoke and so forth. After things died down, Arthur turned to me and said: "Why get excited about anything that doesn't go straight up?"'

During his stay at Las Cruces, Arthur met many local space enthusiasts; one such enthusiast was Clyde Tombaugh, the man who had discovered the planet Pluto in 1930.

'He met Tombaugh and everyone else at the base because he gave a lecture to the local section of the American Rocket Society,' says Stine, 'about his book, space travel and what-have-you.' Arthur was in his second term as chairman of the British Interplanetary Society, the activities of which he would often mention to his audiences. He always managed to sign up a few new members this way.

Next Arthur made for California. His time in Los Angeles was hectic and he loved it that way. He appeared on several radio and TV shows to promote *The Exploration of Space* and he spoke to various groups, including the Los Angeles Science Fiction Society and a more specific audience at the Radiation Laboratory at Berkeley. It was here that Arthur met Luis Alvarez for the first time, having just missed him in England during the war.

He remembers walking inside the windings of the Berkeley Bevatron while there. 'I have a theory that when they switch on that magnet San Francisco will think 1906 has happened again,' he wrote in his fanzine trip summary.

The machines he saw were not confined to the subatomic microworld. Arthur also visited the great California telescopes at Mount Palomar and Mount Wilson.

'Probably the most dramatic moment of my entire trip came when I went up four storeys in an elevator, stepped out on to a balcony – and found myself facing the 200-inch telescope,' Arthur told the fans. His guide was Fritz Zwicky, the astrophysicist who predicted neutron stars and discovered supernovae.

He also rode a bucket with Dr Richardson of Mount Wilson to the top of the 150-foot tower telescope.

An unusual honour was bestowed on Arthur when he was in the San Francisco area. Some 150 scientists and space enthusiasts gathered at an Oakland banquet of the Elves', Gnomes' and Little Men's Science Fiction Chowder and Marching Society to hear Clarke speak and pay tribute to him for his contribution to the general public's understanding of space and its future promise. George Finigan, research chemist and Society chairman, presented Arthur with the third annual Invisible Little Man Award. The trophy was a base of a statue with a pair of mysterious footprints above the inscription. That was it; no statue was affixed to the base.

While Clarke's general policy is never to discuss politics or the international situation in his speeches, on this occasion he did mention that his first visit to America coincided with the Republican National Convention and used this fact to discuss the future of space.

'Of course this first televised national party convention interested me,' he said, 'because, when we get a relay chain of space stations established twenty-two thousand miles above the equator, television service can extend over the whole planet. But I did not expect the Republican Party to take official cognizance of the topics the science fiction writers love to mull over.

'Imagine my surprise when convention chairman Joe Martin talked about spaceships and interplanetary travel in his opening address. After that, nothing could drag me away from the convention programme. Maybe one of the elves or gnomes had got Martin's special ear in a smoke-filled room.'

There were some memorable visits to other writers and science fiction devotees before returning to New York. He met 'Mr Science Fiction', Forrest J. Ackerman, the genre's number one fan who discovered science fiction way back in 1926 with the October issue of *Amazing Stories* and has been a serious fan and collector ever since.

'He came to what is called the Los Angeles Science Fantasy Society and gave a talk one evening,' Forrey recalls. 'I mainly remember his strange pronunciation of the word "Moon".'

Lunch with Ray Bradbury was one of the highlights of his Los Angeles visit. Ray's *Martian Chronicles* was published in 1950, followed by *The Illustrated Man* in 1951.

'Arthur came over to the house,' says Ray, 'and we had a wonderful chance to get to know one another. We had a lot to talk about. I think I was working on the screenplay for *It Came from Outer Space* that summer.'

A photograph taken during their meeting shows Ray Bradbury holding up a copy of Arthur C. Clarke's *The Exploration of Space*. Why did Ray hold up (and in a modest way promote) a copy of Arthur's book?

'Because he asked me,' says Ray, leading into a hearty laugh. 'And he's a very pleasant guy. I don't consider that we're competitive. I think we're friends.'

A visit to Paramount Studios provided some Hollywood stars for Arthur to meet, and he had lunch with George Pal who was shooting *The War of the Worlds* at the time. He also visited the set. 'I saw Pal doing some of the special effects,' says Arthur, 'which you couldn't do nowadays. The Paramount technicians were nervously trying out the death-rays which were so important to the film.'

In mid-July, after these varied activities under the California sun, Arthur flew back to New York. He spent about a week in the city seeing friends and conducting some business, and then he returned to England by air on 1 August 1952.

The first of many journeys to and throughout the United States had come to an end, but his literary reputation in America was just beginning its long climb to prominence.

CHAPTER 8

Writer, with Wife

I think Mr Clarke is the happiest writer I
have ever met.

— J. B. Priestley

Everyone can make mistakes; it's easy to
misjudge your distance when you're driving
by earthlight.

— *A Fall of Moondust*

The American adventures over, Arthur returned home to 88 Nightingale Road and his Remington portable typewriter.

'We set aside two rooms for Arthur,' says Fred Clarke. 'A big
room upstairs in the front of the house became his study, and a
smaller adjoining room was his bedroom. Arthur got on very well
with my wife, Dot. She was a trained secretary and did a lot of his
typing. She cooked. She did all his entertaining. If anybody turned
up unexpectedly to see him, there would always be coffee or a meal
ready to serve. He took a very dim view of me when I let her go off
with somebody else.'

Dorothy remembers Arthur's unique and enviable view of the
mundane chores of daily life. 'He didn't want to have anything to do
with what he called the "mechanics of life". And so Fred and I looked
after him. Fred did the painting and repairs, and I did the washing,
ironing and entertained his guests and so on.

'Arthur was a very disciplined writer,' says Dot. 'He would get up
at about half past seven, get washed and dressed and then come down
and have breakfast. After having breakfast and reading about three
or four newspapers, he'd say "Right!", and upstairs to his study he'd
go. By nine o'clock he'd be thumping away at his typewriter.

'The pattern was that I'd get on with chores and take him up a cup
of coffee at about eleven o'clock and bring my notebook along. He
then dictated letters while we had our coffee. Once in a while, if I'd
get sidetracked with chores, he'd come down at about quarter past
eleven and say, "Dot, are we going to have some coffee?"

'Arthur, like so many of us, was a creature of habit. He used to emerge from his study when his stomach called. He'd come down for lunch, but then he'd go straight up again and work till five or six o'clock. We'd have an evening meal, and invariably he went back up to his study, whether he was listening to his music or reading or whatever he was doing.

'As he got toward the end of a book, his working pattern accelerated. He'd be up at seven, be typing at quarter to eight and he'd still be typing at nine o'clock at night – as if he were telling himself, "I've got to get it out."

'The vision I have of Arthur,' says Dot, 'which always makes me laugh and which was always the same, was when he'd come downstairs and say to me, "I've finished it! I've finished it!"

'And I'd say, "Wonderful!"

'"Right. That's it. I'm not going to do anything else."

'He'd then mooch around a bit and go off upstairs again. About an hour later, he'd come down and sort of gently kick the wall and say, "This is terrible. I've got nothing to do. I have to start another book."

'I once asked him about inspiration, and he said, "No, no. You go up there and work. It's a job. You put a piece of paper in the typewriter and you get on with it." And that's what Arthur did.

'He also said to me during those early days that as soon as his writing became a chore he was going to stop. So obviously it's still a pleasure to him or else he wouldn't be doing it. He may feel compelled to do it, but he enjoys it. He was never happier than when he was writing.'

After the excitement and successes of the US trip, there was motivation aplenty to keep his literary roll going. He settled into his second floor study and wrote. As always, there were several in-progress writing projects. The most important, however, and the one to which he devoted much of his time, was an intense effort on a new novel. It would prove to be one of the most important he would ever write: *Childhood's End*.

Arthur also had many BIS duties to accomplish. These took him to Stuttgart, to the Third Congress of the International Astronautical Federation in late September and early October 1952, where he met Dr Theodore von Karman, the famous aerodynamicist, and Count Guido von Pirquet, one of the first men to recognise the future promise of space stations.

That autumn Arthur also met film producer William MacQuitty

for the first time. MacQuitty is best known for his 1958 film *A Night to Remember*, about the sinking of the *Titanic*.

'I met Arthur at Pinewood Studios,' says Bill MacQuitty. 'I wanted to make a film of one of his stories, and eventually [many years later] we settled on his book, *A Fall of Moondust*, the lunar equivalent of a submarine disaster. I failed to persuade the Rank Organisation to back the film, but I formed a lasting friendship with Arthur. He had a sparkling interest in nature and was always bubbling over with challenging ideas.'

Almost four decades later, in 1989, Bill MacQuitty and his wife visited Arthur in Sri Lanka and took in the sights. When they dropped into Barnes Place one last time to say goodbye, Arthur said smiling, 'I have news for you. Michael Deakin has just phoned from America to say that he wants to film *A Fall of Moondust* – how about that? Full circle!'

'Lucky chap,' said Bill. 'Wish I'd got it.'

The International Mark Twain Society made Arthur C. Clarke an honorary member and cited his juvenile adventure book, *Islands in the Sky*, which was published both in Britain and the United States in late 1952. He dedicated it to his young friend Ian Macauley in Atlanta. The dedication read, 'For Ian, from an Elizabethan to a Georgian'.

Earlier in the year Arthur had begun working on Part I of *Childhood's End*. His trip to the United States then took priority, and he didn't get back to work on the novel until late August. The origins of what many readers and critics still consider Arthur C. Clarke's best novel go back to July 1946 when he wrote the short story 'Guardian Angel' before he began his studies at King's College.

'I submitted it to *Astounding* [and] it was promptly rejected by John W. Campbell, Jr,' Arthur admitted in a short introduction to the story when it was reprinted in the early 1980s. 'I would like to find that letter, because I wonder if John asked whether I had borrowed my aliens from his own story, "The Mightiest Machine". (In a word, Yes . . .)'

He rewrote the story in 1947 and sent it to Scott Meredith to market. After a few rejections Scott asked James Blish, who was then working at the agency, to rewrite it. Blish did a rewrite, added a new ending, and the piece went into the marketplace once again. This version was sold and published in the April 1950 issue of *Famous Fantastic Mysteries*.

How did Arthur feel about Blish's ending? 'I thought it was rather good, but I didn't even know about it for a long time; this was rather naughty of Scott,' Arthur says, laughing.

So it was in February 1952 that Arthur went back and expanded 'Guardian Angel', which became Part I, 'Earth and the Overlords', of *Childhood's End*. By December he had the first draft finished and in late January 1953, as he planned his second trip to the States, he continued to revise and polish the manuscript. Some four decades later, in 1990, he was still at it. He wrote a new prologue, shorter than the original, to bring the novel up to date in the Space Age that had not yet been born in 1953.

Arthur went to the United States for the second time in April 1953. His ultimate destination was Clearwater, Florida, where his friend Dr George Grisinger lived. Grisinger was an admirer of Arthur's *Exploration of Space* and had invited him to the 'Sunshine State'. This was a great location for scuba-diving and Arthur was enthusiastic about trying it. He also wanted to visit his other friends in Washington, DC, and Atlanta en route to the Tampa area. But first he stopped in New York for a few days to conduct business and see Manhattan friends. It was during this time that he met his new publishers.

Even as Scott Meredith searched for the right publisher for his novel, Arthur continued to revise and polish the first draft of *Childhood's End*. In early 1953, the agency was negotiating with Pocket Books, which had bought reprint rights to *The Sands of Mars*. No agreement was reached, however, and Meredith moved on to another publisher. This was Ballantine Books, which had recently been founded by Ian and Betty Ballantine. Their editor, Bernard Shir-Cliff, recommended that they sign up everything Arthur had to offer at that point. An agreement was negotiated and the Ballantines bought three Clarke books: *Childhood's End*, *Expedition to Earth* and *Prelude to Space*. Thus began a uniquely creative relationship between publisher and author that would give birth to some important books, including a genuine classic.

'As a new house, we were evolving our own thinking on a broad fighting front,' says Ian Ballantine. 'We were dealing with the fact that hardcover publishers ignored large audiences. The reality was that hardcover publishers didn't know anything. When we were at Bantam before starting Ballantine Books, we sought writers who wrote about what was going to happen next. Arthur is somebody who's very interested in what's going to happen next and what he's doing next. That's why we were very much in gait with Arthur.

'My belief was that the young people had perceived how much

more complex everything was than their culture gave it credit for. They wanted to stretch their imaginations. That's why they were interested in books such as *Childhood's End* and *The Lord of the Rings*.

'The editorial cliché at that time was quite the opposite,' says Ian. 'That science fiction and fantasy was something for kids. We took the opposite view, and were given recognition for a broadness of interest from the community of authors. I think Arthur's work contributed mightily to that. He wasn't interested in tricks; he was instead interested in what it really would be like if you literally lived in space.'

'When we started Ballantine Books,' says Betty, 'we were quite determined that we were going to do science fiction in book form. Publish it seriously. So somebody had to become cognizant of what was then current. I did an awful lot of reading in the science fiction magazines, read them cover to cover, marking up every story. And Fred Pohl introduced us to several people in the field such as Fletcher Pratt and Lester del Rey. That's how we started. And the results were books such as Arthur's *Childhood's End* and Ray Bradbury's *Fahrenheit 451* – which, by the way, were published within months of one another in 1953.'

During his New York stay, Arthur went to the Ballantine offices on 37th Street to attend a meeting with Ian, Betty and Bernie. The subject of the meeting was the sequence in which Arthur's next three books would be released. Each book would be published in mass market paperback and hardcover editions simultaneously – one of the many publishing innovations of Ballantine Books. The main edition would be the paperback; the hardcover, printed from the same plates, would have a more modest print run. On the back cover and in the front matter of the paperback these words appeared: 'This is an original novel – not a reprint. A hardbound edition of this book priced at $2.00 may be obtained from your local bookstore.' The mass paperback edition sold for thirty-five cents.

But which of the three books should be published first?

'We wanted to do *Childhood's End* first,' Ian recalls, 'but Arthur didn't think we should. Arthur thought that *Childhood's End* should wait, that it was a hard book to publish.

'Betty and Bernie and I sat there and said in so many words, "You're crazy!" We all believed it should be first because it was so important a book, an original novel that had never been published before. It made publishing sense to do a novel which had stature and some heft to it.'

Everyone agreed, including Bernard Shir-Cliff, Arthur's editor, who remembers the first time he read the manuscript of *Childhood's End*.

'I was excited and nervous at the same time. It's like watching someone crossing Niagara Falls on a tightrope and you don't want him to fall off,' says Shir-Cliff. 'You get to the ending and you realise he's written himself into a very difficult spot. And you say, "How is he ever going to bring anything off and end it satisfactorily?"'

Of the many Clarke books the Ballantines published, the only one Arthur ever had misgivings about was *Childhood's End*.

'He was of two minds about what ending he wanted,' recalls Betty Ballantine. 'He had written two endings. But that's the only time I've ever known him to have any doubts at all about what he was writing.'

The doubts may have reflected ambivalence on Arthur's part about his novel's paranormal theme and humanity's transcendental union with the superior extra-terrestrial intelligence of the Overmind. In this respect it was not science fiction based on science which he came to advocate and represent.

'When this book was written in the early fifties, I was still quite impressed by the evidence for what is generally called the paranormal,' Arthur said. Today, he admits to being 'an almost total sceptic'. Why? Because he has seen too many claims exposed as fakes. Says Arthur, 'It has been a long, and sometimes embarrassing, learning process.'

No matter; it was a powerfully used theme in *Childhood's End*, and tens of thousands of readers have been emotionally jolted by its implications.

Whatever the reason for Arthur's hesitation about releasing *Childhood's End* before his other two books, he ultimately went along with Ballantine's preferred publishing sequence. First *Childhood's End* would be released; then the volume of short stories, *Expedition to Earth*; and third an earlier novel, *Prelude to Space*, which was to be published by arrangement with Gnome Press.

'Arthur was not known as a novelist before *Childhood's End* was published,' says Bernie Shir-Cliff. 'He was fairly well known in the science fiction field because he was a frequent contributor to the major magazines. This was a breakthrough for Arthur as a writer. We realised right away that as soon as we published this novel all his work would have a much wider appeal.'

On his way to Florida after his meeting with the Ballantines, Arthur spent time with the Durants in the Washington area. During *this* stay he got his own glasses of water and Pip served hot meals only – no matter what the temperature and humidity read. Later, after

Childhood's End was published, Arthur sent an inscribed copy to Fred and Pip: 'With many thanks for putting me up and putting up with me while I wrote the last chapter!'

Not that the last chapter was completed at Hollin Hills. It wasn't. Arthur was still working on it when he visited Ian Macauley in Atlanta.

Arthur and Ian had both lost their fathers at an early age, and perhaps this visit influenced Arthur in writing the powerful scene when George Greggson says a silent goodbye to his son Jeff as he leaves for ever to become part of the Overmind, the transcendent intelligence into which human consciousness is absorbed.

> There was a mist before his eyes which made it hard to see. But it was Jeff – he was sure of that: George could recognise his son now, as he stood with one foot already on the metal gangway . . . Nor would George ever know if Jeff had turned towards them by pure chance – or if he knew, in those last moments while he was still their son, that they stood watching him as he passed into the land that they could never enter.

'We got to know one another,' says Macauley, 'and discussed all kinds of ideas – life, marriage, racial problems and so on. At that time I was very concerned with the racial problems in the South. Segregation existed, and I was working against it. I belonged to certain anti-segregation groups and was very active. Of course I discussed all this with Arthur. He was writing *Childhood's End* at the time, and these discussions about racial problems may have influenced him. I'd like to think that perhaps this is why he chose to make the last person on Earth [Jan Rodricks] a black person.'

'It could well be,' Arthur reflects, when asked about this. 'It's perfectly possible. I never met any blacks before I went to America. However, when I was a small boy I went to my Aunt Nellie once and protested. In a sad tone of voice, I said, "My friend Johnnie has got a black auntie." I sounded deprived.'

Arthur went on to Florida and stayed with Helen and George Grisinger in their Clearwater home while he explored the Florida waters.

'I was carrying with me my first underwater camera – a Leica – in a cylindrical plastic case I'd purchased from a *Life* magazine photographer,' Arthur recalls. 'A whole bunch of us went diving in Tampa Bay on a wreck – a very undisciplined bunch of divers, I might add. It was on this dive that I saw my first big groupers. Some of them got speared, I'm sorry to say. We then crossed Florida in George's boat, the *Ah Phooey*, with his little son, Buddy, who later became a submarine commander. We went across and all the way down to the Keys, but not quite to Key West. I remember doing some diving at places along the Keys such as Marathon and Tavernier, but my big diving was in Weeki-Wachi Springs north of Tampa.'

He tested his camera in the crystalline waters of the Springs, and there encountered a challenging subject: 'A fair-sized alligator, hanging languidly in the vertical position with its nostrils just breaking the surface. I'd never met one before, and assumed (correctly) that it wouldn't attack a strange, bubble-blowing creature heading confidently towards it. So I got half a dozen excellent shots before it became camera-shy and fled up the nearest creek.

'The Leica photographic magazine published an article and ran my alligator pictures, but the piece isn't listed anywhere. My story, "The Man Who Ploughed the Sea", was a product of that period, one of the *Tales from the White Hart*.'

After exploring some of the coastal waters off the Keys, Arthur, George Grisinger and their group headed for North Key Largo. It was here that Arthur met Marilyn Torgenson (née Mayfield), a young woman of twenty-two who was working as the social director of the Ocean Reef Harbor Club. Marilyn was from Jacksonville, Florida. She had been married once and had a young son, Phillip. Arthur and Marilyn first met on 28 May 1953.

The sparks flew. 'It was just spontaneous combustion,' says Arthur. 'Electric,' Marilyn adds. It all happened very fast; everyone agrees about that. Arthur wrote to Ian Macauley on 6 June after he flew back to New York City.

> Now for some news which is going to shock you to the core, but which I hope you'll be glad to hear. On the way back, up the Keys, we stayed just two days at North Key Largo. And in that rather short time, I managed to get myself engaged to a simply stunning girl named Marilyn Torgenson. Incredible to relate, she's gone overboard about me, and when I got back to New York, there was a letter waiting for me with photographs, locks of hair, and 'How soon are we going to get together again?' She's flying up from Florida next week, so that we'll have a chance of getting to know each other better than we did for a few hours at Key Largo. If all goes well, we may get married before we go back to England. She's twenty-two years old and was married at seventeen, and has a little boy that's two years old.

'I was absolutely smitten by his looks,' Marilyn says. 'He was a dandy looking man, and he sported a van Dyke beard. He looked stunning. The beard was red, blond and red, almost a copper colour. Do you know how Errol Flynn would wear a moustache and beard contoured to his face? Well, this is what Arthur looked like. He really looked great. I was shocked rigid when he shaved it off after we were married.

'It was a whirlwind courtship. Arthur wanted me to come up there to New York and visit, but that wasn't something a young woman did in those days, go up and stay with a totally eligible man. I just couldn't do that; I would have had to leave my job and everything.

'After he returned to New York, he called me over the telephone and asked me to marry him. He just couldn't stand waiting.'

Within a week of Marilyn's arrival in New York City, she and Arthur were married. Their wedding date was 15 June 1953.

'He didn't want anybody at the wedding,' says Dave Kyle, co-publisher at Gnome Press with Marty Greenberg. 'I said some of us would be happy to go down and witness the ceremony or just be there, but he wanted to keep it simple. The day before the wedding I asked him, "What are you doing tonight?", and when he said nothing in particular, I suggested that we gather together some friends and fans from the Science Fiction Club and have a bachelor party.

'Arthur agreed and I organised it. I got a gallon of wine, some cheese and crackers, and that was it. There wasn't much money in those days. About five of us – Arthur, Ian Macauley, Carl Olsen, David Ish and myself – gathered in Arthur's hotel room at the Roosevelt.

'You could hardly call it a sophisticated gathering. There was nothing stereotypical about it; no blue movies or vulgar jokes. It was a chit-chat situation – friendly, intimate, gosh-wow, almost juvenile – about what Arthur was doing in America and what his plans were. And we talked about science fiction and Arthur's relation to it. It didn't last long; I'd say about two hours. We all were science fiction people and there was a feeling of being close. It's a very strange kind of brotherhood – unique and unusual.

'What we didn't talk about was marriage in general or his soon-to-be wife, Marilyn.'

The wedding took place in Manhattan's City Hall. 'My first publisher, Marty Greenberg, was there as witness,' says Arthur. 'And there was another witness, a little guy named Murray who was a sort of gopher for the Scott Meredith Agency.'

'Marilyn was a strikingly beautiful girl,' says Scott Meredith, 'and Arthur was absolutely smitten by her. It happened so fast. He called me one day and told me he had met her. Then, before I knew it, he was married.'

His brother Fred remembers him telling the family. 'The day he got married he rang Mother in Somerset and told her, "I've just got married. This is Marilyn." He then put her on the line. Mum was surprised and I'm sure a bit worried too, particularly as he had only known her for less than a month.'

Arthur took his new bride to meet his New York friends. Everyone agreed: Marilyn was a beautiful woman. Everyone was also concerned: what kind of future could this relationship have which went from first meeting to marriage in less than three weeks?

Marjorie May, one of Arthur's Manhattan friends, remembers him bringing Marilyn to meet her. 'I thought she was attractive, but I wasn't drawn to her particularly,' says Marjorie. 'And since he met her and married her in a matter of a very few days, I thought he had married too quickly. I saw them off to England when they went back in the summer of 1953. I was rather taken aback that she was leaving her little boy behind with her parents. He was pretty young to leave behind.'

For their honeymoon in the States, Arthur and Marilyn travelled to the Pocono Mountains in Pennsylvania and stayed at the Mount Airy Lodge. Marilyn had worked there as social director before going to Key Largo.

'It was just a tiny place at that time,' Marilyn remembers. 'I don't know how many days we stayed there, but he had to proofread *Childhood's End* when we were there. It was urgent that he do this and I was caught up with all the old people I knew, so it didn't really matter.'

The newlyweds returned to England in mid-July. David Fowke, Arthur's college friend, met them upon their arrival.

'Val Cleaver and I both went along to Heathrow. We were interested to meet Arthur's new wife, so we picked them up at the airport and then we all went back to Nightingale Road and had a meal together.

'Marilyn had a lively sort of personality,' says Fowke. 'She didn't have similar interests to Arthur and would have had difficulty in keeping up with him intellectually. My guess is that he found Marilyn attractive. He also has quite a soft spot for people who have had things go wrong for them. Marilyn had been previously married and divorced. She had a small son. So here was a woman who might have been treated harshly and whose small boy needed some additional support. That's my guess.'

There's little doubt that Arthur wanted to be a father to the boy, and he anticipated having a family of his own with Marilyn. The idea of fathering, in fact, was deeply appealing to Arthur.

'A boy needs his father,' thinks the character Heywood Floyd in *2010*, while he is billions of miles away from Earth on the mission to Jupiter – another example in Clarke's fiction of an immense gulf of distance and time separating father and son. In many ways, Arthur tried to close that gap in his own life.

A bash was thrown for Arthur and Marilyn at the White Horse pub in Fetter Lane soon after their arrival in London, and his fellow writers and sf fans all gathered to greet and congratulate the newlyweds. Ted Carnell, editor of the magazine *New Worlds*, presented Marilyn with a beautiful bouquet of flowers. But that was not the only surprise.

Word was out that Arthur's North American-grown beard was not appreciated by his wife (had she grown tired of it?), and that's why he had shaved it off. His cronies playfully rubbed this in by appearing with gummed-on beards of various periods and styles – Elizabethan, Victorian and Edwardian. Marilyn, according to witnesses, was not particularly amused.

Less than a week after their return to England Arthur and Marilyn went down to Ballifants for a weekend so she could meet his mother and the rest of the family.

'His mother was very pleasant and nice,' recalls Marilyn. 'And Arthur's sister and younger brother too.'

If Nora or any other family members had real misgivings about such a quick marriage, such feelings were not expressed during Marilyn's first visit. Meanwhile, Arthur and Marilyn were having their own misgivings. The relationship was beginning to have problems.

'By the end of a month,' says Fred Clarke, 'it was pretty obvious that it was a completely unsuitable marriage. Marilyn had no friends in England; she knew no one. She was a lively girl. After all, she had been a social organiser at the hotel. Her job in life was enjoying herself and helping other people to enjoy themselves. Arthur is – and I'm much the same – an unsociable animal. When we want to write or get on with what we're doing, we don't want anybody coming in and saying, "Darling I love you" or whatever, because it throws you. No matter how much darling loves you. And if you're in the middle of a complicated sentence, you're more likely to say, "For God's sake, clear off."

'Arthur had never been to a dance in his life. He was mostly interested in high-brow music, his writing and, of course, reading, two of which are silent hobbies and occupations. The last thing Marilyn wanted was lots and lots of silence.

'My first wife, Dot, who was Arthur's secretary during the early fifties, took her shopping. Marilyn was always going up to Arthur and saying, "I want some cash. I'm going to buy a dress. I'm going to buy this, I'm going to buy that."'

Although the writing was clearly on the wall, the show went on for some time.

The Clarkes flew to Zurich in August 1953, where the International Astronautical Federation Congress was being held that year. They stayed at the Touring Hotel Garni and spent some time with Fred Ordway and his wife Maruja, and Les and Lynn Shepherd. Outwardly the Clarkes' relationship appeared fine.

In October a reporter by the name of Jane Harker interviewed Marilyn and wrote an article about the newlyweds for the *Wood Green Observer* headlined: 'A husband in the clouds.'

Mrs Marilyn Clarke, American wife of Arthur C. Clarke, chairman of the British Interplanetary Society and science-fiction writer, finds it [being married to a husband in the clouds] 'fascinating'.

'Sometimes when he looks at me I know he doesn't even see me. He's way up on another planet,' she said.

Harker asked Marilyn if she was able to help her husband with his work.

'Yes, by listening,' she said. Although he sometimes writes all day in the 'den' upstairs without saying a word – except, perhaps, 'I don't know,' when Marilyn says, 'Here's your coffee' – he does like to talk about his work with his wife as often as possible.

'He sits on a pouffe and types on a coffee table – sometimes I go in the room and I can't locate him at first.'

'When Arthur does come down from "his other world",' says Marilyn, 'it's wonderful. He'd give me anything I asked for.'

What better person than Arthur to give her the Moon?

And, unlike some more earth-bound men, he never forgets the monthly 'anniversary' of their wedding.

At that moment Arthur looked round the door to say hello, and disappeared up to the den again.

'I'm going to buy him a spacesuit for Christmas,' said Marilyn fondly, 'with controls adjustable from Earth. I don't want to lose him!'

Behind this mask for the media, there were frequent verbal battles and sulking going on between the newlyweds.

Fred Clarke recalls the rising tension between them at 88 Nightingale Road.

'When Marilyn had a row with Arthur, which was quite frequent, she'd clear out of the house and go off to Arthur's friends, the Shepherds, without any warning, and spend a night or so there. And Les Shepherd, a very nice chap, and his wife Lynn tried to smooth things over.

'Marilyn used to drape herself around Les and fall all over him, you see. After one of these sessions, Lyn asked her husband, "What does it feel like to have a beautiful woman draped over you?" And Les said, "My dear, her bones stick into me."

'If poor Marilyn had known that that's the only effect she was having . . . She was a good-looking girl, but as thin as a rake.'

The incompatibility was not superficial; it was deep and fundamental. Arthur wrote most of the time, of course, which is why he produced so much important work in the 1950s. His young bride didn't know how to fill her time when he was busy. She soon realised that this was very different from the free time they had spent together in Key Largo and Manhattan.

'I had no idea what a writer's life was like. At that point I was extremely unsophisticated and unworldly. Arthur was totally involved in his work, to the exclusion of everything else. He used to sit at the table – it didn't matter if it was breakfast or lunch or dinner – and he would read most of the time he was eating.'

Because Marilyn already had a son, Arthur assumed there would be children and she would give him an heir. Soon after the marriage, however, he was shocked to learn that Marilyn could no longer bear children because of complications which had arisen involving a tear in her womb after the birth of her son. That the marriage could produce no offspring was an additional blow to the union. And although Arthur was particularly fond of her boy, the arrangement which Marilyn reached with the boy's father eventually resulted in the boy remaining with the father.

Arthur was very upset by these events. His brother Fred says, 'He would have made a wonderful father, and he was always good with our children and enjoyed them. I remember Les Shepherd saying that Arthur used to talk with his small son about rockets and space travel. Once he explained to the boy all about the re-entry of rockets, and Les realised it was the first time *he* understood it well – and he had a doctorate in science from Cambridge! Arthur can make complex things simple so that everybody can understand them.'

Childhood's End was officially published in the United States in August 1953. It was published in Britain the following year by Sidgwick & Jackson. The novel's title had an obvious relevance to Arthur's life at the time: his bachelorhood had also come to an end. As the novel appeared to critical acclaim, the marriage slowly continued to disintegrate. The consequences of a hasty, emotional decision were becoming painfully apparent.

The dedication in the front matter of *Childhood's End* was telling: 'To Marilyn, For letting me read the proofs on our honeymoon.'

Upon publication, the prestigious *New York Times* ran two reviews, one in the daily *Times* and one in the Sunday *Book Review* section. William Du Bois wrote in the *Times* on 27 August that the novel was 'mixed by a master's hand' and continued the accolade: 'A first-rate tour de force that is well worth the attention of every thoughtful citizen in this age of anxiety . . . This review can only hint at the stimulation Mr Clarke's novel offers.'

Basil Davenport, the man who had persuaded the Book-of-the-Month Club judges to select Arthur's non-fiction book, *The Exploration of Space*, wrote a glowing review in the *New York Times Book Review*.

> In *Childhood's End*, Arthur C. Clarke joins Olaf Stapledon, C. S. Lewis, and probably one should add H. G. Wells, in the very small group of writers who have used science fiction as the vehicle of philosophic ideas. Having said that, one must hastily add that it is as readable a book, from the point of view of pure narrative, as you are likely to find among today's straight novels.

Childhood's End was an immediate success. The first printing of 210,000 copies sold out in less than two months, and another 100,000 were printed in November. It was on its way to becoming the international classic it is today with more than fifty printings of the US edition alone.

The reception of *Childhood's End* was a boon to Arthur's literary career, but his marriage was not improving. In the autumn of 1953, with Fred and his wife Dot running the household, Marilyn felt like a fifth wheel.

'Arthur's views on marriage at that time were, I think, very vague,' says Marilyn. 'It was almost like a hobby that he really didn't want to get into. He wanted it to be a pastime, but it mustn't in any way interfere with his work. I wanted a *marriage*. It was very difficult for me to try and adjust. Finally I could not cope with it.'

The split between Arthur and Marilyn came as the Christmas season approached in 1953. A discussion about religion provoked the rift.

'I was brought up in the Presbyterian Church,' says Marilyn. 'God, country, all that was important in my upbringing. We were talking and he told me he didn't believe in God and he didn't believe in Christmas. Now that shakes your basic structure, especially if you believe and you think that everybody else does. And at that age you tend to know it all. Now that I think of it, he may have been as profoundly shocked as I was. He may have considered my belief as much a taboo as I considered his not believing. But I couldn't accept it then, and I kept waiting for God to strike him dead. I was just shocked. I couldn't come to terms with it, so I left him.'

Marilyn flew to Paris in late November and then on to Miami in early December. It looked like the marriage was all but officially over less than six months after it had begun.

Momentum continued to build in Arthur's career as a result of his consistent hard work in the late 1940s and early 1950s.

Gnome Press published *Against the Fall of Night* in 1953, the first novel that Arthur had ever begun to write, dating back to his days at Ballifants. Even the book's publication would not put a stop to Arthur's seemingly endless revisions. Still more work would transform it into *The City and the Stars*, published in 1956.

Ballantine Books published their second Arthur C. Clarke book, *Expedition to Earth*, in December 1953. The dedication was 'To Walter Gillings – who must share much of the blame.' Gillings not only bought Arthur's early stories and articles for his *Tales of Wonder*, the first British magazine of science fiction, he also gave him his first typewriter.

As part of Ian and Betty Ballantine's strategy to be the first mainstream publisher of science fiction, they enlisted the help of author and editor Frederik Pohl.

Because the Ballantines were committed to issuing one science fiction title each month, they had to court and build strong relationships with the top authors in the genre. When Frederik Pohl proposed publishing an anthology of the best writers, Ian Ballantine went one step further and suggested that the anthology contain all original stories and that the contributors be paid better than they were by the magazines. This way they could attract the *crème de la crème*.

Star Science Fiction, edited by Pohl, was published in 1953. It was the first volume of original science fiction stories ever published, and it became the first such series when volumes two and three were later issued.

Arthur C. Clarke's contribution was 'The Nine Billion Names of God', indisputably one of Clarke's great short stories, ending with one of the most memorable last lines of literature: 'Overhead, without any fuss, the stars were going out.'

It is a story of apocalypse, rendered with an ironic tone. Two computer engineers have been hired by a sect of Tibetan monks to program and run a computer to help them generate the nine billion names of God, a project they have been working on for three centuries. According to their belief, once their goal is reached God's purpose will be achieved and mankind will have completed its reason for existence.

Their work completed after three months, the westerners have begun their journey home when the stars blink out. Western science directly confronts eastern religion in this famous story, and the mystic rituals prove correct. The fate of humanity is sealed and its ultimate insignificance is dramatised against the immense and mysterious forces of God and the universe.

He had written the story during a rainy weekend in New York City when he was staying at the Roosevelt Hotel in the spring of 1952. 'It was triggered by Lord Dunsany's story about prayer wheels run by water mills in Tibet – a pair of wheels put on the shaft of a dynamo,' Arthur recalls.

Fred Pohl is convinced it's Arthur's best short story, and Arthur himself puts it on his top five list along with 'The Star', 'The Sentinel', 'The Dog Star', and 'Transit of Earth', which he considers 'probably the best short story of all'.

Like all Arthur's editors over the years, Pohl enjoyed working with Arthur because he was a professional writer through and through.

'Arthur is a very graceful and dependable writer,' says Fred. 'His prose is unornamented, but it's lucid, which is a virtue I prize. I always know what he's saying.'

Bernie Shir-Cliff was the editor of Arthur's books published by Ballantine during the 1950s. 'Arthur didn't require much in the way of substantive editing because his prose was always so clean,' says Bernie. 'Maybe sometimes you'd ask him to amplify an incident or something like that, but he knew what his story was about and when it came in it was pretty well lined up.'

In his dedication to the first edition of the 1955 novel *Earthlight* Arthur wrote, 'To Val/who massacred the second draft/And Bernie who slaughtered the third – /but particularly to Marilyn who spent the advance before I got to Chapter 2.' Behind the humour, was there any editorial truth? When asked if he really did slaughter the third draft of *Earthlight*, Bernie replied, 'I probably took out some technical descriptions he loved to do, to keep the story moving. Arthur likes to talk about things. I might say something like, "Arthur, you've got to bring the people back in and get the plot going again."'

When Arthur is asked about his actual process of writing he has very little to say, and what he does say is a head-scratcher.

'You know, it's a strange thing. I don't remember ever writing anything. Not any of my books. It's a hole in my life, a big gap in my existence.'

Betty Ballantine reflects on the balance in Clarke's prose, and how it may relate to his having practically no memory of writing.

'Arthur's work is so thoroughly orchestrated in terms of pacing and tension and excitement. It must be that he does it in the back of his head somewhere.

'Arthur mastered English,' Betty continues. 'He was not a great big flaming talent as a writer, but he was brilliant. His mind was so clear and logical that he could take the English language and control it and use it to express the things he wanted it to do. He had a beautiful consistency and control.'

Marilyn was back in Florida in January 1954 when Arthur decided to visit the United States for the third time. There would be no serious attempt at reconciliation; it was obvious to both of them that the relationship could not be mended.

'The marriage was incompatible from the beginning,' says Arthur. 'It was sufficient proof that I wasn't the marrying type, although I think everybody should marry once. We just each married the wrong person, you see.'

The experience, Arthur admits, was enough to scare him away from ever marrying again. 'While we were together for only a few months before separating, we were legally married for some ten years.' The marriage, in fact, was not legally dissolved until December 1964.

Working out the details of a separation agreement with Marilyn was one reason Arthur had travelled to Florida. But he was also there for the clear waters and good diving, an interest he was spending more and more time pursuing. He attended a meeting of skin-divers in Key Largo and did some diving. He sailed with friends from Key Largo to Miami. 'I've learned a lot of seamanship in a short time,' he wrote his friend Val Cleaver, referring to himself as Horatio H. Clarke.

Arthur also went to New Orleans during this period to see his college chum, David Fowke, whose ship, HMS *Sheffield*, a wartime cruiser, was in port.

'We were stationed in the West Indies,' says Fowke, 'and were doing a tour of ports in the States. We'd gone into New Orleans at the time Arthur was over in America, and we met up there. I arranged for him to take passage with us on the ship from New Orleans around to our next port of call, Pensacola, Florida.'

Business and events also took Arthur north to New York City during his 1954 US visit, and he stopped off to see Ian Macauley in Atlanta on the way. He arrived in Manhattan in late April and appeared on 'The Today Show' and 'The Mary McBride Show' in early May. Arthur's publishers, Ian and Betty Ballantine, held a cocktail party in his honour, and the *Herald Tribune* gave a special luncheon.

More important than these social and promotional dates was Arthur's participation in the Hayden Planetarium's Third Symposium on Space Flight which took place on 4 May. The topic was space travel and world thought.

Soon after Arthur had been appointed co-ordinator of the event, he had begun contacting scientists to speak on various topics.

'I asked who the top guy was on meteorological research, and somebody said Harry Wexler. And so I wrote and asked him to participate,' Arthur recalls. Arthur wanted him to speak about future satellite applications for weather forecasting.

In 1954 Dr Harry Wexler was the Chief of Scientific Services Division, US Weather Bureau. His initial response to Arthur's letter was negative. In fact he thought it was a crazy idea. After all, the planet's weather takes place in the lower levels of the atmosphere –

in the troposphere. Arthur then suggested that Dr Wexler prove how ridiculous the idea was and make that the subject of his talk.

This was the turning point. Wexler failed to prove anything of the sort. Instead he became an enthusiastic proponent of the concept of using satellites to forecast the weather.

'Wexler's first reaction is the right one for a scientist,' says Arthur, 'you know, when he gets thrown some crazy idea. I challenged him, and he accepted the challenge. I admire him for it.'

Thanks to Wexler's scepticism and Arthur's challenge, a new branch of meteorology was born. Harry Wexler became the driving force in using rockets and satellites for meteorological research and operations – one of the most important international endeavours of science today.

As he often did during his US trips, Arthur paid a visit to his friends Fred and Pip Durant. One summer afternoon in 1954 Arthur dropped by Fred's Washington office. As president of the International Astronautical Federation at the time, Fred Durant often called meetings. So Arthur was not surprised when people began arriving. What did surprise him was how highly distinguished the scientists were.

'There was Dr Wernher von Braun, Dr Fred Singer, Dr Fred Whipple of Harvard Observatory, and several scientists from the Office of Naval Research. They were clearly gathering together for the same purpose, and they became very tongue-tied when I tried, as tactfully as possible, to discover what that was.

'Not until more than two years later did I find out that this was the first conference to initiate Project Orbiter, a confidential project of the Office of Naval Research to launch a small satellite vehicle.'

Eventually, through the complex machinations of Washington politics, Project Vanguard won favour and support, and Project Orbiter went into cold storage – and history.

Arthur and Wernher von Braun, whom Arthur had met a year earlier in New York City, were both guests at the Durants.

'They spent the night at our home,' recalls Fred Durant. 'All they did was talk about skin-diving into the early morning hours. And Arthur indoctrinated Wernher, who became a true believer. Within a few months von Braun got his scuba certificate.'

Wernher von Braun, the man most responsible for building the giant *Saturn* rocket that would take men to the Moon, happily acknowledged his friend's influence. 'It was Arthur who introduced me to the sport that has rapidly become my favourite – skin-diving,' von Braun wrote in his introduction to Clarke's *The Challenge of the*

Sea published in 1960. 'I believe that man's insatiable longing for knowledge of what lies beneath the sea stems from the same source as that which prompts him to wonder whether there is life on Mars. Daily, we are learning more and more about the wonders of the sea and the solar system. But we have merely scratched the surface of both.'

When Arthur sailed back to England on the *Mauretania* on 6 July 1954, he knew his next ocean voyage would be a much longer one. He had already decided to join his friend, Mike Wilson, on a diving expedition to the Great Barrier Reef in Australia.

'If you want to continue your mental and emotional growth,' Clarke told an interviewer, 'every so often you must surprise yourself (and your friends) by changing the pattern of your life and interests.'

Upon his return to England, Arthur resumed his writing discipline and Society duties, but his new driving vision was the upcoming adventure he had planned.

The Pacific and Orient *Himalaya* set sail for Australia from London in the winter of 1954.

'I can still remember watching the feeble sun sink into the smoke of the London docks as I sailed away from winter for ever. Twelve hours by jet is too short a time in which to relish such a miracle.'

Arthur's intellectual adventures were soon to be replaced with the physical challenges of diving beneath the Coral Sea along the Great Barrier Reef, confronting real dangers rather than the imagined cliff-hangers of a novel's plot.

CHAPTER 9

Bound for Down Under

It's a wonderful feeling, slowly warming up
as you go through the Mediterranean.
– Letter to Val Cleaver, 13 June 1960

The SS *Himalaya* sailed south from London, around Spain and Portugal, then headed east across the Mediterranean. Arthur had a non-fiction book contract, *The Coast of Coral* in his pocket, and the adventures ahead would decide what shape that narrative would take. He had photographic equipment which would supply the photographs, including underwater shots, for this book and other future projects. But the genuine excitement came from *not* knowing what adventures and experiences to expect. That was the thrill of the unknown, calling Arthur Clarke to far horizons. And he felt a new sense of freedom and hope as he left his sad marriage behind him and sailed to distant lands.

There was an opportunity to go ashore at Port Said before entering the Suez Canal, but after a quick look at what it might have to offer Arthur decided to skip it. He had set some goals for himself before reaching Australia, and he wanted to get on with them.

'A good deal of my time was spent at the bottom of the *Himalaya*'s swimming pool, hoping to improve the capacity of my lungs,' says Arthur. He knew that underwater breathing equipment might not be available in the more remote regions of the Great Barrier Reef, and this proved to be true. 'Eventually I was able to stay submerged for almost four minutes but then gave up out of consideration for the other passengers, who viewed my activities with increasing alarm.'

This was a dangerous exercise, Arthur admits, and many divers have killed themselves in the process. It is a 'trick of hyperventilation', he says, 'flushing out the CO_2 in the lungs by taking deep, rapid breaths, thus inhibiting the normal breathing reflex and destroying, for several minutes, any further desire for oxygen. Hyperventilation can also produce permanent brain damage. My God, do you suppose . . . ?'

He wrote to his buddies at the Globe pub in London (they'd followed the bartender there from the White Horse) and sent them a two-page summary of his journey. In it he bragged that he was doing more than holding his breath. 'I spent the first three minutes of my record dive working out plot details on my next novel, and quite forgot the passage of time. As a result I had to beat off would-be rescuers. Might have managed four minutes without that altercation.'

On the literary side, Arthur did some pleasure reading and completed Tolkien's *The Lord of the Rings*. He also spent a great many hours *again* revising his youthful novel, *Against the Fall of Night*, with which he'd become increasingly dissatisfied. Twenty years had gone by since the story was first conceived, and many scientific developments had not been incorporated in the earlier novel which had been completed in 1946.

'In particular,' wrote Arthur in his 1955 preface, 'certain developments in information theory suggested revolutions in the human way of life even more profound than those which atomic energy is already introducing, and I wished to incorporate these into the book I had attempted, but so far failed, to write.'

Arthur's ship arrived in Colombo, the main port of Ceylon, and remained in the harbour for half a day. This gave him an opportunity for some local sightseeing with two people whom mutual friends had suggested he look up.

'Colombo was my first real introduction to the mysterious east, and I am very favourably impressed by Ceylon,' Arthur wrote his compatriots at the Globe pub. 'Was met at the dock by Major Raven-Hart, a fabulous character who is a sculptor, ex-radar expert, Buddhist, sf fan (several *Galaxy* rejection slips) and author (ten books published). He took me to a Buddhist temple which though small was quite impressive and beautifully decorated.'

Arthur put Major R. Raven-Hart on his short 'unforgettable characters' list, and the honour was validated when Arthur wrote about the Major more than twenty years later in *The View from Serendip*.

During Arthur's half day in Ceylon another friendship began. 'In Colombo I also met Rodney Jonklaas, Deputy Superintendent of the Zoo and a famous spearfisher. He was hunting last year with Bill MacQuitty (producer of *The Beachcomber* and *Above the Waves*) when a shark stole all the fish he'd shot and had attached to his waist. He thought it was Bill nudging him . . .'

Jonklaas, a trained zoologist, was the only skin-diver Clarke had met who *never* used a snorkel. 'I think he can breath through the back of his neck,' said Arthur.

'Rodney suggested that if I survived the perils of the Great Barrier Reef I should come back to explore the seas of Ceylon.'

But the future was uncertain as Clarke sailed out of Colombo harbour towards Australia and the unknown dangers of the Great Barrier Reef. He made no promises to return to Ceylon, and he certainly had no idea that one day it would become his home.

Many of Arthur C. Clarke's fans and friends wondered why he decided to give up space for the sea in 1954.

'I now realise,' says Arthur, 'that it was my interest in astronautics that led me to the ocean. Both involve exploration, of course – but that's not the only reason. When the first skin-diving equipment started to appear in the late 1940s, I suddenly saw that here was a cheap and simple way of imitating one of the most magical aspects of space flight – weightlessness.'

The SS *Himalaya* sailed south-east across the Indian Ocean to the west coast of Australia. Its first port was Fremantle, south of Perth, and passengers had a chance to take in the sights, but Arthur was distracted upon arrival.

'Saw little of Fremantle, my first port of call in Aussie,' he reported to his fellow space (and sea) cadets at the Globe. 'There were three reporters and two cameramen waiting for me. As luck would have it, my arrival coincided with a plague of flying saucers. Think I was able to shoot down a few,' he wrote, referring to his considerable experience in finding rational explanations for unidentified flying objects.

The ship was again at sea, sailing along Australia's southern coast, when Arthur celebrated his thirty-seventh birthday. There may not have been too much sandy-coloured hair left on the top of his head, but he felt vigorous enough and 'able to cope with most of the requirements of [my] new occupation,' he wrote, citing his impressive breath-holding record. Then on 18 December he arrived in the south-east port of Melbourne, and it was here that he met Mike Wilson.

Mike had left England in early 1954 and had been in Australia for ten months, making contacts in the diving and pearling business (and diving for pearls himself), acting as a film extra and chatting up the ladies, leaving 'at least one fractured heart in every major Australian city'. This reputation was nothing new for Wilson – only the continent had changed. 'He's accumulated some stunning girlfriends,'

Arthur informed the Globe crowd, 'one of whom is on the cover of a national magazine this week, and several of whom are probably now watching the calendar with some anxiety.

'We spent a couple of days in Melbourne and were able to greet a few of the local science fiction fans, all of whom would have been quite at home in the Globe. They told us just what the Sydney fans were like; that had a familiar sound, too . . .

'We did one very important piece of business in Melbourne,' he went on. 'The manufacturers of the Aussie *Porpoise* apparatus, which is a great advance on the aqualung, are giving us three units and their new air-compressor for nothing but depreciation charges.'

A short sea voyage north, and the adventurous odd couple arrived in Sydney a few days before Christmas. The *Himalaya* sailed through the morning mists of Sydney Harbour and passed beneath the great bridge. At last – the final landing for Arthur. The Great Barrier Reef still may have been more than a thousand miles away, but it began to dominate their thoughts as they started planning and training in earnest for their expedition.

One aqualung and five underwater cameras were in Arthur's luggage and Mike had brought two more aqualungs from England. So along with the newer *Porpoise* diving equipment on loan to them, they had a good start on the equipment needed for their journey to the reef. The trip north, however, was still a few months away because they had to make additional preparations and also wait for the end of the cyclone season and fair weather.

Sydney was a beautiful city, Arthur thought. 'We have been very lucky to get excellent lodgings on the northern hills overlooking the harbour,' he told Globe fans. Their boarding house was near Balmoral Beach, a sandy stretch with a group of strangely sculptured rocks at one end.

'I had had my first swim in Australian waters off these rocks – on a sun-scorched Christmas Day. I got very sunburnt, which is something that never happened to me in England at this time of year.'

He experienced more than sunburn during a swim on New Year's Day. 'I met my first big shark at close quarters yesterday,' he wrote Val Cleaver. 'I was swimming about thirty feet offshore, in one of the bays around Sydney. Visibility about fifteen feet. Had just chased a small shark into the kelp when the big boy started circling me at the limit of visibility. He went around me once, with a beautiful, effortless movement. Then I swam towards him in the hope of getting a good look and he shot away. He must have been the best part of ten feet long. I must be getting a bit blasé, since all I felt at the time was "Goody – a shark!"'

After three months of preparation, Arthur and Mike were ready to embark on their expedition to the Great Barrier Reef – the largest coral reef on planet Earth, stretching more than a thousand miles along Australia's Queensland coast. The cyclone season was over, and on 23 March the two men loaded the Chevy and began the first leg of their journey. Heron Island, one of the Capricorn group, was their destination.

'It now looks as if we will leave Brisbane for Heron Island (off Rockhampton) at Easter,' Arthur wrote Val Cleaver. 'The Great Barrier Reef Committee has a small research station there, and I have got permission to stay at it . . . Heron is the southernmost of the Reef islands, and one of the best.'

Oval-shaped and about half a mile long, the island is densely covered with a forest of pisonia and pandanus trees, except where clearings have been cut for the buildings. As the tides rise and fall, Heron Island undergoes a transformation. Only the small forested sand key is visible above the sea at high tide, but when the tide is low the island enlarges a hundred times as the vast, flat reef becomes exposed.

'We had planned to stay . . . for no more than three weeks before moving further north along the Queensland coast,' wrote Arthur. 'As it turned out we stayed on Heron Island not three weeks but six.'

Inclement weather was the reason for the extension. There were only four perfect days and another four that were acceptable for productive underwater work. The rest of the time it was overcast or a gale was blowing or the water was churned up and dirty. For ten days the rain never ceased, and Arthur and Mike were forced to remain in their primitive hut.

'We are just going to stick here until we have all the material we need,' Arthur wrote Val Cleaver, 'even if we see no more of the reef. So far, in about six days actual diving, we have obtained both black and white and colour shots better than any I've ever seen reproduced.

'We're particularly pleased to have got from the US a dozen rolls of the new Ektachrome colour film, three times as fast as any other on the market. Processed our first few rolls last night, with exceptional results.'

In early June 1955 Arthur and Mike packed up their thousand-plus pounds of gear, boarded the *Capre*, and sailed back to the mainland. They would head north and continue their exploration of the Great Barrier Reef before returning to Heron two months later.

'I was to see many other islands – some more beautiful and more romantic,' wrote Arthur, 'but for the rest of my life the words "Great Barrier Reef" will always conjure up a certain submerged coral garden forty feet down and half a mile out from Heron Island.'

Mike and Arthur wanted to sail the more than thousand-mile length of the reef, but time and money made this impossible. Instead they drove back to Brisbane and then flew north in a DC-4, touching down at Cairns, the last town of any size on the coast, on 15 June. The reef was a mere ten miles off the mainland at this point, but their plan was to stay a few days and continue northward.

It was another five hundred miles to their destination – the extreme northern tip of Australia, Cape York, and the Torres Strait beyond. The reef continued into Torres Strait, the body of water between Australia and New Guinea, which was scattered with many small islands.

The last leg north was flown in a DC-3. Arthur and Mike landed on Horn Island's airstrip, which had been built during World War II. Half an hour later they boarded a launch with all their gear and headed across the narrow channel to Thursday Island.

Because it is surrounded by many other islands, Thursday Island offers protection from the open sea. The Fisheries Research Vessel *Gahleru* was in port, as were a dozen or so commercial pearling luggers. The *Gahleru* would become Arthur and Mike's home for much of their stay in the Torres Strait.

On one of its expeditions the *Gahleru* pointed west toward the Gulf of Carpentaria, stopping engines off Crab Island and drifting so that the divers, including Arthur, could work the bottom for shells.

Arthur's lead weights were adjusted and he went down the ladder into the water. Mike held him at a depth of ten feet so he could clear his ears. Then the life line was played out, allowing him to sink to about sixty feet.

'I did not enjoy losing my freedom of vertical movement,' Arthur wrote, 'which I had always taken for granted in all previous dives I had ever made. Now I was weighted down, and had to depend upon someone on the surface when I wanted to move upward. But this could not be helped; a diver who has to walk along the bottom has to be heavily weighted; otherwise he will drift away in the slightest current.'

For a while Arthur watched the helmeted divers search for pearl oysters, and then he decided to surface and get a camera. He went straight to the bottom on the second descent and experienced the reassuring 'click' in the right ear, but not the left. Immediately he was in severe pain, and no amount of blowing or yelling into his mask helped.

'Soon after I had reached the bottom there was a curious soft explosion inside my ear,' says Arthur. 'The feeling of pressure vanished immediately and I was able to take notice of my surroundings once more.'

The drifting *Gahleru* was dragging Clarke along the sea bed. During his ear pain, he had become somewhat tangled up in the life line, air hose and camera straps, but had managed to unravel himself. He stayed down observing for a short while, took a few photos and then surfaced.

'As I came back to the surface, I once again became aware of pain in my ears – and suddenly realised that my face mask was full of blood. I must have been a fairly gory sight when I removed the mask.'

Mike threw a bucket of water in his face and told him he had probably punctured an eardrum. Arthur was sceptical because he could still hear perfectly, but soon understood that this was the only explanation.

Their adventures in the Torres Strait over, Arthur and Mike flew back to Brisbane, arriving on 6 July. Arthur was eager to 'start on the fifty thousand words of *Coast of Coral* still to be done'.

Later in the month the *Capre* sailed thirty miles off the coast of Queensland and delivered Arthur and Mike Wilson to Heron Island for the second time. Luck was with them: the long spell of bad weather was coming to an end, even if the coral waters were a bit colder.

'We now have some beautiful underwater colour shots,' he wrote Val, 'though still no sharks . . .

'The weather here has been good to excellent, with several perfect days. I've been annoyed by a cracked rib, but it hasn't interfered with diving. Did it climbing over the side with an aqualung on my back.'

While the sea had dominated Arthur's life for the first seven months of 1955, some electromagnetic waves reached his wooden hut on Heron Island on 29 July that profoundly influenced his lifelong dream of space travel.

'Coming in from a morning's dive along the reef, I happened to switch on the radio and was transfixed by the news that President Eisenhower had authorised the launching of scientific satellites during the International Geophysical Year.'

Upon hearing the news, Arthur immediately thought of the 1951 meeting in London of the International Astronautic Federation, when

Val Cleaver, Fred Singer (an American physicist who was then a science attaché with the US Office of Naval Research) and he were thinking of ways to get the public and governments interested in scientific satellites.

After a few rounds of drinks at the Arts Theatre one night, one of them suggested that what they needed first was a snappy name for such a satellite programme. After some doodling they came up with the abbreviation MOUSE, which stood for 'Minimum Orbital Unmanned Satellite of Earth'.

'In the next few months,' Arthur later wrote, 'Fred produced a blizzard of papers describing what MOUSE (better still, MICE) could do; his predictions were uncannily accurate, and every one of them has since come true. The publicity campaign was extremely successful, and MOUSE appeared in technical journals all over the world.'

As remote as Arthur was at the time, he knew it was a historic moment for space and went to considerable difficulty and expense to cable Fred Singer: 'Congratulations from the bottom of the Barrier Reef. May the MOUSE bring forth a mountain.'

In the days remaining on Heron Island, Mike and Arthur hunted for turtles and explored new areas such as Wistari Reef, a mile away, and then Masthead Island, an hour and a half away by boat. During their explorations, they found and captured a three-hundred-pound turtle, which was eventually put into a small pool on Heron Island.

They were back in Sydney by late August, at which time Arthur despatched eighty thousand words of *Coast of Coral* to his publisher. A month later, as he and Mike prepared to leave Australia, Arthur brought Val, who was always the first person to read and evaluate his work, up to date on his literary affairs.

Harper's are very enthusiastic about *Coast of Coral*, but feel that a bit too much of it is underwater and want more general adventures. I've told 'em that the contract was for an 'Underwater Book on the Great Barrier Reef', and that in fact only a third is specifically underwater anyway. Also that all our printable adventures went into it!

They seem in a hurry and want the photos as quickly as possible. Harcourt Brace also seem determined to let no grass grow under their feet. I had proofs of *The City and the Stars* on *airmail* paper two weeks ago, and bunged them back. For once (ahem) I am quite confident that this is far and away my best book, and you'd bloody well better like it as this time you don't have to share the dedication with anyone.

I have *no* plans for writing in the immediate future – hurrah! Otherwise the long-term situation remains the same – *The Deep Range, Imperial Earth* and two or three short-story collections in between. On the non-fiction side, much depends on the success or otherwise of *Coast of Coral* . . .

I look forward to a few months with no major project hanging round my neck; that's one reason why I'd like to fix a lecture tour – it would stop me writing. Not to mention its more positive aspects in the way of cash and publicity.

There was also some news about what would become one of Arthur's most famous short stories. '"The Star" was sold to some obscure US sf mag [*Infinity Science Fiction* in early 1955] for $80. None of the slicks would touch it – *Saturday Evening Post* thought it was "blasphemous". Let's see if it does better in the UK.'

Says Brian Aldiss, novelist and historian of science fiction, 'I've always admired "The Star" for that absolutely outrageous and grabby opening sentence, "It is three thousand light years to the Vatican." I think that stands as the great opening line of all time. It acts like a kind of pun in that it creates connections between really two conflicting systems of belief – the scientific and religious. And in that way I think it embodies a great deal of Arthur's philosophy. Looked at in that light, it's not altogether different from the famous closing line of "The Nine Billion Names of God". Again you have the two conflicting systems. And a lot of Arthur's work is right there on that kind of crossroads.'

Arthur was pleased with a good review of *Earthlight* by Francis McComas which appeared in the *New York Times*, 'saying that I am, "beyond cavil, our ablest practitioner of science fiction". "Our"?' Arthur asked his London friend.

Before leaving Australia Arthur and Mike put on two public showings of their films and slides of the reef, which were well received. Kodak did a window display of their black and white photos on the main street in Sydney.

'They look terrific,' Arthur wrote. 'We can hardly believe we took them! Expect they'll soon stop traffic.'

Arthur and Mike left Australia in early October, and as their Quantas Constellation climbed out over the Pacific, they cast their eyes northward up the coast towards the Great Barrier Reef. It was one of the most unique formations on the planet, 'the mightiest single work of living creatures on the face of the Earth', Arthur wrote in his 1963 adventure novel *Dolphin Island*. His Australian experiences would serve his work well over time. Heron Island was a central locale in his 1957 novel, *The Deep Range*, and it was also used as a model, though not by name, for *Dolphin Island*, which included several descriptions and experiences that were also in his letters to Val Cleaver.

Towards the end of *The Coast of Coral*, published in 1956, Arthur emphasised the reef's importance and its future promise.

'In an age which is seeking new frontiers, the Great Barrier Reef provides one of the few unexploited – indeed, largely unexplored – regions still remaining on this planet. In at least three major fields of human activity – commerce, science and recreation – it offers opportunities which it would be hard to match elsewhere.'

CHAPTER 10

Around the World to Ceylon

> Beautiful night last night. Southern Cross (a
> very feeble constellation) just above the
> front gate, with Alpha Centauri beside it. It
> always gives me an odd feeling to look at
> Alpha and to realise that's the next stop.
>   – Letter to Val Cleaver, 1955

The isle of Ceylon beckoned. The beautiful memory of a single afternoon in December 1954 enticed Arthur to return. He and Mike
decided that their next underwater adventure would be in the crystal
waters of the Indian Ocean off Ceylon's coast. But first they needed
to attend to some business affairs in the United States and England.

New York City was the longest stay on their around-the-world
journey – about seven weeks. The primary reason for taking the long
eastern route to Ceylon was that they wanted to deliver their hard-
got, irreplaceable colour slides and photographs to their publishers.

Scott Meredith and Arthur spoke of the three new books to be
published in the coming year, 1956. *The Coast of Coral* would be
published in the spring, and two works of fiction would be released
in the first half of the year: *The City and the Stars* and a collection of
short stories from the 1940s and 1950s, *Reach for Tomorrow*.

At this time Scott Meredith referred Arthur to a lecture agency in
Manhattan that could start him on the lecture circuit. He wrote to
Val in mid-October about this promising new connection.

> Both Mike and I have been offered separate contracts by the
> Colston Leigh Lecture Agency, biggest in the world, which
> handles Cousteau, Mrs Roosevelt, Joyce Cary, Ogden Nash,
> General Romulo, Peter II of Yugoslavia, Sir Harold Scott and
> a few others. They want me to do sf and astronautics; Mike will
> cover the underwater side. The head of the agency has since told
> Scott that he thinks I'm one of the best prospects they've had
> for years. What pleases me even more, though, is that they've
> grabbed Mike. They propose to give him a dry run with the

Princeton Businessman's Association to see how he performs. All this should demonstrate rather eloquently that Mike has changed a bit since you last saw him!

The contracts cover a three-year period; we will have to be in the US for three to four-month tours either in the autumn or spring, starting probably Oct 56. It will be an interesting experiment, anyway . . .

In addition to making business arrangements, Arthur and Mike needed to prepare for the underwater expedition to Ceylon. They decided to avoid supply problems by ordering all their equipment in New York and having it shipped over by the same agent who handled such matters for the American Museum's Hayden Planetarium.

Arnie Post of Richard's Sporting Goods was a tremendous help in choosing the best hardware for their needs, and he and Arthur became friends. Arnie let them test whatever equipment they wished on his boat *The Flying Frogman*. They bought twin-cylinder aqualungs and a Cornelius air compressor. This allowed them to pump up their tanks wherever they could and gave them complete independence.

They also upgraded their underwater camera equipment when Arnie Post showed them a Rolleimarin – a superb quality underwater housing for the Rolleiflex. The results of this acquisition were magnificently apparent in the colour plates published in 1957 in *The Reefs of Taprobane*.

The seven weeks in New York flew by. Arthur enjoyed seeing his friends in Manhattan and telling them stories about his Australian adventures. He connected with everyone who was in town, including Isaac Asimov, Olga Druce, David Kyle and Marjorie May. He also attended some unique events on this transit through the city. He was, for example, lucky enough to be at the world premiere of Sam Goldwyn's *Guys and Dolls*; and he visited the *Omnibus* set at the CBS studio and saw Alistair Cooke introduce Antonio and his dancers.

He also visited the Durants one weekend. They had moved to the Boston area because Fred had taken a position with Arthur D. Little, a consulting firm.

Arthur and Mike left for London on 20 November 1955, just in time to miss the first winter blizzard to hit New York.

Further preparations for Ceylon were made in England during December. This was more of a business than pleasure visit, although Arthur did see his family and friends. He and Mike had learned in Australia that weather was the dominant factor in any underwater expedition, and they set their own deadlines accordingly.

'We knew that the earlier in the year we could get to Ceylon,' says Arthur, 'the better our chances of success.'

They also knew that dependable transportation in Ceylon was a real problem, and Arthur solved it by purchasing a Land-Rover which was shipped over.

Underwater motion picture cameras and sundry equipment were other essential needs. After shopping around, they decided that the electrically driven Beaulieu, in the case designed by Dimitri Rebikoff, was the best camera in their price range. Rebikoff was a famous French underwater engineer and photographer who had designed several underwater cameras and their accessories. Mike immediately went to Paris to meet this expert, and then followed him to Cannes to see his workshop.

Finally everything was ready and they set sail on the Orient liner *Orcades* in the first week in January. It was still mild and pleasant when they saw the sun setting behind the cranes of Tilbury dock, and they knew that the blue seas and palm-fringed beaches of Ceylon were only two weeks away.

The *Orcades* sailed the same eastern route to the Indian Ocean as the *Himalaya* had a year before, with a few additional ports-of-call in the Mediterranean, including Naples and Capri. At Gibraltar Arthur had fun calculating what a dropped H-bomb would do to the great mass of rock.

'We went ashore for a few hours at Gib,' he wrote Val, 'and again at Naples. Here I paid my first visit to a brothel; it was a small, one-storeyed building divided into cramped little cubicles with some most interesting mural paintings. Before you get any wrong ideas I'd better add that it went out of business suddenly in AD 69 when Vesuvius woke up.'

One night they saw a spectacular sight: 'A thin line of fire crawling down the sky – the lava flow from Etna, reminding all who saw it that the forces which overthrew Pompeii were still sleeping beneath this land.'

Mike Wilson wasn't too pleased with the average age of the women travelling first class: it was about sixty. His style was cramped because all of the unattached females were in tourist class. At least he enjoyed going through the Suez Canal and seeing some of the places he remembered from his army days there, including a police station he blew up.

The port of Aden with its great oil refinery once again reminded Arthur of a scene from a science fiction story.

'The feeling that I was on a strange planet was heightened when I went ashore and drove into the town, which is situated inside the crater of a huge volcano. If the sky were black instead of blue, the illusion that one was on the Moon would be almost perfect.'

Mary, Arthur's sister, was stationed at Aden as an officer nurse in the RAF. 'Arthur came ashore only for a few hours,' she says. 'We did some shopping in Steamer Point, and I think we took him to Crater to see the supposed Well of the Queen of Sheba. He thought the colony looked like the mountains of the Moon, especially Crater and Little Aden, the BP Oil Refinery.

'Later we went on board and had tea in his cabin, looked at a lot of photographs, particularly lovely ones of pearls taken in Australia, and nearly missed the last boat ashore.'

During the rest of the voyage across the Indian Ocean, Arthur and Mike spent much of their time lying in the sun. This built up their protective suntan which was essential when swimming and diving in tropical waters. Arthur, of course, regularly played table tennis and regularly won.

When the *Orcades* arrived in Ceylon's port of Colombo their friend Rodney Jonklaas was there to greet and help them. Many people, including Arthur, considered Jonklaas 'one of the world's leading underwater hunters', and his adventures off Ceylon are legendary.

By now Jonklaas was working for Ceylon's Department of Fisheries, and he managed to arrange his schedule so he could guide Arthur and Mike to the most promising underwater locations on the island – and this man knew most, if not all, of them.

Thanks to Rodney, they also located a promising abode on land after a temporary stay at a Colombo hotel. The flat was located in Bambalapitiya ('plain of the bamboo forest'), a Colombo suburb about three miles from the centre of the town, and came with a garage for the Land-Rover, which remained outside because the diving and photographic gear had priority and took up the entire garage floor. It was a bargain, says Arthur, 'a small but pleasant apartment and a first-class cook-servant, all at an inclusive cost of about ninety dollars a month'.

Somewhat sensitive to any suggestion of neocolonialism, Arthur defends the practice of hiring servants.

'In the East, of course, a servant is a necessity, not a luxury. Carolis [their first houseboy] probably saved us more money when he went shopping than we paid him in wages. The local shopkeepers would have made quite a killing had we two British innocents dealt with them direct.'

Arthur's first few months in Ceylon, even apart from the diving expeditions, were fascinating and intellectually exciting. Because he loved to learn and explore (an essential and dominant trait of his personality), all the cultural differences, as well as the island's history, stimulated his mind and imagination. The Ceylonese place names, for example, were 'terrifyingly polysyllabic' to Arthur and next to impossible to pronounce.

'I mumbled for about a week before I could tell a cab driver where I lived,' says Arthur, and he admits to the necessity of having to practise pronouncing such tongue-twisters as Illuppadichchenai or Kahatagasdigiliya.

The diversity of people and life styles in the Colombo streets – yellow-robed Buddhist monks, urchins selling lottery tickets, the rickshaws, the old London buses, tourists and businessmen from all over the world – added to the intrigue.

One aspect of Ceylon, however, to which Arthur could never adapt (although Mike had no trouble with it), was the hot food.

'With my first cautious nibble, something went wrong with my windpipe and I felt as if I were a couple of hundred feet down with a broken aqualung.' He has never strayed from the basic British diet which emphasises meat and potatoes.

In February Arthur wrote to Val that he felt at peace and at home in Ceylon. He liked the people, the climate and the cost of living.

'Mike also seems happy here, though he still gets moody and bad-tempered from time to time. He is full of enthusiasm and ideas, and determined to make the expedition a success. However mad we may occasionally get with each other, we can't imagine not being to-gether.'

In another letter to Val, Arthur talked about 'life's ability to give one a "come-uppance". I'm acting on the assumption that if you work hard and produce all you can, which I am doing now, you are making the best insurance against disaster. And Mike and I are now really working together as a team, as well as making the allowances necessary for our somewhat clashing personalities! In fact, it has been a very long time since I have been so contented with life . . . pause while I wait for the roof to fall in.'

During the first half of 1956, Arthur absorbed Ceylon's long recorded history, which goes back some three thousand years and which he would later bring to his fiction, especially *The Fountains of Paradise*. He visited the ancient capital of Ceylon, Anuradhapura, located in the north central region. It had been Ceylon's capital for a thousand years, where ninety Sinhalese kings reigned, until invaders from India overran it and the Sinhalese built a second capital, Polon-naruwa, some sixty miles away.

Of more recent times, Arthur learned about the progressive occupations of the Portuguese, who left their religion – and much spilled blood; the Dutch, who left their architecture and law; and the British who left their language and commerce. Only the British, who were politely asked to go, left in a civilised way, without violence.

Ceylon's population is dominated by the Sinhalese, predominantly Buddhist, although there have been some Christian families for several generations. The second largest group, found mostly in the northern part of the island, is the Tamils. They practise Hinduism and some are aggressively separatist. The real and perceived grievances of the Tamils against the Sinhalese, and vice versa, have brought terror, death and destruction to Ceylon over the past decades, and Arthur has witnessed the suffering it has brought to the tear-shaped isle he has come to love.

But as well as learning about Ceylon's history Arthur was doing what he had come here for. Within a few days of their arrival, he and Mike loaded the Land-Rover and headed south, under the expert guidance of Rodney Jonklaas, to some of the best diving locations off the coast of Ceylon. This would be the first of several treks in early 1956 (later ones would take them north and west).

Akurala Reef, about fifty miles south of Colombo, was their first stop and they quickly learned that the sharks off Ceylon's coast were less aggressive than those in the waters of the Great Barrier Reef. The underwater cameras clicked, and after a few hours they were back on shore developing their film.

'We had the satisfaction of seeing our first shark close-ups,' wrote Arthur, 'and knowing that our visit to the Akurala Reef had given us results which we had never been able to obtain during a whole year in Australia.'

Arthur and Mike made the acquaintance of one of Ceylon's leading photographers, Jo Ebert, who was also the Shipping Master for Colombo. Under his supervision was a complete register, going back a hundred years, of all the sunken ships off the coast. This became a main resource for their diving adventures.

Before summer Arthur and Mike explored six underwater wrecks, two of which had gone down off the Akurala Reef. One of these, the *Earl of Shaftesbury*, had sunk in 1893. Nearby they also dived to investigate the *Conch*, one of the first oil tankers of the Shell Company which hit the rocks and sank in 1903, leaving its huge spill of oil spreading over the reef.

On another occasion they explored a Danish wreck which had gone down in 1939. The *Elsia* was a cargo passenger ship which caught fire and was abandoned. Because it was relatively close to shore, the water was dirty and photography was out. Arthur went down to have a quick look without his aqualung.

'I took a deep breath and plunged down towards the enigmatic blur lying beneath our boat. Before I had run short of air, I found myself *inside* a ship. The *Elsia* appeared to have split open, revealing all her internal machinery . . . Pipes and cables snaked everywhere, sometimes looking alarmingly like giant tentacles.'

The next day the crew went out beyond the *Elsia* to the Rala Gala Reef (also known as Wave Rock because of the ten-footers it creates). The water clarity was amazing. 'It was the first time I had ever encountered visibility of over a hundred feet in the open sea,' says Arthur. Soon after Rodney speared his first pompano and Arthur and Mike got their cameras ready, expecting sharks, which immediately appeared, although most of them were small and camera-shy – with one notable exception.

'I was relaxing twenty feet down when I saw a large shark coming straight towards me, almost on a collision course,' wrote Arthur. 'I quickly whipped the camera up to my eye, praying that my air would hold out until the shark reached me . . .

'At the last minute he swerved to my left; I clicked the shutter and then realised that I was completely out of air.'

Arthur came up gasping, but he had got his photograph and the shark was not seen again.

They spent four hours in the water off Rala Gala Reef that spring afternoon. When they returned to the coastal village of Weligama, Mike and Rodney wanted more fish for dinner and headed out into the bay again. But Arthur was bushed and did not want to contradict his basic philosophy of water activity.

'The whole secret of underwater sightseeing – and indeed of diving in general – is summed up in what is known in physics as the Principle of Least Action,' writes Arthur. 'Never exert yourself unnecessarily: the universe doesn't.'

As the sun set, Arthur practised what he preached by relaxing on the veranda of the resthouse at Weligama Bay, overlooking the curving shoreline commonly agreed to be one of the most beautiful spots on Ceylon's coast.

'The scene was so peaceful and so completely relaxing that I was able to enjoy it without the feeling – from which professional writers are seldom free – that I really ought to be working on something, it didn't matter what. For an hour or so I had escaped from the tyranny of the typewriter, and that was an achievement well worth the journey to Ceylon.'

Weligama, on the southern tip of the island, will always hold a memorable spot in Arthur's heart. It was there he first learned to wear a sarong – the traditional native wrap-around garb for males, 'a simple tube of cloth about four feet long and seven feet in circumference'. He took an immediate liking to its convenience and comfort, and henceforth advertised its benefits by wearing one on various occasions during his world travels.

After heading east along Ceylon's southern coast for another thirty miles and spending some time in the waters off the fishing village of Tangalle (which became an important place in their lives a few years later), Arthur and Mike decided to return to Colombo. They had been away for almost two weeks. On the way back, they stopped at the small town and harbour of Galle, which according to some historians of the Bible is the Tarshish of the Old Testament where Solomon's ships were provisioned as they set forth to find riches of gold and ivory.

In more recent history, August 1883, all the sunken wrecks in the Galle harbour were dramatically exposed when an extraordinary event occurred: all the water drained out of the harbour in a matter of minutes. It was caused by a powerful wave moving west, originating more than a thousand miles away and formed by the cataclysmic volcanic explosion of Krakatoa in the Pacific off Java. Because of Galle's sheltered location on the far side of Ceylon, relative to Krakatoa, no devastating tidal wave returned; instead it came like a swift, smooth tide, once more covering the many shipwrecks on the harbour floor.

But there were more than ancient wrecks to explore. On 5 March 1956 the Greek freighter *Aenos*, carrying six thousand tons of manganese, struck Rala Gala Reef north of Galle and went down. The crew was rescued by local fishermen, who then proceeded to loot the bridge and boat deck – the only portions of the ship not submerged.

Five days later Arthur, Mike, Rodney and a few other friends arrived on the scene with their diving equipment to see what they could bring up from beneath the waves. The diving conditions were not ideal, however, because the flow from the nearby mouth of the Gintota River created unclear water conditions and the monsoon winds were getting stronger.

Rough seas were still battering the *Aenos* so they decided to skin-dive and not use the aqualungs, which would have been a disadvantage and a potential risk. They brought up two wooden chests filled with tools, some water or coffee jugs and other souvenirs.

In addition to these coastal adventures, Arthur was always writing – along the way and even more intensively when they stayed at their flat outside Colombo. He was working on a non-fiction project *The Reefs of Taprobane*, which covered the months in Ceylon, and on a new novel.

After his experiences in Australia and the Great Barrier Reef, Arthur knew he could write an earthbound novel. 'I realised that I now had the background for a whole novel, which was written in Ceylon during the spring of 1956 and published the next year.'

The novel was *The Deep Range*, and its theme was ocean farming and whale ranching. It was dedicated to Mike Wilson, who more than anyone else shared these wanderlust years with Arthur: 'For Mike who led me to the sea.'

Like several other Clarke novels, *The Deep Range* had its start as a short story which Arthur wrote in 1953 and which appeared in the third volume of Frederik Pohl's *Star Science Fiction* series published by Ian and Betty Ballantine in 1954.

Arthur pushed himself to produce as many words as possible in April, May and June 1956. Visions of meetings with his editors in New York in the summer were starting to pop up unexpectedly in his head.

'I've been getting up at 7 every day (5.30 once last week!) and working solidly until about 9.30 p.m. when I usually fold up . . . Average daily output, 2–3 thousand words, and having touched 5.5. How the hell does Simenon do it?'

Also in the spring he had some pleasing literary news: two of his stories, 'Hide and Seek' and 'If I Forget Thee, Oh Earth', were chosen for a college anthology of English literature. Arthur was thrilled. Of the scores of writers included, only two others had two stories included – Dickens and Maugham.

What he wasn't pleased about was the quality of the short-run hardcover edition of *Reach for Tomorrow* that Ballantine Books published. Their main edition, of course, was the paperback, but they published a limited number of hardbacks for libraries from the same plates. This Arthur objected to as 'a scruffy production'. He was going to insist, he told Val, on the same hardcover quality that Harcourt had given to *The City and The Stars*.

On 25 May he dashed off a brief note to Ian Macauley, who was then living in Manhattan.

'Working from 7 a.m. to 10 p.m., trying to finish two books before I leave Ceylon on 30 June. Will be back at my London address until I arrive at the Biltmore on 29 August. Look forward a lot to seeing you again and giving you some of my news.'

But Arthur gave Ian the really big news at the end of the card.

'Have made up my mind – I'm settling in Ceylon and commuting once a year to the US.'

Arthur's circle of friends in Ceylon was expanding, and in a letter to Val he described how comfortable he felt there.

'The contrast between here and England is fantastic, and it's strange to feel free after all these years. Maybe a couple of months a year in Ceylon will be all I can take – will need the remaining ten to recover.'

It was about this time that Arthur met Hector Ekanayake, a young Sinhalese who would become the flyweight champion of Ceylon in the autumn of 1956. He was the youngest flyweight ever, and this kept him from the Olympics.

'Hector was working at a US Agricultural show in Colombo I happened to visit,' says Arthur. 'His father, a police inspector, got him a temporary job there.'

Over the next few years Hector helped with miscellaneous projects around Arthur's place and would sometimes accompany him on trips. Hector eventually learned the underwater business and helped Arthur and Mike on their local adventures. The friendship grew steadily throughout the fifties and sixties, and continues to this day.

Arthur worked hard before leaving on his trip to England and the US. As summer 1956 approached, Ceylon was caught up in a general election. The outcome, to the surprise of many, was that the pro-Western government lost to the left-wing, nationalistic one. This brought forth a controversy over the national language. During the election campaign, both parties agreed that English should be replaced with the majority language, Sinhalese. But the minority Tamils, making up about one-sixth of the population, objected. The antagonism between the Sinhalese and the Tamils, often erupting in violence and death, has continued ever since. Arthur hoped that his newly chosen home would not be 'spoilt by silly politicians and unruly mobs'.

Film director David Lean and his crew were in Ceylon at this time shooting *The Bridge Over the River Kwai*. It didn't take Mike Wilson long to show up on the location when he heard about the shoot.

A member of the film company recalls that this strange character walked on to the set one morning wearing a white marine cap. He walked up to the Columbia representative, introduced himself and told him that he represented the London *Times* and wanted to cover the shooting of the film.

The man from Columbia said he would let him know in a few days, then immediately cabled London for verification. The reply came in from the newspaper. They had never heard of Mike Wilson.

Such character descriptions of Mike as 'absolutely flamboyant' and something of a prankster gain credence in light of this impostor story, and it hinted at the reason for some of the problems Arthur and Mike would have years later.

Mike left for London two weeks before Arthur – in mid-June – at the same time Arthur put two book projects behind him. His *Reefs of Taprobane* manuscript (65,000 words and at least a hundred photos) was shipped to London for typing the same day that he finished writing his novel, *The Deep Range*. These would become his fifteenth and sixteenth published books. Again, he felt the euphoria of finishing, a release from the tremendous self-discipline he had put himself under. He looked forward to two weeks of leisure to catch up on life's miscellany.

He flew to London in early July and used 88 Nightingale Road as his base. Besides visiting Ballifants to see the family, he and Val Cleaver also did some touring. There was plenty of London business to conduct – meetings with his literary agent, accountant, publishers – and friends to see. More than once he dropped into the Globe and saw some of the old gang and some of the new. These pub visits were not just entertainment; they were honest project research as well because his main work in London that summer was to complete *Tales from the White Hart* for publication in 1957.

Arthur wrote another one or two 'White Hart' stories for the volume, and completely edited it as well. Only the preface had to be put off until he had some time in New York City.

Four and a half years earlier – in the spring of 1952 – Arthur had gone to the United States for the first time to promote *The Exploration of Space* and meet the people he had known only through letters. His 1956 trip was memorable because he was about to receive a special honour. During his last few days in London he spent some time polishing the keynote speech he would deliver, then he flew across the Atlantic Ocean once more.

CHAPTER 11

Space-age Dreams

> What we are building now is the nervous
> system of mankind . . . The communi-
> cations network, of which the satellites will
> be nodal points, will enable the conscious-
> ness of our grandchildren to flicker like
> lightning back and forth across the face of
> the planet.
> – 'The World of the Communications
> Satellite'

The World Science Fiction Convention in 1956 was held at the
Biltmore Hotel in New York City during the first few days of September – Labor Day weekend. The convention had been an annual
event since 1939, when the first one took place in Manhattan. Attend-
ance for 1956 was higher than ever before. Wider distribution of the
genre through mass paperback publishing during the early 1950s was
in part responsible for bringing forth a larger crowd than in previous
years. Also, science was catching up with the visions of science fiction
in some technologies. The US announced its plans to launch an artificial satellite in 1955, although no one knew that Sputnik and the
Space Age was just a year away.

David Kyle, co-publisher with Marty Greenberg of Gnome Press,
was the chairman and organiser that year, and he named Arthur C.
Clarke as the guest of honour.

'This was the first time that a non-American was chosen,' says
Kyle. 'And I also pushed and helped put together the bid that took
the convention out of North America for the first time, and the
following year, in 1957, it went to London.'

Robert Bloch, creator of *Psycho* and dozens of other novels, was
toast-master at the event. 'It was certainly one of the first large
Worldcons,' recalls Bloch, 'with between one and two thousand
people attending. The large turnout was very impressive. I know
Arthur met many, many people because this was one of the first
conventions that began to attract large numbers of professional

writers from all over the country. The whole affair was just beginning to be a little bit tainted by commercialism. More dealers were showing up. More editors. More publishers. It began to lose its fannish connotations.

'And I remember remarking to Arthur that when this thing was finished, after the way the fans had been behaving, we had to change the name of the hotel from the Biltmore to the ReBuiltmore.'

Willy Ley, Arthur's old friend who had supplied him with science fiction magazines during the war, was there and led one of the discussion groups. And there was corporate participation, too. People from the Martin Company of Baltimore, prime contractor for the Navy's Project Vanguard, attended, bringing with them a model of the three-stage *Vanguard* rocket vehicle. Arthur was in the process of planning and beginning to write his non-fiction book, *The Making of a Moon*, and the Martin people gave him an open invitation to visit Baltimore and tour their facilities and interview managers.

'I hope to sit on their doorstep for a week or so, picking their brains,' he wrote Val.

Mike Wilson was up to his usual antics at the Biltmore.

'I was fast asleep,' says Arthur, 'and there was a knock on the door. It woke me up. I went and opened the door, and there was this small guy outside; it was Harlan [Ellison]. And he said to me, "Will you please ask Mike Wilson to leave my girl alone?" And I said, "Certainly, Harlan. Goodnight."' With that Arthur went back to sleep.

At the banquet dinner on Sunday evening, Arthur didn't get to speak 'until past my bedtime'. He was sitting between Bob Bloch and the cartoonist Al Capp, so at least things were lively. They joked back and forth for about four hours.

Isaac Asimov was also on the dais, but he wasn't laughing. As a matter of fact he was in considerable pain. 'I had a kidney stone,' Isaac explained. 'Worse yet, the stone managed to get itself into a position where it activated the "I have to urinate" button. I had warned the people who were organising the convention that I would be periodically leaving the dais and said why. Arthur was guest of honour, and when he got up to speak I was determined *not* to leave the dais until he was through lest the audience assume I was demonstrating my disapproval of what he was saying. I turned slightly green, therefore, when he rose with something like thirty sheets of paper.'

Science fiction enthusiasts, Arthur told his audience, were unique: 'No other form of literature arouses such passionate loyalty as does science fiction.' And true enthusiasts, Arthur continued, always combine a sense of wonder and mental flexibility. Arthur went on to defend the genre against its critics whose unconscious logic was all too often, 'I don't understand what this is about, and therefore it's nonsense.'

But Arthur didn't just praise science fiction; he also had some criticism for it. There was 'a great deal of what one can only call ugliness in much modern science fiction', he said. He complained about regretful trends in the field, 'a cult of irrationality has been gaining ground . . . the cults of colliding planets, of airborne crockery [UFOs], and of reincarnated colleens [Bridie Murphy].' Arthur's primary objection was 'that thousands of people are prepared to believe these things *on the sort of evidence that has been put forward*'. He then cited an example of how many eyewitnesses came forward to confirm a UFO sighting which was a deliberate hoax.

He voiced his concern about the 'anti-scientific bias of some current writing', and about the emphasis on future wars and other negative futures, even though science fiction was still a 'basically optimistic and inspiring form of literature'. His plea was for science fiction writers and readers to be more responsible to real science and in educating the public.

'Our society can only continue to exist if there is a revolutionary upgrading of technical and scientific education in the very near future – by which I mean before the end of this century.'

Those gathered at the Biltmore were, said Arthur, 'trustees of a future which we will never see, but which our thoughts and actions will inevitably shape . . . it may seem fanciful to imagine that what we write can affect the future, but that is the literal truth. Who can doubt, for example, that the world's acceptance of space flight is due to the countless works of fiction on this theme? . . . I am quite sure that by writing about space flight we have brought its realisation nearer by decades. Perhaps even more important, we have helped the public to appreciate what it will mean when it comes.'

No one there could have imagined that the Space Age was just over a year away, and that it would be the Russians who would officially give it birth.

After the Worldcon at the Biltmore, Arthur and Mike Wilson took an apartment at the Hotel Chelsea on 23rd Street in Manhattan. Arthur was impressed that several famous literary personalities had stayed at the Chelsea. Brendan Behan, Dylan Thomas, Mark Twain, Thomas Wolfe, Eugene O'Neill and Arthur Miller were just a few of the writers who had lived there. He enjoyed the place and from then on made it his home base in New York City. If he needed some extra local colour or anecdotal material, the residents of the Chelsea could provide it.

In October he finally had a chance to write the preface to *Tales from the White Hart*. Also during this period he did some last-minute work on his novel, *The Deep Range*. But mostly Arthur travelled and lectured during that autumn and winter. Before the end of 1956, he gave almost two dozen talks in thirteen states, from Massachusetts to Oklahoma, returning to New York whenever possible.

'Lectures are now going very well, and I'm thoroughly enjoying the tour. Have been able to do lots of work, too – have half a dozen story ideas lined up,' he wrote Val in early December. He rode the rails from city to city right into the New Year, and had plenty of time to read, write and think about the future.

Once Arthur referred to himself as 'an unemployed prophet', but for all his powers of scientific forecasting, he was not spreading the word in late 1956 that the Space Age would officially begin the next year. The reason was that he didn't know it himself.

In 1957 Arthur published his most fanciful collection of fiction – *Tales from the White Hart*.

These stories were written between 1953 and 1956, years of tremendous change in Arthur's life. During this period he and Marilyn had got married – obviously too quickly – and permanently separated. Did the writing of the *Tales* perhaps serve as self-administered therapy? Did writing humour, in other words, help keep Arthur Clarke on an even keel during this rough weather of life? Possibly.

Arthur had also travelled extensively for the first time, around the world, up and down the east coast of Australia, in Ceylon and throughout the United States. All these scientific tall tales were set in a fictitious London pub which was closely based on a real one, the White Horse, where he and his friends met to discuss science fiction and space travel. Was this consistent setting symbolic of a secure, dependable and friendly home while he was doing his globe-trotting? Again, it's possible.

Harvey Purvis, the teller of the *Tales,* was certainly a fictive conglomerate of many personalities, but some of the other characters were real, as were their names. Arthur's prewar roommate, Bill Temple, was mentioned a few times and Arthur even put himself into one story – 'What Goes Up'.

Ken Slater, a science fiction fan and customer of the White Horse, remembers the pub meetings well enough.

'Anybody new that came to the pub was always told to ask Arthur to tell them about rockets. Which they would do and then sit back for the short lecture. After Arthur broke into the short lecture, then we'd always strongly advise the newcomer to ask, "Look, what does the rocket push against?" Which immediately brought forth from Arthur the long lecture, you know, the five-guinea version. That was a standard put-on at the White Horse, because if you ever got Arthur on rocketry you could sit back and let the bar listen for up to a couple of hours.'

British writer John Brunner remembers going to the White Horse for the first time.

'It must have been in the summer of 1952. I was a callow seventeen-year-old, going on eighteen,' says Brunner. 'I had just made my second sale to an American magazine and earned a thousand dollars out of my first year as a professional writer. And I celebrated by going to the London Science Fiction Circle at the White Horse. Among the people who were there was Arthur Clarke. Also there were Charles Eric Maine, Bill Temple, Sam Youd and others.

'What I remember mainly about that evening, though, was the fact that I was in the presence of people whose work I had frequently read in magazines and, in one or two cases, in book form. And they were very polite to me. I came back thinking, "Wow, I've just met these people. They're selling writers. And I'm one too. Gosh." A terrible thing to happen to a teenager, of course.

'That the Circle members took to meeting regularly at the White Horse on Thursday evenings was a tradition that goes back a very long way, to the time when science fiction had to be paid for in dollars because there was so little of it about. American magazines were extremely hard to find. People would go and literally trade books and magazines they'd read for ones they hadn't.

'The landlord [Lew, to whom *Tales* is dedicated] was such a popular character that when he moved to another pub the entire London Science Fiction Circle moved with him. And that's how we moved to the Globe in Hatton Garden.'

Arthur fictionalised this real move at the conclusion of the last story in *Tales*: '. . . we all followed Drew lock, stock and barrel – particularly barrel – to his new establishment . . . the Sphere.'

Most readers could easily use one of Arthur's favourite expressions to describe this book: 'Great fun!' And Arthur no doubt had some fun while writing it. The critics agreed and welcomed its publication in January 1957 with such words and phrases as 'hilarious', 'wholly

137

delightful', 'high diversion, amusement and amazement', and a 'light and frothy conglomeration of side-splitters'.

During January and February Arthur continued his lecture circuit in the United States and travelled as far as Vancouver, Washington. He enjoyed American trains and the reading time his travelling provided. Whenever he spoke in the vicinity of a fellow writer or a well-known science fiction fan, he would often be invited to stay at the person's home. This was just fine with Arthur, who appreciated the lower overhead and would use some of the savings to entertain or show his appreciation.

Ted Thomas, a Pennsylvania attorney whose hobby is science fiction, recalls one such occasion.

'He was giving lectures in my area, so I suggested that he stay with us if he wanted. That way he'd have a base. We met at the first Milford Science Fiction Writers' Conference,' recalls Ted.

'Well, I got his book, the *Exploration of the Moon*, with drawings by his friend R. A. Smith. I got it because I had an idea to write a story. It was one of my very early stories and its title was "A Far Look", which was soon published in *Astounding*.

'What I did to write this story was to assume that everything Arthur and his artist friend said about the Moon in their book was gospel, and I had gone through that book, annotating and making notes in the margins and used them to develop a storyline.

'Now even to this day I don't know why I did it, unless it was an attempt to be funny, but somewhere toward the end of the book Arthur had written something about the "colour" of something. He of course spelled it the English way. And I put a note next to the margin, "Can't spell color."

'When Arthur was staying with us at the apartment I said, "Here, use my desk. I've got to go to the office all day." He had some writing to do. So he was at the desk working, and there was a bookcase alongside it. He saw his book, pulled it out, and then got intrigued, as you can imagine, with my notations in the margins. In the meantime my wife was out in the kitchen doing dishes . . . There she was, minding her own business doing dishes, and all of a sudden Arthur is in the kitchen, holding this book, steaming.

'"Doesn't he know that in England we spell colour c-o-l-o-u-r?" he told her. My wife, of course, had no idea what all this was about. Well, we finally got it straightened out. I thought it was funny as hell.'

After four lectures out west in early February Arthur got off the road for a while and did some writing in New York City. Between

February and April he wrote the short story 'The Songs of Distant Earth', which would gestate and become a novel more than two decades later.

'For some reason, at the beginning of that momentous year [1957, when the Space Age began] a phrase lodged in my mind and wouldn't go away; it echoed round and round my skull as persistently as the last movement of Sibelius' Second Symphony.'

That phrase was 'The Songs of Distant Earth'. This is a classic example of when a few words, magically and subjectively imbued with meaning, are the genesis of a creative effort.

'Was it possible,' Arthur asked himself, 'to write a completely realistic story using an interstellar – as opposed to a "merely" inter-planetary – background?'

This question was based on the scientific fact that 'we are 99.99 per cent certain that it will always be impossible to travel faster than light, which means that journeys to even the nearest star systems will take decades'.

The answer to Arthur's question was *yes*, a hard science fiction story about interstellar travel *could* be written; and not just a story, but a complete novel.

Of course this question is important to Arthur because it is the basis for his primary commitment to science fiction as opposed to fantasy – and *his* definition of both. *Star Wars* (and Arthur, like every-body else, loved it as entertainment) could have its characters and spaceships jump from star to star as fantasy, but the story was *not* science fiction.

'Now, I like fantasy every bit as much as science fiction,' he says, 'but I recognise the distinction between the genres . . . Fantasy is something that couldn't happen in the real world (though often you wish it would); science fiction is something that really could happen (though often you'd be sorry if it did).'

Both the short story, and later the novel 'The Songs of Distant Earth', contain well-wrought and often moving prose: 'They stared at each other across the wrinkled sand, each wondering at the miracle that had brought them together out of the immensity of time and space.' Arthur's peopled, interstellar story first appeared in a collec-tion of short fiction published in early 1958, *The Other Side of the Sky*.

No major book of Clarke's fiction, apart from *Tales from the White Hart*, was published in 1957. Appropriate to the historic event of *Sputnik*, it was more of a non-fiction year for Arthur C. Clarke.

Besides lecturing in the United States in the autumn of 1957,

Arthur worked hard that year on two non-fiction titles for Harper & Brothers: *The Making of a Moon* (published in mid-1957 before *Sputnik*) and *Voice Across the Sea* (issued in the latter half of 1958).

That both of these books were out of print at the beginning of the 1990s had only to do with their topicality and relevance to the last half of the 1950s. In fact, Arthur came to realise that his fiction would, with few exceptions, outlast his non-fiction from the long-term perspective of his complete corpus. In the 1970s he deliberately focused and devoted his creative time to novels and avoided any non-fiction contracts that were not collections of earlier work.

When Arthur began writing *The Making of a Moon*, he had no idea that *Sputnik 1* would be launched a few months after the book's publication. Had he been able to predict the near future and have access to the Russian space programme, his book could have been published a year or two later and titled 'The Making of the Moons', juxtaposing the Russian and American satellite programmes. But without such a prediction he wrote what was sensible and relevant non-fiction in early 1957: a history of the US Earth satellite programme and Project Vanguard, just one scientific endeavour of many planned for the International Geophysical Year (IGY) which officially ran from July 1957 to December 1958.

Voice Across the Sea was a history of the first telephone cable across the Atlantic, which was completed and christened in 1954. Another mid-century history, this book had the advantage of not being immediately outdated by the rush of technological events. It would be more than two decades before optic cables began to dominate land and sea communications lines.

In the autumn of 1957 Arthur flew to Barcelona to attend the International Astronautical Federation conference and see his friends in the astronautical community. Delegates from about twenty countries were present. Then, catching most of the world off-guard, history was made. The Russians had orbited *Sputnik 1*, the world's first artificial satellite.

'I was woken up by a call from the London *Daily Express*,' says Arthur. 'It was a complete shock; I had not anticipated it in the least. But I knew it would change the modern world.

'I then called the rest of the British delegation, and I didn't get to sleep again for the rest of that night.'

Arthur's friend Fred Durant recalls that the news was slow to reach Spain. 'The head of the Soviet delegation was Leonid Sedov. We saw him at the airport on Saturday afternoon, and we knew nothing about the launch because in Spain under Franco they didn't allow British papers in until they had been censored or reviewed. So a lot of us didn't know about it until later, when people came from England and the States with the news.

'We saw Sedov that evening at a reception and of course congratulated him. We also sent a cablegram of congratulations to the president of the Soviet Academy of Sciences,' says Durant.

Arthur had a good laugh at the same Saturday reception, the day after Russia's *Sputnik 1* spectacular.

'I'll always remember what one of the Russian delegates said during a conversation. It really struck me. When I mentioned *Sputnik 1* weighed about 150 pounds, she said, "It can't be that big. *Pravda* must be wrong."

'Back then, you rarely heard Russians say *Pravda* was wrong. Of course it was even heavier [184.3 pounds].'

The Space Age was born, and even Arthur, who had dreamed about it for so long and had devoted his life to helping it become a reality, had not predicted that it would arrive so soon.

He returned to London and worked for a few weeks before flying to the United States to give some lectures in November and December. He had plenty of new stories for his audiences.

CHAPTER 12

Two-culture Traveller

> I've said half jokingly that as much as I love
> America – and I have a great many friends
> there – the only thing that will get me back
> is when there's a seat in a space shuttle for
> me.
>
> – *OMNI* Interview, 1979

After the United States failed twice in launching its Navy *Vanguard* satellites, the alternative *Jupiter-C* rocket successfully placed America's *Explorer 1* satellite in orbit on 1 February 1958. It was Arthur's friend, Wernher von Braun, who led the US Army team in their successful *Jupiter-C* launch.

While the space race was just beginning to fire up between the superpowers, Arthur C. Clarke was on the road again in America, lecturing for the first three months of 1958. He delivered some forty-eight lectures in fifteen states, this time about a topical subject close to his heart – Earth satellites.

Holiday magazine featured a Clarke piece about his road tour in their October issue: 'USA: A Spaceman Rides the Lecture Circuit'. Wrote Arthur, 'In my 1958 season, thanks to the unexpected co-operation of the Kremlin, I started my tour not merely one up but two up on my audiences. Both *Sputniks* were circling the Earth when I delivered my first talk on satellites; gone for ever, consequently, was the opinionated little man in the front row who was quite sure that space travel was impossible – because no one had ever done it before. Sometimes I miss him; it used to be more fun when there was at least one person in the audience who thought I was crazy, and didn't hesitate to say so.'

Arthur spoke anywhere he was invited, including business associations, universities, women's clubs, churches, libraries, YMCAs and so on. In his *Holiday* article he asked himself why he hadn't yet been invited to a prison, and speculated that 'perhaps the subject of space flight is considered too escapist'.

After a dozen or so lectures, Arthur usually knew what questions were coming. In early 1958 it wasn't difficult to anticipate one of the most frequently asked: 'Why didn't we put up a satellite first?' There were several reasons, of course, not the least of which was Washington politics, but it *wasn't*, Arthur emphasised, because the Russians had the expertise of more German rocket scientists. Rather it was the US that got the leading rocket men after World War II.

The lecture circuit had one major surprise for Arthur: nowhere did he find religious opposition to the idea of space travel. Was it because his audiences were generally well-educated and pro-science and research to begin with? Probably. But had there been some aggressive attacks from the over-zealous believers, Arthur would have replied with his common-sense perspective: there was no basic difference between exploring the solar system and universe and exploring planet Earth.

Even Pope Pius XII had stated formally that the exploration of space, once the means of doing so had been discovered, was fulfilling mankind's God-given potentialities. There was no doubt that the Catholic Church welcomed and accepted the soon-to-come Space Age.

'It is hard to believe that anyone, whatever his religious faith, can seriously disagree with this argument,' wrote Arthur. 'Any path to knowledge is a path to God – or to Reality, whichever word one prefers to use.'

The main theme of Arthur's lectures in the 1950s (and many thereafter) was that an immense revolution would be taking place within a decade, or certainly no more than a generation.

'We are living, I told audiences from New Hampshire to New Mexico, in a moment unique in all history – the last days of Man's existence as a citizen of a single planet.'

Arthur then created an analogy that became famous when the *Eagle* landed on the Moon a decade later and Armstrong and Aldrin left their historic bootprints in the lunar soil. Wernher von Braun gave a variation on Arthur's analogy to the media:

'What is happening now is nothing less than the next stage in evolution, comparable to the time, perhaps a billion years ago, when life came out of the sea and conquered the land.'

The concept was similar to one written by the great Russian space pioneer, Konstantin Tsiolkovsky, of which Arthur confesses he wasn't aware at the time he wrote his aeonic view: 'The Earth is the cradle of Mankind – but you cannot live in a cradle for ever.'

The subject of flying saucers or UFOs aroused debate at most of Clarke's lectures. Arthur was both 'astonished' and 'disturbed' by the extreme interest. True believers in flying saucers did not always take kindly to Arthur's healthy scepticism and scientific approach. No stranger to UFOs, Arthur has seen far too many to believe in them as ET spaceships. His lecture approach to this subject was to describe several of his sightings – all extremely credible and initially mysterious – and then explain what they were proved to be.

Three examples he often gave audiences were: a line of brilliant silver discs along the horizon were actually seagulls' wings acting like mirrors reflecting sunlight; what looked like an aerial jellyfish or silken cloud in the late summer sky was actually a mass of sunlit gossamer threads discarded by spiders; a flying object, spitting sparks and flames, was a burning golfball ejected from a trash can by its own highly combustible and energy-torqued rubber bands. And he had more. He presented them all objectively, giving detailed sightings and thorough explanations. But there were always some true believers who refused to be convinced by his rationality.

'On one occasion,' says Arthur, 'a lady from the audience asked me if I believe that those who claimed to have met men from flying saucers were liars. She sat down rather abruptly when I replied, "Yes, madam"; not until later did the chairman gleefully inform me that her husband had authored one of the best known of the sacred writings.'

Arthur sighted a 'classical' flying saucer on 17 October 1958 when he was flying up the coast of Italy aboard KLM Flight 826 on his way to Geneva. The aircraft was at an altitude of about ten thousand feet, and it was a bright, hazy day. Arthur was looking at the coastline below, waiting to see Naples and Vesuvius.

'I became aware that a brilliant oval of light was keeping pace with the aircraft a few thousand feet below. It appeared quite solid, though its edges were hazy and seemed to pulsate slightly; they also had a bluish tinge rather like that of a mercury arc. It was impossible to judge its size or distance, but I had the impression that the object was halfway between the aircraft and the ground. Sometimes it was so brilliant that it hurt the eye to look at it directly.'

He watched the UFO for at least ten minutes. It was a solid disc, with no transparency at all, and its shape and size were constant as it kept station beneath the aircraft. Other passengers also saw it; several even took photographs of it. Arthur wouldn't take his eyes off it, and he finally won the wait.

'I was able to keep it in sight until it disintegrated and slowly faded from view, like a cloud breaking up beneath the sun. By that time there was no question of its identity.

'It was a mock sun, or "sun dog", caused by the presence of an invisible layer of ice crystals between the aircraft and the ground.'

This was another good sighting to describe to his lecture audiences. He also imparted his humorous rule for UFO observers:

'It's not a spaceship unless you can read the Mars registration plate.'

Exhausted after three months on the US lecture circuit, Arthur flew back to England in April. While he was there he participated in a special symposium, 'Britain Enters the Space Age: A Discussion on Guided Missiles and Space Travel'. It was held at the Royal Festival Hall on 14 April 1958. Sponsored by the Air League of the British Empire, it took place 'in the gracious presence of HRH Prince Philip, Duke of Edinburgh', who delivered the opening address.

In 1958 Britain had no definite space programme, let alone a time-table, even though the competition was heating up between the US and the USSR.

'I cannot believe that the British people will be content to sit by and watch others explore the universe around us,' said Prince Philip. 'You can be quite certain it is not from any lack of willingness or scientific brain-power. It is simply that research and development for space travel is almighty expensive.

'We could only go in for this if we were prepared to make very considerable sacrifices in other directions,' the Prince told the young audience from universities, technical schools and the military services.

There were four speakers besides Prince Philip, and A. C. Clarke had the final position. His main themes were the coming revolution in space-age communications; the exploration of space as the next evolutionary step; and an eventual interplanetary civilisation. Also during his speech Arthur returned to the point Prince Philip had made about the tremendous cost of exploring space.

'If anyone thinks that space research is beyond the resources of this country,' Arthur said with conviction, 'I should like to point out that the money thrown away in developing aircraft types which were scrapped even before they flew could have put a British satellite into space before *Sputnik 1*.' He came up with a cost per person that would allow Britain to compete with Russia and the United States – about 'a shilling a head a week' he said.

Later, Arthur and Prince Philip chatted for a while and, according to Arthur, got 'into a brisk argument on the subject of UFOs . . . I expressed surprise that he seemed to take them seriously.'

Before leaving London Arthur spent time with his good friend, Val Cleaver. 'We saw *Sputnik 2* on the last four nights of its existence,' he told Sam Youd. 'It was an awe-inspiring sight – the brightest thing in the sky – and I'm looking forward to spotting number three.'

By May 1958 Arthur was back in Ceylon. He had settled in to a new address, 20 Rheinland Place, and was on a disciplined writing schedule again, working mostly on articles for *Holiday* magazine, some of which were reprinted in his 1959 essay collection *The Challenge of the Spaceship*. And he was thinking about future novels.

'The one I am now working on will be my first non-sf; it's based on my RAF experiences,' he wrote to Sam Youd. 'It's about time someone did a novel about the early days of radar. I feel that I have now lost my amateur status, as my twenty-first book comes out this autumn . . . Now that I've accumulated this stockpile, my aim is less writing and more thinking.'

During the summer of 1958 major violence erupted in Ceylon – the first of many internal conflicts Arthur would experience over the years.

'About two hundred people have been killed in riots,' he wrote Sam, 'and there has been a lot of property damage. Until this week [10 July 1958] there has been a rigid curfew, but that has now been relaxed and things are generally calming down. But it does make one doubtful whether to invest much in the place.'

Arthur was still stuck in the middle of *Glide Path*, his war novel, in mid-August, but some of his frustrated energy was going into a new business enterprise with Mike Wilson.

'We are just floating (if that's the word) Clarke-Wilson Associates, diving consultants,' he told Sam. 'Mike's already done one survey job on a wreck in the Maldives, about four hundred miles west of here. He has brought back some fabulous close-ups of sharks feeding. They have bad table manners.'

In September Mike met a beautiful girl named Elizabeth. One night, after a small get-together with friends at Rheinland Place, Mike took Elizabeth home by cab.

'As he was leaving her place,' Arthur wrote Sam, 'he was attacked by four thugs who bashed him on the head with an iron bar and gave him some nasty scalp wounds which put him in hospital for several days.' Mike might have thought he was being warned off, but he reaffirmed his commitment to Liz by marrying her immediately. 'The entire family is on Mike's side,' continued Arthur, 'inc. Elizabeth's Scots mother, so it's only a matter of time. Meanwhile all sorts of underground campaigns are in progress to smuggle her clothes out of the house past the old man's guard.'

Before September ended, Arthur had written fifty thousand words of *Glide Path* and had made plans to fly to England in October, with

Arthur's first satellite dish, a gift from the government of India and erected by their engineers, was part of the Satellite Instructional Television Experiment (SITE) in the mid-1970s.

Neil Armstrong, the first human to walk on the moon, and Arthur Clarke take a break during NASA's conference on Wallops Island, Virginia, in June 1970.

Below Looking at the work of space artists with cosmonaut Alexei Leonov, the first human ever to 'walk' in space, at a UN space conference in Vienna, August 1968.

Above In front of MGM Studios, Hollywood, after the release of *2001: A Space Odyssey* in 1968.

Below Two visionaries, writer and filmmaker, created a movie that continues to influence film and our images of the future. Arthur and Stanley Kubrick on the set of *2001* in the mid-1960s.

a stop in Geneva to visit Sam Youd and his family who were then residing at Chalet Monnet in Montreux.

Liz was now at Rheinland Place, running the household, and she and Arthur got on well together. It was just the two of them when Mike left for his underwater film lecture tour in the United States. By the time he returned Arthur would be on the road again, sharing his visions of the future with diverse audiences and trying to finish his novel and write some shorter pieces between stops.

As 1958 came to a close, the United States aimed and launched three *Pioneer* spacecraft towards the Moon. The *Pioneer* programme grew out of the International Geophysical Year and was inherited by NASA from the Department of Defense. *Pioneer 1, 2* and *3* failed to reach destination Moon, but they did send back useful data on the atmosphere and radiation belts.

Arthur knew it would not be long before a Russian or American spacecraft crash-landed on the lunar surface.

'I'm getting quite reactionary in my old age,' he wrote Sam as he approached his forty-first birthday in December 1958. 'I think it's rather a pity that we'll soon look for the last time on the virgin Moon.'

Before Christmas Arthur had flown the Atlantic once again (this time in a Comet: 'take off most impressive'), and was handling business in Manhattan. He signed three contracts for short non-fiction books, *The Challenge of the Spaceship*, 1959; *The First Five Fathoms*, 1960; and *The Challenge of the Sea*, 1960.

His unfinished war novel, *Glide Path*, was still in search of a unique identity. It would be a long search, despite his best intentions: 'I also hope (touch wood) to finish *Glide Path* in 1959,' he wrote Val, 'and get started on *Imperial Earth* and a non-fiction book Harpers are very anxious to get, based on my *Crystal Ball* series and incorporating the idea we've often discussed of considering what sf inventions make sense.'

There was time to see friends and a movie now and then. *The Defiant Ones*, starring Sidney Poitier and Tony Curtis, was running in Manhattan. Arthur immediately pronounced it a screen classic.

He travelled to the Boston area for the Christmas holidays, and stayed with Fred and Pip Durant and their family in Concord. Arthur, as always, was made at home, and Pip knitted him a Christmas stocking to hang on a chair with the children's.

A few days after Christmas Isaac Asimov (then at Boston University) and Arthur Kantrowitz (an executive at Avco Corporation and

Fred's boss) came for dinner at the Durants. It was a wonderful evening of talk, Fred recalls, most of which was dominated by the two big names in science fiction.

'Kantrowitz was a brilliant physicist, but he knew nothing about science fiction,' says Fred. 'While Arthur and Isaac threw out ideas back and forth across the room, I can remember Kantrowitz's head just going from left to right, left to right, as if he were watching a tennis match. He was utterly stunned with the brilliance and exciting concepts of these two. And Arthur Clarke would say, "You can have that one, Ike." And Ike would say, "All right, here's one for you . . ."' The two egos of science fiction were one on one, having a great old time.

Back in Manhattan at the Hotel Chelsea, Arthur prepared for his 1959 lecture tour. He was happy that the tour was only half as hectic as the previous year's. His itinerary called for twenty scheduled engagements during the first quarter.

The promise of the Space Age and the benefits of communications and weather satellites were Arthur's major lecture themes early that year. To a Michigan audience in January 1959 he predicted: 'Should the Soviet Union launch a concentrated rocket programme, men will be on the Moon within the next ten years.' The prediction was right, but the country was wrong. It was the 'concentrated rocket programme' of the United States that won the historic triumph in the summer of 1969.

Arthur met Kingsley Amis at Princeton – 'a pleasant, modest guy', he reported to Val – who said to Arthur upon their meeting, 'This is like meeting T. S. Eliot!' Amis was giving six seminars on science fiction which was an unusual thing in those days. His seminars were later published in book form.

When Arthur was speaking in Chicago late in January, he spent some time with the Beat Poets and found himself on a panel protesting about the local censorship of Naked Lunch. 'I had never heard of Burroughs or the Beats,' he told Val, 'but it sounded fun.'

The famous Chicago attorney, Elmer Gertz, who fought the legal battle for Henry Miller's Tropic of Cancer in the United States, was the man who asked Arthur to be on the panel. Gertz was not able to be there, but, he says, 'everyone told me later that Arthur Clarke was convulsively funny. He was like a Bob Hope of the intellectuals.'

Arthur also had the pleasure of spending a weekend with Commander Jacques Cousteau in Boston in February. The occasion was a big skin-divers' convention. The latest project in Cousteau's life,

Arthur learned, was his sea farm in Monaco. During their discussions, Arthur raised the possibility of Cousteau writing a short introduction to his book, *The First Five Fathoms*, and it eventually happened.

Cousteau's film, *The Silent World*, was shown, and Arthur met Roger Caras, the television correspondent, author and wildlife expert, for the first time. Roger was then working for Columbia Pictures in New York City and he had handled the promotion for *The Silent World*.

'I already knew Jacques,' says Roger, 'and Herb Shriner and I (we were very close friends) were invited up to Boston for a party Jacques was giving at the Copley Plaza. Arthur was also at the party, and I was introduced to him by Jacques Cousteau. We got chatting. It was like a meeting of kindred souls, and we went on from there.'

A few years later Roger and Arthur would work for the same boss: Stanley Kubrick.

In the late February Arthur headed south for more lectures in South Carolina and Virginia. He appeared on Dave Garroway's 'Today Show' early one morning with Wernher von Braun and two other guests. They spoke about space and missiles for two hours. 'I seem to be regarded as the philosopher of space flight – that's what they're calling me,' he wrote Val.

The lecture tour for the 1959 season ended in the midwest, with stops in Illinois, Indiana and Ohio. During the question and answer period at one of these talks, a young lady asked Arthur why he liked Ceylon so much.

'I was about to switch on the sound track I had played a hundred times before,' says Arthur, 'when suddenly in my mind's eye I saw those two beaches – both so far away. Do not ask me why it happened then; but in that moment of double vision, I knew the truth.

'The chill northern beach on which I had so often shivered through an English summer afternoon was merely the intimation of an ultimate and unsuspected beauty – the Platonic ideal, as it were, of a childhood dream. Like the three princes of (how appropriately!) Serendip, I had found far more than I was seeking.

'Six thousand miles from where I was born, I had come home.'

Soon after his return to Ceylon in mid-April Arthur was busy preparing for a diving expedition with Mike Wilson and Rodney Jonklaas off Ceylon's south coast. Their destination was the Great Basses Reef, which was almost wholly unexplored because of the rough weather found there ten months of the year. The two good months are March and April, but even this period is not always reliable. In April of

1959, however, luck was with them and they had almost perfect weather for their week of diving and photography.

Thanks to an arrangement with the Imperial Lighthouse Service, they stayed at the Great Basses lighthouse, ten miles out in the Indian Ocean, and used that as their base. They got to the lighthouse aboard the Service's powerboat, the *Pharos*, whose uniquely experienced crew knew how to navigate the treacherous waters and unload people, gear and stores at the lighthouse under all but the worst conditions.

The surge of water made it impossible to do any exploring close to the reef, and so, with their heavy equipment, they had to struggle to reach calmer waters a few hundred feet away, fighting the powerful currents and pulling their rubber dinghy and tanks behind them.

'But,' says Arthur, 'the struggle was worth it. Beneath us was a fantastic fairyland of caves, grottoes, coral-encrusted valleys – and fish in such numbers as I have never met anywhere else in the world. Sometimes they crowded round us so closely that we could see nothing but a solid wall of scales, and had literally to push our way through it.'

Besides a rainbow-rich variety of small tropical fish, the waters were filled with eagle-rays, turtles, angel fish, 300-pound tuna, groupers and sharks. The sharks near the Great Basses Reef were easy to photograph once a fish was speared and its blood spread into the sea. The challenge was to get photos of sharks with one or two divers in the same picture. This was tried by taking up certain positions relative to the speared bait.

'We had sharks all around us – two nine-footers fought over a fish just six feet away from me as I lay on the seabed,' Arthur wrote Val. 'But despite all our efforts, Mike couldn't get me and the sharks in the same picture.'

Perhaps the creatures they saw most were a family of three groupers who often came out of their caves to see what the intruding divers were doing. Groupers, also known as sea bass or sea perch, come in many varieties and sizes – some over a thousand pounds. The heavy in this particular threesome, however, was only 150 pounds, with the others weighing in at about seventy-five and forty pounds.

By handing a speared fish to the big member of the grouper family Rodney began an underwater friendship, and soon the three groupers all had names, from large to small: Ali Baba, Sinbad and Aladdin. The groupers gratefully accepted the free food which Rodney could obtain much easier than they could. In return they would pose for the still and movie cameras. It became a good working relationship, and Rodney trained and fed the actors.

'Usually Ali Baba swam up from the cave,' says Rodney, 'which he regarded as his own private castle, while Sinbad had already joined us from his own territory a few yards to the lee. Aladdin was last on the scene and usually performed his actions after the larger two had had their fill. It was because of this that he displayed such amusing actions of haste, jealousy and peevishness.'

Cameras ready, Rodney began the action of spearing a fish. Once the gun was discharged the grouper swam quickly to the struggling fish. 'If I missed (which was fairly often),' says Rodney, 'the expression of bewilderment displayed by the disappointed grouper was remarkable.'

Three non-union actors who didn't have to remember their lines – what more could the movie crew desire? Mike was able to shoot sixteen mm colour footage of the underwater adventures of the groupers as well as the shark activity. Later, after cutting, this would produce a twenty-five-minute film for the Ceylon Tea Board, *Beneath the Seas of Ceylon*.

'Writing the script, doing some of the camera work and producing sound-effects in the bath was an interesting experience,' Arthur admits, before lapsing into a tongue-in-cheek hyperbole, 'and quite helpful when I had to do the same sort of thing, on a slightly larger budget, with a fellow named Stanley Kubrick.'

But Arthur's first meeting with Kubrick was five years in the future. There were several more books and modest, regional movies to be produced before then.

The quiet life – that's what Arthur hoped to lead for the rest of the year; quiet with a lot of hard work. Besides all the book contracts he had to fulfil, he and Mike were building up their underwater consulting business, Clarke-Wilson Associates, and work was coming in.

'Just acquired demolition gear – I've been sharing my office with fifty pounds of gelignite, whose company I don't appreciate,' he wrote Roger Caras in May. 'But the arrival of the SW Monsoon has just put a stop to diving on this side [west] of the island, and all work has to move over to the other coast.'

Hector Ekanayake, the young boxing champion, began working fulltime for Clarke-Wilson Associates in May 1959, and Rodney Jonklaas also left his job about the same time. Between Mike, Hector and Rodney, they were ready to take on whatever work came their way. One of their first jobs together was to survey underwater obstructions for the Fisheries Department.

Mike also attempted some boat-building during the summer months. 'He hopes to revolutionise the fishing industry with a catamaran he's designing,' Arthur wrote. 'Meanwhile I'm trying to keep sawdust out of the hi-fi set.'

After returning from the Great Basses Reef, Arthur began working on a juvenile book which he was supposed to finish in early June. When published in the spring of 1960 it became *The First Five Fathoms: A Guide to Underwater Adventure* 'with Mike Wilson' added to the authorship line. The book also boasted an introduction by Jacques Cousteau.

After the manuscript and photographs were sent to the publisher Arthur immediately began his twenty-fifth book, 'about all the possible ways of exploiting the sea', which was due to be delivered before the end of 1959. This was *The Challenge of the Sea*, published in 1960, and it too had an introduction by someone famous. Wernher von Braun wrote it and acknowledged that Arthur had introduced him to his favourite sport, skin-diving.

As if that weren't enough, Arthur had the RAF novel *Glide Path* to complete. He was hard at work on it again in September 1959, completely rewriting and retyping it.

'The first draft was partly an *aide-mémoire* to myself,' he told Val, 'and I'll probably only use about half of it.' That estimate was not far from the mark. By the end of September he had written twenty thousand words of new text.

Also during this period, Arthur did some minor work on his first anthology, *Across the Sea of Stars*, which was published in the summer of 1959. This volume contained selected short stories from three previous collections as well as two novels: *Childhood's End* and *Earthlight*. Just prior to its release, Arthur's first collection of essays, *The Challenge of the Spaceship*, was also published. No question about it: the Clarke corpus was gaining momentum as the historic decade of the 1960s was about to dawn.

At the end of October Arthur moved in to a new house in Colombo. Its address was 47/5 Gregory's Road.

'Our new house is a beauty,' he wrote Val, '47/5 is a common local convention. It means that forty-seven is a lane and we are the fifth house in it. Actually we are at the end of the lane, nicely secluded. As soon as possible I'll take some shots of it, but photography has been out of the question while the darkroom is being installed.'

Arthur was settling in once more: 'I hope to be here right through 1960, repairing my shattered finances (if possible).'

That would be a bigger job than he thought.

CHAPTER 13

Writing his Way Out

I am in a slight stupor at the moment, having written 3,500 words of the novel yesterday, much of it in a kind of automatic frenzy
. . . I was scared to go on with the story as
my brain was racing too fast and I thought
I'd better stop. Very odd feeling.
– Letter to Val Cleaver, 17 October 1960

When New Year's Day 1960 was celebrated no one knew how momentous the coming decade would be. Not even Arthur cared to predict when the first man would orbit the Earth, set foot on the Moon, or descend almost thirty-six thousand feet beneath the Pacific Ocean to the bottom of the Challenger Deep – all near future events. (The latter was accomplished in early 1960 by Naval Lieutenant Don Walsh in the bathyscaphe *Trieste*.) Arthur was thinking and writing more about the far future – beyond the year 2000 – than the current decade. He was beginning to write speculative essays which would become *Profiles of the Future*.

His most important new magazine market in the 1960s was *Playboy*, for both fiction and non-fiction. The May 1960 issue ran 'I Remember Babylon', an important *and* entertaining piece about possible abuse of the coming communications satellites. The story, written in October 1959, was unique because Arthur C. Clarke was one of its two main characters, and the first scene at the Soviet Embassy was no doubt based on a similar social event. He even gave passing mention to Mike Wilson and his wife Elizabeth who were attending the fictional embassy gala, and *Playboy* ran a colour photo of the threesome with the piece.

'Mixing fact and fiction was a deliberate experiment,' he told Val in April, promising to send him a copy of the story he was then calling 'Blue Network'.

Gene Hartford, the American character in the story, planned to launch an independent communications satellite in orbit and broadcast pornography and other decadent programmes direct to American homes.

Said Hartford, 'We'll be using America's own decadence as a weapon against her, and it's a weapon for which there's no defence.'

The story does have a message, Arthur admits, even though he usually agrees with Samuel Goldwyn's advice that people with messages should use Western Union. 'It was written in the pre-*Telstar* days, with the deliberate intent of making the public think seriously about communications satellites,' says Arthur. 'Only a few years after *Playboy* published this cautionary tale, I was watching the launch of *Early Bird* by closed-circuit TV at Comsat Headquarters.'

In August 1960, three months after the story's publication, the *Echo 1* satellite was launched. This huge aluminium-coated balloon was the precursor of communications satellites. While it was rather primitive and could only passively bounce off signals (unlike the *Early Bird* which could receive, amplify and retransmit them), it nevertheless marked the beginning of the communications revolution. Millions saw it as a bright star arcing across the night sky – a true symbol of the new Space Age.

It was Arthur's friend, John Robinson Pierce, who had first proposed passive and active communication satellites in 1954; *Echo 1* embodied his ideas. In fact the East Coast ground station for the *Echo* satellite programme was constructed by his division at Bell Laboratories.

A week after the launch the Bell Telephone Laboratories announced that they had made the first transatlantic wireless code transmission via *Echo 1* from Holmdel, New Jersey, to Issyles-Moulineaux in France.

That this new technology could be abused was an extremely important message at the outset of the Space Age. Thirty years later, as the 1990s began, several law suits were filed against an American company that broadcast X-rated pornographic programming direct to satellite dish owners who subscribed to their service. Arthur's story foresaw such problems even before *Telstar 1* telecast the first TV images across the Atlantic in 1962.

Only three other Clarke short stories were published in 1960. The non-fiction side of the opus leger dominated that year. *Holiday* magazine published his essay 'Riding on Air', which would become a chapter in *Profiles of the Future*. *Playboy* followed with another (and several more before the book was published in England in late 1962).

The diving expeditions and other activities during the late 1950s had definitely cut into Arthur's literary output – as compared to his own past prolificacy, of course. He wrote hard in 1960, but some unexpected problems made literary life more difficult. And the underwater work which Arthur financed, then called 'Submarine Safaris', became an unpredictable source of income for Mike Wilson, Rodney Jonklaas and Hector Ekanayake.

Mike was doing more and more photography, however, and he landed an excellent photographic assignment for *Time* magazine early in the year, which took him to Sumatra and Borneo to cover missionary activities in the jungle. Also in the first quarter of 1960 several good diving jobs came in for Hector and Rodney, so they were at least supporting themselves, which wasn't always the case.

The new house in Gregory's Road, a bungalow, offered some badly needed extra space, and that made life a bit less chaotic. The main room was huge, some fifty feet long, and the other rooms leading off it were also good-sized. These included two bedrooms, Arthur's office, a spare bedroom which Rodney used as an office, a darkroom (with stereophonic sound), the kitchen, the servants' room and toilet, two bathrooms and a large garage which was used as a workshop.

But Arthur's attitude to his work and life in early 1960 was basically down; it appeared that he was going through some kind of mid-life crisis.

His literary output was, at least temporarily, also on the wane. Giving Val an update on *Imperial Earth* (a novel first conceived in the early 1950s), he was not at all hopeful about its progress: 'Doubt if I'll ever do it now. Put it aside for several years anyway. (I've written three thousand words of it in five years!) . . .

'I seem to have lost all interest in novels, and know better than to try to force the matter. It'll come when it will come: if it doesn't, I could hardly care less. I've always enjoyed essays and short stories much more, and now I'm beginning to feel I'm a fool to write anything else both from the financial *and* the influential point of view.

'I know all the arguments in favour of novels, and *hope* I'll do one again some time. But I've several years' accumulated backlog of story and article ideas I want to work through: that should take most of this year, and when I'm fed up with short pieces I hope I'll feel like tackling another major work. I have the "Breakthroughs in Science" book [*Profiles of the Future*] half-promised to Harper, but intend to write that in article form anyway.

'Also the economics of novels doesn't make any sense – unless you land a movie sale, or are a Nevil Shute.'

Besides the better pay for magazine articles than books (comparing initial income and number of words written), the large audiences for magazines such as *Playboy* and *Holiday* (about one million each at that time) also appealed to Arthur. He knew he could never reach that many people with a book – at least not in the first few printings.

The ultimate sign of trouble, though, was when he confessed to Val, 'I've largely lost interest in sf . . .' For anyone who had ever experienced Arthur's genuine, unwavering enthusiasm, this attitude was a shock and could only be explained as a temporary aberration – a rare downer in his personality which no doubt would turn upward. The only question became 'When?', and the answer was rather non-committal when Val asked him how he was feeling in April.

'It varies in a way which doesn't seem to have a definite period and probably depends on what I've eaten. Sometimes I feel on top of the world and full of energy; at other times everything is too much bother. I was cheered by your remark that I looked thinner in the photo – then remembered that it was taken four years ago!'

Arthur was working, but for the twelve hours a day he was putting in (with time out for meals), he wasn't writing as much as he wanted. Details of the diving business were the problem. Arthur got stuck with many of them because Mike and Rodney were both almost equally 'hopeless at accounts'.

When he was able to write Arthur worked on short stories such as 'Summertime on Icarus', which he hoped to bring together in a short story collection. Arthur considered 'Summertime' to be a suspense-action story, 'quite a tough piece full of technicalities (though all explained) about a man trapped on Icarus at perihelion and doomed to be cooked at dawn'. When the *Saturday Evening Post* hesitated to buy it (although they didn't say no), Scott Meredith promptly sold it to *Vogue* and told Arthur, 'This will shake the *Post* to the core.'

In early July Arthur's brother Fred phoned from England to say hello. 'I spoke to all the family. It made me quite homesick, and in the unlikely event that I can raise the cash I may try to come home for a short time in '61 or '62,' he wrote Val.

In late July Ceylon held its election and a new prime minister, Mrs Sirimavo Bandaranayake, was chosen. The future political situation was still somewhat up in the air, however, and Arthur expressed his worries to Val.

'It will be some weeks before we see how things work out, but we now have to face up to the fact that we may have to close down here at a moment's notice.

'The awkward thing is that this has happened just when we were about broke and the overdraft was due for repayment. If the bank won't extend it, we've had it and will have to sell up.'

A month later, in August, matters were even worse: 'All hell has broken loose here,' he told Val, 'and we are too exhausted and upset even to think, let alone write. We have run into all sorts of snags, personal and financial . . . not to mention political.'

First of all, *Glide Path* was finally rejected after Arthur had done two major rewrites – the first time that one of his books had ever been turned down (although many of his short stories had to be moved around in search of the right publisher). The latest revision had gone to Scott Meredith in July. He then passed it along to Bill Jovanovich, the president of Harcourt, who turned it down within a few days.

'After Macmillan and Harper turned the novel down,' says Scott, 'I then reported this to Arthur, who asked for the script back to work further on it.'

The news really threw Arthur.

'That means I've gambled several thousand dollars and lost; I'd been relying on that to pull us out of the hole,' he told Val. 'I could have earned at least ten thousand dollars in the same writing time.'

His financial situation, he told his friend, was too complicated to describe, but it came down to the fact that he was getting heavily taxed in Ceylon and elsewhere.

'If the worst comes to the worst, we may be wiped out any minute.' All the earnings he brought into Ceylon were not wasted, he explained to Val, but went into the house, the VW bus, the diving gear, the cameras and motion picture equipment. The change of government, however, put the demand for their underwater and other services very much in doubt.

'The worst of it is, having to run round seeing lawyers, accountants and govt officials leaves me completely exhausted for writing, though I have been able to get off several pieces recently. So it's a vicious circle.'

There was still hope that a few things would break right. Several diving jobs could come through at any time, allowing Hector and Rodney to pull their own weight in the underwater diving, salvage and tourist business.

'And any moment, of course, I may sell something to Hollywood! But the big trouble is that we have absolutely no reserve to carry us over the sticky patches.'

There was at least one good thing coming out of all the troubles: Arthur was losing weight from the stress.

★

When in doubt, write. The same man who had lost interest in novels earlier in the year was fifty thousand words into a new one by mid-October – a novel he hadn't even thought of six weeks earlier.

'I decided to do a short story to make some money quickly, and it just blew up in my face. I am working from seven thirty a.m. to around nine p.m. on it, have cancelled all lectures etc and have only been to a movie once in the last month. The reason for this pressure is not merely the financial situation but something that causes me even more worry, though a quite unnecessary one. This is the fact that I contracted to deliver my new Harper book [*Indian Ocean Adventure*] on 1 October – and it isn't even started.'

Arthur continued to fret about missing his contractual deadline in a November letter to Sam Youd.

'I've had the advance, and being a conscientious type (unlike many authors) this somewhat weighs on my mind.'

Another reason for the writing marathon was that the lawyers were leaving him alone (for the time being), and he took advantage of the lull. Once they started bothering him again it would be impossible to produce much work. No doubt the solicitors knew enough to leave him be and let him work hard.

The stress in the household produced by financial woes had slackened by autumn 1960, probably because everyone finally understood that there were no quick fixes; solutions to their problems would take some time. Arthur told Val that things on the personal front were quite happy again.

'Liz is now rather pear-shaped and wearing what I call her Calamity Gown. Only two months to go,' he wrote in October. 'The only gloom comes from Hector, whose girl has been lured or dragged away by her parents and now doesn't write to him.'

Hector had had his share of disappointments in 1960. After becoming the youngest boxer ever to become flyweight champion of Ceylon, he'd gone on to the boxing finals for his weight class in the Rome Olympics. In April he knocked out one of his opponents in the first round, but ultimately he didn't survive the Olympic finals.

'He doesn't seem too upset about it,' Arthur told Val. 'One good thing is that now he's not training every day he is much more useful to Clarke-Wilson Associates.'

Val had asked Arthur about the common root 'ayake' in Sinhalese names. It means 'chief', Arthur said. '*Dahanayake* = chief of ten. (*Ekanayake* = chief of one!)'

The Colombo premiere of Mike's first film *Beneath the Seas of*

Ceylon was a success: 'Almost a thousand turned up and many were unable to get seats,' Arthur told Val. There was the hope that a sale of extra copies to the Ceylon Tea Board could help with the financial difficulties.

Arthur was writing hard, pounding away at the keys until he had nothing left to give his new novel. Sometimes he just had to stop.

'I am in a slight stupor at the moment,' he wrote Val on 17 October 1960, 'having written 3,500 words of the novel yesterday, much of it in a kind of automatic frenzy. In fact one reason why you're getting this letter now is that I was scared to go on with the story as my brain was racing too fast and I thought I'd better stop. Very odd feeling.'

For most of three months – September, October and November – Arthur put himself under intense pressure and had the novel completed by 21 November 1960. Thus *A Fall of Moondust* was written in a short period, without a contract or even the knowledge or interest of a publisher. It was conceived as a short story and, with the frenetic energy of impending desperation, became a novel. This act of will was Arthur's way of regaining his confidence as a writer.

Perhaps it is symbolic that the passengers and crew of the novel's Dust-Cruiser *Selene* are buried alive beneath the Moon's surface. *A Fall of Moondust* is a survival story, at a time its author was struggling to survive himself.

Almost without exception Val Cleaver gave all of Arthur's manuscripts a thorough critique, and Arthur put a high value on his friend's opinion. Val was therefore the lucky recipient of two Clarke novels in December 1960 – *Moondust* and *Glide Path*.

Arthur was so confident about *Moondust* that he asked Val to 'run through it' and then rush it over to his English agent, David Higham. 'No need for the usual detailed analysis – unless of course you want to,' he wrote in early December. 'Where I *would* like the analysis,' he said, still scratching his head and soothing his ego, 'is on *Glide Path*.'

He had just learned that his British publisher, Gollancz, also turned down *Glide Path*, but this time he got to see a copy of the reader's report which helped to restore his morale (along with the fact that the same publisher was enthusiastically publishing his collection of short stories, *The Other Side of the Sky*).

'Though by no means altogether flattering,' he said of the report, 'it proves that I've done exactly what I set out to do in this book; the point of argument is whether it was worth doing. (The reader says: "The wartime atmosphere is excellent, but how stale it all seems. I wonder why the author put all this work into such a passé theme.")'

Despite the rejection from Gollancz David Higham said he would continue to try to sell it, if that's what Arthur wanted. Arthur's response was that his new novel, *Moondust*, should now take priority.

At the end of 1960 there were a few more uplifting notes. Harcourt, Brace offered a contract for a second anthology, *From the Ocean, From the Stars*, which included two novels (*The Deep Range* and *City and the Stars*, and his collection of short stories, *The Other Side of the Sky*). This produced an unexpected cheque, and Scott Meredith had collected another one from Gnome Press. 'These two cheques,' Arthur wrote Val, 'have saved our bacon – for the time being – but I don't like having to rely on unexpected windfalls.'

Arthur now focused his efforts on *Indian Ocean Adventure* for Harper & Brothers, which was already two months overdue. The book was about the autumn 1959 expedition to Great Basses Reef and it wasn't going to involve that many words; Arthur thought he could write it in a month. What's more, photographs were ready to select, even if Mike might have to enlarge some. His estimate was close: he completed the text on New Year's Eve.

During the November 1960 US election, Arthur was playing host to Pat Weaver, creator of the 'Today Show' and former president of NBC. At the time of his visit Pat was Chairman of McCann-Erickson International, one of the largest advertising companies in the world.

'I was a great admirer of Arthur's fiction,' says Weaver. 'I was down in Australia, finalising a deal to open a joint agency in Australia, and I just called him up and said, "Are you going to be there?" He said, "Yes." So I stopped in Colombo for two or three days. I met all of his friends. It was most enjoyable.' They visited the ancient port of Galle and stood on the ramparts of the old fortress.

Arthur wrote Val, 'He decided to spend three days here just to find why we liked the place so much. By great good luck, the weather was lovely – it poured before and after – and we all had a fine time, driving him down the coast, chewing the rag. Then we listened to the election results direct on the SW [shortwave radio] while sitting by the sea at Mount Lavinia. Though Pat's firm has the Republican Party account (!) and he is Nelson Rockefeller's adviser, his pleasure at the result was not too well concealed.'

By the end of the year it was decided that the underwater business would be handed over to Rodney Jonklaas. Mike wanted to concentrate on his photography and film-making, but agreed to help Rodney with any big projects that came along.

Mike and Liz's baby, a girl, was stillborn on 23 December and sadness descended on the household. Mike was terribly upset and became very ill the next day with a kidney infection and was delirious for some time. He was too sick to pick up his wife at the hospital. Hector brought Liz home. 'She's pale but composed,' Arthur told Val, 'and said to me, "The growing-up process finished yesterday." She spoke for them both.'

The same day the bad news came from the hospital, Arthur received a cable from William Jovanovich, president of Harcourt, Brace, saying, 'New novel [*Moondust*] superb repeat superb. I am anxious to publish as soon as feasible.' And Scott Meredith said it was his 'greatest book yet'.

'Keep your fingers crossed,' he told Val in a letter he wrote on Christmas Day. 'This book may pull us out of the hole.'

Everyone at Gregory's Road was relieved that 1960 was over.

CHAPTER 14

Treasure and Rockets

It was one of the unforgettable moments
of a lifetime, for I knew then that I was
staring at something that very few men
have ever seen – genuine, honest-to-
goodness treasure.
— *Treasure of the Great Reef*

The rising rocket appeals to instincts older
than reason; the gulf it bridges is not only
that between world and world – but the
deeper chasm between heart and brain . . .
— 'The Eve of Apollo'

Still in the euphoric afterglow of completing *A Fall of Moondust* in
early 1961 and receiving high praise from Scott Meredith and Harcourt, Arthur wasn't going to let the rejection of *Glide Path* throw
him off.

Upon receipt of Val's critique of the novel, he decided to let the
manuscript and Val's comments 'mature in the wood'.

'I will await developments with DHA [David Higham Associates]
and perhaps in a year or two I may decide whether to do an additional
re-write or whether to let the book stand as it is, with the faults which
you list and with which I agree . . . In any case I am quite convinced
it will be published eventually even in the present form and I'm
certainly not ashamed of it in that version.'

At the beginning of 1961, Arthur had been giving his future writing
projects some careful thought.

'I am pretty firm in my resolve to write only what I *want* to write,
and I'm sure is worth writing,' he told Val, enclosing in the same
letter a list of his next ten book projects, 'not necessarily in proposed
chronological order, but roughly so'.

The list included three collections, the problematic *Glide Path* and
the promising *A Fall of Moondust*. Also there was *Breakthroughs in*

Science ('Title just used by Ike Asimov!!),' he scribbled to Val in the margin. Arthur was hard at work on this in January 1961.

'Have done about twelve thousand words, but it involves a great deal of research that is impossible here, and I think I can only complete it in London and NY,' he wrote. 'At the moment I am having a lot of fun dealing with some of the false prophets of the past, to put the reader in the right frame of mind.'

Arthur knew this project was much more than adding some new essays to old ones. 'I think this book (now provisionally retitled *Profiles of the Future*) may be my most important non-fiction since *EoS* [*Exploration of Space*]. I hope to finish the rough draft by the middle of the year.'

Meanwhile, on the other business front, as Mike got more deeply involved in film-making projects he dropped the boat-building activities of Clarke-Wilson Associates. What started out as a hobby with the purchase of their first movie camera soon became a way of producing income for the business partnership in underwater work. Believing that Wilson's talent should be encouraged, Clarke financed the film-making ventures. Both he and Wilson did the scriptwriting and other production chores.

The Ceylon Tea Propaganda Board paid £1,800 for the first ten prints of the twenty-five-minute-long *Beneath the Seas of Ceylon*, his first production venture. If the Board ordered a few more copies, the project soon would be in the black.

The second movie-making venture was scheduled for spring 1962, and Mike, now restored to health, was in a big hurry to complete it, 'working like a demon'.

Arthur told Val about Mike's latest film project. 'The film will be a fifteen-minute fantasy about a small boy who finds a genie in a bottle and gets his wish – an aqualung. The underwater sequences will involve the boy and our pet giant groupers (who we hope will remember us).'

Neither Arthur nor Rodney Jonklaas accompanied Mike on his spring 1961 expedition to Great Basses as they had two years earlier. Arthur had more than enough writing to keep him chained to the typewriter, and he wasn't too enthusiastic about roughing it again in the lighthouse and on the reef. Rodney was working on an underwater survey of the Maldive Islands.

Mike's on-location swimmers were two teenage American boys, Bobby Kriegel and Mark Smith, whom Mike had met the previous year. He had taught them how to scuba-dive.

Dick Kriegel, Bobby's father, was a training officer at the US Operation Mission in Ceylon. He says, 'The boys were like ducks, very confident. They were excellent swimmers and they had become competent divers. They were trained for the open sea and the more treacherous waters of the Indian Ocean.'

'After a very few lessons,' says Arthur, 'Mike was confident that they could tackle all ordinary underwater jobs quite safely, and wouldn't lose their heads in an emergency.'

The film's script was not complicated (it starred one boy and some fish), and Mike wrote it for Mark Smith, who was smaller and looked younger than Bobby Kriegel, and for the three groupers who were named during the 1959 dive: Ali Baba, Sinbad and Aladdin.

Mike and his two young apprentices loaded up the Volkswagen Microbus and headed south to the Great Basses Reef, arriving at the village of Kirinda on 12 March 1961 from where they caught the power launch, *Pharos*, that took them to the lighthouse.

Mike and the boys did a lot of diving and underwater filming during the next week. They would jump off the edge of the reef and swim out some hundred yards to where the groupers were. They towed a large inner tube behind them, with the cameras and aqua-lungs attached. Once on location they anchored this temporary dock, and got to work on their underwater set.

Sinbad, Ali Baba and Aladdin were still there after two years, and as long as they were well fed they co-operated for the camera. A big shark was seen at a distance, but it was not aggressive and caused no alarm. Only a less-than-friendly grouper chased them once and another time their friendly film star Sinbad got greedy and tried to swallow Mark's arm up to the elbow. No real harm was done, though. Sinbad's small teeth left a few minor scars and Mark was proud of them – his battle scars from the deep.

The weather was good most days, and Mike was getting the film he needed. On 22 March the sea was calm. It was too calm for photography because there was no current to clear away the sand in the water. Since no filming was possible, Mike and the boys decided to explore another reef about a thousand feet away from the light-house. This became a holiday; without their photographic and aqua-lung gear they were underwater tourists. The free time was a pleasure; the new territory exciting. They explored for a few hours.

'They were thinking of turning back when Mike spotted something on the seabed that he had been looking for, in vain, for many years,' Arthur wrote later. 'It was an old cannon – a very tiny one, only about two feet long – shining brightly in the sunlight as if it had been lost only yesterday.' Mike knew that, depending on how the ship had hit, there might be more of the wreck on the coast side of the reef.

'After we got to the other side the first thing we saw was a shiny cannon [swivel gun],' recalls Bobby Kriegel, 'about two and a half feet long, sitting on the edge of a big canyon; and it was worn smooth by the water . . .'

The wreck's wooden hull had probably long ago decayed and vanished, but they knew – even without that – there must be more to discover. They made a second dive in the afternoon. This time they brought their aqualungs so they could stay down longer on the seabed and explore more thoroughly. Soon they found a large, five-foot cannon, two huge tangled anchors and a massive pile of twelve or more large iron cannons.

'Mike was hitting everything he saw with his knife,' says Mark Smith. 'Then he came over to us and showed us the cannon, and Bob pointed out something shining right near it. Mike examined it and then yelled . . . "Silver!" underwater with his mouthpiece on!' The treasure of the Great Basses had been found – the first Indian Ocean treasure ever recovered.

Mike and the boys returned to Colombo four days later. Arthur had just sent half the manuscript of *Profiles of the Future* to Scott Meredith and was taking a breather, relaxing and reading Lawrence Durrell's *Alexandria Quartet*. He had finished *Balthazar* and found it 'brilliant and amusing'.

When Arthur asked Mike and the boys how it had gone, they mumbled a few non-committal words as they staggered into his office carrying a battered tin trunk. Mike locked the door behind them.

'Look at this,' he said mysteriously, throwing open the lid of the trunk. Arthur gazed in and saw two small bronze cannons.

'My God, you've found an old wreck!' he cried as Mike lifted out the guns to show him what was underneath.

'At first, I thought I was looking at dirty lumps of coral,' says Arthur, 'about the size of coconuts. Then I realised just what those lumps were; and I was too astonished to say anything.

'It was one of the unforgettable moments of a lifetime, for I knew then that I was staring at something that very few men have ever seen – genuine, honest-to-goodness treasure. These unimpressive looking lumps were masses of coins – hundreds of them, cemented together.'

Arthur bent down to pick up one of the lumps; he could hardly lift it. Besides the lumps there were also hundreds of loose coins, and all had Arabic letters on them.

After the initial excitement subsided, they discussed their plan of action and decided to contact their lawyer and inform the boys' parents.

Later that evening Arthur's adrenalin was still flowing. 'Well, Mike has done it at last!' he wrote Val. 'I'm too excited to go to bed, and this letter will probably be a bit incoherent. You may even think I'm drunk or pulling your leg!'

He then went on to summarise the treasure story for his friend.

'We've always dreamed of this, and never found anything but busted-up tankers. Mike says there's more where these came from. I've just weighed the lumps and they come to 115 pounds. So I'm sitting here in my office with a hundredweight of treasure at my feet, wondering if it's all a dream, and what will happen next! . . .'

The Muslim coins, research soon determined, were rupees that were minted at Surat in north-west India in 1702 during the reign of the Mogul emperor Aurangzeb. During the eighteenth century these coins were common currency for a large area of Asia. Because all bore the same Muslim date and appeared to be brand new, it was most likely that the ship carrying them had come directly from India. And since all the large clumps contained exactly a thousand coins it was obvious that they had been packed in bags of a thousand, but the bags had disintegrated long ago.

'The Smithsonian is quite interested and would like to buy one of the lumps which weighs some twenty-five pounds,' Arthur wrote Val.

There could be many more silver lumps of treasure beneath the waves of Great Basses Reef, and the decision was made that they would mount an ambitious expedition the following spring.

While the treasure continued to provide most of the excitement around Gregory's Road (even though it was a closely guarded secret), the literary side of Arthur's life continued to provide some modest uplifting news from time to time. His British publisher, Gollancz, published his short story collection *The Other Side of the Sky* in March, two years after the US edition first appeared. It contained some of his great stories, including 'The Nine Billion Names of God' and 'The Star', and Arthur was especially flattered when Victor Gollancz himself praised the volume on the press release: 'This is a superb book. I am inclined to think that "The Star" may be the finest short story I have ever read.'

During the spring of 1961 Arthur was anxiously awaiting the fate of *A Fall of Moondust*, to see what kind of serial rights might be sold. And while there was some film interest shown in England, Arthur knew from experience that before any contract was signed it was no more than pie in the sky. 'I refuse to do any daydreaming on the subject,' he told Val.

Russia and the United States, meanwhile, were making the ancient dreams of space flight actually fly. On 12 April 1961 Yuri Gagarin was strapped into the *Vostok 1* spacecraft mounted atop Russia's A-1 rocket and roared into orbit. He became the first human in history to orbit planet Earth and witness two sunrises in just under two hours.

'Well, the Russians have certainly done it now!' wrote Arthur. 'The Mercury people must be feeling sick, however much a brave face they put on it. And if they kill one of the US astronauts, it will be exactly like the Vanguard situation again. I hope Major G took some nice snaps with his box Brownie. Doesn't he look like Lindberg!'

Less than a month later, Alan B. Shepard Jr rode his *Freedom 7* spacecraft on a successful suborbital flight. This was America's first manned space flight, and if nothing else it showed that the US couldn't yet be written off even if Russia was winning the historic firsts.

'I was pleased that the Americans got their first astronaut back safely – although slightly overshadowed by Yuri, it's still a fine feat, and I feel they've earned some success. I'm glad to see, however, that there is no disposition to claim that it's bigger than it is.'

Arthur heard Shepard's flight on the short wave, although not very clearly. 'Hope it shames the Russians into being more forthcoming,' he wrote Val.

President Kennedy's famous to-the-Moon speech was made in late May 1961, and Arthur speculated to Val that it might have some effect on his British friend's on-again, off-again rocket project at Rolls-Royce: 'Or will the country just turn over in its sleep?'

Russian rocketry, and its impressive feats, appeared to be more on his mind in June when he had an 'incredibly vivid dream'.

'I was going through Russia in a bus, and we passed within a few hundred yards of one of their launching vehicles,' he wrote Val. 'It was a couple of hundred feet high, three or four stages (come to think of it, the original stimulus was probably that recent photo of the *Saturn* mock-up – I've just realised that). But it was apparently made of overlapping boilerplate, with the rivets quite prominent!

'But the funniest thing is that the next incident (after a friendly argument with a Russian soldier sitting beside me, who rather objected to my intense use of binoculars as the bus drove past the rocket) was a meeting with you in which I carefully described the beast, and we decided that I *hadn't* dreamed the whole thing!!!! Work that one out . . .'

Dreams of space flight and of treasure were coming true in 1961. What else could a writer hope for? A bit of peace and quiet would have suited Arthur just fine.

In early summer he told his friend Sam Youd that, because of Mike's growing film-making business, there were as many as ten people in the house at one time. Then there were five dogs, including his beloved Laika who often curled up by Arthur's feet. And there was more.

'Mike and Liz got married the other evening – in the eyes of the church,' Arthur wrote Sam in June. 'They've also adopted a little boy, a month old.

'All is quiet here at the moment (except for the baby), despite anything you may have read in the UK press. There has been trouble, but only on a very small scale, in limited areas.'

Still not clear of his cashflow crisis Arthur was working 'like a galley slave', putting in fifteen or sixteen hours a day at the typewriter.

'I've been turning out about two articles or short stories a week as I have to get together at least $3000 *above* normal income to make the US trip possible. And I've just lost a solid week as Irwin Hersey asked me to do an article on 'Space and the Spirit of Man' for the special SFRN [Space Flight Report to the Nation] issue of *Astronautics*. This has proved diabolically difficult, simply because it's very hard to think of anything along these lines I've not already written. (At least once!)'

Some cheer did come from two magazines that summer: *Reader's Digest* bought *A Fall of Moondust* for their Condensed Books, and *Playboy* bought four more pieces about the future.

Mike's film *Boy Beneath the Sea* was being edited in June and July and would soon be completed. Technicolor blew up a hundred feet of the sixteen mm print to thirty-five, and the quality was superb. This was good news because it meant that all the underwater footage could be used commercially in a variety of possible ways. And Mike's next ambitious project – a first full-length Sinhalese colour movie – already had a shooting script. The cameras would roll by early July on Ceylon's east coast, at Trincomalee. Mike's newfound vocation as film-maker, thanks to Arthur's backing, was keeping him busy.

It was about this time that Arthur learned from his brother Fred that he and Dot were having problems with their marriage. Arthur was quite upset.

'I'm sorry to say that my brother and sister-in-law have separated,' he wrote Sam, 'and Dorothy has gone off with my little nieces, of whom I'm very fond and was looking forward to spending some time with this summer. Luckily they're still in Wood Green and I hope to see them all. This has been a great blow to the family – the Clarkes do not seem too successful at their marriages. The casualty rate is now fifty per cent.'

By July 1961 Arthur had his travel plans to England and the United States set: early August, London; late August, New York. He hadn't left Ceylon for two years, so he was eager to see friends and family in England, talk to his agents, editors and publishers on both sides of the Atlantic, and see his aerospace colleagues at two conventions in the United States.

After spending most of August in London and Somerset – including a ten-day touring trip with Val Cleaver – he arrived in New York on 31 August and began his business rounds in Manhattan.

Among the many people he saw in New York was Hugo Gernsback (1884–1967), the pioneer editor and publisher of science fiction who was often referred to as 'the father of magazine science fiction' and who has been honoured by having the Hugos, the annual achievement awards in the genre, named after him. Born in Luxembourg, Gernsback spent most of his life in the United States and he was the man who coined the term 'science fiction'.

'We met at his 14th Street office and went out for lunch. I remember his old-world charm (and that he never owed me for any stories). Later he wrote complaining that I'd used the phrase "orbital post office" in an article on comsats without crediting him for its invention: he gave a reference to his first use. I shot him down in flames by pointing out it was used *earlier* in *Profiles of the Future* – which was dedicated to him! He apologised handsomely, and sent me his amusing Xmas mini-mag to the end of his life.'

In late September Arthur went to Washington, DC, to attend the Twelfth International Astronautical Congress and was pleased that an editor wanted to print his speech even before he gave it. '*Horizon* is holding up the presses to get my IAF speech into the January issue – so even when I am writing for nothing I eventually get paid for it!' he wrote Val. 'I've been up two nights working on the revision.'

He delivered the speech, 'The Social Consequences of Communications Satellites', to the symposium on Space Law at the Congress in early October 1961. He spoke about the revolution in communications which was underway. 'For communications satellites will enable us, in effect, to move almost instantaneously to any part of the world . . . Indeed, by the end of this century all terrestrial calls may be local calls and may be billed at a flat standard rate,' he said – an idea he would use again in his novel *2061: Odyssey Three*. The speech described the information age of the last quarter of the twentieth century and the inevitable future of the global village as it would be in the 1990s: 'No dictatorship can build a wall high enough to stop its citizens listening to the voices from the stars.' Arthur was talking intelligently and lucidly about the future of comsats almost four years before *Early Bird*, the first commercial communications satellite, was launched in April 1965.

Arthur spent a lot of time at the IAF Congress with the Soviet expert on astronautics, L. I. Sedov, then Chairman of the USSR Commission on Astronautics. After Arthur had seen the Soviet film, *With Gagarin to the Stars*, he said to him, 'Pity the rocket you see at the end of the Gagarin film isn't G's [Gagarin's].' Sedov's nonplussed reply: 'Well, from a distance all big rockets look the same.'

While in Washington Arthur visited Mendel Peterson at the Smithsonian, the man to whom he had sent one of the thousand-rupee silver lumps Mike Wilson and the boys had found earlier in the year. (Most of the lumps were given away as souvenirs. Although Arthur only got $2–3000 as a tax credit for the Smithsonian silver, silver lump current assessments value all of them at up to $40,000.) Arthur and Mendel then went together to the National Geographic Society and met Luis Marden, who had discovered the *Bounty* wreck off Pitcairn. Arthur hoped that, depending on what the next expedition uncovered, *National Geographic* might want to run a story about the Great Basses wreck.

Arthur returned to New York City for the American Rocket Society's big conference, 'Space Flight Report to the Nation'. The meeting was held at the Coliseum and was combined with the Space Flight Exposition of hundreds of exhibits, including a giant *Saturn F.1* rocket motor.

'Looks like I have a lot of homework to do!' he told Val, on learning that he would appear on television on two successive nights. He was 'flattered and shattered' to be asked to participate in both the US and USSR space programme reviews. Security, however, excluded Sedov or other Russians from participating.

The show went well; it had the biggest audience in the American Rocket Society's history. Arthur went out of his way to generate controversy. 'I had spent several weeks concocting these [questions], which were designed to bring my panel nicely to the boil.' He even asked General Schriever (head of the US Air Force missile programme) how to begin integrating the US and USSR space programmes! (This was at a time when the space race was still escalating.)

Vice-President Lyndon B. Johnson was there and Arthur met him.

'He gave a speech,' says Arthur, 'and someone passed on to him the suggestion I had made in an earlier meeting that we ought to get *Syncom* ready in time for the Tokyo Olympics. I think that's what triggered that chain of events.'

That 'someone' was Dr William Pickering, director of the Jet Propulsion Laboratory, who was in the front row of the audience when Arthur was moderating a panel discussion. Pickering liked the idea so much that he did indeed pass it on to Vice-President Johnson, who also liked it. Johnson even departed from a prepared banquet speech he gave the next evening and mentioned the idea.

The final result was that the White House asked Comsat to coordinate arrangements for televising live the 1964 Olympic ceremonies from Tokyo to the United States. The signals were sent via *Syncom 3* and the US Navy Earth station at Point Mugu, California. Not as many people saw the historic broadcast as had been hoped because the networks did not want to upset their existing programme schedules and advertising commitments. This event, however, heralded the new era which would officially begin when *Early Bird* started commercial operation in April 1965.

After 'The Space Flight Report to the Nation' conference was concluded, Arthur was happy to leave rocket and space business behind him for the rest of his stay in Manhattan. In the few days remaining *Newsweek* magazine conducted an interview with him which was published in their 30 October 1961 issue as 'Clarke of Ceylon'.

'At a time when Washington and Moscow have become the citadels of science, Clarke has managed to turn his back on both and chronicle the new age from Colombo, Ceylon,' wrote the magazine, before going on to describe his 'pioneering principles' for communications satellites. Arthur acknowledged that 'the communication satellite was the most important idea of my life. Had I realised how quickly it would materialise, I might have patented it. Of course I had the idea before I saw commercial TV.' A last wry phrase from Arthur C. Clarke.

Arthur flew back to London in late October. During his brief stay, he filled Val in on the two conferences, and on 6 November left for Ceylon. He was going to round off the year by meeting the first man in space, Yuri Gagarin.

The most famous man in the world in 1961, and the first man to leave it, Gagarin arrived in Colombo aboard his own four-engine jet on 6 December. There was major publicity for his arrival, and his schedule was crowded.

'I was walking back to my house,' says Arthur. 'I'd just been playing table tennis at the Otter's, the local athletic club, and was about to cross the main road (then Buller's Road, now renamed Bauddaloka Mawatha). Suddenly a police escort came in sight, followed by a car containing a group of dignitaries . . .

'My gaze locked on to a single figure, and instantly there flashed into my mind a phrase that was used more than a hundred years ago, when President Lincoln was assassinated: "Now he belongs to the ages."

'That was my first glimpse of Yuri Gagarin; I never guessed how soon, and how tragically, the same quotation would apply to him.' (Colonel Yuri Gagarin died in the crash of a jet trainer on 27 March 1968, some eight months before *Apollo 8* made its historic flight around the Moon in December of that year.)

Because of Gagarin's tight itinerary it was impossible to spend any real time with him, but Arthur did manage to speak briefly to him after a public lecture the Colonel gave. He asked him the same question he had asked Professor Sedov in Washington: 'Why doesn't your film show your rocket?'

At least Gagarin's answer was somewhat more forthcoming than Sedov's.

'Well, when we can destroy all our war weapons then we'll be able to show it,' Gagarin answered.

They chatted a bit longer, with the help of an interpreter, and Arthur saw him as 'a cheerful, friendly and in no way unusual young man, quite untouched by destiny'.

Before Gagarin left, Arthur gave him a copy of *Indian Ocean Adventure*. The choice was made with the knowledge that all the men chosen in the first groups of cosmonauts and astronauts had an interest in underwater exploration.

Several weeks later, after Gagarin had completed his international tour, Arthur received a signed copy of his autobiography. It read, 'To Arthur Clarke, this souvenir of our cosmic voyage and our meeting in Ceylon – Y. Gagarin.'

It was a great way to end an historic year.

CHAPTER 15

Paralysis to Praise

I was convinced that my spine was being
slowly bent backwards until it was about to
snap. In other interludes, I was dying of
thirst while being buried in desiccated dust.
— *Treasure of the Great Reef*

Their only hope [children of the Third
World] of a better future lies in science combined with wisdom and foresight. I shall be
happy indeed if any writings of mine have
helped toward this goal.
— 'Kalinga Award Speech'

Good weather allowing, the Great Basses Reef was Arthur's destination for spring 1962; he wasn't going to miss it this year. He needed
some adventure and experiences to fill those not-yet-begun books he
had promised publishers.

At a shipyard in the centre of Colombo the hull of the twenty-
eight-foot *Ranmuthu Duwa* (meaning 'island of pearls and gold') was
taking shape, but there were no engines yet.

Mike Wilson had convinced Arthur that this was an important
investment for the return expedition to Great Basses and its treasure,
and for the future of their underwater business. The boat's name was
taken from the film, *Island of Pearls and Gold.*

'By this time,' says Arthur, 'it was not clear whether the movie
was going to pay for the boat or the boat for the movie.'

A special and compact air compressor was ordered and delivered
and two 'Redshank' rubber dinghies also arrived, generously donated
by the Avon Rubber Company.

'The first trials of the boat should be in a couple of weeks,' he
wrote Roger Caras in late February 1962, 'and then we'll set to sea.'

Preparations went forth. On the last day of February Arthur was
shopping in Pettah, the Colombo bazaar, buying equipment for the
boat, when fate took a rather uncompromising stand.

'Leaving one store, I misjudged the height of a doorway and crashed the top of my head against the lintel. It took me a few minutes to recover, and I had a painful scalp wound; but I felt none the worse. After I stopped cursing, I got on my motor scooter, drove three miles home, played several vigorous games of table tennis, and ate a hearty dinner – my last for many months.'

That night he became violently sick, but he believed that it was some kind of temporary stomach ailment. His condition didn't improve. Still, he didn't think it necessary to call a doctor and spent a few days in bed, convinced that his body would rally and destroy the mysterious intruder. It didn't happen.

Finally the doctor was called, but by the time he arrived Arthur was in trouble. 'I was almost completely paralysed and could barely breathe,' he says.

He vaguely remembers being carried to the hospital, where he remained delirious for several days.

'A plastic collar fastened round my neck gave me the worst nights I have ever endured, for I was convinced that my spine was being slowly bent backwards until it was about to snap. In other interludes, I was dying of thirst while being buried in desiccated dust (I can still taste the dust).'

When Arthur finally came out of his delirium, he had no strength or body control whatsoever.

'Though I could just move one arm and one leg, I could do nothing with them. The greatest feat I could achieve, after long deliberation and careful planning, was a slow roll from my back on to one side . . .

'Although I could breathe without much trouble when perfectly relaxed, the slightest exertion left me gasping. I could not speak more than two or three words without panting for breath. Having my face washed was a frightful ordeal; I could barely endure the brief passage of the suffocating sponge over my nose.'

He wouldn't be seeing the Great Basses Reef any time soon – that was certain. The expedition was cancelled.

Arthur spent six weeks in a private hospital, helpless and unable to feed and bathe himself. In mid-April he was carried home, but he was wholly dependent on Hector or one of several male nurses to help him move. At least he could sit, propped up in a chair, with some help. He was terribly weak, yet he was determined not to let this bad luck keep him down. What's more, he could read and write, two life-sustaining activities for any writer. And while he was still extremely weak, he noticed a gradual improvement. Things weren't all that bleak.

'My slow but steady recovery was like a new birth; for all its worries and unpleasantness, it was a voyage of discovery I am glad to have made,' he later wrote. 'There was the day when I could sit up in bed unaided; there was the day when I could reach the bathroom by myself; there was the day (a good deal later), when I could *leave* the bathroom by myself; there was the day when I could rise from a chair using both arms, then one arm, then *no* arms. And finally I was able to walk, with the aid of two sticks, for as much as a dozen yards.'

In mid-April, when Arthur was lying helpless in bed, he got a real boost. The news came that he had won the Kalinga Prize for Science Writing, which was administered by UNESCO. This prestigious award, given for the popularisation of science, was a tremendous psychological benefit; he credits it with accelerating his recovery. Its annual award of a thousand pounds, donated by B. Patnaik, the Indian statesman and industrialist, helped pull him through his convalescence too – and the falling balance in his bank account.

Mike's adventures in Technicolor movie-making were costing Arthur a bundle, as was their custom-built boat for the now cancelled Great Basses expedition. The contract delivery dates with Harper & Brothers to write two books about the treasure had to be amended. They wouldn't see Great Basses and the treasure again until 1963 at the earliest. The additional advance money paid upon delivery of the manuscripts and photographs was therefore delayed.

The Kalinga Prize money came in handy, and Arthur hoped to be well enough to attend the ceremony in New Delhi in the autumn. It was the tenth award; he was flattered to be in the distinguished company of past winners, a list including Bertrand Russell, Sir Julian Huxley and George Gamow.

By early May 1962 he still couldn't stand or sit up without assistance, but once someone propped him up on his feet he could walk up to a hundred yards. He was, he told Sam Youd, 'immensely improved', and by the end of May he could get to his feet without assistance and walk a hundred yards at a time 'with only one stick'. He said he was in no discomfort.

'I should be almost recovered in a few months, but the left arm may never come quite back to normal,' he wrote Sam. 'It's been a weird experience and has just chopped a couple of months out of my life. But doubtless I'll be able to use it in due course as I was able to do a lot of reading and think of a lot of plots.'

Arthur could even joke about it – always a sure sign of renewed spirits. Explaining his long silence to Sam, he said: 'At the end of February I conducted an unsuccessful experiment to see if two objects could occupy the same space at the same time. One was a doorway and the other my head.'

By July Arthur only had about half his normal strength, but at least he could walk for considerable distances. Because of his dramatic improvement – from complete helplessness to self-propulsion – he was no longer terribly worried about his future health prospects, although the reasons for his illness were still unclear.

That summer he began writing an adventure novel for youngsters, and in less than two months he had produced *Dolphin Island* in which he drew upon his rich experiences on Heron Island, the rest of the Great Barrier Reef and the coast of Ceylon.

'I wrote a couple of pages every day in pencil,' says Arthur, 'propped up in my chair – and got my secretary [Pauline de Silva] to type them out while I could still remember what the squiggles meant. *Dolphin Island* went very smoothly, being completed in six weeks, but when it was finished I felt rather sad. I could not help thinking that it was probably my farewell to the sea, which had given me so many strange, wonderful and exciting experiences.'

In *Dolphin Island*, the character of Professor Kazan becomes a mentor to the young adventurer, Johnny Clinton:

'Though he never stopped to think about it, the island had become the home he had never known, and the professor a replacement for the father he could scarcely remember.' Once again, a 'son' finds his 'father' in Clarke's fiction.

The novel, with its vivid maritime depictions and its good pacing and suspense, wasn't just a good read for Arthur's intended audience of boys. Even today it is enjoyed by people of all age groups.

During the first half of 1962 Mike was working on his third film, *Ranmuthu Duwa (Island of Pearls and Gold)*. It was the story, in part, of a twelve-year-old skin diver and the same groupers that appeared in *Beneath the Seas of Ceylon* (the ones Rodney Jonklaas had trained during their 1959 trip to the Great Basses).

Mike spent several weeks in London at the Technicolor studios working on the final editing of what would become the first Sinhalese colour movie. As the Colombo premiere drew near in the early summer, Arthur was hoping for the best – a success which would establish Mike as a big name in the Oriental film industry.

'I'm still astonished,' he wrote Sam, 'that we've been able to make a two and a half hour, thirty-five mm Eastmancolor movie with our modest resources. Of course, we had some help from the bank and the distributors, but even so – keep your fingers crossed: if this film doesn't appeal to the locals, we've had it.'

What they got was a Ceylonese success. Arthur wrote, '*Ranmuthu Duwa* turned out to be a smash hit, and its catchy songs were soon blaring out of every radio. Within a few months it had been seen by a million people – a tenth of the population of the country – and had created a great reservoir of good will for us. Wherever we went members of our diving team who had played parts in the movie were recognised and cheered (if they were Good Guys) or hissed (if they weren't). Hector played the villain and did such a good job he was sometimes despised by those who didn't know him!'

By the autumn of 1962, the film had broken all records for Ceylon and was running in twelve cinemas. Arthur had no illusions, however, about it being an international commercial success.

'The photography really is superb,' he wrote Roger Caras in November, 'and though the story is a bit hammy, it's just the thing needed for not very highbrow audiences. I've seen it three times and still enjoy it. We're working on versions in other languages and, who knows, one day there may be a cut-down English version.'

Arthur, however, had not been in Ceylon to witness every moment of Mike's triumph. In August he gave in to the gentle pressure from family and friends and returned to England. He had assured those closest to him that he was out of danger and on the mend, but everyone agreed that he ought to get the medical opinion of British specialists about his condition.

His Comet aircraft landed in London on 12 August, and brother Fred was there to help him down the gangway and take him back to 88 Nightingale Road.

The British doctors who examined Arthur disagreed with their Ceylonese colleagues. Their diagnosis: he had polio. The specialists in Ceylon, however, had assured Arthur that it was the bang on the head that had caused the paralysis.

'There is not much that a mere patient can do when the experts disagree,' Arthur said at the time; 'I would have preferred polio, which was likely to gain me more sympathy than my own carelessness.'

He wasn't certain which doctors to believe until years later, in 1988, American doctors at Johns Hopkins thoroughly examined him. After a battery of tests and a biopsy from his leg, the doctors proved that he was suffering from post-polio syndrome, a relatively new diagnosis even in the late 1980s.

But all Arthur knew in the summer of 1962 was that his health was

Arthur and his mother at the London première of
2001: A Space Odyssey.

Right In Hollywood, with
writer friends Robert Bloch
and Ray Bradbury, May
1984.

Below Wernher von Braun
and Arthur C. Clarke at the
Wallops Island conference,
June 1970.

Below Buckminster Fuller and Arthur
discuss the future on CBS Television,
June 1970.

Above As his satellite dish points skyward, the 'father' of communications satellites looks down from his home terrace.

Left Ready to go pearling off the Australian coast during his 1954–5 expedition to the Great Barrier Reef.

Below His underwater adventures in Australia and Ceylon changed the direction of his life and work. Here he discovers a huge propeller from an underwater wreck off the coast of Ceylon.

continuing to improve. A visit to Ballifants cheered him. Besides seeing his mother and some local friends, the scenes of his childhood and youth brought forth memories. Perhaps he understood one truth in his life, which he expressed in *The Fountains of Paradise* some seventeen years afterwards: 'The dreams of childhood had been far surpassed by the reality of adult life.'

'Six quiet weeks in England did me a lot of good,' says Arthur. 'At least I arrived using two sticks and left with only one, when I flew to New Delhi at the end of September to receive the Kalinga Prize.'

Although Arthur had lived in Ceylon for five years, this was his first trip to India. One sure way of bonding to a nation is to have it honour you with a prestigious prize and hand you a cheque as well. Writers, whose literary and financial fortunes rise and fall like the ocean tides, are especially grateful for such recognition.

He flew first class to New Delhi on a third-class ticket ('I think BOAC was embarrassed to have a VIP in steerage'), and saw the great Himalayas flash with lightning storms.

M. Rene Maheu, acting director-general of UNESCO, presented Arthur with the prize. Arthur also met the donor, B. Patnaik, and many other officials, politicians and scientists. And he managed to stand while giving his speech.

'In addition to the pride I personally feel on receiving the Kalinga Prize,' he told his audience, 'I would like to think that it is a tribute to the field of literature in which I have specialised – science fiction.'

He had published about as much fiction as non-fiction in his writing career, he told them, and defended science fiction against scientists who 'lose no opportunity of criticising it'.

Arthur spoke not just about science fiction's educational value, but of its inspirational value as well – how the best science fiction has opened up the wonders of the universe for young people and sparked their interest in science.

'Many distinguished scientists have paid tribute to the influence of these great masters [Verne and Wells],' said Arthur, 'and a careful survey would, I believe, reveal that science fiction is a major factor in launching many youngsters on a scientific career.'

Science fiction has had an enormous influence on astronautics, Arthur said. 'The four greatest pioneers of space flight – Tsiolkovsky, Oberth, Goddard and Von Braun – *all* wrote science fiction to propagate their ideas (though they did not always get it published!).'

The hope of a better future, Arthur concluded, 'lies in science combined with wisdom and foresight. I shall be happy indeed if any writings of mine have helped toward this goal.'

Upon his return to Ceylon in early October 1962, Arthur was determined to take things easy until he was fit again. This non-exertion pact with himself did not apply to mental activities, however, and he put himself on a disciplined work schedule writing several magazine pieces for *Playboy*, *Holiday* and the *New York Times Magazine*. *Playboy* continued to serialise some of the essays which would be published in *Profiles of the Future*.

He also had good news about the juvenile novel, *Dolphin Island*. The Junior Literary Guild chose it to offer its members, his publisher, Holt, Rinehart, told him.

Of his physical condition, Arthur wrote, 'I am now able to walk quite well but am still extremely weak and convalescence will be a long job. Goodness knows when I'll be back in the States – I shall not be doing any travelling again for a long time if I can help it.'

The exception, of course, was a local trip to the Great Basses Reef and a visit to the treasure wreck he had missed in 1961. If he was strong enough, he wanted to accompany Mike in the spring of 1963. This would give him the taste of adventure he needed, and hope for the New Year.

CHAPTER 16

Silver and Books

Meanwhile I remain the most successful
writer in the world who's never had a movie
made.
 – Letter to Sam Youd, 24 October 1963

Ten months after the paralysis struck Arthur down, he was still weak.
His doctors had anticipated a slow recovery, and his body proved
them correct. Basic arm movements continued to be difficult for him
in January 1963.

Arthur's health was the crucial element in his bid to join the Great
Basses Reef expedition in the spring, and he began working out to
build up his strength.

'I exercised and trained and struggled to lift minute weights with
my moribund left triceps. By the beginning of March – exactly a year
after the accident – I had made up my mind that I *would* go to the
Great Basses. I did not expect that I would be able to dive, but I was
sure that I could watch operations without getting in the way.'

Arthur was greatly encouraged when he discovered that he could
manage an aqualung and breathe comfortably under water. This gave
him an added incentive to keep up his disciplined exercise schedule.

While he was preparing his body for the Great Basses trip, his mind
was firing away also. He was back revising *Glide Path* for the third
time. Arthur was determined to do whatever was necessary to get
this difficult novel off his back and into the bookshops.

He and Julian Muller, his editor at Harcourt, Brace, discussed ways
in which the book could be improved.

'It had all the ingredients of a fairly exciting novel,' recalls Julian,
'but it had to be reshaped by giving a different emphasis to certain
parts, and suspense had to be developed in certain portions of the
narrative, by holding it up, in typical fictional form, for later revelation. All I did was, essentially, make structural suggestions which
Arthur picked up – I can't claim too much credit for it.'

Glide Path was Arthur's thirtieth book and his only autobiographical novel to date. He was hoping for the best when he sent it off to New York this time.

Within a month of receiving the manuscript Harcourt scheduled the book for their autumn list. Relief at last! *Glide Path's* tortuous road to publication was coming to an end.

On 14 February 1963 *Syncom 2* was launched and became the first artificial satellite to go into a geosynchronous orbit. Arthur's 1945 vision had become hardware in a stationary orbit above the Earth.

His forecasts were even longer term in *Profiles of the Future*, which was published in the United States early in 1963. Reviewers (including fellow science fiction writers Isaac Asimov, Brian Aldiss and Fritz Leiber) praised the book and confirmed Arthur's opinion that it would be his most important non-fiction work since *The Exploration of Space* a decade earlier.

A number of critics placed Clarke and this book in the tradition of English futurists and considered *Profiles* as a pioneering effort in future studies. The book, wrote Asimov, gave 'all of us a chance to raise our eyes from the ground and to contemplate the scenery ahead'. Fritz Leiber viewed it in a historical context as 'a splendid introduction to the devices and concepts which the science fiction writers of the past half-century have been exploring with controlled imaginations'.

Profiles of the Future was not a narrative listing pie-in-the-sky predictions. Instead, Arthur carefully described what he would and would not do in the book, admitting that he was limiting himself, for the most part, to the future of technology.

'All attempts to predict the future in any detail appear ludicrous within a few years,' he wrote in an updated introduction to *Profiles* in 1983. 'This book has a more realistic, yet at the same time more ambitious, aim. It does not try to describe *the* future, but to define the boundaries within which possible futures must lie.'

Profiles offered the best of rational speculation based on the limits of natural laws and discredited any loose imaginations that cast aside the truths and methods of science.

And as an extra bonus readers were presented with Arthur C. Clarke's First Law. The Second and Third Laws were later pulled out of the text and given the status of 'laws'. The revised US edition of *Profiles of the Future* then mentioned all three for the first time, although on different pages. Here they are, gathered together:

Clarke's First Law: When a distinguished but elderly scientist says that something is possible, he is almost certainly right. When he says it is impossible, he is very probably wrong.

Clarke's Second Law: The only way to find the limits of the possible is by going beyond them to the impossible.

Clarke's Third Law: Any sufficiently advanced technology is indistinguishable from magic.

Profiles of the Future has been, and continues to be, an influential book for all those interested in science, technology and the future. Some thirty years after its original publication, it still stands out from the dozens of less important books that attempted to imitate it.

For Gene Roddenberry, creator of television's *Star Trek, Profiles* had an impact.

'I read *Childhood's End*, of course, and was mightily moved by it,' said Roddenberry. 'And I should say that *Profiles of the Future* was the next most important Clarke work in my life because a great deal of what I did on *Star Trek* was guided by that.'

It is difficult not to think of the famous Roddenberry line, 'Beam me up, Scottie,' when reading chapter seven of *Profiles*, 'World without Distance', about teleportation. Arthur was never one to underestimate the power of popular culture and ever hopeful that it could be used to dispel some of the abundant ignorance of the inhabitants of planet Earth.

When the weather for the south coast looked good in the middle of March 1963, Mike Wilson, Rodney Jonklaas and two boatmen sailed *Ranmuthu* out of Colombo harbour and headed down the coast. Arthur, Hector and the others followed by land a few days later, with all the additional equipment in tow.

The small harbour of Tangalle was the closest protected anchorage to the reef (although Kirinda Beach was the final coastal destination), and the land and sea parties met at a resthouse on the water's edge of the small bay where *Ranmuthu* anchored.

Their newly built boat had chugged into the bay on half an engine. Both water cooling pumps had broken down, but there were new parts in Arthur's group's luggage and the repairs were made.

Their jumping off point to the Great Basses, as on their earlier trips, was the fishing village of Kirinda some forty miles further along the coast. But the weather turned bad, and they had to remain at Tangalle.

When the weather did not improve in the next few days, it was decided that it was a waste of time and money for the entire team to remain. Arthur and Mike returned to Colombo, while Rodney and the two boatmen remained behind to watch over *Ranmuthu* and the equipment.

Back in Colombo, a baby daughter, Anne, was born to Elizabeth and Mike in late March. Then an unexpected letter arrived on 1 April from Peter Throckmorton, the archaeologist who discovered and excavated a Bronze Age trader off the Turkish coast which had last sailed in about 1300 BC. His letter asked that he be notified if anything of historical importance became known off the coast of Ceylon.

Arthur and Mike immediately cabled Throckmorton, asking the long shot that he might be free and able to join them. Before long he answered that he was and would be coming.

Soon after Peter Throckmorton's arrival in early April, they received reports of good weather on the south coast and set off once more in their quest for the silver beneath the sea.

After more frustrations, including a broken exhaust pipe which was none-too-easily repaired, the *Ranmuthu* finally arrived safely at Kirinda with Mike, Peter and the two boatmen aboard. They rendezvoused with the shore party – Arthur, Hector, Rodney, a cook and a photographer. The treasure waited only ten miles off shore.

When *Ranmuthu* headed out to the reef the next morning, Arthur climbed the small hill overlooking Kirinda Beach and set up his three-and-a-half inch Questar telescope.

'Though Mike had pressed me to come, I was not aboard. The boat was already crowded, and this first day I decided to stay on land. I was still extremely weak, and if anything went wrong I would only be in the way.'

Arthur became the unofficial on-shore observer on the first day of the expedition to the treasure wreck. There was no competition; he was the only one who brought along a telescope.

He even wrote an *aide-mémoire* on comsats while on Kirinda's shore. Requested by UNESCO, its purpose was to provide guidelines for a special 1963 Geneva conference on space communications called by the International Telecommunication Union. It was reprinted several times as 'The World of the Communications Satellite', making its most popular appearance in his volume of essays, *Voices from the Sky* (1965).

Arthur could see *Ranmuthu*'s canvas awning ten miles out in the Indian Ocean, and while she looked submerged in the boiling surf, he knew that this was an illusion of perspective. The boat was actually anchored a few hundred yards away from the harsh surf of the reef.

Meanwhile, Mike and Peter had located the wreck, but Rodney had to turn back because of a defective regulator.

'I very quickly recognised the plateau where we found the second bronze cannon two years previously,' says Mike, 'and led Peter right to the spot. I swam the whole length of the wreck with Peter, showing him the cannon, the anchors and finally the place where we'd found the silver.'

After replenishing their air, they went down again.

'We dived around a bit,' recalls Mike, 'and since we had such a long swim, about two hundred yards through very hard conditions, we didn't feel much like carrying anything back with us. We had a very good look at the site, made some measurements, drove some pitons in, left some equipment on the spot and came back with Laza in the dinghy around the reef to the *Ranmuthu*.'

The second morning Arthur was aboard *Ranmuthu* when she sailed to the reef. It was 14 April 1963. He didn't feel strong enough to handle an aqualung, so he decided to don flippers, face mask, gloves and a weight belt and do some snorkelling while staying attached to the rubber dinghy which was stationed not too far from the wreck site. The water was clear and Arthur could see Mike, Rodney and Peter at work below.

'Mike was chipping away, with hammer and chisel, at the half-exposed cannon, while Peter was swimming along the wreck unrolling a tape measure. He was engaged in the very difficult but important operation of mapping the site, by measuring the distance between the numbered metal tags he had wired to prominent objects such as anchors and cannon.'

No significant new finds were discovered that morning, Mike confirmed during a midday break aboard the *Ranmuthu*.

'I think we got most of it last time. There doesn't seem to be much more,' Mike said.

Was this possible? Arthur wondered. No treasure left?

After a snack of hot cocoa and biscuits, Mike and Peter made their second dive to the wreck. Later still, about mid-afternoon, Peter continued his systematic investigation while Mike and Rodney paddled one of the rubber dinghies over to visit the lighthouse. Peter was alone when he got lucky. He found the mother lode.

'There's at least a ton there,' he told Arthur on the *Ranmuthu*, having rowed back to impart his exciting news and replenish his air.

Arthur's face lit up. He was excited. The expedition was worth it after all. He couldn't wait to break the news to Mike and Rodney when they returned from the lighthouse.

'I was greeted with that grin Arthur has when he's happy about something,' says Mike.

As soon as Arthur told him, he grabbed a new lung and headed back to the reef to find Peter and get directions to the mother lode.

Besides the many coin masses (once bags of silver coins that had congealed) they brought up a 331-pound bronze cannon with the help of Peter's Port-A-Lift balloon, which became a powerful lifting tool when inflated under water. Other items brought up included wooden pistol stocks, rusty hand grenades, a copper serving plate, cannon balls, a bronze pestle and so forth. Peter's further investigation indicated that it was a twenty-two or twenty-four-gun ship, much larger than they'd originally thought.

Their last dive on Great Basses was on 21 April and Arthur went along. Snorkelling near the surface he could clearly see the activities below. Mike and Peter had found still more silver, 'a couple of lumps as big as your head'.

'I had a perfect bird's-eye view of the salvage operation,' says Arthur. 'I was watching something which, I suppose, not more than a handful of living men have seen – the lifting of treasure from the seabed, at the actual moment of discovery.'

The next day the divers drove back to Colombo. All the salvage from the wreck had to be classified, photographed and preserved in a manner consistent with good archaeological methods. This had to be done quickly with Peter's expert guidance because he had to return to Greece and prepare for yet another expedition.

Arthur's priority was to weigh the accumulated silver from the 1961 and 1963 expeditions. It came to about 350 pounds of silver coins, including the clump that went to the Smithsonian.

The treasure remained in a chest in Arthur's office while the research into the ship, its origins and its cargo continued, and while the legal aspects of the discovery in international waters were clarified and confirmed.

In late April, Arthur's treasure-hunting experiences still fresh, he began work on a new book, *The Treasure of the Great Reef*. He also found time for some short stories. In May he wrote a story for *Boy's Life*, originally titled 'Sunjammer' but reprinted several times as 'Wind from the Sun'. Three more stories, including 'The Secret', were completed in June.

The summer brought good news for Arthur. He was proud to learn that he was going to be included in the 1964 edition of *Who's Who*. He was also pleased to discover that *A Fall of Moondust* had been made a selection of the Science Fiction Book Club. And to top it all off, in July he found out that he was being awarded the Stuart Ballantine Gold Medal from the Franklin Institute in Philadelphia. This would be one more reason, along with publishing and lecture business, to visit the United States in the autumn.

Arthur sat in front of the typewriter and wrote for most of July and August, and then flew to England on 31 August. He stayed at 88 Nightingale Road with his brother Fred and Fred's new wife.

'This was the visit when Arthur gave my wife, Sylvia, a beautiful little poodle called Dusty,' Fred recalls, 'which was short for *A Fall of Moondust.*'

The mass media beckoned and on 10 September Arthur went to the BBC studios and filmed an episode of 'The Sky at Night' with host and friend Patrick Moore. The programme (which was broadcast on 6 January 1964) focused on 'Bases on the Moon', and Patrick introduced Arthur to the television audience as the man who'd first put forward the concept of a communications satellite in 1945.

Arthur bravely made some forecasts at the end of the programme about what would happen in the future. The first flight around the Moon, he predicted, would be made in 1967 (he was a year early). The first manned Moon landing he put at between 1970 and 1972 (just six months off), although he qualified it by saying that 'there is a chance that it will come earlier – perhaps even in 1968'. The first flight around Mars (1980) and the first landing there (1990) were far from the mark (assuming he meant manned missions and not the unmanned *Viking* spacecraft of 1977). His forecasts of a lunar base (1975) and Mars base (about 2000) were too optimistic, extrapolating as he did from the tremendous 'space race' momentum of the early sixties which resulted from *Sputnik 1*.

What is important here is that Arthur's 1963 short-term forecasts, those within ten years, were generally accurate; those beyond a decade were far from the target. Arthur had proved a point he'd made almost ten years earlier in *The Exploration of the Moon*: '. . . the further we try and see into the future, the more our prediction will depart from reality when it comes about'.

There was also some treasure business to attend to during his London stay. Says brother Fred: 'On Friday 13 September I took Arthur to meet Dr Walker at the British Museum to identify the coins. As we went down the long corridors they had to unlock and lock again several sets of doors as we went through them, arriving finally in the room which held all the museum's silver.

'We showed them one of the big lumps of silver coins; they had never seen anything like that. They were able to identify the rupee coins, but they had never seen the half-rupee ones, one of which Arthur donated to the Museum.'

Late in September, Arthur and Val Cleaver flew over to Paris to attend an astronautics conference, and then on 8 October Arthur was once more crossing the Atlantic to the country that first embraced his work.

It was one of his shortest US visits, lasting about two weeks, and he decided not to push too hard.

'I was determined to take it easy and accepted *no* TV or radio,' he wrote Sam Youd. (Even twenty months after the paralysis he tired easily, and got breathless on the shortest flight of stairs.) He went on to describe his US experiences, including his acceptance of the Stuart Ballantine Medal from the Franklin Institute in Philadelphia.

He was impressed with the award ('a nice hunk of gold') which was presented to him for 'his soundly based and prophetic early concept of the application of satellites in the primary human endeavour of communication'. Among the notables at the Franklin Institute ceremony was the Chairman of the Atomic Energy Commission, Glenn Seaborg.

While in the Philadelphia area, Arthur visited General Electric's space research facility at Valley Forge.

'Highlight of the trip,' he told Sam, 'was watching four men on day ten of a thirty-day mission in the gigantic space chamber at GE's space technology labs. And listening to the *Syncom* test tapes.'

Arthur's New York City business was fruitful.

'Time-Life have just commissioned me to do a book on space in their beautifully produced Science Series,' Arthur wrote to Sam. 'When it's finished, they'll fly me over for the final polishing, so I'll get a free trip to the US out of it as well. It's quite a short book and should be fun to write, unless I have trouble with the fifty or sixty editors who seem to be involved.'

This became *Man in Space*, and was published in 1964 ('With the editors of *Life*').

Television claimed Arthur again when he returned to England, and he found himself at the BBC in late October waiting for the back-projection equipment to be repaired. He was there to work on a programme in the 'Adventure' series, 'The Treasure of the Great Reef', which would be broadcast in early January 1964.

Sam Youd wrote that he enjoyed the telecast and offered his opinion that the show was stolen 'by that cute little Disney-type baby shark'.

'Baby shark, my foot,' Arthur wrote back. 'It was six feet long, if it was an inch . . .'

On 3 November he flew east to Ceylon, and found the hearth and home in an acceptable state.

Glide Path was published in the autumn – at last! – after all the frustrations Arthur had gone through. The *New York Herald Tribune*'s reviewer looked at the novel's overall theme of testing and developing a new technology – ground control approach radar.

'*Glide Path* describes this final phase of the project through the eyes of one of the "team", a young radar officer. The method is mainly anecdotal with sketches of flying types – Anglo-American "boffins" (scientists) and airdrome officers – rather than genuine character development . . .

'Arthur Clarke writes with knowledge and authority. He has a gift for making scientific intricacies intelligible without recourse to jargon, and he has an obvious familiarity with the folkways of engineers and scientists.'

It was a positive review. Not a rave, but certainly nothing to hang one's head about. Arthur felt a tremendous sense of relief whenever he was able to put a book behind him. The publication of this novel offered more relief than usual.

Towards the end of 1963 two possible movie options were under discussion. There was 'major' interest in *Childhood's End*, but this was hardly the first time. There had been talk of a film version of his 1953 novel for a decade. And there was a small option being offered for *A Fall of Moondust*.

These prospects were summarised in a November letter to Sam Youd. Arthur closed by saying, 'Meanwhile I remain the most successful writer in the world who's never had a movie made.'

This claim would be short-lived; Stanley Kubrick was thinking about what he should do after *Dr Strangelove*.

CHAPTER 17

The Genesis of 2001: A Space Odyssey

'Our next speaker is the only person I know
who can be unambiguously introduced by a
four-digit number – 2001.' And there was a
standing ovation.
  – MIT Symposium on the 100th Anniversary of the telephone, March 1976

That tens of thousands of people still carry vivid images in their
minds from the great film *2001: A Space Odyssey* more than twenty
years after it first appeared on the screen is proof of its lasting artistic
power. Even today its influence is frequently seen in new films,
television programmes and advertising in several media. Some of the
classical music adapted to its soundtrack is now all but universally
associated with the future. And film giants Steven Spielberg and
George Lucas have both acknowledged its influence on their space
movies with cosmic and extra-terrestrial themes.

The famous collaboration between Stanley Kubrick and Arthur C.
Clarke on the film classic *2001*, and the novel upon which the film
was based, began by chance. It was one of those lucky connections.

'I was having lunch with Stanley at Trader Vic's,' recalls Roger
Caras, who was then working for Columbia Pictures and who would
later become public relations director for the film. 'It was just as *Dr
Strangelove* was coming out [February 1964].'

'What are you going to do next?' Caras asked Kubrick.

'You'd laugh,' Stanley said.

'No, I wouldn't. What are you going to do?'

'I'm going to do something on ETs,' Stanley said, looking to see
if Caras knew what that meant.

'That's fantastic,' said Caras. 'As a matter of fact I'm doing a radio
show on extra-terrestrials tonight.'

Their lively conversation continued, and then Caras asked Kubrick
who the writer was going to be. Kubrick didn't know yet.

'I'm reading everything by everybody.'

This, Caras knew, was exactly what Stanley would do. He'd pick the top twenty-five science fiction writers, have his assistant pull together everything they'd ever written and read it. That was the thorough way Stanley approached his projects.

'Why waste your time?' Caras asked. 'Why not just start with the best?'

'Who?' Kubrick asked him.

'Arthur C. Clarke,' Caras replied.

'But I understand he's a recluse, a nut who lives in a tree in India some place,' said Kubrick.

Roger Caras put that rumour to rest. 'Like hell. He's not a recluse or a nut. He just lives quietly in Sri Lanka.'

Kubrick then asked Caras if he knew Clarke.

'Extremely well,' Caras told him. 'We were introduced by Jacques Cousteau years ago.'

'Jesus, get in touch with him, will you?' Kubrick asked.

Caras said he would and soon cabled Arthur in Ceylon. Caras recalls the cable's wording as:

STANLEY KUBRICK – 'DR STRANGELOVE', 'PATHS OF GLORY', ET CETERA, INTERESTED IN DOING FILM ON ET'S. INTERESTED IN YOU. ARE YOU INTERESTED? THOUGHT YOU WERE RECLUSE.

Arthur replied rather promptly with his own cable to Roger:

FRIGHTFULLY INTERESTED IN WORKING WITH ENFANT TERRIBLE. CONTACT MY AGENT. WHAT MAKES KUBRICK THINK I'M A RECLUSE?

Roger Caras passed the information on to Scott Meredith, who then began to define the first stages of the project with Clarke and Kubrick. For Caras, that was the last he would hear of Kubrick's ET film project until well into 1964.

Scott Meredith knew Stanley Kubrick. He'd first met him in the early 1960s, when he sold him the film option rights to a novel by one of his clients, Peter George.

'*The Red Alert* was a voice-of-doom novel,' says Meredith, 'which was published by one of the small paperback publishers. We sold *Red Alert* to the movies in June 1959 for a thousand dollars. This was a little motion picture deal for a very minor book. Just an outright deal. It then went through three or four different hands. This fellow sold it to that fellow for the same thousand dollars, and then this fellow sold it to someone else. None of these people could get financing to make a film. The final owner came to us in the early 1960s and said that he couldn't find the money to make the picture. He wanted us to represent him and wanted us to sell the film option rights once again.

'We resold the rights for $3500 on behalf of the owner to a small company which became Polaris Productions – Stanley Kubrick's company. That's how I first met Stanley,' says Meredith. 'And the film which evolved out of Peter George's novel became *Dr Strangelove* – rather a famous film. A serious book became a satire on the screen.'

After Scott learned of Arthur's interest in Kubrick's next film project, he called and discussed things with Stanley who suggested that the next step was to select some of Clarke's stories that could be considered resources for the screenplay. Kubrick then wrote to Clarke directly in Ceylon.

Arthur received the letter in March 1964.

'He wanted to do the proverbial "really good" science fiction movie,' says Arthur. The letter went on to describe Kubrick's main interests in confronting the question of extra-terrestrials.

'(1) The reasons for believing in the existence of intelligent extra-terrestrial life. (2) The impact (and perhaps even lack of impact in some quarters) such discovery would have on Earth in the near future.'

The letter further aroused Arthur's interest in the project. He had seen Kubrick's *Lolita* and was impressed by it, and everyone was talking about the just-released *Dr Strangelove*, although he hadn't seen that yet.

Arthur wanted to meet Kubrick and discuss the project further the next time he was in the States.

'By a fortunate coincidence I was due in New York almost immediately, to complete work on the Time-Life Science Library's *Man and Space*, the main text of which I had written in Colombo.'

The preparations for Arthur's trip included searching through his published fiction for ideas that could be used in the film.

'I very quickly settled on a short story called "The Sentinel", written over the 1948 Christmas holiday for a BBC contest. It was this story's idea which I suggested in my reply to Stanley Kubrick as the take-off point for a movie. The finding – and triggering – of an intelligence detector, buried on the Moon aeons ago, would give all the excuse we needed for the exploration of the Universe.'

The original story did not win or get placed in the BBC contest when it was written in 1948. But Arthur, whose rule is never to throw any writing away, filed one copy and eventually sent another on to Scott Meredith. Two years later it was sold to the magazine *Ten Story Fantasy* and was published in the spring of 1951 under its original title, 'Sentinel of Eternity'. Then it found a new life in 1964 and became *one* of the sources for the extra-terrestrial theme of *2001: A Space Odyssey*.

'I am continually annoyed by careless references to "The Sentinel" as "the story on which *2001* is based"; it bears about as much relation to the movie as an acorn to the resultant full-grown oak. Considerably less, in fact, because ideas from several other stories were also incorporated. Even the elements that Stanley Kubrick and I *did* actually use were considerably modified.'

The extra-terrestrial artifact in the story, for example, was not the black monolith of the film but instead a 'glittering, roughly pyramidal structure, twice as high as a man, that was set in the rock like a gigantic, many-faceted jewel'. The artifact's location on the Moon was also different from the film. Instead of Mare Crisium in the book it became Crater Tycho, which Arthur considered the 'most spectacular of all lunar craters'. Tycho had the additional attraction that it can actually be seen from the Earth at full Moon.

Arthur travelled from Ceylon to New York via London in April 1964. During his brief visit in London he took the opportunity to see *Dr Strangelove*.

'I was happy to find that it lived up to the reviews,' he said later. He also believed the film's 'technical virtuosity' boded well for the even more ambitious cinematic space epic that was gestating in Kubrick's mind.

On 22 April 1964 Arthur met Stanley Kubrick for lunch at Trader Vic's in the Plaza Hotel. This was the same day that the New York World's Fair opened.

Stanley arrived for the luncheon on time, Arthur recalls, describing him as a 'rather quiet, average-height New Yorker', not yet sporting the full beard which he had during the making of *2001*. He had little or no colour in his cheeks, Arthur noted, because he was very much a night person – a fact which would soon become apparent in their working relationship.

It was immediately obvious to Arthur that Stanley Kubrick had already absorbed a tremendous amount of science fiction and general scientific fact prior to their first meeting. Kubrick grasped new ideas, no matter how complex, almost immediately, and Arthur realised at once that this man's creative curiosity seemed to encompass everything.

Arthur remembers well the marathon discussion during their first day together.

'We talked for eight solid hours about science fiction, *Dr Strangelove*, flying saucers, politics, the space programme, Senator Goldwater – and, of course, the projected next movie.

'Stanley was in some danger of believing in flying saucers,' says Arthur. 'I felt I had arrived just in time to save him from this gruesome fate. Even from the beginning, he had a very clear idea of his ultimate goal. He wanted to make a movie about Man's relation to the Universe – something which had never been attempted, much less achieved, in the history of motion pictures. Stanley was determined to create a work of art which would arouse the emotions of wonder, awe, even, if appropriate, terror.'

After their first meeting, the two men met often and talked extensively during the spring of 1964.

'I was working at Time-Life during the day and moonlighting with Stanley in the evenings, and as the Time-Life job phased out Stanley phased in. We talked for weeks and weeks – sometimes for ten hours at a time – and we wandered all over New York. We went to the Guggenheim and to Central Park, and even to the World's Fair. We talked at Stanley's apartment, in restaurants and automats, movie houses and art galleries. We considered and discarded literally hundreds of ideas. Besides talking endlessly, we had a look at the competition.'

There was none, of course, according to Stanley. In Arthur's opinion there had been several good ('or at least interesting') early science fiction movies. His list included *Destination Moon* (the collaborative effort of his writer friend Robert Heinlein and producer George Pal), *The Day the Earth Stood Still*, *Forbidden Planet*, *The Thing*, and *The War of the Worlds*.

One of the technical advisers on *2001*, Frederick Ordway, remembers Kubrick commenting on several occasions that, for all the brilliance of Arthur C. Clarke, Arthur was totally mesmerised by what Stanley considered grade B or grade C science fiction movies. It was incredible to Stanley that Arthur, who was so precise and so knowledgeable, would go and see a horrible black and white science fiction film and sit there like a school kid.

Needless to say, Stanley was very critical of all the old science fiction films. Even the classic H. G. Wells film, *Things to Come*, which Arthur persuaded Stanley to see, didn't fare too well under Kubrick's critical eye, although it did influence *2001* and was listed in the credits.

194

By May 1964, after seemingly hundreds of hours of talkathons, the two men agreed that 'The Sentinel' was good material and could be used. At first they thought of the story's extra-terrestrial artifact as a climax rather than a jumping-off point. When it was decided that the discovery of the artifact buried on the Moon would be up front in the story line, Arthur reviewed his backlist of published stories for more ideas.

He came up with six additional stories which, along with 'The Sentinel', would become building blocks for the novel and the screenplay. They were 'Breaking Strain', 'Out of the Cradle, Endlessly Orbiting . . .', 'Who's There', 'Into the Comet' and 'Before Eden'.

An early working title of the film, used privately by Stanley and Arthur, was 'How the Solar System was Won'. Stanley next proposed a rather unorthodox approach in producing the screenplay. He and his agent, Louis Blau, had to show the top brass at Metro-Goldwyn-Mayer something of substance in order to get their commitment to finance production. But Stanley had a particular dislike for movie scripts and wanted to present the backers with something completely different.

'He proposed that we sit down and first write the story as a complete novel,' recalls Arthur. 'That way, before embarking on the drudgery of the script, we [could] let our imaginations soar freely by developing the story as a novel upon which the screenplay would eventually be based. We would generate more ideas, Stanley thought, and give the project more body and depth. Though I had never collaborated with anyone before in this way, the idea suited me fine.'

Arthur never considered the novel to be anything but independent and self-contained, even though it was written as the basis for the film proposal and later the screenplay.

'In theory, therefore, the novel would be written (with an eye on the screen) and the script would be derived from this. In practice, the result was far more complex; towards the end, both novel and screenplay were being written simultaneously, with feedback in both directions. Some parts of the novel had their final revisions after we had seen the rushes based on the screenplay based on earlier versions of the novel . . . and so on.'

Although the novel, *2001: A Space Odyssey*, has gone through some fifty printings and has sold three million copies since its publication in July 1968, its complex and intricate relationship to the film is often simplified and even erroneously stated.

'A novel by Arthur C. Clarke based on the screenplay of the MGM film by Stanley Kubrick and Arthur C. Clarke,' reads the back cover copy of a recent printing.

'I felt that when the novel finally appeared it should be "by Arthur Clarke and Stanley Kubrick; based on the screenplay by Stanley Kubrick and Arthur Clarke" – whereas the movie should have the credits reversed. This still seems the nearest approximation to the complicated truth.'

But in the spring of 1964, the writing of the novel had not even begun. Arthur and Stanley continued to brainstorm.

'Stan's a fascinating character – I've been living with his family, very nearly, ever since reaching NY,' Arthur wrote Sam Youd. 'Working with him six to eight hours a day *after* my stint at Time-Life, where I have a lovely office on the thirty-second floor.'

At this early stage both men envisioned the film as 'a kind of semi-documentary about the first pioneering days of the new frontier'. That concept was soon left behind.

The first projected schedule calculated by Stanley for all the work was 'hilariously optimistic', Arthur recalls. His time estimate for all the various tasks, from writing the story to editing the film, added up to about two years.

Arthur reluctantly accepted the fact that his planned return to Ceylon would have to be postponed until enough work was completed for the all-important, one-shot proposal for MGM. It was at this time that he and Kubrick came to an agreement.

'We shook hands on the deal during the evening of 17 May 1964,' says Clarke, 'went out on to the penthouse veranda to relax, and at nine p.m. saw, sailing high above Manhattan, the most spectacular of the dozen UFOs I've observed during the last twenty years.'

Arthur had persuaded Stanley in their initial conversations that UFOs were simply that – unidentified flying objects – and had nothing to do with outer space and extra-terrestrials. And while he could usually identify and explain them fairly quickly, this sighting was an exception.

It looked like a brilliant satellite to Arthur. He checked the listing of satellite passes in the *New York Times*, but there was no such transit at nine p.m.

They both continued to stare at the bright object. It appeared to come to rest at the zenith, remain in that position above Manhattan for about a minute and then sink down to the north.

'I can still remember, rather sheepishly, my feelings of awe and excitement,' says Arthur, 'and also the thought that flashed through my mind: "This is altogether too much of a coincidence. *They* are out to stop us from making this movie."'

Arthur continued to argue that there was a simple explanation, but he couldn't come up with one. Reluctantly, they contacted the Pentagon (reluctantly because the Air Force was still smarting from Kubrick's acclaimed satire on the military, *Dr Strangelove*). They even filled out and submitted the standard sighting form. Besides the Pentagon, Arthur contacted his friends at the Hayden Planetarium and gave them all the relevant details of the sighting. They fired up their computer, and shortly thereafter the mystery was solved.

What they had seen was indeed what Arthur had first suspected: a satellite. It was a transit of the huge *Echo 1* satellite, the hundred-foot inflated balloon with its highly reflective aluminium surface, which had been launched in the summer of 1960. Why the *New York Times* hadn't listed this spectacular appearance, yet had listed two less impressive ones that occurred later the same night, was anybody's guess.

Scott Meredith and Louis Blau began working out the details of a formal legal agreement for Arthur's participation in the *2001* project. This was some eight months before Kubrick had any solid backing from MGM.

'We signed the agreement for Arthur's six stories,' recalls Scott, 'on 20 May 1964. We got $10,000 for the option on these stories, including "The Sentinel".

'By 28 May, "The Sentinel" had been picked, and we signed an agreement for Arthur to write a treatment based on it for $30,000; $15,000 on commencement of principal photography and the other $15,000 on completion.

'Now the "novelisation" deal, as it was thought of at the beginning, was really a collaboration,' says Scott. 'Arthur did all the writing, of course, but Stanley was feeding him ideas every day. The book was a sixty-forty deal, with Arthur getting sixty per cent and Stanley forty per cent. That's continued to this day. The book has made millions; we keep sending Arthur cheques and Stanley cheques. Everything continues to operate because it's a worldwide deal. It must be published in at least forty countries and every time a licence runs out in one of these countries we relicense them.'

Arthur and Stanley continued their brain-storming sessions throughout the entire film production. They usually met at Stanley's place while in New York, but sometimes at restaurants nearby. In early summer 1964 they were plotting and discussing several possible endings for *2001*. They had ideas aplenty, but they also had a dilemma.

How should they depict extra-terrestrials in the novel and film? One or more of the crew members would come into contact with them, but what would they look like?

Arthur decided to give Carl Sagan a call and solicit his ideas. He and Stanley invited Carl to have dinner with them at Kubrick's New York penthouse.

Sagan was just short of thirty years old, and was then an astrophysicist at the Smithsonian Astrophysical Observatory in Cambridge, Massachusetts.

'They had no idea how to end the movie,' says Carl. 'That's when they called me in to try to resolve a dispute. The key issue was how to portray the extra-terrestrials that would surely be encountered when they go through the Star Gate. Kubrick was arguing that extra-terrestrials would look like humans with some slight differences, maybe à la Mr Spock. And Arthur was arguing, quite properly on general evolutionary grounds, that they would look nothing like us. So I tried to adjudicate as they asked.

'I said it would be a disaster to portray the extra-terrestrials. What ought to be done is to suggest them.

'I argued that the number of individually unlikely events in the evolutionary history of Man was so great that nothing like us is ever likely to evolve again anywhere else in the Universe. I suggested that any explicit representation of an advanced extra-terrestrial being was bound to have at least an element of falseness about it, and that the best solution would be to suggest, rather than explicitly to display, the extra-terrestrials.

'Kubrick's preference had one distinct advantage, an economic one: he could call up Central Casting and ask for twenty extra-terrestrials. With a little make-up he would have his problem solved. The alternative portrayal, whatever it was, was bound to be expensive.'

How the film and novel actually would end remained an open question. In fact more than two years later, in September 1966, Arthur was completely rewriting the ending of the novel for what he hoped would be the last time. But in mid-1964 it looked as if the ETs would be suggested rather than depicted.

'Just bought a ream of paper and start work in ten minutes (I hope) on the new novel, which Stanley Kubrick bought a month ago,' Arthur wrote Sam Youd on 19 June. 'I'll be stuck here (or in Hollywood, ugh) for the next year or so, though I hope to commute back to Ceylon occasionally.

'Stanley installed me, with electric typewriter, in his Central Park

West office, but after one day I retreated to my natural environment in the Hotel Chelsea, where I could draw inspiration from the company of Arthur Miller, Allen Ginsberg, Andy Warhol and William Burroughs.'

The Chelsea offered many distractions, but Arthur did his best to avoid them. He wholly dedicated himself to researching and writing the novel that would be used to convince MGM to back the film. He produced between one and two thousand words a day on average during the summer months and into the autumn. He typed on an old grey Smith-Corona in suite 1008 at the Hotel Chelsea, and he lived for the most part on tea, crackers and liver pâté.

'Every other day Stanley and I would get together and compare notes; during this period we went down endless blind alleys and threw away tens of thousands of words. The scope of the story steadily expanded, both in time and space.'

Says Roger Caras, 'Arthur and Stanley were very interesting foils. There was some slight conflict in that Arthur goes to bed very early. He gets very tired, and typically nine to nine thirty is his bedtime. Stanley goes to bed about three in the morning and sleeps till about three in the afternoon. That presented problems sometimes. But when their times meshed, they were terrific foils.'

Arthur recalls, 'The merging of our streams of thought was so effective that, after this lapse of time, I am no longer sure who originated what ideas.'

During the latter half of 1964 the ambitious theme of a space odyssey began to emerge – what Stanley referred to as a 'theme of mythic grandeur'. The universe was depicted as a vast cosmic ocean upon which mankind would sail, evolve and discover new worlds. It represented the last ever-expanding frontier for mankind's exploratory voyages.

In Arthur's 1958 book of essays, *The Challenge of the Spaceship*, he concluded with a poetic envoi, set in italics, which captures the essence of what he and Stanley were exploring in *2001*:

Across the gulf of centuries, the blind smile of Homer is turned upon our age. Along the echoing corridors of time, the roar of the rockets merges now with the creak of the wind-taut rigging. For somewhere in the world today, still unconscious of his destiny, walks the boy who will be the first Odysseus of the Age of Space . . .

'We set out,' says Arthur, 'with the deliberate intention of creating a myth. The Odyssean parallel was in our minds from the beginning, long before the film's title was chosen.'

As early as 1965 Arthur went around quietly saying that there was a surprise in store for Metro-Goldwyn-Mayer executives. 'MGM doesn't know it yet, but they've footed the bill for the first six-million-dollar religious film.'

Ultimately it was the mythic elements in *2001* that created the controversy and assured its status as a classic in film history.

But in 1964 Stanley Kubrick had his worries. The robot probe *Ranger 7* impacted on the surface of the Moon on 1 August, and both he and Arthur stayed up late to see the TV close-ups. The reality of what these space probes could discover got Stanley worrying about the *Mariner 4* space probe and what it might find as it flew by Mars in July of 1965. What if signs of life were discovered on the Red Planet? Such a discovery could wreck their story line.

'This was typical of Stanley's ability to worry about possibilities no one else would think of,' says Arthur. 'He always acts on the assumption that if something *can* go wrong, it will; ditto if it can't.'

Later on, once MGM had committed to the film, Stanley actually tried to insure the studio against the risk of extra-terrestrial life being discovered. He consulted Lloyd's of London, but dropped the idea when he found out how much the premium would be.

'Stanley decided,' says Arthur, 'to take his chance with the Universe.'

During October and November both men were grappling with the material which would become the evolutionary sequence that begins both the novel and the film. Background research included Arthur reading Louis Leakey's *Adam's Ancestors* and Robert Ardrey's *African Genesis*. Arthur also spent time with Dr Harry Shapiro, director of the anthropology division at the American Museum of Natural History in New York.

The day before Christmas Arthur was at his Smith-Corona labouring on what he believed to be the final pages of the first draft. He wanted to have them ready as a Christmas present for Stanley. When Stanley read them he was delighted with the last chapters. 'We've extended the range of science fiction,' he told Arthur. And so their grand myth was further defined as the New Year approached.

It was Arthur's belief, fleeting though it was, that the novel was essentially complete then, and that the screenplay would be developed from it in a rather straightforward way. This was far from the truth, but the early draft of the manuscript combined with Stanley Kubrick's track record, then rated excellent with the recent success of *Dr Strangelove*, were all Louis Blau needed to sell the project to MGM.

'I took the treatment they had,' recalls Blau, 'and presented it to MGM to read. They had a two- or three-day deadline during which they had to come back to me, and that's how I made the deal. What they saw was not in the form of a classic screenplay, with detailed camera directions, but rather a manuscript of a novel. Stanley never uses a traditional screenplay like some directors who want to know all the stage details. Instead he keeps working up to and through his shooting to make sure it's better all the time.'

The executives at Metro-Goldwyn-Mayer decided to finance the film, then called *Journey Beyond the Stars*, to the tune of six million dollars.

The final title was chosen less than two months later. 'Stanley selected *2001: A Space Odyssey* in April 1965,' says Arthur, 'and as far as I can recall it was entirely his idea.'

This future date naturally evolved during the hundreds of hours of discussions in 1964. The year 2001 – a setting which was thirty-five years in the future when MGM decided to finance production – was far enough away in time to ensure that the film's future realism wouldn't be undercut by reality.

Fred Ordway, one of the two principal astronautic advisers (along with Harry Lange) whom Kubrick contacted at Arthur's suggestion, remembers '2001' coming up as a potential title.

'Stanley asked me if we should say "two thousand and one" or "twenty o one" like we say "nineteen o one",' says Ordway. 'And we decided that "two thousand and one" sounded better. We often wondered among ourselves whether the fact that the film was called "Two-Thousand-*and*-one" would have an influence on the English language when we got into the twenty-first century.'

Revision of the novel continued throughout the spring of 1965, and entire chunks of text, earlier thought to be essential to the final plot, were discarded as the story line constantly changed.

As Arthur revised and wrote new sections of the novel, Stanley began directing the film project – hiring the staff, initiating design work, negotiating agreements with actors and the technical people who were preparing everything to begin production in England.

'My primary job was still polishing the novel,' says Arthur, 'though I was constantly involved in technical discussions with the artists and production staff.'

In March Arthur stood his ground against Kubrick attempting to bring Dr Poole back from the dead after the computer HAL killed him off.

'I'm afraid,' he scribbled in his notebook, 'Stanley's obsession with immortality has overcome his artistic instincts.'

When most of Part III was ready for typing in May, Arthur was again encouraged. He had also completed the 'Universe' chapter and the 'Floating Island' sequence, both of which were later cut from the novel. At the same time, Arthur realised how much of the material he'd abandoned earlier could be incorporated into the final version.

Kubrick assembled the pre-production team in New York during the first half of 1965. It included Stanley's assistant from England, Ray Lovejoy, artist-designer Tony Pratt, secretary Judy Minoff, technical advisers Frederick Ordway and Harry Lange, executive producer Victor Lyndon, art director Tony Masters, Masters' associate John Hoesli and artist-designer Richard P. McKenna.

Roger Caras also appeared on the scene again in the spring. He hadn't heard from Arthur or Stanley since their exchange of cables.

'One day the phone rang and it was Arthur,' says Caras. 'I said, "Hey, Arthur, when did you get in town?" And he told me that he had been in the city for nearly a year, working on the new project.

'I spoke to Arthur for a few minutes, and then Stanley came on the phone. "Do you want to come to England with us and make a movie?" he asked. It was a Sunday night, about eleven thirty, which is late for Arthur. I called over to my wife and said, "Jill, do you want to move to England?" And she said, "Sure."

'So the next day I resigned from Columbia Pictures after ten years and prepared to move to England with Arthur and Stanley and the rest of the team. I had become the director of publicity for *2001: A Space Odyssey*.'

A telling fact about the relationship between Clarke and Kubrick is that Stanley began setting down conditions from the beginning – not that that surprised anyone who knew him. Even Arthur admitted that, as far as the film was concerned, Kubrick had 'total control', but it was for the good of the picture. 'He knew exactly what he was doing,' says Arthur, 'and he was absolutely right. I have tremendous regard for Kubrick. He's a genius – there's no question about that. A force of nature.'

'In plain fact,' says Roger Caras, 'Stanley Kubrick is probably the only person in the last forty years that Arthur has had to take a back seat to. Kubrick is the more famous of the two; Kubrick is much more the forceful personality of the two. Kubrick says yes, Kubrick says no; it is yes or no. Arthur says yes, Arthur says no; it is maybe.

Arthur is so easily coerced by people he likes because he's so kind. Stanley's nowhere near as generous or as soft-hearted, although he is a kind man.'

Arthur and Stanley had what Roger Caras called a good 'cerebral marriage'. They stimulated one another with a constant flow of ideas and challenges during their creative conversations.

'Arthur became very fond of Kubrick,' says Fred Ordway. 'They seemed to get along quite well together, and it was a tremendous and exciting experience for Arthur.'

And frustrating. There was no way the novel could be completed before the film was finalised. Arthur made changes, then more changes. The only certainty appeared to be additional changes. Once Arthur jokingly suggested that they push the release date back to 2002 or further.

Both the novel and screenplay were in a state of flux when the pre-production team began moving to England in the summer of 1965 to prepare for actual filming. The design and research work that had been completed in Manhattan, as well as some of the special effects footage used in Commander Bowman's final voyage through space and time, was packed up and sent to the MGM studios at Borehamwood north of London.

Arthur left Manhattan in late June and returned to Ceylon after more than a year away. He remained there for the month of July before travelling to London and rejoining Stanley and the film company. As he always did while in London, he stayed at 88 Nightingale Road with his brother Fred and Fred's wife.

The production company had expanded dramatically since its move from New York. The art department had graduated from preliminary sketches, drawings and models to actually constructing the large sets. Once in Borehamwood, Arthur's time was 'equally divided between the apparently never-ending chore of developing ideas with Stanley, polishing the novel, and almost daily consultations at the studio'.

In early September 1965 Kubrick was thinking about a major story change. He wanted to substitute the planet Saturn for Jupiter as the destination for the spaceship *Discovery*. Kubrick's desire for the change was based on aesthetics – the beauty of Saturn's rings and the many spectacular special effects that could be created as the spaceship flew among them. He asked his technical adviser, Fred Ordway, to research the Ringed Planet.

'I prepared the memo,' says Ordway. 'Kubrick was delighted and

Clarke backed the change with great enthusiasm. Arthur then brilliantly wrote Jupiter out and Saturn in. Everybody got excited about the change – except the special-effects people who went ape.'

Eventually this major change proved to be too much for the special-effects group which was already under tremendous pressure. Douglas Trumbull, who was in charge of special effects, got his way – no Saturn.

For the film, therefore, Jupiter remained the destination planet for spaceship *Discovery*, but Arthur retained Saturn in the novel and this became one of the major plot differences between the book and the movie.

In autumn 1965 the ending of *2001* was still unapparent to Stanley and Arthur. Both men were searching for a memorable conclusion to their mythic journey.

In late August Arthur had 'suddenly realised how the novel *should* end, with Bowman standing beside the alien ship'. Stanley was not convinced, however, and the search continued.

'The ending was altered shortly before shooting it,' says Kubrick. 'In the original, there was no transformation of Bowman. He just wandered around the room and finally saw the artifact. But this didn't seem like it was satisfying enough, or interesting enough, and we constantly searched for ideas until we finally came up with the ending as you see it.'

On 3 October, during a telephone conversation with Stanley, Arthur presented his latest ideas for an ending and one of them clicked.

'Bowman will regress to infancy,' Arthur noted afterwards, 'and we'll see him at the end as a baby in orbit. Stanley called again later, still very enthusiastic. Hope this isn't false optimism: I feel cautiously encouraged myself.'

Two days later, after much creative brooding, Arthur came up with a logical reason why Bowman should appear as a baby at the end of the film. 'It's his image of himself at this stage of his development. And perhaps the Cosmic Consciousness has a sense of humour. Phoned these ideas to Stan, who wasn't too impressed, but I'm happy now.'

In the novel the Star-Child detonates the nuclear weapons orbiting planet Earth. This concept actually went to the shooting-script stage for the film, but was finally cancelled. Both Stanley and Arthur agreed that it was too similar to Kubrick's ending in *Dr Strangelove*.

By mid-October, Stanley had decided to kill off the entire crew of *Discovery*. Only Commander Bowman would survive. This was drastic, Arthur thought, but it also seemed right somehow. 'After all, Odysseus was the sole survivor,' he remarked.

Even at this late date, with filming only weeks away, Kubrick was considering major changes that, if pursued, would have had serious ripple effects throughout the entire production effort. Fred Clarke remembers Stanley calling Arthur late one night towards the end of October.

'Stanley had decided to change the type of drive used on the spaceship to what we call the ion drive. This was a new form of propulsion which he thought might be used in the year 2001. But Arthur said that the production crew had been building the spaceship set for three months using the old system and that the new ion drive would mean an entirely different design.'

There were other spaceship sets besides the interplanetary *Discovery*. One was the Earth orbit ship, *Orion III*, which Arthur visited in November with Stanley and the design staff. His presence in this case may have been unfortunate, however – at least in the short run. During the visit to this set, he 'happened to remark that the cockpit looked like a Chinese restaurant. Stan said that killed it instantly for him and called for revisions.' Arthur noted, 'Must keep away from the Art Department for a few days.'

December came and Kubrick was under mounting pressure to start filming before the end of 1965. The growing tension was felt by everyone. Fred Ordway believed that Kubrick, under the circumstances, became less friendly to everyone working around him. Ordway, as technical adviser, brought in design recommendations from US industry for equipment on the sets, but Stanley often was not satisfied.

'Many design aspects of the vehicles in the film changed regularly,' says Ordway. 'It became impossible at times to finalise anything. And we were faced with the fact that the screenplay had a definite tendency to change rather rapidly.'

All of this was the price of Stanley Kubrick's creativity – fighting his way through chaos toward a new unity, forging a contemporary celluloid myth.

The New Year was only days away, and everyone involved in the film was under the gun. Arthur worked right through the Christmas holiday, including 25 December, and sent the fresh manuscript pages over to Stanley the next day.

'He called to say that he didn't think much of the dialogue,' says Arthur. 'I agreed.'

This was the first indication that the screenplay dialogue was a problem for Kubrick, and that he would solve it in an innovative way

– by getting rid of much of it and substituting silence and music.

But he couldn't get rid of the shooting schedule.

While most of the film was shot at the MGM studios in Boreham-wood, the first days were done at Shepperton because it was the only studio in England large enough to build the huge excavation site (which was 150 feet in diameter) in the Moon's Tycho Crater. Kubrick had no flexibility at all with this sequence; the set had to be torn down by 7 January to make way for another production. Time to shoot or die.

CHAPTER 18

A Cosmic Classic

Arthur somehow manages to capture the
hopeless but admirable human desire to
know things that can really never be known.

I don't like to talk about *2001* much, because
it's essentially a non-verbal experience. It
attempts to communicate more to the subconscious and to feelings than it does to the
intellect.

— Stanley Kubrick

Filming of *2001: A Space Odyssey* began on 29 December 1965 at
Shepperton.

'About a hundred technicians were milling around,' Arthur wrote
in his diary. 'I spent some time with Stanley, reworking the script –
in fact we continued through lunch together. I also met the actors, and
felt quite the proper expert when they started asking me astronomical
questions. I stayed until four p.m. – not actual shooting by then,
but they were getting near it. The spacesuits, back-packs, etc. are
beautifully done, and TMA 1 [Tycho Magnetic Anomaly 1 Exca-
vation] is quite impressive – though someone had smeared the black
finish [of the monolith] and Stanley went on a rampage when I
pointed it out to him.'

The black rectangular monolith was not the easiest prop to move.
It was a three-ton block of lucite (the largest piece ever cast) which
was later painted black and hauled on to the excavation set by a crane.

Roger Caras was on hand for the first day's shooting on the Moon
set.

'There was a scene where the scientists come walking down the
ramp into the excavation,' Roger recalls. 'Stanley wanted a dolly shot
with the camera in front of them, backing away as they walked down
the ramp.

'Well, the SuperPanavision seventy-millimetre camera is a big,
heavy machine, and the operating cameraman couldn't do the shot

the way Stanley wanted it because the slope was steep and the ramp was made of corrugated steel, which was too rough for the dolly wheels.

'Stanley was going to get the shot he wanted despite the problems. He decided to shoot the scene himself. He took the SuperPanavision camera, hand-held it, had two or three people behind him to guide him and keep him from going over backwards from the weight of the camera, and he walked down the ramp backwards. Stanley physically shot the whole scene, taking over the operating camera-man's job.'

'He's one of the rare film-makers who can do it all,' says Louis Blau. 'He knows the duties of everybody from the lowest grip or electrician on up to the cameraman and the art director – and everybody else.'

Even the old pros were amazed by Kubrick's total commitment to the project and his depth of knowledge in all areas, technical and artistic.

Even though filming had begun, Arthur was still writing. He wrote the dramatic confrontation with HAL, the 9000 computer, on 8 January and knew immediately that he was producing one of the most exciting scenes in the book.

'I got quite scared,' he says, 'when the computer started going nuts, being alone in the room with my electric typewriter.' These emotions were transferred from print to film in the powerful scene showing HAL's slow death. Film critic Andrew Sarras praised its emotional power: 'I have never seen the death of the mind rendered more profoundly or poetically,' he later wrote in the *Village Voice*.

Clarke and Kubrick managed to resolve most of the remaining questions of plot during a long discussion in mid-January. By 17 January Arthur had completed the first draft of the last chapters. He felt that the end was in sight, but cautioned himself that this would be the third time he'd felt that way.

A few days before Arthur returned to Ceylon for a month and a half, in early February 1966, he viewed a demonstration film which Stanley had produced for the MGM executives.

'Stan spliced together a few scenes to give the studio heads some idea of what was going on. He used Mendelssohn's *Midsummer Night's Dream* for the weightless scenes, and Vaughan Williams' *Antarctica Symphony* for the lunar sequence and the Star Gate special effects, with stunning results. I reeled out convinced that we had a masterpiece on our hands – if Stan could keep it up.'

As busy as Kubrick was filming in the spring of 1966, he still had time to request more work on the novel and screenplay, although Arthur had returned to Colombo. Stanley cabled Arthur in mid-March and requested some 'poetic Clarkian narration' on HAL's breakdown, which was written and sent off to him the same day. This turned out to be another rush job that was never used.

Revision work on the novel continued during late March. Arthur considered his final draft finished in early April 1966, before he flew from Ceylon to Lawrence, Kansas, to speak at the centennial celebration at the University of Kansas. His host was Professor James Gunn, a fellow science fiction author, and he would be in the distinguished company of people like Bucky Fuller and Pat Weaver who were also good friends.

'I met Arthur at the airport,' says Gunn. 'And one of the publicists who was working on *2001* also met him there. We had dinner at the airport. He showed us some production stills he had brought along with him, and he showed them with considerable pride. Arthur was glowing. He thought it was going to be a great film.

'But he was complaining a bit also, irritated that Kubrick would not let the book be contracted. He wanted to get it out at the time the movie was released. And he was unhappy that Kubrick would not let him release the manuscript and get his portion of the proceeds.

'I remember he was still suffering from the consequences of his variously diagnosed disease which caused his paralysis. He was having some trouble breathing when he exerted himself. When he gave his speech ["Explorations in Tomorrow"], he did pause to breathe a few times, and he used his stool to sit on as I recall.'

Towards the end of his speech Arthur speculated about the future of 'ultra-intelligent machines' and the possibility that any advanced extra-terrestrials might be non-organic. '[This would] make them highly suited for interstellar flight because machines don't mind waiting around for thousands of years. They don't mind vacuum conditions; in fact they probably prefer them. They don't mind high accelerations. So if we do have any visitors from space I suggest they won't come in spaceships, they will be spaceships.'

Besides strongly anticipating his 1973 novel, *Rendezvous with Rama*, this portion of his Kansas speech also presents a plausible rationale behind the decision not to depict the extra-terrestrials in the film or novel *2001: A Space Odyssey*.

The question of the book's publication was very much on Arthur's mind at this time. He had to have some kind of resolution.

'I cabled Stanley to say that I was heading back to London to make final arrangements for the publication of the novel. He replied, "Don't bother – it's not ready yet."'

But Arthur *was* bothered, and Kubrick's discouraging words did not stop him. He desperately wanted to get the book into the market place because he had been working on it for almost two years and still had not received a publisher's advance. He flew back to London and went to the studio.

'Stanley himself raised the subject of a publication date,' says Arthur. 'I asked him if he were deliberately delaying publication of the book until the film was out, so it would not appear that the film was based on the book. He made a genuine protestation that he was not up to that. He said he believed that the book needed further work, and he did not then have the time to read it. He also explained that the general release of the film would not be until late in 1967 or even 1968. And when it did first open, it would be running only in a few Cinerama houses, which would give us some more breathing space.'

It was, as Arthur put it, 'Stanley's way', and not much could be done about it, although Arthur kept trying to convince him, right into early summer, that the manuscript should go to the publisher and the publishing process begin.

'I maintained that *I* was the writer and he should rely on my judgement; what would he say if I wanted to edit the film?'

Finally, in June, Stanley suggested a compromise which Arthur knew was at least a step in the right direction. Kubrick promised to read the manuscript and give Arthur a list of improvements he wanted. He kept his word in July by sending a long memorandum of queries, observations and constructive criticism. The memorandum was nine pages long. This was enough for Scott Meredith to begin negotiating a contract with Dell/Delacorte Press.

But two months later, when Arthur was in Ceylon, nothing had really changed. 'I gather that there has been a friendly meeting between Louis [Blau] and Dell,' Arthur wrote Sam Youd in September. 'They have agreed to wait but I can't afford to. Altogether, apart from the fact that I still don't know when and if I'll ever get any part of the novel advance (Stan talks of delivery in February!), I have *lost* about fifteen thousand dollars in commissions I've had to turn down while working on the revisions.'

Arthur was fighting for his financial life because of the delayed book contract. He was in debt and had to borrow money.

In December 1966 he wrote to Roger Caras saying that the book contract was still in limbo, and everything depended on Stanley's co-operation.

Bob and Ginny Heinlein
visiting Arthur in Sri
Lanka, 1980.

Steven Spielberg and
Harrison Ford visit Arthur
in May 1983, after filming
Temple of Doom in Sri
Lanka. *Left to right*: Valerie
and Cherene Ekanayake,
Steven Spielberg, Harrison
Ford, and Arthur.

Visiting Stanley Kubrick at
his Hertfordshire home.

Talking with ex-astronauts Buzz Aldrin (*right*) and
Michael Collins in Riyadh after receiving the Special
Achievements Award from the Association of Space
Explorers in 1989.

Below At a desert feast a day after the awards ceremony, several
guests, including Arthur, took turns holding this magnificent
falcon. Here Michael Collins takes his turn.

'He keeps promising he will send me his revisions but I have received nothing and I don't know what the situation is.'

'It was,' says Arthur, 'a very sad period for me. When Stanley finally approved the book for publication two years later, not a word had been changed. There seems to be a right way to do things, a wrong way and Stanley's way.' It was unintentional; Kubrick genuinely wanted to make his contribution to the manuscript, but his heavy work schedule made it impossible.

Originally, Stanley had indicated to Dell that they might have an approved and signed contract in February 1967, but there was no news from Stanley that month. He wasn't answering the cables Arthur sent. Dell, however, decided to go ahead and send a contract to Scott Meredith, who then forwarded it to Kubrick for signature. He didn't sign it. His reason for the delay, as before, was that he was not yet completely satisfied with the manuscript and wanted to make additional revisions when his schedule permitted. Dell eventually got tired of waiting for the novel *and* the film, which would give book sales a healthy boost. By mid-1967 corporate patience had run out.

'The *2001* novel contract is cancelled,' Arthur wrote Sam in June 1967. 'I've never had a penny . . . Stanley refuses to release it until he has tinkered with the dialogue . . . and he's too busy to do so! As a result, I'm fifty thousand dollars in debt.'

Arthur had to wait until the spring of 1968, just before the film went on general release, for Kubrick to approve publication of the novel. Scott Meredith went back to Dell but the president, Helen Myer, wasn't interested, having decided the book would not be successful. Eventually it went to Sidney Kramer at New American Library and it was not until July, three months after the film's release, that *2001* was actually published. It was published in the UK by Hutchinson.

One of Kubrick's goals in creating *2001: A Space Odyssey* was to take special effects in film to new heights of expertise. He wanted to make the effects look completely realistic, and it took him a year and a half to shoot the many scenes.

'I had to invent all the time,' says Kubrick. 'It was necessary to conceive, design and engineer completely new techniques. We ran through 205 special-effects shots. The last ones were arriving in Hollywood as the negative printing was being done.'

Kubrick says it took eighteen months and $6.5 million out of a $10.5 million (originally $6 million) total budget to create the special effects. These are what caused the film to go over budget and the release to be delayed.

One of the most expensive and important pieces of hardware for the final film was a giant centrifuge, which weighed forty tons and was capable of rotating at a variable speed of up to three miles per hour. This rotation speed had nothing to do with creating artificial gravity as it would have in space, of course, but rather gave Kubrick an entirely new range of photographic effects for the interior of the *Discovery*.

A British firm, the Vickers Armstrong Engineering Group, designed and manufactured the centrifuge to order at a cost of $300,000, a huge sum back in the mid-1960s. It took six months to build. No sound stage (this was only one of eleven used for filming *2001*) had seen anything like it before; it looked like a heavy-duty ferris wheel located in the middle of an airplane hangar.

The centrifuge was thirty-eight feet in diameter, and its exterior was densely covered with cables and lights. Its interior was eight feet wide. Two large ducts at either end brought in the air conditioning. Everything had to be bolted to the floor, both the set constructions (computer console, medical dispensary, shower, recreation area and five hibernation 'beds', called hibernacula in the film) and all the camera and lighting equipment.

Camera work in the centrifuge began in March 1966, but because this set was so unusual and complex there were many difficulties and delays. Kubrick had originally planned to shoot the main scenes in 130 days, but shooting in the centrifuge slowed down progress and added about a week. It was slow work because all the cameras and lights had to be arranged for each new sequence, and each time this took hours to accomplish.

The centrifuge set was also dangerous, and the fire hazard was real.

'When the actors were inside,' says Roger Caras, 'they were sealed in. They went in through the bottom and then the trap door was closed. There was a fire rescue unit on the set at all times. They would have dry runs and rehearsals of how to get the actors out should anything catch fire.

'There was a lot of electricity and flammable set elements like wood and plastic. Had there been a fire inside that machine, it could have been a flash fire like the one in *Apollo 1* that killed the three astronauts.

'There were special bolts, strategically placed, which could be hit with sledge hammers and cause the actors to drop out. The actors were always on the bottom of the centrifuge, you see. The camera moved and the machine moved, but the actors were always at the bottom, only about four or five feet above the sound stage.

'Another thing. All the lighting inside travelled with it. So all the spotlights, although they were designed to be relatively stationary, were going upside down and around on the merry-go-round. This did something weird to the filaments and the bulbs kept exploding. Everyone on the set had to be under shields, including Stanley, because the goddamn bulbs were exploding and showering the stage with glass.

'During one shoot (maybe the jogging scene) the camera, which was travelling around inside the centrifuge, tore loose and fell thirty-odd feet to the floor and nearly killed the actors in there. It was a dangerous set.'

Another innovation on the centrifuge set was closed-circuit television. Kubrick installed the system so he could see what was going on inside and direct the activities without actually being sealed in with the actors, although he sometimes was. A large console was located to one side of the centrifuge, and there were three television receivers and six microphones among all the switches, levers and lights.

Kubrick spent an enormous amount of time, money and energy making sure everything was scientifically feasible. Even all the dials and gauges in *Discovery* and the other spacecraft had the benefit of expert advice for their design, many of which were never even seen in the final film. There were also sixteen rear-screen projectors mounted on the exterior of the centrifuge. When filming began, all of them were synchronised and feeding images to the interior set. They activated the screens in the command module and projected various information on to each of them.

Jeremy Bernstein, science writer for the *New Yorker*, visited the centrifuge sound stage in March 1966 and was overwhelmed by the strange structure and the dozens of different activities going on. After being led to the trapdoor at the bottom of the centrifuge, he peered into the brilliantly lit interior and saw Kubrick staring into the huge camera's viewfinder with complete concentration.

'Keir Dullea, dressed in shorts and a white T-shirt, and covered by a blue blanket, was lying in an open hibernaculum on the rising curve of the floor. He was apparently comfortably asleep and Kubrick was telling him to wake up as simply as possible. "Just open your eyes," he said. "Let's not have any stirring, yawning and rubbing."'

When one of the lights burned out and had to be replaced, Kubrick noticed Bernstein for the first time, staring at the furniture of *Discovery*'s dining quarters bolted to the top of the centrifuge. He assured him that it was well secured and invited him to climb in.

Derek Cracknell, the film's first assistant director, then handed a Polaroid to Kubrick through the trapdoor.

'Here's your Polaroid, guv,' he said. Why did Kubrick need a Polaroid? Bernstein wanted to know. Kubrick explained that he and Geoffrey Unsworth, his director of photography, had figured out a correlation between how the lighting appeared on the Polaroid shots and the setting on the movie camera. This allowed him to check for subtle lighting effects on his colour film.

When Bernstein asked Kubrick if it was usual for directors to become so involved in the details of camera work, Kubrick answered that he had never seen another film director work.

The burned-out light was replaced, Keir Dullea climbed back into the hibernaculum, and Kubrick and his crew went back to the wake-up scene. For this scene, the centrifuge was not rotating. After Kubrick relinquished the SuperPanavision seventy-millimetre camera to his cameraman, they filmed Dullea waking up. He simply opened his eyes.

Standing in for HAL, Kubrick fed his actor the lines which expressed good morning greetings and asked what he wanted for breakfast. Director and actor repeated the scene five times. Kubrick was finally satisfied that he had it right and climbed out of the centrifuge.

He was immediately surrounded by a lot of people, one of whom told him there was an animal trainer and his animal waiting outside. Stanley went to speak to the trainer and inspect a giant black pig which was to appear in one of the prehistoric scenes which begin the movie. Stanley approved the black pig. All in a day's work at the movies.

The director answered several other questions, gave some directions and then climbed into his private blue trailer located on the set.

'Maybe the company can get back some of its investment selling guided tours of the centrifuge,' Stanley light-heartedly told Bernstein. Smile or not, this was a sure clue that some of the MGM money men were starting to grumble.

In late May 1966 Arthur flew to the States for general promotion and public relations duties for *2001: A Space Odyssey*. There were times when he had no choice but to leave England for a period of time because of his status as a British citizen who had an official residence abroad.

Fred Ordway can remember Arthur telling Kubrick about the problem. 'Look Stan, I've got to go. My accountant is driving me crazy. I can't be in Britain any more.'

During this particular trip, Arthur met some nervous MGM executives and attempted to reassure them about Kubrick's budget-busting production. MGM had commissioned a promotion short in 1966, *The Making of 2001*, which was to be shown to film distributors and leaders in high-tech industries who could lend expertise or some other form of support to the production. Arthur was one of its stars, and scenes of Arthur and Tom Buck of *Look* magazine were shot at the Grumman Corporation plant in Bethpage, New York, during his visit.

The Making of 2001 was produced by Craven Film Corporation during 1966 and had no connection with the later book, *The Making of Kubrick's 2001*, edited by Jerome Agel and published in 1970, two years after the film was released. This promotion film was the first indication to the outside world of what Stanley Kubrick had been doing since *Dr Strangelove*.

'It is the year 2001,' begins the promo film's narrator. 'You are on your way to a space station on routine business. You have been travelling less than an hour and have remembered to call your office. Now you transmit your thoughts across space electronically.

'You receive your answer transmitted directly to the built-in television screen in your case. This is but one example of what life will be like in the year 2001.'

So begins *The Making of 2001*, which then goes on to interview Kubrick's technical advisers, Frederick Ordway and Harry Lange, who talk about everything they are doing to 'ensure the scientific integrity of the film'. Ordway names many of the major corporations like IBM and GE that have been regularly consulted.

Later in the film, Arthur Clarke and Tom Buck are shown in front of NASA's Lunar Excursion Module at the Grumman Corporation plant where it was being built.

Arthur addresses the camera. 'We're in the final assembly building of the LEM, which will take two American astronauts down to the surface of the Moon. And in *2001* Stanley Kubrick and I have set ourselves several objectives. We hope to relate to the public the wonder and beauty and promise of the new age of exploration which is opening up before the human race. We want to convey the message that perhaps our Earth is not the only abode of life. Our sun which shines on this planet is one of a hundred billion circling in the Milky Way. How many of those shine upon our equals or our masters out there in the depths of space? That's a question that *2001* asks and seeks to answer.'

As the filming of *2001* progressed, the screenplay's dialogue became less and less important to Kubrick. He was, after all, trying to visualise for his audience an experience that was beyond words. Less than a third of the final film has dialogue (forty-six minutes out of a total running time of 141 minutes), and approximately half an hour goes by before the first words are spoken by a receptionist aboard *Space Station V* to Dr Heywood Floyd: 'Here you are, sir. Main level, please.'

'I tried to work things out,' says Kubrick, 'so that nothing important was said in the dialogue, and that anything important in the film be translated in terms of action.'

This goal, itself controversial, evolved over time as the writing and filming progressed.

The lead actor, Keir Dullea, who played Commander Bowman in the film, certainly noticed the change.

'Any similarity between the script I first read and the movie is purely coincidental,' Dullea says. 'All I saw was a science fiction story with a very visual approach.'

Ray Bradbury thought the film's dialogue 'banal to the point of extinction'. When an interviewer told Bradbury that this was probably intentional on Kubrick's part, Bradbury replied: 'I hope not. I'd like to believe Kubrick is more intelligent than that. I just think he's a bad writer who got in the way of Arthur C. Clarke, who is a wonderful writer.'

Asked in 1989 if his opinion had changed in two decades, Bradbury said no. 'If I could write the dialogue, then I would write scenes for the actors up front before you kill them. Then you've got some friction going, you've got a plot going for you, and you've got an antagonist. I would make more of a contest all the way along with HAL.

'I love the film – that's why I criticise it,' says Bradbury. 'I've seen it six times just to check my feelings. The film is still too long. I could go in and edit it for him tomorrow and make it into a better film, except that what is missing is humanity. There are no sympathetic characters. The popsicle people whom HAL kills off, you never find out who they are so you don't care.

'But the film is historically important and broke ground as far as space travel is concerned. The photography is glorious, and the music, and we'll never forget the excitement of seeing it for the first time for the good parts.'

Stanley Kubrick explained his position regarding the dialogue to the *New York Times*.

'There are certain areas of feeling and reality which are notably inaccessible to words. Non-verbal forms of expression such as music and painting can get at these areas, but words are a terrible straitjacket. It's interesting how many prisoners of that straitjacket resent its being loosened.'

Fred Ordway argued strongly for using voice-over narration in the 'Dawn of Man' sequence, which became the prologue, as well as in the final scenes in the film.

'I thought it was excellent dialogue prepared by Arthur, and I think it would have added immensely to the film,' says Ordway, 'but Kubrick didn't want that. And of course Kubrick knocked out a lot of dialogue that was already there. Originally the stewardesses and the pilots were talking, but Kubrick knocked it out and put music over. Apparently his purpose was to keep it almost a silent film. But a lot of people in the audience would have been less mystified about the film's meaning if the dialogue and narration had remained.'

That the meaning of *2001* would be less mysterious, of course, went against Kubrick's and Clarke's intent – at least in retrospect.

'This is what makes *2001* so unique,' says Clarke. 'It poses metaphysical, philosophical and even religious questions. I don't pretend we have the answers. But the questions are certainly worth thinking about.

'*2001: A Space Odyssey* is about man's past and future life in space. It's about concern with man's hierarchy in the Universe, which is probably pretty low. It's about the reactions of humanity to the discovery of higher intelligence in the universe.'

Stanley Kubrick says, 'I don't like to talk about *2001* much, because it's essentially a non-verbal experience. It attempts to communicate more to the subconscious and to feelings than it does to the intellect. I think clearly that there's a basic problem with people who are not paying attention with their eyes. They're listening. And they don't get much from listening to this film. Those who won't believe their eyes won't be able to appreciate this film.'

The importance of music and soundtrack to *2001* was first indicated in 1966, when Kubrick spliced together a few early takes for a demonstration film that he wanted to show MGM executives. Music of Felix Mendelssohn and Vaughan Williams was laid over scenes of weightlessness, the lunar excavation and some of the special effects of the Star Gate journey. This emphasis on image and music was maintained during the entire production and survived the long post-production period.

'Stan and I used *Carmina Burana* a lot for atmosphere during writing,' Arthur once wrote to Sam Youd. 'We tried to hire [Carl] Orff, but he was too old to tackle a major new project.'

The film opened with Richard Strauss' powerful *Thus Spake Zarathustra*, which led into the prehistoric 'Dawn of Man' African sequence. All action shots in the sequence were filmed in England in the autumn of 1967 with a large-scale front projection system of African transparencies thrown from in front of the screen. This was another innovation first used in *2001*. It was invented and described by science fiction writer Murray Leinster in the mid-1960s, and Arthur was impressed when he saw it demonstrated.

'I can still recall my amazement when Stanley showed me the principle of front-projection in the MGM Studio at Elstree,' says Arthur. 'We stood at one end of the set, facing the huge screen of retro-reflective ("cat's-eye") material covering the far wall. Stanley lit a match – and its image came straight back at us, its brilliance apparently undiminished after a journey of more than a hundred feet.'

The music of another Strauss was used later in the film. Johann Strauss's waltz, 'The Blue Danube', became the soundtrack for the famous evolutionary jump to the space station vista. Kubrick chose Herbert von Karajan's interpretation of the piece.

'It's hard to find anything much better than "The Blue Danube" for depicting grace and beauty in turning,' says Kubrick. 'It also gets about as far away as you can get from the cliché of space music.'

His choice again of Richard Strauss' *Zarathustra* for the end of the 'Dawn of Man' sequence, when Moon Watcher appears to understand how he can use the bone he holds, is another powerful moment in the film, signifying that an evolutionary leap is about to take place. As the film evolved, music became more important than dialogue and replaced it.

Arthur remembers when the last scene in the 'Dawn of Man' was filmed, the one in which Moon Watcher smashes the animal skulls and then throws his bone weapon up into the air. The memorable transition from twirling bone to similar-shaped spaceship becomes what Arthur has called 'the longest flash-forward in the history of movies – three million years'.

This scene was the only one in *2001* that was filmed on location and not in the studio. The location, however, was only a few hundred yards away from the studio in a nearby field.

'A small platform had been set up,' says Arthur, 'and Moon Watcher (Dan Richter) was sitting on this, surrounded by bones. Cars and buses were going by at the end of the field, but as this was a low-angle shot against the sky they didn't get in the way – though Stanley did have to pause for an occasional airplane.

'The shot was repeated so many times, and Dan smashed so many bones, that I was afraid we were going to run out of wart-hog (or tapir) skulls. But eventually Stanley was satisfied, and as we walked back to the studio he began to throw bones up in the air. At first I thought this was sheer *joie de vivre*, but he started to film them with a hand-held camera – no easy task.

'When he had finished filming the bones whirling against the sky, Stanley resumed the walk back to the studio; but now he had got hold of a broom and started tossing *that* up into the air.'

This was the creative genesis of the film's famous three-million-year flash-forward – from a primitive prehistoric tool tossed in the air to a sophisticated space machine of the future.

The principal shooting of live action for *2001: A Space Odyssey* had been completed during the first six months of 1966. Kubrick, in fact, had planned twenty-six weeks to shoot the main scenes, and even though the shooting in the centrifuge had delayed the schedule for about a week he came close to attaining his goal.

There was still a tremendous amount of post-production work, however, which had to be finished. The intricate, time-consuming and all-important special effects needed to be designed and filmed. Most of this work was done during the last half of 1966, all of 1967 and the first few months of 1968 before the film was released.

Arthur was not at the MGM studios every day he was in England. He often worked at 88 Nightingale Road, and communicated by phone with Stanley and other members of the production team. He also travelled during this period, returning to Ceylon and visiting the United States at least twice.

In January 1967 Arthur was at his Ceylonese home in Gregory's Road writing a piece for *Life* magazine and blocking out his travel and commitments for the year. He was also busy writing publicity essays for the film, ten in all, which he sent to Stanley.

In addition, Arthur had a contract for *The Promise of Space* which he had to deliver by the autumn of 1967 – the same time he was scheduled to begin another lecture tour (thirty-five cities this time) in the United States.

'I'm now in a blissful state of ex-pregnancy,' Arthur wrote to Sam Youd in late August, 'having just sent off 95,000 w + 20 tables + 25 figs + 1000 plates, replacing *all* my existing (& obsolete) space books.'

By mid-December Arthur had concluded his American lecture tour and had returned to England just in time to celebrate his birthday – '(ugh!) my 50th!!!' He also attended a symposium on science fiction films put on by the British Film Institute.

With the New Year came the release of *2001*. At long last the cosmic film odyssey was about to go public.

When preview audiences saw the original uncut version of *2001* – which ran for two hours and forty-one minutes – it was not uncommon to hear people criticising it as too long and boring.

'Stanley also sensed it was too long,' says Roger Caras. 'He hadn't seen the film complete with music and sound effects until about a week before it opened. But he couldn't decide on the cuts until he observed a live audience and could get an idea of the squirm factor. He walked up and down the side aisles and across the back endlessly during the screening to see where they were squirming – and that's where he made his cuts.'

After the premieres in Washington, New York and Los Angeles, which took place during the first four days of April, Kubrick cut the original print on 5 April in New York City. He made all the cuts himself; no one asked him to.

'I just felt,' says Kubrick, 'as I looked at it and looked at it that I could see places all the way through where I could tighten up, and I took out nineteen minutes.'

'It took thirty individual cuts to make up the nineteen minutes,' recalls Caras, 'and they came from several different scenes, including the Dawn of Man, *Orion III* spaceship to orbit, Space Station V, exercising in the centrifuge of *Discovery*, and Poole's (actor Gary Lockwood's) space pod exiting from *Discovery*. There was a whole sequence in the space station that was cut. A village square inside the station, with shops and a playground with children running around – that came out. And Gary Lockwood's "breathing" sequence outside the spaceship, before he was killed by HAL, was greatly shortened.'

Kubrick did not believe that the cuts made a crucial difference: 'I think it just affected some marginal people. The people who like it like it no matter what its length, and the same holds true for the people who hate it.'

The film *did* provoke extreme reactions – from both the general movie-going public and professional film critics. There seemed to be no middle-of-the-road response. There were some critics, however, who after seeing the movie a second time changed their opinion from negative to positive. This was, if not unprecedented, at least rare in the world of film criticism.

After the first Washington, DC, press preview Arthur overheard someone say, 'Well, that's the end of Stanley Kubrick.' Several days later, at the world premiere, there was another cynical prediction from an MGM executive. It was 2 April 1968, the day President Johnson announced he would not be seeking another term. The executive, thinking of then MGM president Robert H. O'Brien, said, 'Well, today we lost two presidents.'

'The most remarkable thing about *2001*,' Arthur said, 'is that it is doing so well without any concession to popular taste. Kubrick never once said, "Let's not let the popcorn set get away." It's so uncompromising that people realise it deals with much bigger issues than science alone.'

The New York critics were, as a group, less kind than reviewers in Washington and Los Angeles, although Penelope Gilliatt of the *New Yorker* wrote that '*2001: A Space Odyssey* is some sort of great film, and an unforgettable endeavour'. Less kind was Renata Adler writing in *The New York Times*: 'The movie is so completely absorbed in its own problems, its use of colour and space, its fanatical devotion to science fiction detail, that it is somewhere between hypnotic and immensely boring.'

John Lennon of the Beatles was one who thought it was hypnotic. 'I see it every week,' he said jokingly.

One critic made the tongue-in-cheek suggestion that the film was produced so *Life* magazine could have a major photo spread at the time of release – which it did.

The film, said *Life*, 'dazzles the eyes and gnaws at the mind'. The article went on to summarise and explain the movie, as well as inform readers about the complexity of creating some of the scenes and special effects.

Generally, *Life* was kind to *2001*, as well it might be considering the fact that it had its own special screening on 29 March 1968 – before any of the press previews for the VIPs and film critics in New York and Washington.

Why such favoured status? The reason probably dates back to spring 1964, when Arthur and Stanley were brainstorming the project. During one of their sessions they asked Albert Rosenfeld, *Life*'s science editor, to join them at Stanley's apartment.

'They were plotting their movie,' says Rosenfeld, 'and Kubrick was bouncing ideas off Clarke, who sat there, a mild, scholarly-looking man, full of facts and crinkly with humour. Clarke possesses equally large fonts of imagination and scientific information. This has produced a body of science fiction and technical material that is not only distinguished but also prophetic . . . The two thought that, as *Life*'s science editor, my brain might yield some stray, useful bit of information.'

It also yielded, four years later, some invaluable publicity in a major magazine. Although *Life*'s coverage was neutral, controversy over the film raged in other quarters.

Wrote John Allen in the *Christian Science Monitor*, 'Whenever the thunder of critical controversy rips through the air, one thing is certain: lightning has struck. Stanley Kubrick's *2001: A Space Odyssey* is just such a bolt of brilliant, high-voltage cinema.'

The *Chicago Daily News* critic, Sam Lesner, was one of the critics whose opinion changed after seeing the film again.

'I have seen Stanley Kubrick's mind-bending, maddening, awesome, debilitating, demoniacal, dehumanising, and miraculous extra-terrestrial fantasy-drama twice. At first I thought Kubrick had flipped his lid. Now I believe he is a genius.'

For each word of praise, there was always another of criticism. One particularly nasty review came from Pauline Kael, writing in *Harper's Magazine*.

'It's fun to think about Kubrick really doing every dumb thing he wanted to do, building enormous science fiction sets and equipment, never even bothering to figure out what he was going to do with them. In some ways it's the biggest amateur movie of them all, complete even to the amateur-movie obligatory scene – the director's little daughter (in curls) telling daddy what kind of present she wants. It's a monumentally unimaginative movie.'

Rumour had it that Kubrick flew into a rage once or twice after seeing reviews such as this.

Arthur, on the other hand, was having fun with all the controversy. In fact he added to it sometimes. Soon after the film's release he made a statement about *2001* that disturbed the MGM executives: 'If anyone understands it on the first viewing, we've failed in our intention.'

When asked what he thought of Arthur's statement, Kubrick said he disagreed with it. 'I believe he made it facetiously,' said Kubrick. 'The very nature of the visual experience in *2001* is to give the viewer an instantaneous, visceral, reaction that does not – and should not – require further amplification. Just speaking generally, however, I would say that there are elements in any good film that would increase the viewer's interest and appreciation on a second viewing.'

Arthur rejects Kubrick's characterisation of his comment as 'facetious'. Says Clarke, 'I still stand by this remark, which does not mean one can't *enjoy* the movie completely the first time around. What I meant was, of course, that because we were dealing with the mystery of the universe, and with powers and forces greater than man's comprehension, then by definition they could not be totally understandable. Yet there is at least one logical structure – and sometimes more than one – behind everything that happens on the screen in *2001*, and the ending does not consist of random enigmas, some simple-minded critics to the contrary. (You will find my interpretation in the novel; it is not necessarily Kubrick's. Nor is his necessarily the "right" one – whatever that means.)'

Of all the praise *2001* received during its first six months Arthur was most flattered by a comment from Alexei Leonov, the Russian cosmonaut and first man in the world to leave his spaceship and 'walk' in space. Arthur met Leonov in Vienna in August 1968. The occasion was the United Nations Conference on Peaceful Uses of Space. It was also the European premiere of *2001: A Space Odyssey*.

After seeing the film Leonov remarked, 'Now I feel I've been in space twice.'

Neil Armstrong, the first man to set foot on the Moon, saw the movie before *Apollo 11* blasted off from Earth in July 1969. 'It was a particularly fine production,' says Armstrong, 'with exceptionally accurate portrayals of space flight conditions and visual effects.'

The *Apollo 8* astronauts – Frank Borman, James Lovell and William Anders – who made the first, history-making circumnavigation of the Moon in December 1968, also saw *2001* before they departed Earth.

After seeing the film, Anders had an idea for his upcoming mission: 'I remember thinking it might be worth a chuckle to mention finding a monolith during our *Apollo* flight.'

When Arthur heard this story he wished Bill Anders had followed through with his idea and has never quite forgiven him for not doing so.

At long last *2001* the novel was published. It had been a frustrating period for Arthur but that was over. Now he was having a wonderful time on the lecture circuit and promotion trail during the raging controversy over Stanley's movie. All the talk, of course, was about the film not the novel, but it helped sell copies.

'I always used to tell people, "Read the book, see the film and repeat the dose as often as necessary",' says Arthur.

Book reviewers were generally in favour of the novel, which was almost always seen in relation to the film.

The *New York Times* said that 'all of it becomes clear and convincing in the novel'. The *Washington Post* praised 'Clarke's conception [which] soars and takes you along, stretching your imagination as only good fiction can do'. The *Post* also said 'The book does something that the Stanley Kubrick movie cannot: it leaves the vision to your imagination – and an awesome vision it is.'

Physicist Freeman Dyson, of the Institute for Advanced Study in Princeton, liked the novel and urged others to read it. 'All the parts of the movie that are vague and unintelligible, especially the beginning and the end, become clear and convincing in the book. So I recommend to my middle-aged friends who find the movie bewildering that they should read the book; their teenage kids don't need to.'

The desire of befuddled fans to make sense of the film helped book sales. Many buyers agreed with Herbert Kenny of the *Boston Globe* who said that 'since the motion picture has its baffling moments, a perusal of the book will help, and indeed, the motion picture helps elucidate the book'.

During the novel's first year there were more than a million paperback copies in print. As a result, many of Arthur C. Clarke's other books enjoyed increased sales. During the following year, 1969, three more printings of *Childhood's End* were published. The name of Arthur C. Clarke became known to large numbers of people outside the science and science fiction communities. His reputation was now truly international.

2001, the film, was nominated for four Academy Awards, including best picture. The controversy surrounding the movie was good for the box office, but it didn't help win best-picture votes. The film received one Oscar – for special effects.

'It was a major breakthrough in motion picture production and technology – a good twenty years before its time,' says Roger Caras. 'Everything we've seen since with special effects was born in *2001*. No one dreamed that a film production could go to such heights of technical brilliance.'

Ray Lovejoy, Kubrick's editor on the film, emphasises *2001*'s influence on other film-makers: 'George Lucas was certainly inspired by *2001*. Lucas actually took an ad out somewhere when *Star Wars* first came out, when everyone was praising its special effects, which said that *2001* is still the champion of them all.

'I also did *Aliens* with Jim Cameron,' says Lovejoy, 'and *2001* is the reason Jim went into films. I've met a lot of American technicians who've said exactly that – that this film inspired them to follow the careers they did in the film industry. Many directors I've worked for

have said, "God, you know, *2001* is the reason why I started in films."
And there's a lot of credit to Arthur for that as well. It was his story,
after all.'

Arthur was bitterly disappointed that the Oscar for best screenplay
went to Mel Brooks' *The Producers*. He attended the award ceremonies at the Dorothy Chandler Pavilion in the spring of 1969. 'I
tore up one of the best speeches of thanks never delivered. When I ran
into Mel Brooks years later, I snarled: "Mel – you stole my Oscar."'
But Mel Brooks made the perfect reply, Arthur recalls. 'He said,
"You're a genius." That, of course, instantly put things right!'

How does Arthur C. Clarke view the *2001* phenomenon that boosted
his reputation worldwide and eventually brought tens of thousands
of readers to his other work?

His agent, Scott Meredith, puts it this way: 'Ginger Rogers has
made seventy-three pictures and nine of those pictures were with
Fred Astaire. She is so identified with the Astaire pictures that she
hates the very mention of them.

'You have the same situation with Arthur and *2001*. When I'm
interviewed, and they ask about famous clients, I mention Arthur
Clarke and they say, "Oh yes, the *2001* man." Well, of course he's a
lot more than that. It's easy to understand why *2001* isn't Arthur's
favourite book.'

'My favourite work, my best work, is *The Songs of Distant Earth*,'
said Arthur in 1989. '*2061: Odyssey Three* is much better than *2001* or
2010. *2001* is not a very good book. It was written entirely to make a
movie and was really nothing more than a glorified screenplay.'

Many of his millions of readers would disagree with him and
defend *2001*, the novel, as a worthy work in its own right.

What does Stanley Kubrick have to say about his one-time collaborator?

'As an artist,' says Kubrick, 'Arthur's ability to impart poignancy
to a dying ocean or an intelligent vapour is unique. He has the kind
of mind of which the world can never have enough, an array of
imagination, intelligence, knowledge and a quirkish curiosity which
often uncovers more than the first three qualities.'

CHAPTER 19

The Moon Age Begins

We could – with great expense and difficulty, it is true – reach the moon even with
today's technologies.
  – *The Exploration of the Moon* (1954)

They stood looking up at the stars and the
waxing Earth.
  – *Earthlight* (1955)

'When I published my first space novel [*Prelude to Space*] in the early
1950s, I very optimistically imagined a lunar landing in 1978,' says
Arthur Clarke. 'I didn't really believe it would be done so soon, but
I wanted to boost my morale by pretending that it might happen in
my own lifetime.'

Arthur was even more conservative in response to a survey taken
in 1953, when he was one of sixty-five scientists and writers who
were asked to predict the date for the first manned flight to the Moon
or another planet. His prediction for manned lunar flight was 1985.

'He never thought we would land a man on the Moon in the
sixties,' says Thomas Paine, NASA's Administrator during the historic flight of *Apollo 11*. Arthur didn't foresee the 'space race' between
the United States and Russia.

'There were two things that almost everybody missed,' says Paine.
'First, nobody foresaw the scale of the effort that would be required.
If you think back on the science fiction in the twenties, thirties and
forties, there was always an inventor who went out to his garage,
fiddled around with some gunks and goos, and miraculously invented
a propellant or an antigravity device so that he and the neighbour's
daughter could fly to the Moon in something he put together over
the weekend. It was always a very small-scale effort based on a highly
inventive breakthrough.

'On the contrary, space flight turned out to be a very large effort
that required a great deal of organisation and co-ordination of whole
industries and economies.

'The other thing that everybody missed, however (and I think the two are related), is the fact that by the 1960s two of the world economies – the Soviet Union and the United States – would be quite large enough to afford this at around one or two per cent of their gross national products. This and the fact that these nations decided to compete is what would propel us to the Moon.

'The hardest point for people today to realise when trying to predict the settlement of Mars in 2020 or so,' says Paine, 'is how enormous the world's gross national product is going to be by then.'

Four years had gone into the making of *2001*, the film and the book, during which time the US space programme, with its vast resources and pool of talent, had developed, built and tested the hardware that would fly men to the Moon.

In 1966 Arthur Clarke and two of his friends, Thomas Buck, an editor at *Look* magazine, and Thomas Craven, president of Thomas Craven Film Corporation, founded an organisation called Spaceward Corporation. Its purpose was to educate the public, primarily through television films but also through various related projects, about the benefits of space exploration and other inventive science programmes.

Their initial project was a ninety-minute film, *The Promise of Space*, which would lead into six other shorter complementary films concentrating on specific subjects such as health, communication and education – all of which were to be written by Arthur Clarke. The lead film would be adapted from Arthur's non-fiction book of the same title.

All three partners in Spaceward were actively seeking media and corporate backing for their proposed series of films. Arthur's frequent public speaking engagements and visits to aerospace corporations helped the cause. Eventually Spaceward gained some degree of support from more than a dozen aerospace corporations. This backing made it possible to produce the footage for the ninety-minute lead film, but in the end Spaceward failed to win the support of a major television network.

'*The Promise of Space* was dead in the water by the early seventies,' says Michael Craven, who now heads Thomas Craven Films. 'The networks controlled everything then. Independent film producers had little chance of selling their productions to the networks.'

Despite the earnest efforts of the three Spaceward partners, who put countless hours into the project, the film never reached the large audience for which it was intended.

★

Arthur passed up an invitation to witness the launch of *Apollo 8* at Christmas 1968. He wanted, and needed, to spend time at his home in Ceylon. He was very excited, however, about the historic first circumnavigation of the Moon by a manned spacecraft and eagerly followed it.

'I am sitting glued to the short-wave radio following the progress of *Apollo 8*,' he wrote Tom Craven. 'I wish I could have been in the States – it must have been a wonderful thing to watch on TV. Still, I will see the later and even more ambitious shots.' This was the beginning of the Moon Age, and Arthur C. Clarke's adopted island paradise did not yet receive television.

A local newspaper reporter interviewed Arthur, who saw yet another golden opportunity to educate the public. He turned on his radio, and 'Voice of America' came through loud and clear with *Apollo 8* mission coverage.

'How many people have powerful radios to pick up these transmissions?' Arthur asked the journalist. 'If not for this, I would be unable to sit in my garden, listen to the radio, look up into the sky and hear the voices of the astronauts speaking from outer space.'

And what of television? Arthur went on to say that television would come to the underdeveloped countries through communications satellites. A year later, in 1969, *Intelsat III* began service over the Indian Ocean region. This established the Earth's first global communication system, its messages travelling at the speed of light. The entire planet was finally served with just three satellites in geo-stationary orbit – the same system that Arthur C. Clarke had first envisioned in 1945.

'Television is of tremendous educational value for countries that lack experienced teachers, for a few good teachers could educate classes of millions through the medium of television. That is why I always stress that television *must* come to countries such as India and Ceylon.'

The journalist was left with a Clarkean vision of an evolving global communications network – mankind's nervous system, linking together the entire human race.

In late January Arthur played host to Jeremy Bernstein, the *New Yorker* science writer who had visited the centrifuge during the making of *2001*. He had come to Ceylon to do a profile on Arthur for the magazine. It was Arthur's opinion that Jeremy had gathered enough material for a whole book. The piece, entitled 'Profiles: Out of the Ego Chamber', appeared in the *New Yorker* in early August 1969, just weeks after the successful *Apollo 11* mission that landed men on the Moon. It was the most complete overview of Arthur's life and work that had yet appeared. Appropriately it honoured Clarke's decades-long vision at one of the great moments in history.

After completing his spring lecture tour in the US Arthur flew to Rio de Janeiro for a World Science Fiction Symposium and film festival.

Says Frederik Pohl, 'The sf Symposium was only an added afterthought to a major world film festival, and the city was full of superstars and starlets.' Among the writers there were Poul Anderson, Forry Ackermann, A. E. van Vogt, Bob Bloch, Brian Aldiss and J. G. Ballard. The film festival symposium was hosted by Brazil's Instituto Nacional do Cinema. Arthur arrived on 27 March 1969.

'Clarke seemed to have a bully good time there,' says Sam Moskowitz, historian, editor and long-time fan of science fiction. 'And why not? They were feeding him *and* feeding his ego.'

Among the international film notables present was the famous German director, Fritz Lang, whose 1929 film classic, *The Woman in the Moon* ('Die Frau im Mond'), invented the rocket countdown to create a dramatic plot device.

'The most vivid memory of Rio de Janeiro,' says Arthur, 'is meeting Fritz Lang. He was a very old man then and had a black eye patch. At school in the thirties, before I left for London, I used to arrange film shows. Fritz's *Metropolis* was one of those I remember screening.

'I'll tell you who else was there,' Arthur continues. 'George Pal. George Pal who made *Destination Moon, War of the Worlds* and all those great space films. That was the last time I saw dear old George.'

When Arthur gave a lecture on astronomy in Arizona in the first half of 1969 Gene Roddenberry, the creator of *Star Trek*, travelled from Los Angeles to hear him.

'That was an indication of my respect for him,' Gene said. 'I went there, just planning to be a member of the audience. I not only met this great man, but was persuaded by him to continue my *Star Trek* projects despite the entertainment industry's labelling the production an unbelievable concept and a failure. Arthur prophesied that when humans walked on the Moon it would cause a revolutionary change in attitudes toward space.'

Gene in large part credited Arthur with saving his career.

'At the time, I wasn't getting a lot of assignments because of the so-called failure of *Star Trek*. It was a case of develop a separate or additional income, or begin to lose my house and insurance policies. Arthur put me in touch with Bill Leigh [Clarke's lecture agent], and encouraged me to make use of the lecture platform.

'I visited the lecture bureau in New York City and Bill senior said, "Arthur tells me he thought it would be amusing if you recounted some of your adventures in television land." And, you know, I had the feeling that television was not something Leigh was close to. The feeling I got was, "If Arthur recommends you, of course we shall try to handle you."

'So I went out on my first lecture. Leigh, of course, had no way of knowing that the college students were really gung ho for *Star Trek*. Instead of a hundred people showing up, two thousand did! The auditorium was not large enough, and so I spoke a second time for those who couldn't get in the first time.

'I then began lecturing regularly,' said Roddenberry, 'and there was more money in it than the Leigh agency had predicted. This continued for a number of years, to steadily increasing audiences as *Star Trek* became more and more popular.

'Arthur has been very helpful to me in the *Star Trek* films I've done. He's backed me. When Paramount started to do a *Star Trek* film about religion and finding God in the galaxy, I wrote to Arthur. He in turn wrote to Paramount and said he thought it was nonsense. It's one thing for me to say something to Paramount, but when Arthur Clarke says it that's stronger.'

Gene Roddenberry's *Star Trek: The Next Generation* holds a distinct record.

'It's the first time a show has ever come back to television and been a success,' said Gene. 'And I give many thanks to Arthur for helping.'

CHAPTER 20

Man on the Moon

I still have in my mind the image of that
beautiful ship going up; and it's curious,
although it's three miles away it seems enormous . . . In my memory I can only see the
rocket filling the sky, although of course I
know it was only a fairly small visual image.
  – Arthur Clarke to Walter Cronkite,
              16 July 1969

There's an existential justice in the fact that Arthur C. Clarke helped
to cover the historic launch and Moon landing of *Apollo 11* for CBS
News. Arthur had been thinking seriously about going to the Moon
for more than a quarter of a century before the *Eagle* landed in the
Sea of Tranquillity on Sunday 20 July 1969. There was no other
place he could possibly have been than at Cape Kennedy when *Apollo
11* shook Florida's coast and blasted off to the Moon.

The CBS News coverage of the *Apollo 11* mission was an unprecedented forty-six hours over a period of eight days. An estimated half
a million people had come to view the launch of the great *Saturn V*
rocket. The press site, with some three thousand people, had never
been more crowded. Eventually it was estimated that six hundred
million people or more (one-sixth of the world's population at the
time) watched as *Apollo 11*'s lunar excursion module, the *Eagle*,
landed on the Moon's surface and its commander, Neil Armstrong,
later became the first human being to set foot in the powdery lunar
dust.

Lift-off of the gigantic *Saturn V* came at 9:32 EDT, Wednesday 16
July 1969. None of the hundreds of thousands of witnesses would
forget the deafening roar and the brilliant, all-but-blinding flame that
descended from the rocket as it climbed into the sky.

G. Harry Stine, a science adviser for CBS, was with Arthur during
the launch.

'We went outside,' Stine says. 'Just the two of us, and stood side by side in front of the CBS studio building, and we watched *Apollo 11* leave for the Moon. That was a thrill. Arthur didn't say anything; I didn't say anything. We watched it disappear in the sky and then went back to work. We were only outside for about a minute.'

Arthur remembers something else: at some point the tears started coming. 'I hadn't cried for twenty years. Afterwards I happened to run into Eric Sevareid, and he was crying too,' says Arthur.

Later, on camera, Walter Cronkite asked Arthur what he thought of the flight so far.

'Well,' said Arthur, 'it is one of the most thrilling things I've ever seen. I still have in my mind the image of that beautiful ship going up; and it's curious, although it's three miles away it seems enormous, it seems as though it's only a few hundred yards away. Where it rises the rest of the landscape vanishes. In my memory I can only see the rocket filling the sky, although of course I know it was only a fairly small visual image.'

Clarke went on to speculate about the near future, and what developments we might expect in the next ten years.

'We've got to see the development of reusable spacecraft,' he said, four years before the Space Shuttle programme was announced by President Nixon. 'I mean, spectacular and beautiful as the *Saturn V* is, it's a fantastic way of doing the job. It's like the *Queen Elizabeth* sailing with three passengers and sinking after the maiden voyage, except that the *Saturn V* costs more than the *Queen Elizabeth*. We've got to have spaceships we can use over and over again as often as we use a conventional airliner. The reusable space transporter is the next thing we have to get.'

About three hours after the launch, spaceship and crew were over Australia preparing to fire their third stage engines, which would thrust them out of their Earth orbit.

Commander Neil Armstrong verified a successful third stage firing shortly after noon. They had reached a velocity of 35,579 feet per second. Neil Armstrong, Buzz Aldrin and Michael Collins were curving towards their rendezvous with the Moon.

Sunday 20 July was the day the *Eagle* would set down on the lunar surface. CBS planned for thirty-two hours of continuous coverage, anchored in New York City's Studio 41 (the network's largest), and it included guests, remote interviews and simulations from all over the United States, and people's reaction to the historic event from all over the world.

The set design in Studio 41 was, some people opined, as far out as the event being covered. A painting of our Milky Way galaxy was the background behind Walter Cronkite's anchor desk, which was built twenty-four feet above the floor. Why so elevated? Because an important assistant, 'a second Hal' computer, was built below to help support the anchor with visuals. Dick Hoagland, science adviser to CBS, explains.

'We created a programmable, monstrous "electro-optical device". Walter and all the guests and consultants who participated were ultimately assisted by this system, which could be loaded with a variety of film clips and stills, all on motion picture film – exactly like the display screens in the original *Discovery* spaceship of *2001* . . . The thing was *huge*. The screens faced outward, directly under them [Walter and his guests], allowing the audience to see what was projected, mixed, inputted, et cetera, as background to the discussions occurring "up on top".

'Even if Arthur was aware of all this – the fact that he was broadcasting from the summit of a "semi-intelligent, multi-screen projection system" – I doubt whether he was ever made aware that this "Rube Goldberg device behemoth" was deliberately created in the image, and specifically named in honour, of his Hal.'

Before the Moon landing correspondent Harry Reasoner conducted a discussion in Studio 41 between Arthur C. Clarke and Kurt Vonnegut, Jr. Arthur was one of the foremost proponents of a manned space programme, and at every opportunity he vigorously defended the *Apollo* missions and future space exploration. Vonnegut, the so-called black humorist, took the opposing view, making the case that resources should be used to solve problems on planet Earth. Their exchange never got hostile.

Reasoner spoke of the many people who questioned the vast expenditures of the *Apollo* programme, and asked Clarke if he often faced this attitude.

'Yes,' Arthur replied. 'I'm always running into it. Of course, anything one does could be done better in some other way. If you build a school it means you can't build a hospital. There's always a question of priorities. But I think in the long run the money that's been put into the space programme is one of the best investments this country has ever made, because you're going to get back a so-called "spin-off" which NASA's always talking about, which is important but not as important as the real thing. This is a down payment on the future of mankind. It's as simple as that.'

'Well,' said Vonnegut, overlooking Arthur's last point, 'I've been interested in this "spin-off" for a long time. I've been led to believe that the ball of my ballpoint pen and Teflon were spin-offs. And now I find out that Teflon was a spin-off from World War II. So that only leaves the point on my ballpoint pen.'

The ballpoint pen, Arthur said, existed before the space programme, at least in its terrestrial version. He was right; it was patented in 1938 by Laszlo Biró, a Hungarian.

'But the real spin-offs are going to be largely in the next decade or so,' Arthur emphasised. 'Many of them haven't really come into use. But the spin-off is going to be more knowledge rather than hardware. The ability to do new things which we weren't able to do before. Because the space programme used such an enormous technology, it's going to really revolutionise life and make it much easier all over the world.'

That evening, Neil Armstrong and Buzz Aldrin landed on the Moon after a dramatic descent. A television camera broadcast live from the Moon's surface and captured the bouncing Moon walks and the deployment of experiments. Tens of millions of people from all over the planet were enthralled. Arthur C. Clarke was one of them. He had dreamed of this moment for most of his life.

'When the *Eagle* landed, I was sitting beside Walter and Wally,' Arthur recalls. 'I wasn't on camera at that moment. For me it was as if time had stopped.'

Later, during the Moon walk, Arthur noticed one of the studio technicians sitting in front of a TV monitor. The words 'Live from the Moon' ran across the bottom of the screen as the two ghostly figures went about their lunar explorations. What astonished Arthur, whose lifelong dream was playing out before his eyes, was that the technician was ignoring the historic events taking place on the monitor before him. 'He was reading the racing reports in the newspaper,' Arthur chuckles, 'during this live coverage from the Moon. I still have the photograph,' he says.

When the walk was over Cronkite discussed the future of space with Arthur and fellow writer Robert Heinlein.

When asked, Heinlein wouldn't predict any specifics of future space exploration, but he was convinced it would be done in a big way, going out to all the planets and eventually to the stars.

'We're going out indefinitely,' said Heinlein. 'There's just one equation that everybody knows: $E = MC^2$. It proves the potentiality whereby man can live anywhere where there is mass. He doesn't have to have any other requirement but mass, with the technology that we now have. And this human race will do so.'

Arthur agreed. He then went on to express once again his vision of global unity, his United Nations of the World, that he had been espousing and hoping for since the 1940s. 'And when they do go out, just as when they came to this country, they'll forget their original nationalities. We're going to see them going out into space as nations which will develop new ideas.'

The *Eagle* lifted off from Tranquillity Base in the early afternoon of 21 July. While the long rendezvous process took place between the *Eagle* and *Columbia* the CBS television audience was treated to a special film narrated by Orson Welles. Titled a *History of Space Journeys*, it included clips from a variety of films, such as a 1902 French movie version of *A Trip to the Moon* by Jules Verne; some footage from Fritz Lang's German film, *The Woman on the Moon* ['Die Frau im Mond']; clips from Buck Rogers and Flash Gordon films; and scenes from George Pal's *Destination Moon* and Kubrick's and Clarke's *2001: A Space Odyssey*.

The great and authoritative voice of Orson Welles concluded his narration: 'Now, the Moon has yielded, not merely to man's imagination, but to his actual presence. But for the science fiction writers and film-makers, there remain other challenges to pose to man.'

Walter Cronkite and Arthur Clarke, at the anchor desk, spoke about the short film they had just seen.

'It really is remarkable how close all of this came to reality,' said Cronkite. 'The only thing they didn't seem to contemplate was that the United Nations was going to be in the act, and we would have a space treaty. We wouldn't be claiming the Moon. But in a sense we did, in claiming it for all mankind, as opposed to claiming it for the United States itself.'

'I wrote about that trend twenty years ago,' Arthur said, 'in my first lunar landing novel [*Prelude to Space*]. I coined the phrase, "We shall take no frontiers into space." And I think that's the way it will be.'

Cronkite then asked Arthur what was next for science fiction writers. Would they still write space stories or would they write about earthbound concerns? Biological problems, for example.

'You know,' said Arthur, 'it's a fallacy to imagine, as some stupid people do, that because we've been to the Moon that's the end of science fiction. The more we discover about space, the more possibilities there are for really long-range, and yet soundly based science fiction . . . I'm looking forward to the next few years, when I absorb all this, to do my best science fiction.'

★

In mid-November 1969 Arthur returned to New York to participate in the CBS News coverage of *Apollo 12*, the second manned mission to the Moon. The *Intrepid* separated from *Yankee Clipper* and landed on the Moon's Ocean of Storms on 19 November. Pete Conrad and Al Bean worked on the Moon, while Dick Gordon watched over the mother ship in Moon orbit. A few months later they would be on a world tour together, and when they reached Ceylon and its beautiful tropical shores they would be regally entertained by Arthur C. Clarke.

A unique gathering took place at CBS during the *Apollo 12* coverage. Dick Hoagland remembers Walter Cronkite, Arthur Clarke, Wally Schirra, a scientist by the name of Paul Gast and himself together in the green room of Studio 41.

'Paul Gast was like an Arthur Clarke of the hard science world,' says Hoagland. 'He had little vials of real lunar material with him, and I remember we all stood in a circle, like a druid circle – Walter, Arthur, Wally, Gast and I – and we held these vials with ancient Moon soil in our palms, soil that was 3.8 billion years old and had been brought back from the Moon just a few months before on *Apollo 11*. We didn't need to say anything.'

CHAPTER 21

Jetting for the Future

What the railroads and the telegraph did here
a century ago, the jets and the communications satellites are doing now to all the
world.
　　　　　　　　－ State Department, August 1971

In the long run, the Comsat will be mightier
than the ICBM.
　　　　　　　　－ *The Promise of Space* (1968)

The UNESCO Space Communications Conference was held in Paris
in early December 1969, and Arthur flew over to attend and deliver
his speech 'Beyond Babel'. The speech was reprinted in *Report on
Planet Three and Other Speculations*, published in 1972 with the subtitle,
'The Century of the Communications Satellite'.

His address focused on the future of telecommunications, including
comsats, and forecast how they would affect the home, the city, the
state and the world. The tremendous potential of educational satellites
(edsats) and other types of applications satellites (weather, Earth
resources) was discussed. It was a positive vision of the future, ending
with Arthur's frequently expressed hope of unifying the peoples of
planet Earth through advanced communications systems. It was the
right message for the UNESCO conference and for the holiday
season.

The gruelling schedule Arthur had kept during the last months of
1969 wore him down, and he became ill upon his return to Ceylon.

'I had to check into the nursing home for several days,' he wrote
Tom Craven in mid-January, 'but there was nothing wrong with
me except the flu, and though I am still rather shaky I am slowly
recovering.'

Shaky or not, he began writing one of his favourite stories, 'Transit
of Earth', on 16 January which would be published for the first time
a year later in the January 1971 issue of *Playboy* magazine. It was

eventually reprinted in various collections, including his own short story collection, *The Wind from the Sun*.

The basis of this story was astronomical fact. In theory a person on Mars could actually observe the black disc of planet Earth moving across the face of the sun at certain future times. This was 'hard' science fiction, the type of story Arthur liked and for which he is so well known. He admitted that, even in his university days of applied mathematics, the prediction of such an astronomical event was beyond his powers of computation. He gave credit to Jean Meeus, a Belgian astronomer, who computed and predicted such a transit in a scientific paper published in 1962.

When the Salt Lake City Planetarium presented a dramatisation of 'Transit of Earth' a few years later, and pronounced it a success, Arthur was pleased. He always got a special kick when any of his work was produced in another medium.

The pace had quickened again by February 1970. A film crew from the Encyclopaedia Britannica arrived on the tenth and shot footage for an NBC special which EB was sponsoring. Arthur was host and narrator for the programme *The Unexplained*, which was broadcast in April.

Roger Caras and another film crew arrived in March, and Angus Wilson and J. B. Priestley and his wife came to stay early in the year. (It was Priestley who later wrote in his autobiography, 'I think Mr Clarke is the happiest writer I have ever met'.) Then the three *Apollo 12* crew members arrived.

Arthur was delighted to hear from the American Embassy that the astronauts were planning to extend their stay because of him. The fact that Arthur and Hector were planning to take them skin-diving in the beautiful coastal waters of north-east Ceylon no doubt influenced their decision.

As they were preparing to go down and explore an old wreck in Trincomalee Harbour, Arthur handed astronaut Alan Bean one of the underwater cameras.

'I begged him: "Alan – *please* don't point it at the sun."' Arthur was referring to the time on the Moon's surface when Alan accidentally pointed the TV camera at the sun, and it was destroyed and unusable for the entire mission.

The jest didn't fly. 'He did not seem much amused,' says Arthur.

Nonetheless, they had a wonderful time on the diving expedition. 'They liked it so much,' said Arthur, 'it was a job to get them back on the plane.'

★

A long list of commitments soon put Arthur back in the air to the United States. He lectured for three weeks in April, swinging through Arizona, California and Montana at the same time the *Apollo 13* mission was taking place. Arthur wrote that he was 'sick to have missed covering *Apollo 13* with CBS TV, but enormously relieved that they got back even without my help'.

At the end of April Arthur spent several days in New York at the Hotel Chelsea brainstorming with Alan Watts to produce an interview for *Playboy* magazine which was featured in the January 1971 issue, along with the story 'Transit of Earth', as 'At the Interface: Technology and Mysticism'.

They were, said the *Playboy* editor, 'to engage in a dialogue on man and his world'. After three days there was an over-abundance of dialogue generated on to magnetic tape that would be transcribed and shaped into the final piece.

'I have a long-standing bias against religion that may be reflected in my comments,' Arthur told Alan Watts near the beginning of their long dialogue. He could not forgive religions for the atrocities and wars over time, he said, focusing more on this subject than in other interviews.

Many people 'confuse religion with a belief in God', he went on. 'Buddhists don't necessarily believe in a god or a supreme being at all, whereas one could easily believe in a supreme being and not have any religion.' Elsewhere Arthur has said that any valid theology must await our contact with extra-terrestrial intelligences.

'Fundamentally, I'm an optimist and I believe that the future is not predetermined, that to some extent we can determine our own destiny. By thinking about the future and its possibilities, we do have a chance of averting the more disastrous one. This is why I believe that the interest in the future that is so common now is a good thing. There are suspect ways of looking at the future of course – astrology, divination, that sort of thing.'

It was a rather friendly exchange between Arthur and Alan. Arthur Clarke's concluding words were: 'The purpose of the Universe, Alan, is the perpetual astonishment of mankind.' To which Alan Watts responded, 'That's as likely as any other purpose I've ever heard about . . .'

April marked the publication of *First on the Moon*, the official book on the historic *Apollo 11* Moon mission. It's authorship was credited to the three astronauts, Armstrong, Aldrin and Collins, although much of the assembling of the text was left to Little, Brown editors. Arthur had been chosen to write the epilogue, 'Beyond *Apollo*', which he had done during the summer months of 1969. The epilogue closes with one of Arthur C. Clarke's most famous quotes, which is often repeated with slight variations:

> For it may be that the old astrologers had the truth exactly reversed, when they believed that the stars controlled the destinies of men.
> The time may come when men control the destinies of stars.

Dr Thomas O. Paine became the head of NASA in the spring of 1969, just months before *Apollo 11* landed on the Moon. After the missions of *Apollo 11*, *12* and *13* Paine organised a meeting in July 1970.

'President Nixon asked NASA to give some thought to where we would go after *Apollo*,' says Paine, 'and so I authorised a retreat at NASA's launch centre out on Wallop's Island. We got together about two or three dozen people who were carefully selected to be long-range, imaginative, creative thinkers.

'Arthur was invited because he had shown a remarkable ability over the years to identify what was going to be terribly important in the future.

'I have a nice picture of Arthur standing there with von Braun, George Mueller, Neil Armstrong and all the bright lights from NASA.'

Arthur remembers meeting Neil Armstrong for the first time.

'It was on the way to this NASA affair. I was boarding a private bus in Washington, and when I stepped into the bus I saw him. He was sitting quietly in the bus next to the NASA public relations man, on one of the aisle seats just ahead of me. I'm afraid I gaped like a schoolgirl seeing her favourite film star or rock idol . . . A slow, embarrassed smile spread across his face; and the senior NASA official sitting next to him, whom I'd completely ignored, said rather testily: "Hello, Arthur – I'm here as well!"'

Later during the conference Arthur asked Neil Armstrong about the controversial 'a' so many people had failed to hear in his historic words upon stepping on the Moon, 'That's one small step for *a* man, one giant leap for mankind.' Even Mission Control's audio recording had failed to pick up the *a*.

Neil's somewhat exasperated reply was, 'That's what I *intended* to say, and that's what I *thought* I said.'

Tokyo was host city for the International Science Fiction Symposium in 1970. Writer Frederik Pohl recalls who was there.

'I represented the US,' he says, 'Judy Merril Canada, Brian Aldiss England, and Arthur the world in general. There were also four Soviet writers – Yuli Kagarlitski, Eremy Parnov, Vasili Zacharchenko and I don't remember the other one's name – and, of course, several dozen Japanese ones.

'The Japanese arranged an evening event after we arrived, where all of us were expected to either give a little talk or perform in some way. We were invited to make fools of ourselves. It was an icebreaker and worked very well. I remember that Arthur did a sort of Polynesian dance for them.'

One of the Japanese present, a professor of physics and engineering, had designed a rocket train.

'We saw a film of this rocket train,' says Arthur, 'a very small scale model of it, and the thing took off the track and went flying in all directions. Brian Aldiss or I (I can't remember which) christened it the "Kamikaze Express". The inventor was a distinguished Japanese aeronautical engineer. I think he was the guy who designed the Zero – one of the famous wartime fighters.

'Anyway, I went around telling everybody this was the Kamikaze Express. To my great embarrassment, the next day this guy came up to me, pointed to me, and said, "Ha, ha, Kamikaze Express! Ha, ha, Kamikaze Express!" This was the inventor himself who had heard the name. He seemed quite amused, but I was embarrassed.'

'We were looked after by Japanese writers and translators,' says Brian Aldiss. 'Our chairman was an illustrious man by the name of Sakyo Komatsu. He's a very powerful man indeed in the circles in which he moves.

'On one occasion,' says Aldiss, 'we were taken to stay for the night at a hotel on Lake Biwako. Very, very pleasant. Everyone was relaxing after a rather hard day, and we persuaded Arthur to have a little dry sherry. And he seemed to be enjoying himself, but finally he looked at his watch and he said, "Well, it's ten o'clock and I have a golden rule, that at ten o'clock, no matter how good the company, I go to bed." And with that, he got up, said his good nights and went up to bed. And I couldn't help noticing that he had only half-finished his little dry sherry. I was interested to see that he only wanted a sip or two, of society as it were.'

In a December 1970 letter to friend and fellow writer Sam Youd, Arthur took inventory of his life. He told his friend how difficult it was becoming to leave his adopted homeland of Ceylon, 'despite political and economic problems here'. Arthur went on:

Besides this house (where I have a library – all my books, at last – cameras, telescope, computer, I have a very nice brand new place on an unbelievably beautiful bay seventy miles S with a coral reef outside the front door . . .

I guess I am lucky – everything of mine is in print, except the very early non-fiction space books, which have been absorbed by later editions. The fiction goes on for ever. Even my 1947 *Prelude to Space* has just come out with a post-*Apollo* preface, encapsulating it like Jules Verne. This is one of the reasons I'm writing no more non-fiction . . . at least for a few years.

I could have retired years ago if I was content to live reasonably and not commute round the world twice a year. I have to get out of Ceylon six months in the year as the tax situation is impossible – there's no treaty with the US or UK. I can't pay tax in *three* countries . . . hence my mobility. Anyway, I like lecturing, and since *2001* I've become a minor cult hero on campus.

As 1970 came to a close, Arthur was hard at work on what he called 'the new *2001* book'. This would become *The Lost Worlds of 2001*, a miscellany, really, including out-takes from the novel *2001*, assorted entries of the period from his journal, and several short introductions to the material. The book was Scott Meredith's idea, and Arthur certainly approved. It would give new life to the cut text he had once laboured over.

Gore Vidal, the American novelist, was Arthur's first visitor in the New Year. On 6 January 1971 they lunched with the American Ambassador, Dr Strauz-Huppe. The next day he and Hector took Vidal and some other friends to the south coast and showed them their base for diving operations at Unawatuna, near Galle.

'We were driving down the main road going south, and there was a Ceylon Transport Board bus in front of us. Suddenly the entire back axle and differential came out and started cartwheeling down the road toward us, like a drum majorette's baton. And it came to rest only a few feet ahead of the car. An extraordinary thing. Luckily no one got hurt.' Arthur jokingly admitted afterward: 'As a hundred kilograms of metal bounced closer and closer, I unselfishly prayed that the world of letters would not sustain a major loss.'

Later in January Arthur began to write his rather long short story 'A Meeting with Medusa', which first appeared in *Playboy* in December 1971. It would go on to win a *Playboy* editorial award as well as the Nebula award from the Science Fiction Writers of

Above An audience with the Pope, October 1984.

Below Meeting with Prime Minister Rajiv Gandhi before delivering his Jawaharlal Nehru Memorial Lecture in India, November 1986.

At the Hollywood première of the film *2010*, December 1984. *Left to right*: director Peter Hyams, Arthur, Ray Bradbury and Gene Roddenberry.

Ready to greet the Queen and receive his honour: Commander of the British Empire. Buckingham Palace, October 1989.

Meeting Queen Elizabeth and Prince Philip at the British High Commissioner's Residence in Colombo, Sri Lanka, in the early 1980s.

America. It was written for one reason, Arthur confesses. 'Over the previous decade I had accumulated some fifty thousand words of short stories, and needed another fifteen thousand to make up a complete volume.'

The Wind from the Sun, published in 1972, became that volume and 'A Meeting with Medusa' was the final story.

'Medusa was', says Arthur, 'the last story I ever wrote before concentrating entirely on novels.'

His beloved tropical island, still officially known as Ceylon in 1971, had a political crisis when Arthur was on a spring lecture tour in the United States. On 4 April several thousand insurgents attempted to take over the country. This was at a time when the 'island of thirteen million people appeared reasonably contented under a government which had been elected by a large majority', Arthur wrote later. The well-trained insurgent force attacked many of the provincial police stations and easily overwhelmed them. Arms and ammunition were stolen, and the rebels continued their fight and were able to control some rural areas for short periods.

While there had been some signs of unrest, the government was caught off guard. 'It appealed for help – which promptly started to arrive from a remarkable variety of sources,' wrote Arthur. 'The countries which rushed to the aid of Ceylon included the United Kingdom, the United States, India *and* Pakistan, the United Arab Republic, Yugoslavia – and China. Ceylon is a land without enemies; however, she frequently exasperates her friends.'

Within a few weeks the insurrection was put down and the bitter fighting ended. Fifteen thousand rebels and suspects were rounded up and put in prison camps, eventually to be released. Those identified as leaders, though, were brought to trial.

'Most of them appear to have been young idealists and left-wing extremists, dissatisfied with the progress that the government they had helped to elect had made towards solving its social problems,' he wrote later. The country had more or less returned to normal by the end of 1971, but periodic problems and bloodshed have continued.

While Arthur was in California on the western leg of his lecture tour he visited his old friends, Bob and Ginny Heinlein. He also stopped at the North American Rockwell plant and saw the mock-ups of the space shuttle and an early design version of a space station.

Shortly after, Arthur wrote a letter to the editor of the *New York Times* and it was printed under the heading 'Space Shuttle: Key to

Future' on 22 May 1971. After stating that 'many of the solutions of our present social and environmental problems lie partly in space', and citing the tremendous benefits of an educational satellite project in India, Arthur brought forth the example of the $50 million Orbiting Astronomical Observatory which failed soon after it reached orbit because of a minor circuit defect.

'A man with a screwdriver might have been able to fix it,' Arthur wrote to the editor, anticipating the first satellite repair in orbit by more than twelve years. 'As our applications satellites become larger and more complex, space shuttles will be essential not only to orbit them, but to carry the technicians who must check, service and repair them.' Arthur Clarke went on record and cast his vote for the space shuttle about half a year before President Nixon announced that the nation and NASA would proceed with the shuttle programme.

Arthur went to New York to cover the *Apollo 15* mission with Walter Cronkite on 30 and 31 July – the two days during which astronauts Dave Scott and Jim Irwin landed the lunar module *Falcon* on the Moon and explored its surface. It was the first time a lunar roving vehicle was used. The vehicle allowed them to cover seventeen miles on the Moon's surface during their stay. One of the craters they drove past they named 'Earthlight' after Arthur's 1955 novel.

This was the longest *Apollo* mission to date, more than twelve days, and Arthur flew to Houston and the Johnson Space Center for the splashdown coverage. He got the complete VIP tour of the facilities when he was there, including mission control and various training facilities, and had dinner with astronauts Joe Allen and Phil Chapman.

Allen was a long-time fan of Clarke's and had read several of his books as a youth. More than once he acknowledged that Arthur had had a major influence on his decision to become an astronaut. 'When I was a boy,' Allen wrote to Clarke, 'you infected me with both the writing bug *and* the space bug but neglected to tell me how difficult either undertaking can be.'

In August 1971 Arthur was guest speaker at a US Department of State affair, hosted by Secretary of State William Rogers. Another prominent guest was former First Lady Mamie Eisenhower. The first voice ever beamed to Earth from a communications satellite was that of her husband, President Dwight Eisenhower, in December 1958.

'We are here,' said Secretary Rogers, 'to sign a constitutional instrument, a permanent charter, for man's first international co-operative effort in space. I doubt that even the most optimistic of prophets, even Arthur C. Clarke, would have predicted in August 1964 that on this seventh anniversary of the establishment of the international arrangements for Intelsat, we would be gathered here to sign the definitive arrangements for an organisation of eighty nations, an organisation which already has in being global satellite systems interconnecting people on six continents.'

This agreement created an international partnership in telecommunications and brought Arthur Clarke's dream of a united family of man one step closer to reality.

'Do we have the imagination and the statesmanship to use this new tool for the benefit of all mankind?' Arthur asked the audience gathered at the Department of State. 'Or will it be used merely to peddle detergents and propaganda?

'I am an optimist; anyone interested in the future has to be. I believe that communications satellites can unite mankind. Let me remind you that, whatever the history books say, this great country was created a little more than a hundred years ago by two inventions. Without them, the United States was impossible; with them, it was inevitable. Those inventions, of course, were the railroad and the electric telegraph.

'Today, we are seeing, on a global scale, an almost exact parallel to that situation. What the railroads and the telegraph did here a century ago, the jets and the communications satellites are doing now to all the world.

'I hope you will remember this analogy in the years ahead. For today, whether you intend it or not, whether you wish it or not – you have signed far more than just another intergovernmental agreement.

'You have just signed a first draft of the Articles of Federation of the United States of Earth.'

As the *Mariner 9* spacecraft neared its encounter with Mars on 12 November 1971, Arthur was en route to the Jet Propulsion Laboratory in Pasadena, California, to participate in a conference. There he would join his old friends, Ray Bradbury, Carl Sagan, Bruce Murray and Walter Sullivan to discuss Mars on the historic occasion of the *Mariner 9* encounter. The fact that a planetwide dust storm obscured the surface of Mars as the robot spacecraft approached left plenty of room for the imagination in the JPL discussions.

Walter Sullivan of the *New York Times* was moderator, and he introduced everyone, including Arthur, who began by paying tribute to early science fiction writers like Edgar Rice Burroughs, Stanley G. Weinbaum, Percival Lowell and H. G. Wells, all of whom contributed to the myth of Mars.

'It was Edgar Rice Burroughs who turned me on,' says Arthur, 'and I think he is a much *underrated* writer.' He went on to make some comments about Lowell, the man who believed that Mars had a sophisticated network of canals, and got a lot of other people to believe it too. Arthur referred to Lowell as 'our Boston brahmin'.

'Whatever we can say about Lowell's observational abilities, we can't deny his propagandistic power, and I think he deserves credit at least for keeping the idea of planetary astronomy alive and active during a period when perhaps it might have been neglected.'

Arthur then told the audience about his recent visit to Lowell Observatory and how he'd actually looked through Lowell's twenty-six-inch telescope. 'He's buried right beside it; his tomb is in the shape of the observatory,' he said. 'Whatever nonsense he wrote, I hope that one day we will name something on Mars after him.'

Arthur would make no predictions about the real Mars that *Mariner 9* would reveal once the vast dust storm abated. What was important to remember, he said, was that 'the frontier of our knowledge is moving inevitably outwards.

'We're discovering, and this is a big surprise, that the Moon, and I believe Mars, and parts of Mercury, and especially space itself, are essentially benign environments – to our technology, not necessarily to organic life. Certainly benign as compared with the Antarctic or the oceanic abyss, where we have already been. This is an idea which the public still hasn't got yet, but it's a fact.

'I think the biological frontier may very well move past Mars out to Jupiter, which I think is where the action is. Carl [Sagan], you've gone on record as saying that Jupiter may be a more hospitable home for life than any other place, *including* Earth itself. It would be very exciting if this turns out to be true.

'I will end by making one prediction. Whether or not there is life on Mars now, there will be by the end of this century.'

Ray Bradbury remembers the conference. 'Every single person there had had his life changed by Burroughs,' says Ray. 'We all discovered that we had grown up on Edgar Rice Burroughs. The chemistry between Walter Sullivan and Arthur and Carl Sagan and myself, and Bruce Murray (who was then head of the Jet Propulsion Lab) was so wonderful that at the end of a day of talks and lectures and what-have-you, it all fell together. Somebody said, "By God, we've got a book here." It was so fabulous,' says Ray, 'that it turned into a book.'

Besides the transcript of the discussion, the participants added their more considered thoughts a year later, after the dust storm had subsided and the cameras of *Mariner 9* sent back images of the real Mars with all its wonders. The book, *Mars and the Mind of Man*, was published two years later in the summer of 1973.

CHAPTER 22

Set of the Sails

> The dreams of childhood had been far sur-
> passed by the reality of adult life.
> — *The Fountains of Paradise*

The ever-growing corpus of Clarke's work gained momentum in
1972, and four new books were published – three fiction and one
non-fiction.

A sixth volume of short stories, *The Wind from the Sun*, was released
early in the year, the first such collection to come out since 1967. It
contained eighteen stories, all written in the 1960s. In the preface
Arthur told his readers, 'I was tempted to give it the subtitle "The
Last of Clarke" – not through any intimations of mortality (I have
every intention of seeing what *really* happens in the year 2001), but
because I seem to be doing less and less writing, and more and more
talking, travelling, filming and skin-diving.'

A collection of non-fiction pieces was also issued in the first half
of 1972. *Report on Planet Three and Other Speculations* included work
mostly from the 1950s and 1960s, as well as some reprinted speeches.

Victor Gollancz, Clarke's British publisher, issued another collection of short stories late in the year: *Of Time and Stars: The Worlds of
Arthur C. Clarke*. The volume was distinguished by a J. B. Priestley
introduction and included several early classic stories such as 'The
Sentinel', 'The Fires Within' and 'The Nine Billion Names of God'.

'From the first he seems to have fallen in love with space,' wrote
Priestley in the introduction, 'and as soon as I met him I was aware
of his genuine tremendous enthusiasm. (He is also a great gadget
man, and if a robot had served lunch I would hardly have been
surprised.) It must be this enthusiasm that gives him such an astonishing air of youth, suggesting a man in his thirties and not already in
his middle fifties.'

Priestley dropped the age down even more when he wrote about
his visit to Ceylon and described Arthur as a man with the 'heart and

mind of a boy of sixteen'. When Sam Youd quoted this, Arthur quipped, 'Actually, nineteen is nearer my mark.'

The fourth collection published in 1972 was *The Lost Worlds of 2001*, which brought together all the chapters or segments that had been cut from the novel *2001*.

In February 1972 Arthur spent two weeks in India at a conference on communication satellites in Ahmadabad. A month later, on 14 March, he spoke before a Goddard dinner audience in Washington, DC. The title of his address was 'The Last Revolution', and he mentioned his trip to India.

'I was standing on a lonely hilltop in Ahmadabad, beneath the sixty-foot dish of the Experimental Satellite Ground Station – a quarter of a second, via synchronous orbit, from Calcutta and all other cities of India,' Arthur told his audience. 'As I am sure you know, in 1974 the satellite ATS-F will be parked over the subcontinent for one year, and for the first time it will be possible to televise information on health, improved agriculture, family planning, into the remotest villages, to millions who can neither read nor write.'

Satellite communications were rapidly changing the world, Arthur explained. 'The TV coverage of President Nixon's China trip was in some ways as significant as the visit itself. It marked the crumbling of the last communications barrier on this Earth. The wiring of the global electronic village is now complete.

'But not all the fittings are yet installed,' he went on. 'When they are, the world will be changed beyond recognition. How many of us can remember the age before the coming of radio? Already, it is hard to recall life without television. Yet the changes wrought by radio and TV are trivial compared to those that are coming. This fact is so overwhelmingly obvious that it is almost impossible to grasp it.'

Arthur C. Clarke, born to a post office family, was the messenger for the future.

In early autumn Arthur was back in Ceylon putting the finishing touches to a new novel, *Rendezvous with Rama*.

'I am working flat out on polishing the novel,' he wrote Tom Craven on 7 September, 'which is a huge job – though now merely a matter of time since all the problems are solved.'

Three months later, on 19 December 1972 the last men to visit the Moon in the twentieth century returned home to planet Earth. As the three *Apollo 17* astronauts, Eugene Cernan, Ronald Evans and Harrison Schmitt splashed down in the Pacific, one of humanity's most daring adventures was coming to an end. The great *Apollo* voyages to the Moon were over.

Post-*Apollo* apathy reigned supreme, signalling the abrupt US retreat from the Moon. For most people the thrill and drama of *Apollo 11* could never be repeated, and a ho-hum attitude was common for most space missions, manned and unmanned. Few people recognised that a vigorous space programme was a powerful and important driver of cutting-edge technology that would benefit all sectors of the economy.

Arthur left Ceylon in late February 1973 and spent a week in London before flying to New York on 7 March. The following week he went to Washington to give a lecture at the Smithsonian.

This lecture, 'Technology and the Limits of Knowledge', was the last in a series sponsored by the Smithsonian Institution's National Museum of History and Technology. The overall theme of the series was 'Technology and the Frontiers of Knowledge'. The lectures were arranged in honour of Frank Nelson Doubleday to celebrate the seventy-fifth anniversary of the publishing company he founded, and they were published in the US by Doubleday & Company as *The Frontiers of Knowledge* in 1975.

The other four speakers in the series were Saul Bellow, Daniel Bell, Edmundo O'Gorman and Sir Peter Medawar. Because the lectures were spread out over a year, the five men were not together to exchange views. And it was only later, when Arthur read the others' speeches, that he learned that Saul Bellow had publicly taken a poke at him.

Bellow, in his lecture, 'Literature in the Age of Technology', took exception to a passage in one of Arthur's essays, 'The Mind of the Machine', which appeared in *Report from Planet Three*. He quotes Clarke, out of context from an admittedly speculative essay, a portion of which concerns itself with the possibility of intelligent machines creating art.

> It has often been suggested that art is a compensation for the deficiencies of the real world; as our knowledge, our power and above all our maturity increase, we will have less and less need for it. If this is true, the ultra-intelligent machine would have no use for it at all.
>
> Even if art turns out to be a dead end, there still remains science . . .

Bellow should have quoted the rest of Arthur's sentence: '. . . there still remains science – the eternal quest for knowledge, which has

brought man to the point where he has created his own successor.'
Wrote Bellow:

This statement by a spokesman of the 'victorious' party is for several reasons extraordinarily silly. First it assumes that art belongs to the childhood of mankind, and that science is identical with maturity. Second, it thinks art is born in weakness and fear. Third, in its happy worship of 'ultra-intelligent' machines, it expresses a marvellous confidence in the ability of such machines to overcome all the deficiencies of the real world. Such optimistic rationalism is charming, in a way . . .

Bellow associated Clarke with a group of 'power-minded theoreticians', and ascribed to him 'the confidence of the great simplifier'. The novelist then goes on to put hypothetical words in Clarke's mouth.

'Mr Clarke says in effect, "Don't worry, dear Pals, if art is a dead end, we still have science . . . Thinking machines will give us all the wisdom and joy we want, in our maturity."'

But of course Arthur didn't say that at all. His essay was designed to get readers thinking. For whatever reason (perhaps for purposes of debate), Saul Bellow was over-reacting, and Arthur did not bother to make a move in his own defence. Of course, he couldn't have done so: he wasn't there when Bellow presented his lecture, and vice versa.

When 'Technology and the Limits of Knowledge' was reprinted in *The View from Serendip* in 1978, he at last referred to Bellow's criticism:

'I count it as a noble (and possibly unique) example of my self-restraint that, though I had the last word [his lecture came after Bellow's], I refrained from comment.

'And still do.'

One long-time admirer of Arthur C. Clarke was in the audience to hear his Smithsonian lecture. His name was Joseph P. Allen, NASA astronaut, who would later fly as a mission specialist on the first operational flight of the space shuttle (after four orbital test missions) in November 1982. This mission on *Columbia* would deploy the first commercial satellite in the shuttle programme.

Allen wrote Arthur a letter of appreciation, telling him that of all the lectures he had heard he had 'enjoyed none more than the one which you delivered for the Smithsonian Institute in March.

'You put into words the thoughts and ideas which I flirt with on occasion, but am never quite able to pin down in such an efficient and straightforward way. Thank goodness you devote some of your energies to helping the scientists and technologists themselves, not to mention everyone else, understand better what they are about.'

Another example of helping people understand was the April 1973 publication of *Beyond Jupiter: The Worlds of Tomorrow*. This beautifully illustrated book was in the tradition of the classic *Conquest of Space*, published in 1949, which presented the unique space art of Chesley Bonestell and the text of rocket expert and science writer Willy Ley. In *Beyond Jupiter*, Arthur Clarke and Chesley Bonestell combined their words and artwork to describe the historic voyages of *Pioneers 10* and *11* to the outer planets *before* the spacecraft made their planetary encounters. In the book's concluding paragraphs, Arthur wrote about these first interstellar robots, saying, 'We should build them well, for one day they may be the only evidence that the human race ever existed.'

In April Arthur flew to St Thomas in the Virgin Islands to join Dr George Mueller, NASA's Administrator for Manned Space Flight at the time, and other NASA managers and members of the Sea-Space Society to participate in a Society conference. There was no way Arthur C. Clarke would miss a meeting which focused on the two major interests in his life – sea and space – especially when the sea was there for him to enjoy.

And he did – until the accident. Arthur was snorkelling with Mueller and about fifteen others off the island of St Thomas.

'I was down around ninety feet,' recalls Mueller. 'And Arthur came swimming down, free-diving, waved to me and then leisurely swam up to the surface. It was about that time that one of my buddies saw he was in trouble and went to help him.'

Arthur had been diving all morning, going down, joining the other divers and then going up again to get a breath of air. During one dive in the afternoon, Arthur remembers taking a photo with his underwater camera of several divers swimming over a wreck below him.

'That was very nearly the last photo I ever took,' he says. 'And I remember saying, "That's enough for today; this will be my last dive." Which it almost was.

'It was a beautiful calm day, lovely day, clear water. I went down. Then on the way up, within ten feet of the surface, I suddenly got vertigo, spinning around in the water, absolutely helpless. My inner ear had gone.

'I had a life jacket, but I couldn't find the ripcord. And then I thought I should try to inflate it, but of course that was ridiculous because I was out of breath. And then I could just feel the beginning of panic; luckily I didn't get there. I hit the quick-release button on the weighted belt, which fell off, and then I popped up instantly to the surface. There were a couple of guys on a life raft only a few yards away. They got me on to the raft, then back to land, and they rushed me to the hospital. It was the narrowest escape I ever had.'

George Mueller swam over to help the two already helping Arthur. 'We finally got him back on board, but he was unable to move. He had to be carried because the vertigo was so bad. We took him into the local hospital and he stayed there overnight. The next morning there wasn't any apparent problem, and so we got him on an airplane and sent him off to New York.'

Once again, the sea had spared Arthur C. Clarke.

Arthur returned to Sri Lanka for most of May, but was back in London on the twenty-seventh and attended a performance of *Messiah* at the Alexandra Palace. Later he flew to New York and then to Acapulco, Mexico, to give a lecture at an IBM convention in early June.

'IBM invited me to spend a week with several hundred of its executives, and my old friends Betsy and Walter Cronkite, at the magnificent Acapulco Princess Hotel, and I was happy to accept. I can also claim to have been the only person to attend an IBM banquet wearing a sarong, which is *male* attire in Sri Lanka.'

Because the Princess Hotel was Howard Hughes' last home, Arthur has always wondered whether the famous recluse was actually in the same building during the gathering.

For recreation, he tried some paragliding over the Pacific. 'I went up a hundred metres or so, towed not by a boat but by a jeep on the sand! My most vivid recollection was the discomfort when I hit the ground again – the sand was red hot. But it was great fun, and I'd like to do it again.'

Later Arthur arranged to have the parachute equipment sent to Ceylon. 'People there will be simply amazed!' he said.

On 23 June Clarke boarded the *Cunard Adventurer* at the New York docks and set sail to the Caribbean on a special cruise to see the total eclipse of the sun. Isaac Asimov was aboard its sister ship, the *Canberra*, which was also sailing to see the eclipse, but from a location off the coast of Africa. Before their ships sailed, Arthur met Isaac on board the *Canberra*.

The *Cunard Adventurer* had a full educational programme and various scientific activities planned for two weeks. There were 550 passengers to learn and to see the eclipse. Wally Schirra and Rusty Schweickart were the two astronauts on board, and there were another dozen experts in the various sciences to give lectures. Arthur gave two, each of which had two parts: 'Life in the Year 2001', Parts I and II, and 'The Promise of Space', Parts I and II.

Kerry O'Quinn, programme director for the cruise, later to become publisher of *Starlog* magazine, remembers hearing Arthur give his first lecture.

'I stood in the back of the large cabaret theatre (converted into a lecture hall),' says O'Quinn, 'and listened as he told an entranced audience his predictions – how communications satellites would bring wonders to the underdeveloped peoples of our planet. He spoke of children in remote parts of India and Africa seeing television for the first time and having their minds fired with curiosity and new possibilities. He spoke of electronic education putting an end to illiteracy, to hunger and even to war. He spoke of hope for the future through science and reason.

'As I stood there and listened, his words touched me profoundly. I heard the thinking of one of the great minds of our century, and I found myself infused with admiration and inspiration.

'I also found myself crying,' O'Quinn says, 'it was such an emotional experience.

'Afterwards I went and had a talk with him and told him that he had brought me to tears. From then on instead of being Mr Clarke, he was Arthur. From that moment on we became soul mates.

'We also had a full movie programme,' says O'Quinn, 'and ran different films every day – mainly science fiction films. Of course we had scheduled several screenings of *2001*, and Arthur would get up on stage and do an introduction to the movie and then answer questions. But he didn't want to talk about the meaning of *2001*. He'd often say something like "Read the book and find out." The film was five years old, and it had a cult following. A lot of the passengers were sort of scientific hippies, and great fans of *2001* and Arthur.'

Kerry O'Quinn remembers one evening when astronaut Wally Schirra and Arthur were sitting at the same table.

'Unknown to us,' he says, 'the two of them were either the world's best or worst punsters. The entire dining room would hear either gales of laughter or loud groans periodically coming from that table. This was a personal contest between Arthur and Wally as to who could make the worst pun.'

The *Adventurer* found clear weather in the Atlantic for the eclipse on 30 June.

'It was a wonderful eclipse,' says O'Quinn. 'It was one of the longest ones possible on Earth – almost seven minutes at its maximum off the coast of Africa. For the *Adventurer*'s location in the Caribbean it was not at its maximum duration, but was more like five minutes long.

'Arthur and I watched it together from the bridge. The Captain tried to stabilise the ship against rocking and tripods, cameras and telescopes covered the decks. We arranged to pass out special glasses for people to view the eclipse and Arthur had brought along some eye patches which he passed out to those of us who were on the bridge. This way we could watch the partial phases, but the one eye with the patch would already be night-adjusted when totality began, just after the bright flash of the diamond ring effect occurs and before the sun's corona suddenly appears and shines out in all directions around the black disc of the Moon. Then, when totality began, you would put the patch over the other eye and let it become night-adjusted.

'It's one of the most spectacular celestial events the solar system offers,' says O'Quinn. 'And there was very much a feeling of love and companionship among all the people on board the ship. A kind of bonding takes place when you share a rare experience like this.'

The cruise ended in San Juan, Puerto Rico, on 4 July. Before Arthur returned to New York he visited the huge radio-radar telescope at Arecibo, whose great antenna dish has made so many important discoveries and has been used in the search for extra-terrestrial life. After the telescope's dish received a new surface a year later a powerful radio transmission was beamed toward one of the densely packed globular clusters in our galaxy, some twenty-five thousand light years away. It is possible that a reply may come in AD 51,974.

Alice Turner, then at *Publishers Weekly* and later the editor at *Playboy* who bought some of Arthur's stories, interviewed Arthur while he was in New York. *Rendezvous with Rama*, his first novel for ten years, had recently been published (by Harcourt, Brace, Jovanovich in the US and Gollancz in the UK) and was receiving excellent reviews. Turner wanted to talk to him about that and his love of science fiction. Arthur was, as always, articulate and cogent.

Science fiction is often called escapism – always in a negative sense. Of course it's not true. Science fiction is virtually the only kind of writing that's dealing with the real problems and possibilities; it's a concerned fiction. It's the mainstream that escapes from these things into small anxieties – away from fact, away from things that threaten or enrich our lives.

It's hard to define science fiction these days, especially since the mainstream seems to be moving in that direction. Traditionally, it's been a form that offered a good story, and I suppose you could call that escapism, in a positive sense. C. S. Lewis, who wrote it himself, said, 'The only people who think there's something wrong with escapism are jailers.'

And what of the current state of science fiction? Turner asked Arthur.

We know so much more now that we don't have to waste time on the petty things of the past. We can use the enormous technological advances in our work. Vision is wider now, and interest has never been deeper.

Rendezvous with Rama was an example of this wider vision. The book won virtually all of science fiction's most important awards in 1973 – the Hugo, Nebula, John W. Campbell and Jupiter Awards for the best novel of the year.

There were accolades galore, including compliments from other big names in the field of science fiction. Isaac Asimov, Robert Heinlein, and Frank Herbert all had praise for the novel. And John Leonard of the *New York Times* judged *Rama* as 'story-telling of the highest order' and praised its 'sense of wonder and breathless suspense'. Continued Leonard, 'Mr Clarke is splendid. As a superior intelligence spins a strange spider-culture out of its bowels, we experience that chilling touch of the alien, the not-quite-knowable, that distinguishes sf at its most technically imaginative.'

Julian Muller, the editor at Harcourt, Brace, Jovanovich, remembers receiving the manuscript.

'It was one of the most intriguing books I had ever dealt with. Arthur's invention in terms of plotting was so extraordinary. And there's almost an explosion of invention in *Rama*. Just the capacity to be able to create that world – it staggers me to think that anyone could. Arthur not only created that kind of image in his own mind, but he was able to articulate it brilliantly.'

Muller recalls that the novel's last line caused a stir: '*The Ramans do everything in threes.*'

'It provoked an enormous amount of mail and much discussion around publishing circles because it obviously suggested a trilogy.

And when I spoke to Arthur about it, Arthur said, "No, it just seemed like a good way to end it. I had no intention of doing a trilogy."'

When *Rama II* was published sixteen years later there was good reason to believe that Arthur's intention had changed.

Before leaving New York, Arthur visited Kurt Vonnegut and his wife-to-be, Jill Krementz. No doubt Kurt's short story 'The Big Space Fuck', published in 1972 in *Again, Dangerous Visions*, edited by Harlan Ellison, was mentioned during their lunch. In the story Arthur received a rather dubious honour. Wrote Vonnegut, 'The ship was named the *Arthur C. Clarke*, in honour of a famous space pioneer.' The spaceship's mission was to impregnate the universe by carrying eight hundred pounds of freeze-dried jism to the Andromeda Galaxy. The mission was 'to make sure that human life would continue to exist somewhere in the universe'.

CHAPTER 23

From Sri Lanka to Titan

> I have always been more interested in the spectacular possibilities of the distant future, and not the practical problems of the day after tomorrow . . . If you take me *too* seriously, you'll go broke – but if you don't take me seriously *enough*, your children will go broke.
>
> – US Congress, Committee on Space
> Science, July 1975

'It will be hell for a few weeks,' Arthur wrote to Tom Craven on 18 November 1973. 'Right in the midst of the moving to the new house now.' A couple of weeks later, Arthur gave Craven an update.

'We have moved and have been cut off from the outside world for two weeks. The house is huge and we are still finding our way around, as well as unpacking fifteen years' junk. To complicate matters we had to fire a houseboy this morning (so we're struggling along on four – you'll weep for us) and we've just had a cable saying that Hector's German girlfriend's mother arrives from Munich in two hours, not tomorrow as expected . . .'

Hector's youngest brother, Leslie Ekanayake, was a tremendous help in bringing order to chaos at Barnes Place, and he eventually went on to manage the large household – no small feat for a young man of twenty-six. Over time Arthur developed a fatherly affection for Leslie.

The new house in Barnes Place in Colombo was bought from Lady de Soysa, the mother of the Bishop of Colombo; it was, in fact, the Anglican Bishop's residence. Quite a change from the much smaller house in Gregory's Road.

A few days before Christmas Arthur, Hector, his youngest brother Leslie and the hired help were still trying to bring order to their new home.

'Fighting to get the mansion operational – there are about three

258

sets of workmen here at any given time, but at least the elevator is working and water flows intermittently. We had our first dinner party here a couple of nights ago – my guests were Bill McQuitty, who made *A Night to Remember* and several other good films, and his family.'

As 1973 came to a close, and Arthur and company were settling in to the new, spacious home, the *Skylab 4* crew continued to orbit overhead in much smaller quarters. There was a *real* space station above planet Earth (primitive though it be) only five years after Clarke's more sophisticated version appeared in the film, *2001*. That it was made and converted from leftover *Apollo* hardware made it no less an historic first.

The *Skylab 4* mission, the longest of three manned *Skylab* flights, began on 16 November 1973. They would keep flying through Christmas and into the New Year, finally returning to Earth on 8 February 1974.

Arthur, of course, remained in literary orbit long after the *Skylab 4* crew landed and regained their earthbound walking legs. He was imagining the characters in his new novel who were born on Saturn's moon, Titan.

'I have finally started work on the new novel after twenty years of note-taking,' Arthur wrote Tom Craven in mid-January, 'and don't get any more money until I deliver it.' He would be writing hard until he finished the first draft of *Imperial Earth*.

By mid-February Arthur had written about ten thousand words. He also was preparing for a lecture in Australia.

'I'm accepting an offer I can't refuse – a lecture at the Sydney Opera House,' he wrote Craven. It was not just the money that Arthur couldn't refuse. More important was the opportunity to leave Sri Lanka, which he had to do several times a year because of Sri Lankan law.

The Australian trip went well and by the end of March Arthur was back in Sri Lanka working night and day on *Imperial Earth*. It progressed so well that he decided to bring forward his late summer trip to England to June. He needed a break, and he had learned that his friend Isaac Asimov would be in London on 14 June to address the British chapter of Mensa. Arthur wasn't about to miss the chance to continue his tradition with Isaac of throwing a few good-natured insults at one another.

Isaac and Arthur first met at the Hydra Club in New York the week before Arthur was married in June 1953. Until Isaac's death it was a unique relationship between two of the world's great science fiction writers and science popularisers.

Said Isaac, 'I love Arthur and I'm sure he loves me, and when we do meet we have a lot of fun. There's no jealousy whatsoever because in the science fiction field or the literary field it's an open-ended game. If I sell a story that doesn't mean that Arthur Clarke can't sell a story, and vice versa. So my success does not depend on his failure, and vice versa. We both are very pleased with our mutual success.'

The June 1974 occasion of Isaac's visit to England took their exchange of friendly insults to new heights.

'I spent several days composing an impromptu collection of carefully contrived insults,' says Arthur, 'duly delivered in the Commonwealth Hall, London, on 14 June. Isaac had no warning; nevertheless . . . *his* riposte gave as good as he received.'

'When he introduced me in London,' said Isaac, 'he was extremely funny, and I made up my mind that when I got up and answered him I too would say things at his expense. And we've been doing it ever since.'

The battle of wits began with Arthur's opening remarks.

'Well, Isaac – I've lost my bet. There *are* more than five people here . . . I'm not going to waste any time *introducing* Isaac Asimov. That would be as pointless as introducing the equator, which, indeed, he's coming to resemble more and more closely.'

Asimov's amazing productivity was the next target for Arthur's insults, and he told the audience that he had discovered, through his 'Private plumber's Unit' in Manhattan, some of Isaac's forthcoming titles, including *Asimov's Guide to Cricket*, *The Asimov Exercise Book* and *Asimov's Kama Sutra*.

'It's an awesome output – and it's not true, as some have suggested, that Isaac is actually a robot himself. If you want proof, ask any of the thirty young ladies at the Globe last Wednesday what they had to do to get his autograph.'

After estimating that Asimov's prolific output at that time was responsible for deforestation to the extent of '5.7 times ten to the sixteenth microhectares', Arthur introduced his friend to the London audience.

Without much time for preparation ('He was also very funny, and he was spontaneous,' says Arthur), Asimov answered in kind, suggesting that Arthur knowingly gives the worst kind of introductions – long and clever ones.

'Let me tell you the kind of guy Arthur is. When he met me on the *Canberra* and he saw that I was perfectly at ease and had overcome my fear of travelling and was standing there with nothing between myself and the sea but some thin steel, he said, "Isaac, at great expense I have persuaded the captain of this ship to show *The Poseidon Adventure.*"' The high-IQ audience loved these childlike antics, and the applause was heartening.

Arthur Clarke enjoyed this; he even got the transcripts of the meeting and put together a short piece, *Introducing Isaac Asimov*, which appeared in the *Magazine of Fantasy and Science Fiction* in early 1975. It was, Arthur wrote to Tom Craven, 'done *con amore* with a perfumed hatchet'.

Fifteen years later, in the summer of 1989, one of the more memorable international insults flew around the planet. *Time* magazine, in its coverage of an airplane crash in Iowa that year, reported that one of the passengers had been reading an Arthur Clarke novel in the last half hour before the fatal crash.

'I sent the *Time* article to Isaac, saying that the man should have been reading an Asimov novel because that would have put him to sleep. Soon I got a letter back from Asimov saying, "Oh no, the passenger should have been reading an Arthur Clarke novel, then death would have been a merciful release!"'

Once Arthur scored points by simply passing on a review of one of Asimov's books.

'Arthur cut it out carefully and mailed it to me, just in case I might miss it otherwise,' said Isaac. 'Someone gave me a bad, bad review for a collection of science essays called *The Relativity of Wrong*, which began, "This is a book which never should have been written" . . . What a friend! How thoughtful Arthur can be sometimes. That's typical. I would do the same for him, believe me.'

Their witty insults were unpredictable, but on one matter Asimov and Clarke came to a mutual agreement upon which they could both depend. It had to do with their writing status: who did what best?

Arthur, in part jest, decided to put whatever rumours of rivalry that might be circulating to rest. Originally it was a verbal agreement between Arthur and Isaac, spoken inside a Manhattan taxi. This was in the early 1970s, and they were racing down Park Avenue to some now forgotten dinner or meeting.

'I remember saying to Arthur that I was perfectly willing to maintain that he was the best science-fiction writer if he would maintain that I was the best science writer, and he said, "Done."

'After Sputnik,' Isaac went on, 'I decided it was patriotic to write on science, but it was something I wanted to do anyway. I was tired of writing fiction. Fiction is much more difficult. Writing novels is the hardest thing,' he admitted a few weeks before his seventieth birthday.

Isaac was less than optimistic about renegotiating the Clarke–Asimov Treaty. 'I don't want to let go of "the best science writer" business,' he said. And so the Treaty was unchanged from when it first appeared as the dedication to Arthur's 1972 essay collection, *Report on Planet Three and other Speculations*:

> In accordance with the terms of the Clarke–Asimov Treaty, the second-best science writer dedicates this book to the second-best science fiction writer.

Asimov says, 'When anyone asks me who my favourite science fiction writer is, they always say, "other than yourself". And I always say Arthur C. Clarke. He's supposed to say I'm the best science writer. God knows if he does.'

'On the whole I've kept my side of the treaty,' Arthur says. Both he and Isaac always acknowledged that it was a treaty between their two rather substantial egos, and they recognised that there was plenty of young talent out there.

'If people were to take votes as to who was the best science fiction writer these days,' said Isaac, 'it's quite possible that neither Clarke nor I would win.'

Asimov reflected on their respective egos: 'I don't think anybody begrudges Arthur his ego. If he thinks he's hot stuff, we've got to admit he is hot stuff. The guys who are offended are the guys who think they are hot stuff and aren't. As I frequently say about myself, people say I'm immodest, but no one says I'm a liar.

'My ego refers only to my writing. I'm very proud of my writing. But not necessarily of me. When it comes to me, I know my faults and failings, and I make no big deal about it. As far as I know, Arthur really has the ego people think I do, but that doesn't stop him from being lovable.'

'The one thing Isaac and I have in common,' says Arthur, 'is that we're almost as good as we think we are.'

Arthur was deeply saddened when he heard the news of Asimov's death in the spring of 1992, and he wrote a goodbye and tribute to his dear friend:

> Many years ago, when introducing Isaac to a MENSA Society meeting in London, I said, 'Ladies and gentlemen – there is only

one Isaac Asimov.' Now there is no Isaac Asimov, and the world is a much poorer place.

Isaac must have been one of the greatest educators who ever lived, with his almost half a thousand books on virtually every aspect of science and culture. His country has lost him at its moment of direst need, for he was a powerful force against the evils which seem to overwhelm it (and much of western society). He stood for knowledge against superstition, tolerance against bigotry, kindness against cruelty – and above all, peace against war. His was one of the most effective voices against the 'new age' nitwits and fundamentalist fanatics who may now be a greater menace than the paper bear of communism ever was.

Isaac's fiction was as important as his non-fiction, because it spread the same ideas on an even wider scale. He virtually invented the science of robotics – and named it before it was born. Without preaching, he showed that knowledge was better than ignorance, and that there were other defences against violence than violence itself.

Finally, and not least, he was great fun. He will be sorely missed by thousands of friends and millions of admirers.

After a few weeks in London to conduct business and see old friends such as Val Cleaver and David Fowke, Arthur flew back to Colombo on 6 July and continued work on *Imperial Earth*.

'I have been very busy – have hardly left the house since I have arrived in Ceylon – but I am now about three-quarters of the way through the novel,' he wrote to Tom Craven in late August 1974. He also told his friend that the Smithsonian and NASA had invited him to a week's conference at the Auchincloss summer house in Rhode Island to discuss the future of space with Wernher von Braun, Margaret Mead and Alistair Cooke. 'They even wanted me to rush across for the *weekend* after the IAF conference [Amsterdam in early October], but I was absolutely adamant. In any case I have to stay out of the US for eighteen months to de-establish myself!'

This was a reference to the fact that Arthur was establishing *non*-residency in the United States and residency in Ceylon in anticipation of the so-called 'Clarke Act' of 1975, which allowed money and goods to be brought into the country without being taxed.

In early September Arthur welcomed his broadcaster friend, Hugh Downs and his wife, Ruth, to Sri Lanka for a five-day visit. Downs, a pioneer broadcaster with fifty-plus years in the business, hosted

NBC's 'Today Show' for ten years from 1962 to 1972, and had Arthur as his guest several times during his tenure. Both Arthur and Hugh have been actively involved in the National Space Institute [now the National Space Society] since it was formed in 1975 and Downs has been president of the organisation since its early days.

'We went to Sigiriya,' Hugh recalls, 'and Arthur showed us one of the frescoes on the vertical rock walls. There's a painting of a woman holding a box with a kind of lattice work (it looked like a grille), a round thing up to her ear. For all the world, it looked like a transistor radio, and Arthur pointed this out to us.'

Arthur mentions this in the 'Sources and Acknowledgements' section of his novel *Fountains of Paradise*, which was published in 1979.

'The attendant is clearly *listening* to the mysterious hinged box she is holding in her right hand. It remains unidentified, the local archaeologists refusing to take seriously my suggestion that it is an early Sinhalese transistor radio.'

At the end of that year, which marked the twentieth anniversary of Arthur first seeing Ceylon, Nora, his eighty-two-year-old mother, visited him. She broke her hip at the Polonnaruwa Resthouse while sightseeing 130 miles away from Colombo, and the hip was pinned at the Frazer Hospital. She seemed to be on the mend as 1975 began.

The beginning of the year had no pressing deadlines for Arthur. He was thinking about visiting his peaceful retreat on the south coast, when he heard some interesting news: his old diving partner, Mike Wilson, had left his wife Liz to become a monk [Siva Swami]. He had not seen either of them for two years.

The Wilsons had moved into their own home for more space when the children came along in the early 1960s. Later in that decade, there had been a cooling off between Mike Wilson and Clarke. Wilson always depended on Clarke for the venture capital to fund his various projects, but his ventures were expensive, necessarily spending and wasting a lot of money. This had been going on for several years before there was a confrontation.

The blow-up actually occurred between Hector Ekanayake (who had become protective of Arthur, especially so after Clarke's paralysis) and Mike Wilson.

'I can remember the falling out,' says Clarke. 'It was a trivial thing, really, but it was the last straw. Mike wanted to borrow an inflatable boat, but Hector wouldn't lend it to him because he believed that Mike wouldn't return it.'

That day the line was drawn and the relationship changed. What was once a close relationship became a distant one.

Arthur's brother Fred arrived for a holiday in early March. Nora's hip gave way completely and nothing could be done for it in Sri Lanka.

'I was only there for three days,' remembers Fred Clarke, 'and had to turn around and bring Mum back to England. Our sister Mary, who's a nurse, arranged for a doctor to do a complete hip replacement, and in a couple of months she was walking around again.

'That's when Arthur decided that she wouldn't be able to live out there [a possibility the family had discussed], and that I'd have to take over the looking after her. And that's when I decided to sell up in London and come down to Somerset.'

This period in the early 1970s served as a personal turning point for Clarke. He finished a book that had been gestating in his mind for twenty years. He adopted a more relaxed attitude toward his writing. And he settled into the new home on Barnes Place. It was the Moon Age that Arthur C. Clarke was living in – one of his earliest and most persistent dreams had come true.

David Higham Associates, Arthur's British literary agency, had good news early in the year. *Rendezvous with Rama* was sold to the Russians.

'Am delighted,' Arthur wrote Craven, 'to hear that *Rama* is the *first* English novel that the Russians have bought under the new copyright agreement.' Andrew Nurnberg, the agent who made the sale, sold the novel while visiting Moscow to sell scientific books. The deal was made with the Mir [Peace] Publishing House and took about eighteen months to complete.

'I consider it a breakthrough for writers in the West,' said Nurnberg. 'The Russians will pay in sterling at nine to ten per cent of the retail price. They will sell fifty thousand copies in hardback at seventy kopecks each. It will certainly be financially worthwhile.'

When the Russian sale was announced, Fred Clarke said that it was an important introduction to a market, even if it represented only 'a drop in the ocean'.

'Arthur's books have been published in the Soviet Union before, but only for blocked roubles, which could only be spent there. As Arthur never visited Russia, he never had any benefit from it.'

The euphoria was somewhat dampened, however, when Arthur read that the Russians take out ninety per cent in tax. 'If this is so,' he wrote Sam Youd in June, 'they certainly won't have any more books of mine, and of course, they won't be able to pirate them now.'

The Russian tax turned out to be thirty per cent of the advance, not ninety per cent as Arthur had heard. Other charges and commissions added another twenty per cent on top of that.

In the same letter to his friend Sam, Arthur announced that he had finally become a permanent resident of Ceylon. 'But I do expect to spend about a month a year in England.' Because of this bestowal of official residency, 1975 was the first year he didn't have to leave the country for six months, and he took advantage of it by spending much of the year pursuing interests and business other than writing. During the first half of the decade, he had been writing steadily and had produced two novels. He was contracted for a third, but not before he took some time away from the typewriter.

He described his relaxed lifestyle to his friend, Tom Craven.

I am now taking things very easy, basking in the warm afterglow of completing *Imperial Earth*. Both UK and US publishers are delighted with it and I am pretty sure it's the best thing I have ever done.

I am now leading a very quiet life – doing lot of reading, playing with Hal Jr [his computer] – hardly going out except for two hours of hectic table tennis every day at the local club. I can now beat (almost) everybody in sight.

Arthur also bragged to Sam Youd about how little he was writing.

'Since I delivered *Imperial Earth* to Gollancz and Harcourt Brace Jovanovich at the end of '74, I have written exactly a thousand words – a book review for the *New York Times*! And that's *all* I intend to do this year.'

The *New York Times* review covered two UFO books ('*UFOs Explained* by Philip J. Klass and *The UFO Controversy in America* by David Michael Jacob) and appeared in late July.

'Klass is a complete sceptic,' wrote Arthur. 'Jacobs thinks that there may be a hard core of phenomena still unexplained by contemporary science.'

The *New York Times* agreed to print a footnote Arthur requested. The footnote, with a mix of Clarke's humour and opinion, rather succinctly stated his position on UFOs.

It read in part, 'He [the reviewer] believes that UFOs need a few decades of benign neglect, and threatens to sue the *Times* if it forwards any correspondence relating to this review.'

'I am happy to say that the *Times* kept its side of the bargain, and I never received a single letter,' says Arthur.

The one lesson so far learned from UFOs, according to Clarke, was that 'they tell us absolutely nothing about intelligence elsewhere; but they do prove how rare it is on Earth'.

The review was reprinted in *The View from Serendip*, a collection of non-fiction pieces published in 1977. In a short introduction, Arthur wrote:

'I am no longer interested in any further books, or letters, *about* UFOs.

'But I am still interested in UFOs themselves.

'Mildly.'

Arthur C. Clarke's basic position on UFOs hasn't really changed since. Show him one, and he'll give it his complete attention.

Two important events in July 1975 took Arthur out of Sri Lanka for most of the month. The first was the launch and rendezvous of Russia's *Soyuz 19* and *Apollo 18* for the first superpower link-up in orbit. The second was his appearance before the House of Representatives Committee on Space Science and Applications, with Chairman Don Fuqua.

Both launches for the *Apollo–Soyuz* Test Project were successful on 15 July. The Russians roared skyward first, about seven hours before *Apollo 18* left the pad at Cape Kennedy. Arthur was in Florida and witnessed the US launch. Afterwards he went to the CBS studios at the Cape, and along with Neil Armstrong helped Walter Cronkite with the coverage.

'Neil Armstrong and I waited while President Ford gave long-winded replies to Walter. I think we finally had a minute each on camera.'

His long-standing and consistent support of international co-operation in space exploration made this a sweet launch for him. Once more his vision was being realised.

The hearings before the Committee on Space Science and Applications were focused on the future of the American space programme, and Arthur appeared on 24 July.

'I was both flattered and apprehensive,' he admitted to the Committee members. 'It was quite one thing to write inspirational prose about the wonders of space exploration in the centuries to come, but it would be quite another to answer even the friendliest interrogator wanting to know, "Yes – but exactly *what* should we be doing in fiscal seventy-seven?"'

Ten witnesses gave their testimony. They included James Fletcher, NASA Administrator; Norman Cousins, editor of *Saturday Review*; Carl Sagan of Cornell; and Gerard O'Neill of Princeton. Other authorities such as Isaac Asimov, Bruce Murray, Bernard Oliver, John Pierce, Edward Teller and Wernher von Braun presented written contributions.

True to form, Arthur praised and promoted his beautiful island of Sri Lanka and mentioned his recently completed, though still unpublished, novel *Imperial Earth*, whose hero actually addresses the US Congress.

Arthur read the portion of his novel in which the protagonist, who has had his expenses paid from Saturn's moon, Titan, speaks to Congress on 4 July 2276. The character's speech even includes some historical perspectives on early centennials, the one celebrated in 1976, for example, which was then a future event (about a year away) for Arthur and the Committee members.

'"In 1976, the conquest of interplanetary space was about to begin,"' Arthur read from his novel.

> By that time, the first men had already reached the Moon, using techniques which today seem unbelievably primitive. Although all historians now agree that the *Apollo* project marked the United States' supreme achievement, and its greatest moment of triumph, it was inspired by political motives that seem ludicrous – indeed, incomprehensible – to our modern minds.

He next spoke about technological forecasting and how important timing was to development of a technology that was both possible and desirable. 'It can be disastrous,' he said, 'to be a premature pioneer.' And he went on to mention the *Great Eastern* steamship of the middle nineteenth century or the Comet jetliner of the twentieth.

'I have always been more interested in the spectacular possibilities of the distant future, and not the practical problems of the day after tomorrow,' he told the Committee members. 'Indeed, I've summed this up in the warning that if you take me *too* seriously, you'll go broke – but if you don't take me seriously *enough*, your children will go broke.'

He spoke of various applications of satellites – communications, weather, Earth resources – and the difficulty of getting the public to understand their importance and to support them. He told the Committee about the ongoing ATS-6 direct broadcast satellite experiment that would in a matter of weeks beam educational information on family planning, hygiene and agricultural methods direct to several thousand small receivers all over India. And he spoke of his strong conviction that the communications revolution would change for ever the geopolitical realities of the planet. History would soon prove him right.

'What we are seeing now – largely as a result of space technology – is the establishment of supernational, global-service organisations in which all governments, in their own sheer self-interest, will simply *have* to co-operate. Intelsat is the obvious prototype,' he told them.

Arthur next spoke to the congressmen about the space shuttle, which wouldn't fly until 1981, and stated how important it was to the future of space exploration. 'It's unfortunate that the shuttle, once touted as the DC-3 of space, has now been degraded for fiscal and other reasons to the DC-1½.' He believed it would provide 'the final convincing demonstration of the need for men in space, not just on occasional sorties but as full-time workers'.

Projecting further into the future, Arthur talked about an advanced propulsion system based on research 'that is going on at the moment to trigger fusion reactions with laser pulses . . . One can imagine microspheres of hydrogen-deuterium being zapped several times a second during the climb through the atmosphere, and at more leisurely intervals thereafter.'

And for the more distant future, he summarised for the Committee members the incredible idea of one day laying a cable from a geostationary satellite high above the Earth all the way down to the surface – a concept which both the Americans and the Russians originated separately.

'And then, in principle, one could send payloads up the cable by simple mechanical means. An electric elevator to space, or a Streetcar Named Heaven,' he said, two years before he began writing *Fountains of Paradise*, his novel which incorporates the concept.

The Committee hearings were winding down. Arthur's cosmic eloquence was in top form when he made his closing remarks.

'It is true that we must cherish and conserve the treasures of this fragile Earth, which we have so shamefully wasted. But if we come to our senses in time, we may yet have a splendid and inspiring role to play, on a stage wider and more marvellous than ever dreamed of by any poet or dramatist of the past. For it may be that the old astrologers had the truth exactly reversed, when they believed that the stars controlled the destinies of men.

'The time may come when men control the destinies of stars.'

Once more he effectively used one of the great, and most famous, Clarke quotes.

In the subsequent, more down-to-earth question period, Arthur told Congressman Fuqua that the United States should work on projects of 'immediate applicability'. Other discussions included how military research can be a primary driver of new technologies (such as the laser) that can be utilised in future space programmes and how the public can be educated about the benefits of the less obvious and more long-term research. Education was the key, everyone agreed.

'I know an awful lot of scientists, and astronauts for that matter, who were turned on by science fiction,' Arthur said. 'This is part of the educational process.

'One reason is that science fiction is usually optimistic. Much modern fiction is very pessimistic, and in the science fiction area you usually do have the feeling that the future can be better than the past, we can do something about the future, we don't have to wait until it comes and clobbers us.'

In closing Arthur emphasised the importance of the vision that is so often the foundation for reality.

'I'm sure we would not have had men on the Moon if it had not been for Wells and Verne and the people who wrote about this and made people think about it. I'm rather proud of the fact that I know several astronauts who became astronauts through reading my books. I feel a considerable responsibility for this myself.'

After another day in Washington, Arthur flew to London for a short stay and then on to Colombo, arriving on 31 July 1975. August would be a special month for Clarke. He was about to receive his largest gift ever, a 'unique and magnificent gift' he called it, presented to him by the government of India.

It was Wernher von Braun who first advised Arthur on the possibility of obtaining a satellite dish from the Indian government to receive signals from the ATS-6 satellite. Sri Lanka, then, in its own modest way, could participate in India's Satellite Instructional Television Experiment (SITE) which began in 1975.

Von Braun was the man who, more than any other person, gave the United States the *Saturn* rocket which took the first men to the Moon. After the *Apollo* programme ended in the early seventies, he became vice-president at Fairchild Industries. Fairchild built the ATS-6.

'The best solution for you,' wrote von Braun in the summer of 1974, 'would be to get a hold of one complete Indian village installation. It consists of antenna, UHF adapter and TV set (plus plug-in power connects). Several thousand of these installations are in production in India proper, so the task is to siphon one off for you.'

Von Braun added that he would be glad to take the matter up with the head of the Indian Space Programme, Dr Satish Dhawan.

'I think they will agree with us,' said von Braun, 'that they could not possibly deprive the inventor of the geosynchronous satellite of the fruits of his own labours!'

The bureaucratic wheels began to turn, and Arthur received a letter from the director of India's Department of Space in April 1975 indicating that the necessary clearances from the Sri Lankan authorities had to be initiated before he could obtain a ground station for 'demonstration purposes'.

A few more months of red tape, and then six Indian engineers arrived at Arthur's house to install his Earth station.

'Lanka's link with unique TV venture' was the headline in the *Ceylon Daily News* on 12 August. 'India's gesture to Arthur Clarke. World's first private home to have reception unit.'

Yash Pal, Director of the Space Applications Centre in Ahmadabad, wrote to Arthur telling him that he would have installed a 'specially made community receiving station to enable you to directly participate in the realisation of your dream of many years ago, because Sri Lanka is far from the beam centre, and in order to provide you with a proper signal, we have fabricated a fifteen-foot diameter antenna instead of the normal ten-foot one and we have also made a special low-noise converter.'

The front-page photo showed the six Indian engineers standing in front of the erected satellite dish on Arthur's balcony at Barnes Place. Arthur stood to the right of them, wrapped in one of his favourite batik sarongs, his right hand holding on to one of the ribs of the satellite dish.

It was the only privately owned Earth satellite station in the world and Arthur's home had the only television set on the island of Sri Lanka in 1976.

A few days later Arthur wrote to Yash Pal, expressing his gratitude, commending the engineers and telling him how he was spreading the good news.

'I am now inviting the Prime Minister, Cabinet, leading government officials etc., to come and see the programmes. Although I shall be leaving Sri Lanka for two months on 20 August, I will make arrangements for continued viewing during my absence.' And, he added, he'd promote India's innovative programme wherever he spoke, including the Nobel Institute Space Symposium in September.

Arthur promised to accommodate a limited number of people at his house to view the Indian educational programme. This 'limited' number, however, proved very difficult to control.

'House now looks like Jodrell Bank,' he wrote Tom Craven on 11 August. 'Getting dozens of visitors a day and it will increase.' He was right about that.

Hugh Downs remembers Arthur telling him how hard it was to cope with all the viewers who came to Barnes Place.

'He told me it was the most expensive gift he ever received,' says Hugh, 'because everybody came there to see the programme and he'd have to serve them drinks. He was buying liquor by the barrel to serve the people who dropped in on him. A wonderful gift, but it cost a lot.'

More than thirty years after Arthur had first conceived of geosynchronous satellites he had an Earth station on his own terrace which would keep him in touch with the rest of the planet.

Clarke also envisioned more distant places in the solar system, like Saturn's moon, Titan. In his novel *Imperial Earth* he attempted to portray its strange environment, which was home to the fictional Makenzie clan. Arthur went on to describe a United States of America three hundred years in the future, 2276, during its quincentennial celebration, and how odd much of it appeared to the hero, Duncan Mackenzie, who had lived his entire life on Titan. Duncan's visit to Earth also involves the fascinating technology of cloning (a hot topic in the mid-1970s) to create the next Makenzie generation that would govern Titan.

The British edition of this novel was published in September 1975. Its subtitle, dropped from the US edition, was 'A Fantasy of Love and Discord'. The US edition was published in early 1976, and it was further revised, with five more chapters added and a few more expanded.

Several reviewers spoke of Clarke's more-than-usual concern for characterisation in *Imperial Earth*, a lack of which critics had pointed out in some of his earlier novels. Arthur admits that he has always been more interested in things and ideas than in people. But he is still sensitive to the criticism that his characters lack depth and has tried to compensate.

'This book has more plot and human interest than Clarke's previous opus *Rendezvous with Rama*,' wrote the reviewer in the *Washington Post*. Gerald Jonas wrote in the *New York Times* that the novel showed Clarke 'at the height of his powers'. Clarke is, says Jonas, 'clearly less interested in "what happens next" than he is in describing a society in which sex has finally been freed from shame or guilt, in which near disaster and the lessons of space colonisation have taught man to live in partnership with nature, in which visitors from one planet must gradually accustom themselves to the gravity of another planet, and so on.'

What pleased Arthur immensely was that another novel was behind him – 'after twenty years work, on and off, and almost the whole of '74 behind the typewriter'. He even thought for a while that *Imperial Earth* would be 'the big one'.

CHAPTER 24

Perturbations in Time

> It was a pity that there was no radar to guide
> one across the trackless seas of life. Every
> man had to find his own way, steered by
> some secret compass of the soul.
> — *Glide Path*

In a year that would be dominated by the US bicentennial festivities, there was also a significant centennial to celebrate. Bell Telephone Company and the Massachusetts Institute of Technology marked the hundredth anniversary of the invention of the telephone with a special programme of symposia in March 1976.

Dr Jerome Weisner, then president of MIT, wrote to Arthur and asked if he would deliver the keynote address.

'Since your remarkable forecast of communication satellites,' wrote Weisner, 'you have been recognised around the world as one of the principal figures in the shaping of modern communication. It would seem most appropriate for you to open the second century of telephony with some thoughts about where it is likely to take mankind.'

Even though Arthur was accepting very few speaking engagements, he replied that he would be happy to accept the offer and travel to Boston.

After a day's stopover in London, Arthur arrived in Boston on 7 March and had two days to relax, explore and see old friends before his presentation on the tenth. He stayed with Marvin Minsky and his wife, Gloria, and was impressed with Minsky's Artificial Intelligence Laboratory at MIT. And Arthur was truly thrilled to meet Dr Edwin Land – the man who invented the Polaroid Land Camera and created a corporation. 'One of the greatest living Americans,' Arthur called him.

He also had a reunion with his old friend, John Pierce, the comsat pioneer who was instrumental in developing the first communications satellites. John knew Arthur from the times he'd visited New

York City in the early 1950s. Pierce was also a science fiction fan and writer. In the late fifties and early sixties he and Arthur attended some of the science fiction conventions together.

A buddy from the radar days of World War II, Bert Fowler, was also in the Boston area. He and Arthur met and talked about the war years, the latest on comsats and other common interests. Fowler went to hear Arthur's speech and remembers the afternoon of 10 March 1976 – one hundred years exactly from the day Alexander Graham Bell invented the telephone on 10 March 1876 in Boston. After lunch speakers from the various workshops were giving their summaries prior to Arthur's lecture.

'They were held in the Kresge Auditorium at MIT,' Fowler says, 'and the room was only fifteen to twenty per cent filled when the experts spoke. Then, about ten minutes before Arthur was scheduled to speak, I became aware that the room had quietly filled up, and about five minutes before the appointed hour every seat was taken. There were people seated in the aisles, and they were lined up several deep along the sides and the back of the auditorium.

'The group that filled up the auditorium was mainly young people,' says Fowler. 'And before that time I had never realised (I had probably taken Arthur too casually) what a cult figure he had become.'

Bert Fowler repeats President Jerome Weisner's introduction of Arthur C. Clarke. 'He said, "Our next speaker is the only person I know who can be unambiguously introduced by a four-digit number – 2001." And then there was a standing ovation.'

In his speech, 'Communications in the Second Century of the Telephone', Arthur spoke of an ideal communications console, a 'comsole' was his coined abbreviation, whereby 'one could have face-to-face interaction with anyone, anywhere on Earth, and send or receive any type of information'.

The comsole could bring forth information at the speed of light from the great libraries of the world. It also would be a sophisticated robot secretary and could have advanced voice recognition capability.

Other favourite Clarke concepts were discussed – wristwatch telephone, 3-D visuals, the immense potential of utilising comsats for education – but the speech offered much more than descriptions of novel technological devices. Arthur also spoke on the philosophy of communications.

'For man is the communicating animal; he demands news, information, entertainment, almost as much as food. In fact, as a functioning human being, he can survive much longer without

275

food – even without water! – than without information, as experiments in sensory deprivation have shown.'

The search for signals from extra-terrestrial intelligence – which looked at communications on an interstellar scale – was Arthur's last topic before his concluding remarks.

'For we can now say, in the widest possible meaning of the phrase, that the purpose of human life is information processing,' Arthur told the MIT audience, following up with the begged question: '"Well, what is the purpose of information processing?"'

'I'm glad you asked me that.'

And with that cliff-hanger ending, his speech celebrating the hundredth anniversary of the birth of the telephone was over.

Ever since Arthur had first come to the United States in 1952 he had been visiting friends and colleagues in and around the nation's capital. This trip was no exception. The sixteenth of March 1976 was the fiftieth anniversary of Robert Goddard's first-in-the-world flight of a liquid-propelled rocket, which left the Earth from his Aunt Effie's cabbage patch in Auburn, Massachusetts.

Many events were planned to celebrate this anniversary, and Arthur travelled from Boston to Washington, DC, to participate. One such event took place at the Museum of Natural History's Gem Room, which held some of the most beautiful gems in the world, including the famous Hope Diamond. Several astronauts and many top brass from NASA were present. So too was Arthur's good friend, Fred Durant, then the Assistant Director, Astronautics, of the new National Air and Space Museum, who had arranged the speeches, ceremonies and dinner.

At one point during the festivities, Durant waved his arm in a gesture which encompassed the entire Gem Room.

'Do you realise that *all* this collection wouldn't pay for my latest exhibit?' he told the gathered guests. The exhibit he had just installed in the great hall of the National Air and Space Museum was the second complete Skylab – the one that had not flown. Arthur guessed that it was worth between a quarter and half a *billion* dollars, 'enough to buy at least a hundred Hope diamonds – even assuming that there was no discount for quantity'.

There were always plenty of people to see – indeed, too many. Arthur's week in Washington included meeting with *Apollo 11* astronaut, Michael Collins, who then headed the new Air and Space Museum; Wernher von Braun, then a vice-president at Fairchild; and fellow writer Ben Bova with whom he visited NASA during

276

Goddard Day on 16 March. Fred and Pip Durant held a reception at their house, a tradition when Arthur was in town.

Next stop, Manhattan, for a week of meetings with friends and colleagues, and he consented to give *Publishers Weekly* an interview.

Arthur C. Clarke could, the interviewer wrote, 'easily be regarded as the grandfather of contemporary science fiction if only he weren't so sprightly, [and he] sees the present as "the golden age" of the genre. Then he adds, with that touch of playful facetiousness that so often occurs in his work: "There have been many golden ages, of course, but up to now they've all been only twelve-carat."'

Asked about his current reading habits, Arthur replied that he reads anything that sounds interesting to him.

'Maybe a quarter of it is good stuff – which I suppose means about one or two per cent of everything that's published . . . In a way I'm sorry for this new generation of science fiction readers. When I was young you could read everything that was written – there were maybe two hardcover books a year, and the rest was the magazine stuff.'

He was a firm believer in traditional story telling, he told his interviewer.

'I'm often accused of being a reactionary old-timer, with no interest in stylistic innovation. And it's true I still think in linear terms. In *Rendezvous with Rama*, for instance, I was trying to prove that the traditional adventure story can still carry everything I want to say. In that sense Conan Doyle's *The Lost World* is a model of what I mean.'

And why is the science fiction genre so popular? he was asked. 'The young today are looking to expand their minds,' he replied, concluding the interview, 'and good science fiction is the only genuine consciousness-expanding drug there is.'

In early May the Padukka Earth station was officially opened in Sri Lanka. 'Our beautiful new Earth station – only twenty miles from Colombo – has an impressive mural which we might use,' Arthur wrote Tom Craven. Plans called for Craven to arrive with a crew late in the year to film several segments of an AT&T prime time television ad with Arthur for the hundredth anniversary of the invention of the telephone. Finally there would be satellite facilities in Sri Lanka that were not located at Arthur's home. This visionary from Somerset was always plugged into the world at large; the new Earth station simply meant he would have an even greater capacity to communicate.

In the summer of 1976 Martian history was made. The planetary explorers *Viking 1* and *2* arrived at Mars during July and August, and the *Viking 1* lander settled on to the rust-coloured sands of the Red Planet on 20 July 1976. A quarter of a century had passed since Clarke's novel, *Sands of Mars*, was first published.

Arthur was thrilled. Man's machines were scouting Mars for the manned missions that would one day follow. Another part of his dream come true.

And there were the more practical aspects of *Viking* technology which Arthur reminded us about, such as how the state-of-the-art hardware could easily be adapted to important remote-sensing satellites in orbit above planet Earth.

'In a very important and fundamental way, when we study Mars we are also studying our own world,' says Arthur, 'and what it may teach us about our planet may one day be a matter of life and death.'

He was referring to the discovery of dried-up river beds on Mars, which meant that large-scale climatic changes had occurred over time on the Red Planet. Where and how had all the water gone? By finding the answers, science could conceivably predict and avoid such an epochal calamity on planet Earth.

In mid-August Arthur wrote to his friend Tom Craven. 'I am hard at work (to my considerable surprise) on the new novel.' Arthur went on to tell Tom about the Non-Aligned Conference which was taking place in Colombo.

'You wouldn't recognise Colombo. I expect to meet Mrs Indira Gandhi next week, but on the whole I am lying low.'

A Tokyo lecture, 'Managing the Universe', took Arthur to Japan in late September for a conference put on by the Dentsu Advertising Agency, one of the largest in the world.

'"Managing the Universe" was mostly off the cuff,' he told Craven, 'though v. carefully prepared. I did write the opening statement to give time for it to be translated into classical Japanese. I used about a hundred NASA ERTS slides [Earth Resources Technology Satellite, later known as Landsat], which made a terrific impact.'

While in Japan, Arthur had the opportunity to meet Edward Heath, the British Prime Minister in the early 1970s.

From Tokyo he flew to Singapore and rendezvoused with Hector who was there shopping for diving equipment and having some dental work done.

'We stayed at the old Raffles which is haunted with ghosts of Maugham and Kipling – it's now the Hotel Chelsea of Singapore,' he told fellow world traveller, Roger Caras. It was here that he first saw Stanley Kubrick's *Barry Lyndon*, which he enjoyed despite the Malay and Chinese subtitles. They returned to Colombo on 7 October, and Arthur immediately attacked his pile of mail.

In a couple of letters to friends he gleefully mentioned turning down a big money project.

'Phone call from NY last night – Paramount and Simon & Schuster offering half a megabuck for novel/screenplay. Couldn't care less and wouldn't be tempted for ten times as much.' He was hard at work on the novel about Sri Lanka he had been planning for many years, which became *The Fountains of Paradise*.

Arthur wanted to prepare for the arrival of his mother and his brother Fred in early December, and he also had some script work to do before Tom Craven and his film crew arrived on 30 November to shoot about twelve minutes of AT&T television commercials. The ads would appear first during a showing of *The Man in the Iron Mask*, and Arthur was in good and playful humour when he wrote to Craven in late October: 'Can't you persuade them to change it to *The Man in the Rubber Mask* and shoot it underwater? Much bigger draw,' he jested.

The commercials would be nearly six minutes long in total and there were six of them. The theme was technological progress leading to the development of new frontiers in telecommunications by the year 2076.

The shoot took place during the first few days in December at three different locations in Sri Lanka: Polonnaruwa, the ancient capital of Ceylon, with its beautiful (although eroded) Buddhist temple called Watadage; Sigiriya (meaning 'Lion rock' in Sinhalese), one of Asia's most photographed archaeological sites; and Black Rock Shrine, where three huge sculptures, including a large reclining Buddha, form a temple.

These were some of the most picturesque locations in Sri Lanka, and they provided the ancient backgrounds before which Arthur C. Clarke would wax eloquent about the future of communications in the twenty-first century and about how people in the year 2076 (the bicentennial year for the invention of the telephone) would have the world at their fingertips.

The last shoot was in Colombo at Arthur's home, which Tom Craven described as 'neo-Somerset Maugham with great square rooms equipped with ceiling fans that stir the moist Colombo air'. The crew was tired from the long drive back, and they gathered around the big table in the dining room for tea and sandwiches.

There was even some unexpected live entertainment when two snake charmers showed up at the front door, and Hector's fiancée Valerie offered to invite them, and their cobras and monkeys, into the garden for a show.

'By the time the final trill of the snake charmer's flute sounded,' Craven recalled, 'the sun had outlined the huge [dish] antenna on the porch roof outside Arthur's bedroom. It made a good setting for his opening statement, so we filmed for several hours until weariness and waning light made us fold our tripods for the day.'

The commercials showed Arthur standing on his balcony next to his satellite dish. 'The Bell System knows that I like thinking about the future,' he began, 'and the second century of the telephone has just begun, so later in the programme I'm going to stick my neck out and speculate about the future of telecommunications a hundred years from now, in the year 2076.'

The locale then changed to Polonnaruwa. Arthur spoke, standing in front of the huge reclining Buddha.

'Five hundred years before Columbus, this was the ancient capital of Ceylon – one of the great cities of the world. Engineers and artists of genius laboured here, men as brilliant as any alive today. But they lacked something that we now take for granted. They could not speak to each other beyond the range of a shout.

'Like almost all men before the nineteenth century, the builders of this city lived in a tiny, isolated world. And then, just a hundred years ago, Alexander Graham Bell changed the whole pattern of society. And yet the communication revolution is only just beginning. Our grandchildren will wonder how we ever managed to run our world with such clumsy, primitive tools. For they will have face-to-face contact with anyone anywhere on Earth, at any time. They will have instant access to all the visual arts of mankind.'

Arthur went on to describe his vision of a positive future.

'All the knowledge of mankind will be available at the touch of a fingertip through the global electronic library,' he said. 'We'll even approach the old science fiction dream of teleportation. You'll be able to send a life-sized, three-dimensional image of yourself to anywhere in the world.

'Technology is not an end in itself. It exists to provide us with what we want. It is our servant, not our master.'

This was an important message. What's more, it reached one of Arthur C. Clarke's largest, all-at-one-time audiences ever – twenty-five million American homes.

★

Tom Craven and his associates wanted Arthur to do more commercials and asked him to commit to making them. The idea of shooting some at Stonehenge was also discussed. Arthur replied to Craven's letter in mid-June 1977.

'The big problem is that I am committed to Bucky Fuller's birthday in Bali on 12 July! So that the earliest I could get to London is the last week in July, and I must return to Colombo by about 10 August at the latest. I have to take off to Prague on 24 September and before then will have to write my Congressional speech and do as much work as possible on the novel . . .'

Arthur's friend Bucky, whom he often crossed paths with on the lecture and conference trail, would be eighty-two years old, and it was one birthday celebration Arthur didn't want to miss. Unfortunately, fate took a painful turn.

'I was going to Bucky's birthday party in July 1977 – he had a big party in Indonesia – but that was just a week after Leslie Ekanayake was killed. Hector's youngest brother. I can't forget that. It is the greatest sadness I have ever known. We all were devastated. We never got over it. I cancelled the trip, of course.

'Leslie had had a row with his girlfriend, I think, and probably wasn't driving carefully. He was on a motorbike, coming back from seeing her. A bus overtaking on the wrong side of the road went right into him. On 4 July . . . He was killed a week before his thirtieth birthday.'

Arthur had grown fond of Leslie during the years at Barnes Place. Leslie was like a son to him in many ways – the son he'd never had.

'There were ten in the family, I believe,' recalls Arthur, 'and Leslie was the youngest and the best. He was the sweetest and best person I have ever known in my life, and his radiant and compassionate spirit completely transcended his rather plain appearance. He was the only man who ever said to me (several times) "I love you" without the slightest hint of embarrassment or mawkishness.

'Leslie was also perhaps the most widely loved person I have ever known. Hundreds came to see him, while we were waiting for his brother and sister in New York to get here for the funeral.'

The grief was deep and long-lasting. Arthur had lost a son. He wrote to and called many of his friends for support. 'We are now picking up the pieces of our lives,' he told Tom Craven less than a week after the funeral. 'Leslie's presence was everywhere; among those who came to pay their respects were weeping beggars, and an Ambassador to the Court of St James.'

More than a year later, in December 1978, he wrote to Sam: 'I don't think we'll ever recover from the loss; it still seems like yesterday.'

Almost eight years after Leslie's death a friend accompanied Arthur to the cemetery. 'He took me to Leslie's grave the day after we arrived in Sri Lanka. A photograph of Leslie was etched into the headstone of the grave. He cried like a baby and told me, "This is where I will be buried, next to Leslie."'

In September, death struck another person close to Arthur. Val Cleaver died unexpectedly. Their friendship dated back to the early London days in the 1930s when the British Interplanetary Society moved its location from Liverpool to London.

'For forty years he had been my closest friend in the UK, and our professional as well as social lives were inextricably intertwined,' Arthur wrote Sam Youd. 'Now that he's gone, I simply don't feel like visiting the UK, or going to the London cinemas and theatres which will always remind me of him. (The last night we met, we saw *Equus*.)'

Arthur had had the utmost confidence and trust in Val Cleaver's professional opinion, which he solicited whenever he completed a manuscript. In fact he concluded his preface to *The Exploration of Space* with an expression of gratitude to 'A. V. Cleaver for his careful reading of the MS and his many valuable, and frequently pungent, suggestions and criticisms'.

On 20 September Arthur flew to London and then drove west to Bishops Lydeard and spent four days at the farm. Before the end of the month he was in Prague, attending the International Aeronautical Federation conference. Next it was off to New York in early October, where he remained for two weeks.

Lester and Judy-Lynn del Rey invited Arthur and Isaac Asimov over for supper one evening. Lester did the cooking and served roast turkey.

Judy-Lynn was genuinely excited about having Arthur and Isaac over at the same time – two of the world's best and best-known writers of science and science fiction. If only Bob Heinlein was there too, she thought. Judy decided on the next best thing.

'Let's call Bob,' she said, and went to her bedroom phone and dialled the number. He was at home, and everyone spoke to him.

'That's the only time I can recall that Heinlein, Clarke and I were on a conference call,' said Isaac, whose exceptional memory brought forth a portion of the talk with Heinlein.

'I said, "Come on, fellows. We've been the *big three* now for decades, and people are getting tired of it. Don't you think, in order to give a break to the other writers, that one of you two (since you're older than I am), should step aside?" And Heinlein said, "Fuck the other writers!"'

That same evening Asimov penned a limerick for Clarke that is still hanging on his office wall:

> Old Arthur C. Clarke of Sri Lanka
> Now sits in the Sun sipping Sanka
>   Enjoying his ease
>   Excepting when he's
> Receiving pleased notes from his banker.

In mid-October Arthur went to Boston to receive the Bradford Washburn Award from the Museum of Science.

This pleased him greatly. 'I'm proud of it, and it's a very handsome lump of gold.' The award was given 'to recognise an outstanding contribution toward public understanding of science, appreciation of its fascination, and of the vital role it plays in all our lives'. It was established in 1964 in honour of the Museum Director, Bradford Washburn.

At the press conference following the award ceremony Arthur emphasised the tremendous changes that had taken place since the late 1930s, when he was 'one of a bunch of crazy Englishmen who used to meet several times a month in London pubs and talk about ways of going to the Moon.

'I saw the subject of space flight go through a complete cycle,' he said. 'One, it's utter nonsense, don't waste my time. Two, it's possible, but isn't worth doing. Three, I said it was a good idea all along. Now in some ways we're back to square one again. But to be fair, we have made some progress. We may have only gone back to square two.'

Coincidentally, the official publication date for the US edition of *The View from Serendip* was the same day Arthur was presented with the award – 17 October 1977. The book was a delightful and wide-ranging collection of essays, many of which concerned his life in Ceylon, and a few others which were reprints of important speeches. The essays and speeches were written over a period of twenty years, but none seemed dated.

Two days later Clarke was in Washington, DC, in the Gold Room of the Sam Rayburn Building, speaking before the 'Congressional Clearinghouse on the Future'. Congressman Charlie Rose had requested that he appear. The topic under discussion was energy for the future – a major preoccupation because of the decade's oil shortages.

There were plenty of Washington officials and friends to meet, and Arthur remained in the capital for a week. He lunched with the recently appointed head of NASA, Robert Frosch, visited Comsat, met Senator Adlai Stevenson and saw Bob and Ginny Heinlein before returning to London on the high road, via Concorde.

King's College, Arthur's alma mater, made him a fellow in 1977, so he had honours bestowed from both sides of the Atlantic. It was, he wrote to Sam Youd, 'about my first UK recognition! That middle C makes everyone assume I'm American, dammit'.

He was back home in Sri Lanka by early November working on *The Fountains of Paradise*, and by 13 December he was able to write in his daily log, 'First draft FOP finished.' Three days later he became sixty years old. It was not the happiest of birthdays. He had made it, but two of his dearest friends had not.

The year 1978 would prove to be unique. It was the only year Arthur did not leave his adopted homeland.

'I've become more and more reluctant to leave Sri Lanka,' he wrote Sam Youd, 'and only did so because the tax situation compelled it. But when they passed what's now generally known as the Clarke Act, I was able to move here for good, tax free. About four years ago I (or rather my company Underwater Safaris) bought a huge house in Colombo's Belgravia (if you can imagine that with palm trees) and as I have everything here that I need, I hardly ever go out – except for a couple of hours to a local club each afternoon to play table tennis.

'Underwater Safaris I leave entirely to my Sinhalese friend Hector Ekanayake and his Australian fiancée Valerie, who share the house with me . . . The company is doing very well – we're now building a couple of twenty-eight-foot dive boats to extend our operations. Among Hector's clients were the entire *Apollo 12* team when they got back from the Moon.'

Of his creative output, Arthur wrote, 'Professionally: the completion of the two books I've been working on for almost twenty years has cleaned out the cupboards in a way I'd never have believed possible. There's simply nothing more I want to write, fiction or non-fiction. And I don't have to if I don't want to.

'I had thought that *Imperial Earth* would be the big one . . . But it turned out that *The Fountains of Paradise* was *the* book, and the one I'll be remembered for, if at all . . .

'I do have one major project looming over me. Yorkshire TV (who did the one-hour documentary on me a few years ago) wants me to host a thirteen-part series on various scientific and other mysteries. They are writing the script and doing all the research; I'll vet, edit and narrate. They've agreed that all the shooting will be done here, if necessary.'

This was Arthur's domestic year. He was happy to remain in the big house in Barnes Place, which he had named 'Leslie's House' in memory of Leslie Ekanayake, his 'only perfect friend of a lifetime' . . .

He was, he admitted, resting on his laurels as 1978 came to a close. He bragged to one interviewer that he hadn't used a typewriter since January and confessed to a secret, humorous fantasy. 'I'm thinking of taking the typewriter down to the reef and photographing it surrounded by fish,' he told Malcolm Kirk, the interviewer/photographer for *OMNI* magazine.

'And at last I have time for a secret ambition I never dreamed I'd really achieve (I'll still need another five years . . .). I'm learning to play the piano!!' He had his first piano lesson on 5 September and stayed with it.

'I spend a half an hour a day on the piano and may appear in public around the year 2001!' Arthur wrote Tom Craven in December, shortly after celebrating his sixty-first birthday.

And to accompany the new music in his life was some good news.

'I've been appointed the Chancellor of the new Technical University here. I still haven't been officially notified, but it's definite. I'm not sure whether this is a life sentence, or whether I'll get time off for good behaviour.'

This appointment came from the President of Sri Lanka, J. R. Jayewardene, and Arthur received it with 'flattered alarm'. Why the alarm? 'My occupation of "resting on my laurels" has been jeopardised,' he wrote to Sam Youd in January. The newly created University of Moratuwa, formerly the University of Colombo, was an engineering campus of two thousand students.

And there was more good news from his British literary agent.

'I've just sold the UK paperback rights of *Fountains* for a record sum – it will pay for the hovercraft that I've now definitely ordered.' It appeared that Arthur would soon be floating – literally – on air!

Playboy magazine published two excerpts from *The Fountains of Paradise* in January and February 1979. (The January issue celebrated *Playboy*'s twenty-fifth anniversary.)

'The January *Playboy* has just come in,' Arthur wrote Sam. 'They've done me proud – except that they give a photo of the temple on Sri Pada (locale of the novel) as my house! I expect a delegation of indignant monks, when they get their subscription copy . . .'

The gaffe, he told Roger Caras, prompted the Colombo newspaper to run the headline, 'Playboy's Biggest Boob.'

Arthur was particularly fond of his latest novel.

'It's the most ambitious thing I have ever done,' he told Martin Walker from the *Guardian*. 'Everything is in it: Buddhist philosophy, ancient history, the ultimate space transport system. It's my magnum opus . . . Two main locales, both in Ceylon, are awe-inspiring places. One of them is Adam's Peak, sacred to every religion. Christians and Muslims say it's Adam's footstep on the summit, Buddhists say it must be Buddha's mark, and the Hindus say the footprint is that of the god Shiva.'

Arthur always felt a sense of elation when he finished a work, and this feeling had a decided influence on how he perceived any recently completed book. He was especially pleased with *Fountains* because his beloved tropical island played such an important part in it. And he was fascinated about how the concept of the 'space elevator' evolved separately, first in Russia and then in the United States, and what its real future potential might be. In theory it could offer an inexpensive and safe method of reaching space – an alternative to the costly and polluting chemical rockets that we still depend on today.

Arthur in fact devoted several pages at the end of the novel (in 'Sources and Acknowledgements') to detail the history of the idea, and he would deliver a major paper on the subject in Germany later in the year.

The theme of space elevators was also the topic of an introduction Arthur wrote in January for another science fiction writer's book – Charles Sheffield's *The Web Between the Worlds*. Such a contribution to another writer's work was a rare act for Arthur Clarke. That *Fountains of Paradise* and this book, published just months later, shared a major technological concept was purely coincidental, but there was concern that some people might misinterpret Sheffield's paperback novel as plagiarism. Arthur's introduction set the record straight.

'A clear case of plagiarism? No – merely an idea whose time has come. And I'm astounded that it hasn't come sooner . . .

'Anyone reading our two books will quickly see that the parallels were dictated by the fundamental mechanics of the subject – though in one major respect we evolved totally different solutions. Dr Sheffield's method of anchoring his "Beanstalk" is hair-raising, and I don't believe it would work.'

★

286

Time magazine asked Arthur to write a piece to mark the tenth anniversary of the first manned landing on the Moon. Published in the 16 July 1979 issue, it was titled, 'The Best Is Yet to Come'. In it, Clarke made the case that mankind reached the Moon earlier than it would have otherwise because of the vision and conviction of just a few people: 'Space travel is a technological mutation that should not really have arrived until the twenty-first century. But thanks to the ambition and genius of Wernher von Braun and Sergei Korolev, and their influence upon individuals as disparate as Kennedy and Khrushchev, the Moon – like the South Pole – was reached half a century ahead of time.'

Arthur's vision of the future, still optimistic, went out to millions of *Time* readers, and he introduced them to his latest technological concept – the space elevator.

'Today's comsats demonstrate how an object can remain poised over a fixed spot on the equator by matching its speed to the turning earth, 22,320 miles below,' he wrote. 'Now imagine a cable, linking the satellite to the ground. Payloads could be hoisted up it by purely mechanical means, reaching orbit without any use of rocket power. The cost of operations could be reduced to a tiny fraction of today's values.'

The same basic message about a new transportation system to space, although much amplified and accompanied with technical details, was presented by Clarke to the Thirtieth Congress of the International Astronautical Federation which met in Munich in September 1979.

CHAPTER 25

Transits/Eclipses

Less than a minute to go now. It's like a
door closing with a great light behind it, a
curved door, hanging up there in space. The
Moon has almost completely covered the
Sun. The last light is beginning to go. Just
a tiny narrow thread of light – that's all.
Going . . . going. Gone.
  – Filming total eclipse at Palam, India,
February 1980

In February 1980 Nora Clarke – mother of Arthur, Fred, Mary and
Michael – died at Dene Court in Somerset.

Arthur couldn't return to England in time. Nor could he have faced
it well had he gone. 'He had said his goodbyes to her at their last
meeting,' says Fred, 'for we knew the end was not far away. Yorkshire TV had arranged a tight schedule, and I saw no reason to hold
up everything until he could have got back to England. Nor would
Mother have expected it under the circumstances.'

The day Nora Clarke was buried, her eldest son was in India with
the Yorkshire Television crew. The crew had arrived in Colombo a
few days earlier and had begun filming some of the introductory
material for the *Mysterious World* series. They followed Arthur to
Hyderabad for more footage.

Fred wrote to Arthur on 15 February about their mother's passing.
'For the last four days she was completely out of pain and at peace.
She slipped quietly away. There were two people beside her all the
time.'

Arthur wrote a brief letter to Tom Craven about Nora's passing.
'Mother died just before I left for India – it was really a great relief
as she had failed badly and her life was becoming a misery to herself
and all around.'

Nora Clarke was gone, but not her indomitable spirit. All four of
her children – reared alone by her after her husband Charles died
nearly fifty years earlier – were well and prospering. And Ballifants,

their farm, remained in the family with her youngest son, Michael, running it as a dairy farm. What else could a good mother want before saying goodbye for the last time?

Arthur booked into the Hyderabad Bantarra Hotel on 15 February 1980. The next day he, John Fairley and the Yorkshire Television crew filmed the total eclipse of the sun in nearby Palam. This became the opening sequence for the Yorkshire TV series, *Arthur C. Clarke's Mysterious World*.

'There's the corona!' Arthur exclaimed as the camera captured solar totality. 'The most glorious sight – a great crown of light – the solar corona. There are streams of light stretching out around it, and very bright bursts of flame near the edge itself . . . I can't see any stars, just Venus and little Mercury.'

The two men responsible for the series, John Fairley and Simon Welfare, first met Arthur in the 1970s, when they were filming a Yorkshire Television documentary, *Arthur C. Clarke: The 2001 Ideas of the Prophet of the Space Age*, produced and directed by Michael Deakin. Deakin, by the way, remains the most active film-maker of Arthur's work after all these years, with plans and rights to film many of the classic stories. In 1990 he created a screenplay of *Fall of Moondust* for the television market.

When Arthur returned from the eclipse in late February, the year was still young and things were hopping. A photographer from *OMNI* magazine visited Arthur on February's extra leap year day to capture some images for future issues. This new popular science magazine ran a lavish artwork spread in April 1980 illustrating Clarke's First, Second and Third Laws, the last of which is perhaps most often quoted: 'Any sufficiently advanced technology is indistinguishable from magic.'

Colombo entertained an unusual ship in early March. 'I visited *The Golden Hind*, or at least the remarkable full-scale replica which sailed into Colombo Harbour,' Arthur remembers. The day after this replica of Sir Francis Drake's famous ship anchored in Sri Lankan waters, Arthur's long-time friend and fellow writer Bob Heinlein and his wife Ginny arrived on the island. They spent a few days relaxing at the bungalow in Unawatuna and then, says Arthur, 'We chartered a plane and flew Bob and Ginny over Sigiriya and Adam's Peak and then on to the Great Basses Reef. Hector and Valerie were at Great Basses then, instructing thirteen Italian divers, and we flew out over the reef and, in the good old RAF tradition, bombed them with toilet paper rolls before flying back up the coast.'

Colombo Harbour, always busy, had the USS *Enterprise* and the SS *Universe*, the sailing university, anchor there in late March. Arthur had sailed on the SS *Universe* in the spring of 1979 and he now made the reacquaintance of Dr Lloyd Lewan and his colleagues who ran the educational programme, 'Semester at Sea'. They discussed future schedules and how Arthur might join them again as a lecturer on future voyages. The sea beckoned, and he agreed to go the following October.

On 19 August Arthur flew to London and remained in England for about a month. All four Clarke children gathered together at Fred's home, Dene Court, and held the annual general meeting of the Rocket Publishing Company. A family portrait was taken during this visit.

'It's really just a report of what I've been doing during the year, and whether we've made a profit or spent more money than Arthur has earned,' says Fred of the annual meetings. 'The meetings usually take about an hour, and then we all go and have a meal together.'

Before Arthur left Somerset on this visit he had a reunion at Ballifants with his dear Aunt Nellie, who had played such an important role during his childhood.

A week later Arthur was back in London. There was a press preview of *Arthur C. Clarke's Mysterious World*, and Arthur met his English literary agent, Jacqueline Korn, lunched with Stanley Kubrick and attended a Mensa conference at Trinity College in Cambridge.

On 10 September Arthur delivered the Second Annual *OMNI* Lecture, 'Towards the Space Elevator', at the Royal Institute. The next day he and Kathy Keeton, *OMNI* magazine's president (and wife of Bob Guccione), flew in a small plane to Goonhilly Downs, the satellite Earth station on the Cornwall coast, to shoot some television ads for the magazine.

'The weather was miserable that day,' says Keeton, 'and there must have been five different weather scenes during the shoot. It rained, the sun shined, it sleeted, it was misty. Besides the big Goonhilly dish in the background, we shot some scenes on the beach.

'Arthur wasn't feeling well, but he kept going all day,' says Keeton. 'He was marvellous.'

Ridley Scott, director of the 1979 film *Alien*, directed the commercials. Variations on the two were created by editing and rearranging the footage. One commercial opened with a view of the Atlantic ocean and pounding surf.

'Here in the sea,' said Arthur, 'billions of years ago, life began an odyssey that would reach across space and time . . . I know that even the sea is not eternal, but the life it spawned will survive, for Man's destiny lies among the stars.' This narration then led into 'the unfolding universe of *OMNI* magazine' – his final words.

As Arthur spoke, a white doorway appeared on the beach with the breaking waves in the background. Arthur then stepped off camera. The door opened, and there was Arthur C. Clarke standing by the same white door and ocean scene. As he talked about Man's destiny among the stars, the door opened once more. This time it was filled with stars. Intimations of the Star Gate in *2001*.

As if the weather problems weren't trouble enough during the filming, they also made the return to London more than merely inconvenient.

'The weather turned so awful at the end of the day,' says Keeton, 'that the plane couldn't take off. So Arthur and I ended up catching this terrible train back to London. It took all night. There was no heat, there was no food – no coffee or tea or anything. We ended up at Paddington Station at about six in the morning.'

For Arthur this was just one of many hassles endured in the cause of spreading good news about science and technology to ever-growing audiences. His message was sharply enhanced and amplified by the very technology he spread the good news about. The timing of his career, Arthur realised, was serendipitous, coinciding as it did with the new mass media of television and paperback book publishing. He was one of the very first writers to appear in both of these media on a regular basis after World War II, and they spread his published work and ideas to hundreds of thousands, then millions, of people.

On 18 October Arthur flew to Jakarta in Indonesia and rendezvoused with the SS *Universe*. The next day they set sail. As the ship passed through the Sundra Strait, between Java and Sumatra, it sailed by Krakatoa, the famous volcano which literally blew itself out of the Pacific when it erupted in August 1883. The soundwaves generated by the explosion travelled three thousand miles and fifty-foot waves crashed upon shores and settlements, causing more than thirty-five thousand deaths.

Arthur loved life aboard ship – especially this one whose passenger students all relished new experiences and enjoyed learning.

'He was our distinguished writer in residence,' says Lloyd Lewan, dean of the 'Semester at Sea' programme. 'He would do the preparatory slide shows and lectures about Sri Lanka – its culture and history and literature – and he would do special programmes. I remember one called "UFOs and Other Nonsense". One evening he played a tape where he introduced Asimov, and Asimov introduced him, and they spoke about science fiction. Another time he lectured on the Great Barrier Reef and his experiences there.'

Somewhere in the Indian Ocean the science fiction film classic *Things to Come* was shown to an appreciative audience, and Arthur added his comments afterwards. A video tape on exponential population growth by a University of Colorado professor was once shown. 'Arthur watched and listened,' said Lloyd, 'and I asked him to react to it. He took the microphone, raised it up to the ceiling speaker, and the sound exponentially screeched across the room. Then he pulled it away and the sound reduced exponentially. Then all he said was, "It's up to the human race." Isn't that powerful?'

Perhaps more than anything else, however, Arthur was elated at the number of potential competitors there were for table tennis. He played a lot, and he won a lot.

The next port of call was Madras, on the south-east coast of India. The ship anchored there on 26 October and the next day Arthur visited Harry Miller and his snakes at the Snake Park.

'I met Harry in the mid-1970s, when I was filming with Tom Craven. He was a photographer specialising in wildlife, and a star reporter of the *Indian Express*. Though Welsh, he's lived in India most of his life and married a Hindu lady. He's had a *National Geographic* cover and has written extensively on animals.

'I stayed with him in the seventies at his cottage outside Madras, and have lots of photographs of that occasion, draped with Harry's snakes. I've seen him on all my visits to Madras, and he's come to Sri Lanka several times.'

On 29 October Arthur delivered a lecture at the Indian Institute of Technology before sailing south and returning to Sri Lanka on 1 November.

The SS *Universe* remained in Colombo Harbour for a few days and one evening Arthur, Lloyd Lewan, the dean, Paul Eckert, the assistant dean, and Roger Moss had a pleasant dinner together before the ship sailed once more.

'Roger Moss was one of the lecturers on the *Universe*,' says Arthur, '(subject: psychology and American Indian sign language). I started the rumour that you hadn't lived until you have seen Roger give his lecture on sex, in *Indian sign language*.'

Arthur sailed on the SS *Universe* several times in the 1980s. He knew this unique travelling educational programme had great value for students; he believed in it, and he even gave a scholarship for one student.

Says Lloyd Lewan, 'I remember sitting with him at breakfast and saying, "Arthur, we have a terrible time coming up with funds to put minorities on the ship." Of course he wanted to help. The result was he gave us a full scholarship for a minority student – a black woman from the University of Pittsburgh. He paid for it completely.'

Voyager 1 flew by Saturn's mysterious moon, Titan, on 11 November. Radar instruments aboard the spacecraft found out that Titan wasn't the largest moon in the solar system after all; it had to give up its title to Jupiter's Ganymede. This great interplanetary robot from Earth thus sent back another cosmic revelation before leaving Saturn and family and sailing out of the solar system for ever.

The communications revolution reached another plateau on 4 December 1980 when *Intelsat V*, the largest comsat ever, was successfully launched on an Atlas Centaur rocket from Cape Kennedy and placed in a geostationary orbit.

Communications satellite technology had come a long way since the launch of *Early Bird*, the world's first commercial comsat, on 6 April 1965, when its capacity was a modest 240 telephone circuits *or* one TV channel. Fifteen years later, in the autumn of 1980, *Intelsat V* had the capacity to handle simultaneously twelve thousand telephone circuits (fifty times that of *Early Bird*) *and* two TV links. Before the end of the 1980s capacity again would be more than doubled with the launch of *Intelsat VI* in 1989.

If better and more communication between nations and individuals was what was needed for global progress, then the future was promising. Technology had put state-of-the-art hardware in space, following Arthur C. Clarke's vision of 1945, and it was improving all the time. If the global family wanted to talk more it had all the 'extra-terrestrial relays' high above Earth it needed by the end of 1980. A decade later, as geopolitics changed old political divisions formed after World War II, it appeared that a lot of chatter and exchange of information had been taking place in Clarke's orbit.

CHAPTER 26

Odyssey's Return

> I showed him [Ambassador Vernon
> Walters] the dedication of *Odyssey Two*,
> which is highly classified until I get back
> from Moscow. (It's going to delight and
> enrage my Russian friends, about fifty-
> fifty.)
>
> – 'Egogram', 4 April 1982

The film business dominated Arthur's activities in early 1981. The
movie *Beddegama* ('Village in the Jungle'), in which Arthur had had
a bit part, opened in Colombo in February. Filmed in Sri Lanka
during the summer of 1979, it was based on Leonard Woolf's book,
The Village in the Jungle, published by the Hogarth Press in 1913.
Clarke played Woolf as a young magistrate in Ceylon, dressed in the
Edwardian colonial clothing of the time. The scenes were shot in the
actual courtroom over which Woolf presided.

'As I sat on the bench in my borrowed judicial robes, I was not in
the least conscious of acting a role; even the camera and lights did
not break the spell. The courtroom was a time machine that had
carried me back to the beginning of the century.'

American producer Julia Phillips descended on Barnes Place with
a movie script in hand about this time. She had an impressive track
record, with such successful credits as *Close Encounters*, *The Sting*
and *Taxi Driver*.

'When I made it clear I wasn't interested (even for quarter of a
million),' Arthur wrote Tom Craven, 'she cheerfully left with *five*
other projects – we'll see what happens. Meanwhile I'm waiting to
hear what Yorkshire TV want me to do next.'

A few weeks before Arthur's friend Walter Cronkite arrived with
a CBS television crew to film a feature for *Walter Cronkite's Universe*
the maiden test flight mission of the space shuttle was flown. Launch
date: 12 April 1981. Commander John Young and pilot Robert
Crippen flew the *Columbia* for thirty-six orbits above the Earth and
tested all the systems. They successfully landed at Edwards Air Force

Base in California on 14 April. The first reusable spaceship was also 'the world's greatest flying machine', according to Commander Young, and history was made.

Walter Cronkite, his wife Betsy and the CBS crew arrived in Colombo in May, and in June Arthur was in Paris addressing the UNESCO Conference on the International Programme for the Development of Communications (IPDC). He was the Sri Lankan delegate, and his talk, 'New Communications and the Developing World', summarised what new communications hardware and services would be available in the next ten years. (It was later reprinted in his 1984 collection of speeches and essays, *1984: Spring, A Choice of Futures*.)

During his presentation he mentioned the recent Cronkite visit and related it to new technology.

'Last month I had the pleasure of showing my old friend Walter Cronkite around Sri Lanka while we filmed one of his "Universe" programmes. I say "filmed", but actually we were using electronic cameras, and it was wonderful to view what we had shot within minutes instead of days.

'However, even the electronic cameraman still has to get his cassettes through an obstacle course of postal authorities and customs officials and censors. But not for much longer; very soon he will need only a small collapsible dish, about the shape and size of a beach umbrella, and he'll be able to beam his pictures up to the nearest satellite, and straight to home.'

More than thirty nations were represented at the conference at UNESCO headquarters in Paris that June.

'I sat next to the Russians and opposite the Americans,' recalls Arthur, 'and had a lot of fun with both.

'UNESCO has been severely, and not always fairly, criticised in many quarters for its assumed attitude towards the free flow of communications – which is what this conference was all about. So I seized the opportunity to point out that it didn't matter *what* the politicians said or did; the issue had already been settled by the engineers.

'Rather to my surprise, the speech was applauded by *all* the delegates. Obviously, some of them hadn't understood what I was saying . . .'

Arthur also spoke about the marvels of future 'electronic educators' – hand-held microprocessing machines that would provide instant access to the information of an entire library and tutoring in any subject. They would be adaptable, through a wide variety of plug-in programmes, to many teaching and learning situations. If the future comes down to what H. G. Wells envisioned as a 'race between education and castastrophe' (a remark which Arthur sometimes quotes), then such micro-teaching machines could give education a real advantage in the race to solve the ever-more complex problems confronting our species.

Joseph Pelton, friend and telecommunications expert, was at the conference. 'This was at the height of Arthur's interest in what can be done with space technology for educational purposes, and this was the thrust of his keynote speech.

'In effect the conference was a US–Sri Lankan initiative. Its purpose was to make a positive response to the need for education and information in the developing countries, rather than the negative connotation about a new world information order where there would be control and censorship of what the developed countries might send to the developing countries, and so on. There was a great deal of tension during the 1970s on that point. And Arthur was right centre stage of some of these major developments in terms of world politics.'

The conference over, Arthur flew across the Channel to London on 23 June. Fred was there to pick him up and they drove directly to Somerset and Dene Court. During the last week in June Simon Welfare and John Fairley visited Bishops Lydeard to discuss the possibility of another Yorkshire TV series. There was other miscellaneous business to conduct, but the really important meeting was to take place in early July in Somerset.

Scott Meredith and his wife Helen arrived from the United States on 1 July 1981. Arthur was expecting to hear one of the greatest appeals of Scott's career. He had come to England to try to convince Arthur to write a sequel to *2001*. One more book for Arthur? This would take some doing, but if anybody could convince Arthur to write another 'last book' it was Scott Meredith; he had had a lot of practice over the years.

'When it came time to force Arthur to write *2010* – and that's exactly what it amounted to – I had told him that I was going to Sri Lanka to see him,' says Scott. 'We had the visit all set and then one of their many revolutions broke out. So we decided to meet on neutral ground, and I went over to Arthur's house in England.'

How did Scott Meredith win Arthur over? 'It was a variety of things,' says Scott. 'Threats, cajoling, flattery. But most important, I think, was when I said, "You know, Arthur, none of us knows what the hell the ending of *2001* was really all about. We don't understand it, we're not sure what you meant, and you owe it to the public and, most of all, Arthur, you owe it to me."

'Arthur was afraid, I think, to tackle *2010* because *2001* was such a success, and he was typecast.

'Well, about the third day Arthur knocked on my door at about six in the morning, waking my wife and me up. As I opened the door, thinking the house was on fire, Arthur stuck his hand out and said, "I'll do it." That's how the thing finally worked.'

'I realised he was right,' Arthur said later, referring to the enigmatic ending of *2001*. 'In *2001* we went to Jupiter, and the finale of the film takes place among the moons of Jupiter. When I wrote the novel those moons were just spots of light we knew nothing whatsoever about. Well, the *Voyager* spacecraft went there only twelve years later. So with the new information about conditions on Europa, Io, Callisto, Ganymede, the moons of Jupiter – and Jupiter itself – that I'm able to work into the new novel, I have a much more realistic background.'

Voyager 1 encountered Jupiter and its moons in the spring of 1979 and flew on to ringed Saturn and its retinue in the autumn of 1980. During the Saturn flyby, radar instruments aboard the spacecraft discovered that Titan wasn't the largest moon in the solar system after all; it had given up its title to Jupiter's Ganymede. Clarke incorporated many of the *Voyager* revelations into the planetary descriptions of *2010*:

'The most extraordinary feature of the Ganymedean landscape was the presence of meandering stripes, built up from scores of parallel furrows a few kilometres apart. This grooved terrain looked as if it had been produced by armies of intoxicated ploughmen, weaving back and forth across the face of the satellite.'

Such detailed descriptions would have been impossible before the *Voyager* flybys, and Clarke took great care to make them accurate in his second odyssey.

'You know,' says Scott, 'Arthur has retired about three hundred times since 1980. He always says, "I've retired." But he's only done these hundred things since he's retired. He works much faster and harder in retirement.'

The fact that this was only a book contract, and did not involve Arthur in a movie obligation in any way, helped Arthur keep his *angst* to a minimum. Just a novel to write – no film, no Kubrick, and none of the big problems of *2001*. And the advance was encouraging, to understate the truth. Within a few months Scott had negotiated a one-book contract for *2010* with the del Reys of Ballantine Books for a million dollars. In the UK, the book would be published by Grafton Books.

Arthur wrote *2010*, the novel, in about nine months – from July 1981 to March 1982. It was a concentrated effort, and luckily there were no major interruptions that ate up weeks of writing time, although Roger Caras and an ABC TV unit arrived to film a segment for '20/20' in early August.

Roger took the opportunity to conduct a long interview with Arthur, which went beyond the scope of the '20/20' segment. A small portion of this off-camera conversation was quoted in Roger's piece, 'Our Man in the Future', published by *Science Digest* in March 1982. During the interview Arthur told Roger one of the secrets to his often successful forecasts.

'If you are an optimist you have a better chance of making a self-fulfilling prophecy,' he said. 'If you say this is a wonderful world and we can make it better, then there is a chance that people will listen to you and do what you say.'

During one of the '20/20' scenes Arthur and Roger rode side by side on elephants – the only time, surprisingly, Arthur had ever ridden on one during his twenty-five years in Sri Lanka. As they swayed rhythmically to their elephants' gaits, they discussed the importance of preserving rare species and preventing their extinction.

'Any creature could ultimately be reproduced from a computer readout,' Arthur said, predicting a time when zoologists could recreate even extinct animals. 'We will eventually have complete codings of anything we're interested in and then can reproduce it.'

He agreed with Roger that a decline of biological diversity threatens future life.

'In biological diversity we have stability,' he said. 'One of our troubles is we can't create large, complex systems that are stable. Nature can and that's one of the things we can learn from nature.'

The '20/20' segment began with a dawn over the Indian Ocean and a brief description of Arthur C. Clarke's adopted country.

'Many of the elements of Sri Lanka, including its mystical and religious elements, even if I don't necessarily agree with them, I respect them and I have worked them into my books,' says Arthur. As he speaks, the ABC camera captures the parade of the Buddha's tooth, the Perahera, a festival in Kandy that is held under the full moon of August.

'But I'm anti-mysticism,' he goes on. 'I'm very anti the sort of lame brains who accept anything fanciful, nonsensical like pyramid power, astrology, which is utter rubbish, much UFOlogy, flying saucers. There's so much garbage floating around and on the news-stands. This is one thing that does worry me about the present mental state of the West . . . At the same time I'm sure there are many very strange things in the universe.'

In another shot Arthur is on the roof of his home in Colombo looking at the Moon through his telescope.

'It's just past half full, and as it happens I'm looking this very second at the two main locations at the opening of 2001. The great crater Clavius, which is a magnificent crater. I can see about a dozen small internal craters. This is where the Moon bus took off at the beginning of 2001 to the crater Tycho, which is just above it, a very sharply defined crater with a beautiful central peak.'

Not many authors can revisit a scene from their novel by peering through a telescope.

'Now working night and day on novel,' Arthur wrote in haste to Roger in mid-November. 'Going well – getting word processor next week to start on final version.'

When 'Archie' (as he christened his Archives III computer) came into his life, Arthur had produced about a hundred pages of 'messy' manuscript on his electric typewriter.

'As soon as I realised what word processing could do, all writing came to an abrupt halt. I was in exactly the same position as an Egyptian scribe who had spent his life carving inscriptions on granite – and suddenly discovered ink and papyrus.'

After hiring someone to key the hundred pages of typescript into Archie's memory, Arthur began writing the rest of 2010 on his word processor.

'I can honestly say that I have never touched a typewriter since that day.'

He was still thrilled about his new computer in the spring of 1982 when he sent his first 'Egogram' to friends.

The marvellous thing about Archie (Archives III, 5 megabytes Winchester disk, Wordstar program) is that he has totally elim-inated the drudgery (mechanical, not mental!) from writing; I could no more imagine going back to a typewriter – I've not touched one since last year – than to a slide-rule after using a pocket calculator. (That's a pretty exact analogy.) Getting rid of carbon paper (ugh!) is another bonus; it gives a wonderful sense of power to know that I have only to press a button and

I can zapp off as many perfect copies as I like of any letter. (Archie's main memory can hold 1,000,000 words; the diskettes about 80,000. But the printer is rather slow – it takes almost a minute to do a 500-word page.) So now I'm writing letters again *for fun* – something I've not done since about 1939 – and I don't even rule out the possibility that I may do another book every few years, if I happen to feel like it (and for no other reason).

Arthur was the first to admit that Archie had 'quite literally changed my life'. He was writing more, and even after the nine-month writing marathon which produced *2010: Odyssey Two*, he was generating a substantial amount of correspondence.

The new novel, he told his friends in early 1982, was unexpected. 'Scott Meredith is entirely to blame (he flew over to UK and slipped something into my coffee at Dene Court.)' But by April the real work was done on *2010*, and Arthur was experiencing his after-delivery euphoria.

Ballantine Books was already thinking about promotion ideas and asked Arthur to commit to promoting the book in New York, where a big publication party was planned, and in Los Angeles.

The US visit was only one of several major trips in 1982. Clarke also learned that he had won the Marconi Fellowship Award and would be going to The Netherlands for the ceremonies in June. After this, he would fly to Moscow – his first visit to the Soviet Union. Summer lecture commitments would also take him to Vienna and Geneva.

The Marconi International Fellowship was created in 1974 to mark the centennial of Guglielmo Marconi's birth, the Italian Nobel Prize winner who invented wireless telegraphy and transmitted messages across the Atlantic. The first fellowship was awarded in 1975. Arthur was its eighth recipient, and he was especially proud to share the honour with some friends who were past winners – John Pierce (1979) and Yash Pal (1980).

The Fellowship Award was granted to individuals who 'have made a significant contribution to the advancement of the technology of communications through discoveries, inventions or innovations in the physical or information sciences or engineering'.

Arthur C. Clarke arrived in Amsterdam on 9 June 1982 and was met at his hotel by Gioia Marconi Braga, Marconi's daughter and founder of the Award. She was accompanied by her husband George

Braga and then Secretary of the Fellowship, Walter Orr Roberts. The Award ceremony was held on 11 June at The Hague in the Hall of the Knights (the Ridderzaal).

Arthur's corporate host, Philips, had arranged an historic exhibit of communications technology. It ranged from early radio equipment dating back to Marconi's day right up to a large model of the latest communication satellite of the early 1980s.

'They had installed a dish in the courtyard to receive TV from a European satellite,' Arthur wrote later in a newsletter, 'and the well-known broadcaster Raymond Baxter greeted us from the Goonhilly Downs Earth Station, reminding us that Marconi conducted his famous Atlantic transmission not far from here . . .'

His Royal Highness Prince Claus presented Arthur with the unique trophy, consisting of 'two orthogonal brass rings, with plastic threads radiating down to them from a circular ring at the top – I assume they represent radio waves beamed somewhere!'

In his acceptance speech Arthur told his distinguished audience how he had come to write his famous *Wireless World* article in 1945 when he was serving as a radar officer in the Royal Air Force. At that time he and other early members of the British Interplanetary Society were trying to revive their organisation which had been inactive during the war.

'So communications and astronautics were inextricably entangled in my mind, with results that now seem inevitable,' he said, modestly emphasising that if he hadn't first proposed geostationary relays someone else soon would have.

'My efforts to promote and publicise the idea may have been much more important than conceiving it,' he went on, again emphasising the practical roles of scientists like John Pierce and Harold Rosen whom he considered the 'true fathers of satellite communications'.

'The world needs uninhibited thinkers not afraid of far-out speculation; it also needs hard-headed, conservative engineers who can make their dreams come true. They complement each other, and progress is impossible without both.'

The Award was accompanied by a $35,000 grant, with which Arthur proposed to establish a Developing World Communications Centre, in co-operation with the government of Sri Lanka, at the University of Moratuwa.

Arthur flew on to Moscow on 14 June, arriving in the evening. He was met at the airport by the Counsellor of the Sri Lanka Embassy, Casie Chetty, and three Russians: Vasili Zacharchenko, editor of *Tekhnika Molodezhi* magazine; Oleg Bitov, translator of Arthur's last two books published in Russia (*Rendezvous with Rama* and *Fountains of Paradise*); and his interpreter and guide, Svetlana Prokhorova.

'Though it was now late evening there was still plenty of light (something I couldn't grow accustomed to after two decades near the equator) so we made a quick trip to Red Square for the usual photos at Lenin's tomb. Then to the huge Ukrania Hotel, where I slept well and woke up to the good news that the Falklands war was over.' (Arthur had his Sony radio, and with some difficulty he could get news from the BBC's World Service.)

The Moscow Space Park, with its impressive displays of spacecraft, was Arthur's first stop the following day. Mounted outside was a huge Vostok rocket.

His interpreter, Svetlana, and an official photographer next accompanied Arthur to 'Star Village' (Zvezdny Gorodok), some fifty kilometres from Moscow. Arthur voluntarily handed over his camera before they entered, but it was given back as soon as they were inside and he was able to photograph whatever he wanted.

At the entrance to the administrative building, Arthur met his good friend Alexei Leonov, cosmonaut and general, and a TV crew. Leonov was the first human to ever 'walk' in space, and he was also the Russian commander of the 1975 *Apollo–Soyuz* mission.

'We greeted each other with bear hugs, and he introduced me to two other cosmonauts I'd met before – Vitaliy Sevastyanov and Valery Lyakov, whom I'd recently taken for a spin in my hovercraft.'

Arthur was next introduced to General Beregovoy, commanding officer of Star Village and one-time pilot for the *Soyuz 3* mission. The general gave an unexpected lecture, illustrated with his own sketches, about mankind harming the environment. After this, Arthur and Alexei exchanged gifts – a set of British Interplanetary Society ties for Alexei and a volume of space art, *Life Among Stars*, by Alexei and fellow artist Andrei Sokolov for Arthur.

Then Alexei took Arthur to see the film, *Our Yuri*, which his host explained had never been screened elsewhere. It showed the cosmonaut's training as well as his family life. Arthur found it 'deeply moving'.

After the movie they visited *Soyuz-Salyut* trainers and crawled inside to be filmed and interviewed by the TV crew.

'I was also inserted, with great hilarity, into an EVA suit and then filmed grinning inanely through the visor.'

Still followed by the TV crew, they proceeded to the Gagarin memorial and then on to Gagarin's own office. It was exactly as Gagarin had left it on 27 March 1968, the day he died when his jet trainer crashed. They had stopped the clock to record his time of death.

'I heard the crash,' Alexei told Arthur sadly. 'We never found out exactly what happened.'

Arthur was then given a fragment of the jet in which the first man to orbit planet Earth had been killed, and a commemorative medal struck in 1981 on the twentieth anniversary of Gagarin's historic flight.

It wasn't until Arthur was a guest for dinner at Alexei and Svetlana Leonov's apartment that the subject of his not-yet-published new novel, *2010: Odyssey Two*, came up. Between toasts, and with the family parrot Lolita occasionally orbiting the room, Arthur told Alexei some exciting news.

'I revealed that most of the action in *2010: Odyssey Two* takes place aboard the spaceship *Cosmonaut Alexei Leonov*. This obviously delighted Alexei, and now most of the Soviet Union has heard, via TV, his ebullient reaction: "Then it must be a good ship!"'

The ultimate compliment delivered, Arthur was still not finished. Through his translator, he expressed his hope to Alexei that the joint mission to Jupiter in the new novel, where Americans and Russians work together and become friends, might in its own small way foster friendship between the two nations. But, he continued, genuine understanding must be based on honesty, and he had to be honest and warn him: 'There were some aspects of the book that would not be well received in the Soviet Union. In particular, the plasma propulsion system for *Leonov* was being invented right now [in the novel], by Russia's most famous scientist, whose moving appeals for peace I greatly admired. He has plenty of time on his hands, being exiled in Gorky . . .

'Alexei gave a wry smile, and we parted affectionately.' Arthur did not, however, reveal his controversial dedication to *2010* at this time. 'I felt it tactless to spell out in detail.'

The dedication read:

> Dedicated, with respectful admiration, to two great
> Russians, both depicted herein:
>
> General Alexei Leonov – Cosmonaut, Hero of the
> Soviet Union, Artist
> and
> Academician Andrei Sakharov – Scientist,
> Nobel Laureate, Humanist

The Clarke entourage drove back to Moscow, and editor Zachar-chenko and Arthur caught the midnight sleeper to Leningrad. TV cameras were there to greet them as they stepped on to the platform the next morning.

'Among those waiting for us I was delighted to meet Yuri Artsuta-nov, inventor of the "space elevator" . . . He seems a shy, modest person, and I hope all the publicity (the cameras invaded his apart-ment when I was there) hasn't upset his life.'

Two days were spent in Leningrad, and Arthur's schedule was hectic. There were two TV interviews, a visit to the local Writers' Union and to Czar Peter's country estate and, of course, to the famous Hermitage with its more than two million exhibits.

On 18 June he returned to Moscow and made his final round of official visits, including stops at Intersputnik and the Ministry of Posts and Telecommunications. That evening he went to Moscow's Writers' Union and met about twenty writers and editors who spe-cialised in science fiction, a very popular genre in the Soviet Union.

On Saturday Arthur had a conference with the director, Sagdeyev, and his top scientists of the Institute of Space Research. When the Russians expressed regret that the Jet Propulsion Laboratory had been forced to take on defence contracts Arthur agreed, but quickly pointed out that the Soviet's military space programme was much more vigorous than that of the United States.

Later that day Arthur was flattered when Nina Kubatieva, a univer-sity student from Novosibirsk, presented him with a copy of her academic thesis 'The Science Fiction Novels of Arthur C. Clarke', and another student who had corresponded with Arthur from time to time, Larisa Mikhaylova, gave him her thesis on 'British and American Science Fiction'.

One more television taping for a Russian science show, and Arthur prepared for departure. Before he left for the Sheremetyevo-2 airport he got a surprise call from Alexei Leonov, wishing him a good flight. Alexei was on his way to the launch site for the next manned Russian mission – the flight of *Soyuz T-6* on 24 June which would rendezvous and dock with *Salyut 7*.

Arthur's interpreter paid him what she considered to be a compli-ment before he left the hotel. 'You're not a bit like an Englishman,' she said with a subtle smile and twinkle in the eye.

Arthur had been in Russia for a week, and he would never forget it. Perhaps in some small way he had brought his vision of a global family closer to reality.

★

The post was piled high when he returned to Colombo on 21 June, and it included the galleys of *2010* – 'with an editorial request that all corrections be phoned to New York within forty-eight hours'.

More deadlines for Arthur, but he had to keep his publishers happy. 'Archie' had been upgraded with a modem, so while the text of *2010* was sent to New York on a disk the corrections would be sent via satellite and international telephone circuits.

'It was a great thrill when, after several false tries, I succeeded in sending a short file called ODYCOR from Colombo to New York,' says Arthur, who ended his back-of-the-book acknowledgements in *2010: Odyssey Two* with that fact: 'Last-minute corrections were transmitted through the Padukka Earth Station and the Indian Ocean Intelsat V.'

Not long after he had cleared away the backlog of correspondence and chores, Arthur was off to Europe to participate in two important conferences.

He was a Sri Lanka delegate to the Second United Nations Conference on the Exploration and Peaceful Uses of Outer Space (UNISPACE 82), which was held in Vienna in early August. Later in the month, he addressed the meeting of the UN Committee on Disarmament in Geneva.

Carl Sagan was also in Vienna attending UNISPACE 82, and Arthur and Carl gave two of the three keynote addresses at the conference. Oleg Gazenko of the Soviet Union gave the third.

'Oleg's my second favourite Russian [after Alexei Leonov],' says Arthur. 'I told him that.'

Clarke's Vienna speech, 'Space Flight – Imagination and Reality', intentionally avoided any politically sensitive issues. The fact that Arthur would be talking about the militarisation of space later in the month to the UN Committee on Disarmament no doubt was a primary reason for this. Also the spacefaring nations had opposed including the subject of space militarisation on the official agenda of UNISPACE 82.

Before leaving the podium, however, Arthur did quote a well-known phrase from his first novel, *Prelude to Space*: 'We will take no frontiers into space.' This succinct statement reflected his unwavering conviction that no territorial disputes should be exported to orbit. Although the UN agenda didn't include the militarisation of space as a topic, it was on the minds of all present. In his opening address the Secretary General of the United Nations mentioned the urgent need to prevent a new arms race in space.

Arthur's 'Space Flight' talk was a well-wrought overview of space fantasies and science fiction dating from Lucian of Samos in AD 160 all the way to Arthur's own *2010: Odyssey Two* (he'd never miss a good PR opportunity). He described and compared means of propulsion over the centuries, and even dug out the first use of the 'spacegun' launcher, made famous by Jules Verne, from a 1728 book *A Trip to the Moon* by the obscure Irish writer, Murtagh McDermot.

Propulsion concepts evolved from the supernatural to the scientific, and Arthur scrutinised the early ones for science and the modern ones for superstition. Only since 1925 did rockets for space flight receive any serious attention.

'It is hard to believe,' he said, 'that this pioneering era is only half a century ago, and that a mere forty years after the flight of the first liquid-fuelled rocket in 1926, men were preparing to go to the Moon.'

The audience heard about Russian Yuri Artsutanov and his 1960 space elevator concept which became a major theme in *Fountains of Paradise*.

'Perhaps you may consider that the space elevator put too much of a strain on the imagination – but without imagination, nothing is ever achieved, as the history of astronautics amply proves . . . It should never be forgotten that, without some foundation of reality, a science fiction would be impossible, and that therefore exact knowledge is the friend, not the enemy, of imagination and fantasy.'

It was Sri Lanka's Ambassador in Geneva, Tissa Jayakoddy, who had asked Arthur to address the UN Committee on Disarmament, and on 31 August Dr Clarke delivered his speech 'War and Peace in the Space Age'.

'My Geneva speech was probably the most important thing I've ever done,' Arthur told a journalist a few months later. 'I'm very proud of that speech. I also had lunch with the American, Soviet and Chinese ambassadors, at the same table. They told me I should have been a diplomat – which I'm not sure is a compliment.'

In his 'War and Peace' speech, he spoke of the complexities and fuzzy lines between military and peaceful uses of technology. For example, scientific satellites that detect minute irregularities in the Earth's gravitational field have been extremely important to those who design intercontinental missiles, and so on. Citing several real-world examples, Arthur made the case that the missile numbers and other military counts can be misleading and can actually result in dangerous and wasteful policy decisions.

'The importance of halting this arms race before it gets truly under way will be emphasised when one realises that these planned ASATs [anti-satellite weapons] are only the primitive precursors of systems now being contemplated.'

Arthur went on to describe an early 'Star Wars' vision, put forth by General D. O. Graham in his 'High Frontier' study, where dozens of orbital fortresses are put in space to intercept enemy ICBMs – at a cost of hundreds of billions of dollars. This was more than six months before President Reagan gave his pro 'Star Wars' speech in the spring of 1983.

'The two superpowers,' said Arthur, 'are both led by intelligent and responsible men, yet they sometimes appear like small boys standing in a pool of gasoline – each trying to acquire more matches than the other, when a single one is more than sufficient.'

His was an eloquent plea for reason, intelligence and well-weighed decisions. Arthur was against 'Star Wars' technology and deployment even before the press had borrowed the Lucas film title or heard of its euphemistic acronym, SDI (Strategic Defense Initiative). Space was international. It should be a place for co-operation not conflict, for the challenges of exploration not war.

Perhaps Arthur's speech in Geneva made such an outcome a bit more likely. Less than a month later, back in Ceylon, he was delighted to learn that his 'War and Peace' speech had been placed in the *Congressional Record* (on 21 September 1982) by Representative George E. Brown of California. It all helped; it all added up. Arthur was pleased.

The official publication date for *2010: Odyssey Two* was set for 15 November 1982, and Arthur agreed to do a two-city promotional tour – New York and Los Angeles – for Ballantine Books.

The famous Rainbow Room on top of the RCA Building in Rockefeller Plaza was the site of the publication party hosted by Ballantine. This was probably the largest-ever gathering of Arthur's friends and publishing colleagues, and he was happy to see them all. The guest list included the Ballantines, the Asimovs, Gioia Marconi Braga, the del Reys, the Durants, Peter Gimbel, Marjorie May, Fred Pohl, Kerry O'Quinn, James Randi, Bernie Shir-Cliff, and dozens more – as many as 100 people.

There was only a rumour about a film version of *2010: Odyssey Two* at the time the novel was published in late 1982. Arthur told a *Washington Post* reporter what he'd told Stanley Kubrick when he'd passed through London en route to New York.

'I called Stanley [who has a percentage interest in any Odyssey projects] and said, "Your job is to stop anybody making it so I won't be bothered."' Arthur was at least half serious at this point. He went on to tell the reporter that too many movies like *Close Encounters* and *ET* (and he loved them, make no mistake) made the reality of space travel, as seen on TV news coverage, disappointing for many people as compared to the 'over-glamorising' which takes place on the silver screen.

Says Scott Meredith, 'The *2010* book contract had nothing to do with the movie deal, of course, movie rights having been reserved for Arthur, with the movie deal made after the book was completed. We submitted first to MGM because they'd made *2001*, and they tried to get the rights under the usual movie contract "sequels" clause, which allows them to acquire author-written sequels for a percentage of the amount paid for the previous movie. We said absolutely not – this is a brand-new and major property, and it's got to be a major new deal.

'There was a lot of fighting back and forth with various executives of MGM, and then they finally capitulated and said "Let's make a new deal." Freddie Fields was then the vice-chairman of MGM and he had an apartment in New York, so he flew in and I drove in and we spent a couple of hours in the apartment and made our deal.

'There were no negotiations with Stanley or Lou Blau [Kubrick's lawyer and agent] on the *2010* movie. Of course, I kept Lou informed of all the negotiations between myself and MGM and with Freddie Fields, and Lou was able to step in at just the right time to finalise things for the footage and Stanley's fees for the productions.'

While Arthur was in Los Angeles promoting his novel he met one old friend he had never seen before.

Fifty-one years after he'd bought the book, *The Conquest of Space*, Clarke finally met its author, David Lasser. This book was a major influence on Arthur when he was growing up. He discovered it the same year that his father died. Back in 1931, Arthur had persuaded his Aunt Nellie to purchase this book for him when he saw it in a shop window in Minehead.

'It was a heartfelt meeting,' recalls Steven Jongeward, Arthur's then assistant. 'It was as if the two of them had known each other for a long time, but this was their first meeting. They were very happy to see one another. Very friendly.'

Arthur left Los Angeles on 24 November and three days later he was back in Colombo at Barnes Place, where he was greeted by family, pets and staff. His new computer friend 'Archie' awaited his commands. It was Archie, after all, who had persuaded Arthur to come out of retirement by eliminating much of the mechanical drudgery of writing. Thanks to Archie, writing had become fun again for Arthur C. Clarke.

CHAPTER 27

World Telecommunications Year

So is it absurdly optimistic to hope that, by
Columbus Day 1992, the United States and
the Soviet Union will have emerged from
their long winter of sterile confrontation?
— Video Presentation to US Senate,
Committee on Foreign Relations,
13 September 1984

The successful launch of the IRAS (Infrared Astronomical Satellite)
mission in January 1983 was praised by the international astronomical
community. It also had special significance for Arthur C. Clarke
because it encompassed two of his lifelong pursuits: astronomy and
international co-operation.

The IRAS satellite conducted the first all-sky survey to search for
cosmic objects emitting infrared radiation, and it eventually pin-
pointed the positions and intensities of more than two hundred thousand of them, including the disc around the star Beta Pictoris — a
possible solar system. The mission was a joint effort between The
Netherlands, the United Kingdom and the United States.

While the IRAS was going through its orientation exercises in
orbit, Arthur was busy digging through his corpus of work for early
technical essays. His brother Fred helped in England by searching
through the stacks of British Interplanetary Society publications and
other journals and magazines in the 'Clarkives' for Arthur's more
technical pieces. Fred then sent them to Sri Lanka for Arthur to
review, select, organise and write introductory material. This would
become *Ascent to Orbit: The Technical Writings of Arthur C. Clarke*,
which was published by John Wiley and Sons.

If there was a recurring and consistent theme to Arthur's life in
1983, it was his active involvement in the global telecommunications
revolution that was continuing to gain momentum on planet Earth.
Indeed 1983 had been declared World Telecommunications Year, and
on 12 February Intelsat celebrated its tenth anniversary. As for his
part, Arthur addressed the United Nations in the spring, communi-

cated with the director of the film *2010* via a computer modem, and had dish antennas installed at his home and at the new technology centre in Sri Lanka that would bear his name.

During this period, Arthur's writing often consisted of adding new words to old – but still relevant – work. In addition to his work on *Ascent to Orbit*, he compiled, edited and annotated a new collection of essays. *Spring of '84* was his working title, but Judy-Lynn del Rey, his editor at Ballantine Books, thought that a transposition of those elements would improve the title and it became *1984: Spring/A Choice of Futures* when it was published the following February.

'Don't blame me for that title: I wanted to call it something completely different,' Arthur told would-be readers elsewhere.

He also worked on a special illustrated volume of his shorter fiction, *The Sentinel*, published in quality paperback format, adding short introductions for each story. It was the first volume in a new Berkley Books series, 'Masterworks of Science Fiction and Fantasy'. The last short piece, which had originally appeared in *OMNI* magazine in 1980, was a three-page film synopsis of his 1957 short story 'The Songs of Distant Earth'. This would also be the year that he would begin to write his interstellar novel by the same name.

In early 1983 Arthur received some great news. 'PBS has finally taken *Mysterious World*,' he wrote his old friend Tom Craven, whose health was failing. At about the same time, Simon Welfare, John Fairley and Yorkshire TV were making plans to film *Arthur C. Clarke's World of Strange Powers*, and publish the tie-in book. Yorkshire Television scheduled to film Arthur's host segments for the new series later in the year.

In the spring Fred Clarke, his wife Babbs, and ninety-two-year-old Aunt Nellie arrived for a visit after spending two weeks in South Africa. Arthur showed the family around historic Galle, while half a world away the maiden voyage of space shuttle *Challenger* rose from the Florida Coast on 4 April. The first shuttle spacewalk took place on the mission.

In early May Arthur had a brief visit from two of Hollywood's most famous men – Steven Spielberg and Harrison Ford.

'We only met briefly,' says Arthur. 'They just dropped in on their way to the airport when they finished shooting *Indiana Jones and the Temple of Doom* here.'

Arthur did bring up the subject of Satyajit Ray's stillborn film project of the late 1960s, *The Alien*, and asked Spielberg if his own *ET* was influenced by Ray's script. (Several people had pointed out certain similarities.)

'Tell Satyajit I was a kid in high school when his script was circulating in Hollywood,' Spielberg told Arthur in a rather indignant, testy tone.

Before they left a few pictures were taken. There they were – Clarke, Ford, Spielberg, Hector's wife Valerie and daughter Cherene (holding an ET doll) – standing in Arthur's study with filled bookshelves in the background. Arthur's forearm rested on Harrison Ford's shoulder.

'I was wearing a genuine ET T-shirt,' Arthur recalls, laughing with childlike glee.

It was not even a month later that Arthur followed his family to England before continuing on to the United States. He arrived in London on May thirteenth and checked into Brown's Hotel in Piccadilly. This is where Arthur sometimes put up when he wasn't in Somerset now that 88 Nightingale Road was sold.

He had only a day to see people and do things in London, and this included a script conference with Simon Welfare and John Fairley for the *Strange Powers* TV series. Then on 15 May, after appearing on an early morning talk show and chatting with Uri Geller (whom he had met several times before), Arthur barely managed to get through a massive traffic jam in time to board Concorde for its flight to New York. One of Arthur's big days was fast approaching.

Arthur had been asked to speak at the United Nations on World Telecommunications Day – 17 May 1983. It was the GTE people who organised it, the same group who were funding a three-part television documentary on the communications revolution, *The Messengers*, which was being directed by David Kennard. Kennard, who filmed the UN speech as part of this project, was a senior producer on Carl Sagan's *Cosmos* as well as co-producer of *The Ascent of Man*. Two weeks earlier he had been in Sri Lanka, working with Arthur and filming some segments for this series.

To befit the occasion, Arthur stayed at the Waldorf Astoria. Somehow his favourite Hotel Chelsea – with its rich literary history and long list of eccentric guests – did not quite complement this august event.

'I was invited to give the keynote address at the United Nations headquarters,' says Arthur, 'and it was a great privilege to stand in the shadow of history and speak from the podium of the General Assembly Chamber itself, although I did not actually address the General Assembly. It was also a weird feeling to stand there on that famous rostrum and see so many of my friends sitting at desks still bearing the names of the UN's 150+ disputatious members.'

'What most impressed me was the sharp contrast of seeing Arthur in Sri Lanka and then a few days later in the General Assembly,' said David Kennard.

'Once Arthur knows you he's a tremendously informal guy, and while we were filming I saw him in every sort of sloppy beach wear. He is a kind of benign slob in terms of his dress. He is at his happiest being a sort of beaming shambles. His style suggests that he's never seen a decent tailor in his life.

'So the single thing I remember on that day of the United Nations speech was to see Arthur in a suit! Suddenly there he was in this extraordinarily natty gentleman's suit and a tied tie looking like an ambassador from the finest nation on earth. When he saw us and the film crew he gave me a big wink and said, "I bet you didn't recognise me, did you?" And I said, "Well, quite honestly, no."

'He's so boyish. Given half a chance, Arthur will have this impish grin and a twinkle in his eye, and he'll always get the good little one-line gag out.'

His UN speech, 'Beyond the Global Village', had no gags as such, but it was given in the afternoon after lunch so the audience was in receptive good humour. And Arthur did deliver a few humorous anecdotes from the history of communications as openers. He told one about the Chief Engineer of the British Post Office who was not impressed when he heard the news of Alexander Graham Bell's invention. Arthur repeated the Chief Engineer's response: '"The Americans," he said loftily, "have need of the telephone – but we do not. We have plenty of messenger boys . . ."'

Dr Clarke spoke about the telecommunications revolution in the developed and undeveloped nations, and what it meant to the future of planet Earth – including a prediction that wristwatch telephones would be coming into general use by 1997. 'They will give you direct access to most of the human race, through the invisible networks girdling our planet.

'The long-heralded Global Village is almost upon us, but it will last for only a flickering moment in the history of mankind. Before we even realise that it has come, it will be superseded – by the Global Family.' The audience applauded, and Arthur relished the ovation.

He remained in Manhattan for a few more days, agreeing to only two interviews. David Hutchinson interviewed him for *Starlog* (Arthur was happy to accommodate his friends at the magazine), and then critic John Leonard, once a leading reviewer for the *New York*

Times, interviewed him in the library of the famous Explorers Club for a segment of a pilot TV show called *First Edition*.

Arthur then went to Washington, DC, to visit the Durants and to participate in another World Communications Year event. Joseph Pelton, then at Intelsat, recalls one event at which Arthur spoke.

'He gave a brief speech at George Washington University in the Lisner Auditorium,' says Joe. 'This was another event sponsored by the US Committee for the World Telecommunications Year. John McLucas and I introduced him, and it was a packed house. He only spoke a few sentences, saying how delighted he was to be there and thanking his hosts. He then agreed to a short question-and-answer period.

'I remember one lady asked, "Arthur, what is the greatest invention of the twentieth century?" And Arthur, without any hesitation said, and this is a paraphrase, of course, "Well, the greatest invention of the twentieth century is just happening now, and it hasn't really entirely happened, but it will have happened by the end of the twentieth century. It is artificial intelligence. With artificial intelligence we are going to be able to do almost everything that we have envisioned and conceived of and need to do – be it interstellar space travel or finding extra-terrestrial life or what-have-you. And it will be ultimately the most practical and important technology – not only for the twentieth century, but maybe for ever – in terms of the evolution of mankind."

'And I think everybody was impressed by that, because they were expecting him to say something like electronics, or space travel or such.'

While in Washington Arthur attended the first board meeting of the newly formed US Foundation for the Arthur C. Clarke Centre for Modern Technologies. This was an offshoot of the ACC Centre in Sri Lanka, which was being initiated with the Marconi Award funds and would be inaugurated in the autumn of 1983.

'When I learned about the creation of the Clarke Centre in Sri Lanka, which I thought was an excellent idea,' says Joe Pelton, 'it occurred to me that some sort of US Foundation to support it was important. I went to Fred Durant first, and he agreed and we put together a board and invited a number of people to participate. Then we convinced John McLucas to be the chairman.'

Among other things discussed at the first board meeting was the forthcoming White House press release announcing the creation of the Foundation. The announcement came on 23 June 1983.

The White House release read in part:

A number of the top communications leaders in the United States, as part of the World Communications Year Observances, are launching a new US Foundation to support THE ARTHUR CLARKE CENTRE for modern technologies, being established in Colombo, Sri Lanka.

Joseph N. Pelton, managing director of the US Council, in his White House announcement of the new foundation, explained: 'The new US Foundation will seek to strengthen the educational, training and R and D programs at the new CLARKE CENTRE.' The prime objective of this CLARKE CENTRE, in fact, will be 'To share the technology with developing countries, particularly in the Asia/Pacific region. This will be done by training technicians, engineers and scientists in "High tech" areas; by R and D programs in new technology appropriate to developing countries; and, possibly, initiating new joint ventures between developing and developed countries.' Projected areas for such new joint ventures might be: earth station manufacturing, ocean thermal energy conversion, and tele-education offerings via satellite.

From Washington, Arthur flew to Monaco to address the senior editors of *Reader's Digest* and then went on to Paris for a visit to the Centre Mondial Informatique before returning to Colombo on 27 May. And the busier half of 1983 was about to begin!

Although the filming of the thirteen-part TV series *Arthur C. Clarke's World of Strange Powers* would take place in 1984, Arthur revised and finalised the scripts in June and July, and edited the spin-off book as well, which also was released in 1984.

'At a generous assessment, approximately half this book is nonsense,' he wrote in the foreword. 'Unfortunately, I don't know *which* half; and neither, despite all claims to the contrary, does anyone else.' When necessary, Arthur always has an acceptable *and* enjoyable way of straddling the fence.

He went on to tell the reader that the book (and television series upon which it was based) nevertheless contained nonsense of the 'very highest quality . . . Anyone studying it can hardly fail to be entertained, amused, sometimes saddened, and always instructed. It teaches a great deal about human psychology and the motives controlling the behaviour of even the most intelligent and rational members of that peculiar species, *H. Sapiens*.'

While Arthur readily acknowledged that both the book and the TV series were inspired and researched by Simon Welfare and John Fairley, he wholeheartedly lent his support to the project as a mixed offering of entertainment and education, while also letting his audience know of his healthy scepticism with good humour.

In his epilogue to *Arthur C. Clarke's World of Strange Powers* he produced a validity scale for strange powers from +5 ('certainly true') to −4 ('certainly untrue') and went on to rate poltergeists as +2 ('possible – worth investigating') and reincarnation as −2 ('almost certainly untrue').

'Human judgment must stop at −3; only God can go to −4,' he wrote, concluding that if half his readers thought of him as a stubborn sceptic and half as a credulous dupe, he would feel he had done his job well.

Painful news came to the Clarke household in early July 1983. Arthur's dear friend, fellow visionary and futurist R. Buckminster Fuller died in Los Angeles on 1 July.

'He died of a heart attack,' says Arthur. 'He was with his wife Anne in her hospital room, where she was dying of cancer.'

Anne Fuller had lapsed into a coma, and doctors at the Good Samaritan Hospital informed Bucky that morning that she would probably never regain consciousness. As Bucky sat at his wife's bedside in the intensive care unit, he suffered a massive heart attack and died that afternoon.

Arthur Clarke and Bucky Fuller had much in common, including being born by the sea and spending their lives sailing the uncharted waters of the future. Arthur commented to several friends how thankful he was that Anne Fuller never knew; neither husband nor wife had to live through one another's death – a gift of fate.

By mid-1983 the MGM/UA movie project *2010: Odyssey Two* was heating up. It was about this time that Peter Hyams first approached Arthur about his involvement on the project – after he had already spoken to Stanley Kubrick about it.

'I was filled with all kinds of reservations,' admits director Peter Hyams. 'The first two people I wanted to contact were Arthur Clarke and Stanley Kubrick. I had a long conversation with Stanley and told him what was going on. If it met with his approval I would do the film; and if it didn't I wouldn't. I certainly would not have thought of doing the film if I had not gotten the blessing of Kubrick. He's one of my idols; simply one of the greatest talents that's ever walked the Earth.

'He more or less said, "Sure. Go do it. I don't care." And another time he said, "Don't be afraid. Just go do your own movie."

'Then I called Arthur, who was a bit prickly when we first started to speak. He was a bit off putting. Then I spoke to him later and said, "Look, Mr Clarke, I've been asked to do this film, and it appears now that I'm going to do this film. There are two ways it can be done. It can be done with you, or it can be done not with you. I cannot conceive of doing it the second way, and I would really love to have you become an integral part of the whole process."'

Ever since Arthur had given up his gruelling, twice-a-year lecture circuit in the 1970s, his primary consideration in taking on any project was whether he could do it without leaving Colombo. Arthur knew he no longer had the energy or the time for a collaboration requiring the kind of lengthy (three-year) total immersion of *2001*. But in 1983 he had his state-of-the-art, instantaneous electronic mail capability.

'It might be fun to see what could be done with the new electronic facilities,' Arthur thought at the time. 'Moreover, I did have a certain responsibility in the matter, and would like to know just what was going on in Culver City, California . . .

'But this time, thanks to the new technology, I would be in complete control of the situation. Sitting quietly in my Colombo home I could do as much or as little work as I liked. I knew nothing about Peter Hyams (though I had been quite impressed by his previous films *Capricorn One* and *Outland*, despite certain reservations), and if I didn't like the guy I could always pull the plug on him.'

Recalls Peter Hyams, 'All of a sudden Arthur did a 180-degree turn and became very sweet. I think he had seen a couple of my films. Then we began this fairly cumbersome business of me calling him and discussing a whole bunch of changes that were made from the book. The film followed certain parts of the book fairly closely, and then deviated a great deal in others – its structure and its politics. Large sections of the book were not dealt with and a whole new section was written for the film – about the Russians and Americans – that had nothing to do with the book. I wanted to set it in a time of enormous conflict between the superpowers. I first discussed that with him, and then we began to talk more and more. Finally we set up the computer link and worked that way.'

As soon as Arthur knew he could stay put and still be as involved as he wished by using his new electronic toys, he had what he wanted and was happy.

'Peter and I started looking at the available systems,' says Arthur, 'and shortly thereafter I received news that a Kaypro II was on the way to me.'

Before the computer modem link was established, Peter remembers quite vividly one regular trans-Pacific telephone conversation with Arthur. It occurred on 30 August 1983.

'There was a thirteen-and-a-half-hour time difference,' says Peter, 'and while I was talking to Arthur in Sri Lanka – it was late evening in Los Angeles – the coverage of the night launch of space shuttle *Challenger* came on my television set.

'Just the idea of talking to somebody in Sri Lanka, least of all Arthur C. Clarke, about a film like *2010* while the space shuttle *Challenger* was launched at night for the first time – I was just overwhelmed by it all, and I started to cry.

'I don't know. Somehow the relationship changed then. He became somebody very dear and very important to me and unbelievably helpful. And somebody with this extraordinary touch of a poet in him. I guess the writing, the communication by writing brought it out in him. He became someone I cared for enormously. And it became my mission to make a film that he liked more than anybody.'

Along with the Kaypro Arthur received a Hayes Smart Modem, which was installed for him. He and Peter Hyams then began to send messages to one another over the international direct dial telephone lines at the speed of light. They began communicating electronically on a daily basis about script problems on *2010* in mid-September, and discussed such matters as the spaceship *Leonov*'s design and its propulsion, Jupiter images and help from JPL, among other things. They continued into the spring of 1984 when Hyams' shooting schedule took over and the modem mail flow dramatically fell off, although even then the link was used quite regularly by Steven Jongeward, Arthur's one-time assistant, who was now working for Peter Hyams and MGM.

November began with a birth in Arthur's extended family. Hector and Valerie's second daughter, Tamara Ekanayake, was born on 2 November, 'giving Cherene a little sister to bully', Arthur wrote.

Preparations for the inauguration of the Arthur C. Clarke Centre for Modern Technologies were proceeding, and the contractors pushed themselves to complete the centre's first modest building in time for the ceremony. Built with Arthur's Marconi Award funds as well as some government support, it was erected just across from the campus of the University of Moratuwa some ten miles south of Colombo.

The site soon received one of three satellite dishes that were donated and erected by a group of Americans from the then booming private satellite industry. Robert Cooper, publisher of *Coop's Satellite Digest*, was the prime mover and organiser of the trip, and he was accompanied by several other industry leaders, company presidents, family members and assorted colleagues (more than twenty in all) who arrived in Colombo in early November to begin installing the dishes.

Besides erecting the twenty-five-foot dish at the Arthur C. Clarke Centre, Bob Cooper and the others installed a fifteen-foot dish donated by Hero Communications at Arthur's home, on his roof terrace, and another thirty-foot dish at the University of Moratuwa. To accomplish this task before the end of November they often worked through the night. All three dish antennas were TVRO (TV Receive-Only) Earth stations.

'This was not only a gift of extraordinary generosity, for which I shall always be grateful,' Arthur wrote friends, 'but an incredible feat of organisation and expertise. Ever since then we have been receiving superb pictures from Russian, Indian and Chinese comsats. (Intelsats? My lawyers have advised me to take the Fifth Amendment.)'

Besides Bob Cooper, who thought of it and brought the entire mission off, the other industry donors were Dave Johnson of Paradigm Manufacturing Inc., Bob Behar of Hero Communications and James Gowen of Antenna Development and Manufacturing, Inc.

The official inauguration ceremony of the Arthur C. Clarke Centre took place on 25 November 1983 at the University of Moratuwa. The Secretary of the Ministry of Higher Education, as well as the deans and professors of the university, gathered at the vice-chancellor's office. There they formed a procession and walked to the Arthur C. Clarke Centre, where the invited guests were seated in the pavilion.

Besides the speeches, the traditional ceremonial customs were carried out, including the boiling pot of milk which was positioned near the entrance to the building.

'At the opening of any new building, there is a pot of milk with a fire built under it,' says Cyril Ponnamperuma, who would be appointed the first director of the centre by the president of Sri Lanka in 1984. 'And if the milk boils over very fast it is a good omen.'

The milk did boil over quickly that day and, according to tradition the future success of the Centre for Modern Technologies was assured. The lighting of the Sri Lankan oil lamp also took place as part of the ceremony.

The ceremony concluded while *Namo Namo Matha* played on the public address system, and then all the guests enjoyed tea at the centre.

Five days later the Inaugural Symposium of the Arthur C. Clarke Centre was held at James George Hall, University of Moratuwa. Chancellor Clarke delivered the keynote address, which was followed by more technical presentations, including Bob Cooper's 'The Development of Low Cost Satellite Technology' and Saman Ediriweera's 'Padukka Earth Station'.

The following week Arthur saw television coverage of the opening of the centre. There he was, Chancellor Clarke, dressed in his purple robes, standing in front of the centre's large satellite dish. His legacy would be more than a literary one.

CHAPTER 28

Nineteen Eighty-four

> The United Nations Organisation is the last
> hope of Mankind . . . It is therefore neces-
> sary to consider in what way the rocket can
> be used as an instrument of world peace
> rather than regional security.
> – 'The Rocket and the Future of Warfare',
> March 1946

The only Big Brother in Arthur C. Clarke's life as 1984 began was
the large listening ear on his terrace – the fifteen-foot satellite dish
donated by Hero Communications. Because it was a receive-only
antenna, there was no need to fear any invasion of his privacy as the
character Winston did in George Orwell's *1984*.

His own personal Earth station was perhaps the largest technological toy with which he'd ever had the pleasure of playing. The first
programme he received was a cricket match in India, broadcast from
a Russian satellite. In mid-January he wrote to Peter Hyams, 'I feel
very happy – after weeks of hunting I've located and identified eight
of the twelve comsats in my sky, though I can only get good TV
from three (two Russian, one Indian). I've also been able to peek at
Intelsat newsfeeds. No wonder I've had no time to think about writing . . . but doubtless my subconscious is bubbling away.'

Back in Hollywood, Hyams was frantically preparing to start
shooting *2010: Odyssey Two*. He had signed Roy Scheider (*The French
Connection, Jaws*, and *All that Jazz*) to the lead role in late 1983, and
this delighted Arthur. Other than the Scheider decision, things were
generally in a state of creative chaos at the MGM/UA studios.

'Federal and state inspectors are hovering around the Esther Williams tank . . . trying to determine if it is suitable for our dolphin,'
Peter transmitted to Arthur in January, as he worked out the problems for the dolphin-in-domicile scene with Roy Scheider. 'It turns
out that you have to bring over three dolphins so no one will get
lonely.'

As Hyams and his MGM team struggled to capture the future on

film, President Ronald Reagan initiated the US space station programme during his State of the Union Address on 25 January. Less
than two weeks later the shooting of *2010* began. At the same time
space shuttle *Challenger* was orbiting the Earth with a crew of five.
Arthur sent a file to Peter at the beginning of February.

'Do you realise that during the next few days the shuttle crew
will be performing, for the first time, what we showed in *2001* – a
non-tethered EVA?'

On 7 February astronaut Bruce McCandless successfully completed
the world's first untethered space walk, using the manned manoeuvring unit (MMU) for the first time. He was a human satellite, orbiting
planet Earth at more than seventeen thousand miles an hour. Many
times Arthur had imagined and written about a variety of similar
mind-boggling experiences in his fiction, where a character finds
himself alone and isolated, floating above a planet or marooned on
its surface.

In fact, one of Clarke's favourite stories, 'Transit of Earth', tells of
a lone survivor on a Mars expedition who is marooned on the Red
Planet. The story's narrator, Evans, is doomed, running out of
oxygen to breathe, but he continues to collect scientific data on the
Earth's transit across the face of the Sun before he dies.

On 11 May 1984 the rare astronomical event described in 'Transit
of Earth' actually took place in the solar system. It was, Arthur wrote
to his friends, 'exactly as described – but without a human spectator.
We'll have to wait until 2084'. If an observer had been on Mars with
appropriate equipment and filters, he could have seen the Earth's tiny
disc move across the face of the Sun, just as it was described in the
story.

But it was his story set in 2010 that required Clarke's attention.
Peter sent Arthur the film script of *2010* and Arthur was pleased,
although he couldn't resist having a little fun. 'I felt like playing a
few tricks on you – like a message from my secretary saying that I
was last seen heading for the airport carrying a gun. But being the
day it is [when shooting begins] and the delicate condition you are
in, I'll say right away that it's a splendid job and you have brilliantly
chiselled out the basic elements of the novel, besides adding quite a
few of your own. I laughed – and cried – in all the right places.'

On 29 February 1984 Arthur flew from Colombo to New Delhi
to deliver the keynote address to the Indian Association for the
Advancement of Science. It was the same basic speech, 'Beyond the
Global Village', that he had given to the United Nations in May of
the previous year.

Upon his return to Sri Lanka, he juggled various projects in various stages of completion (the *Strange Powers* TV series in particular, many portions of which would be filmed in Sri Lanka in June and July), and greeted friends and other guests who would often land on Sri Lanka's shores with little or no notice.

Elmer Gertz was one old friend whose cruise ship, the *Rotterdam*, anchored in Colombo Harbour about this time, and he and his wife visited Arthur for a day. Gertz, well-known Chicago attorney and long-time defender of literary freedom and civil rights, defended the literary works of Henry Miller against lawsuits of obscenity in the 1960s. Arthur had got to know him when his lecture tours took him to Chicago.

Elmer wrote a series of pieces about his world cruise for the *Chicago Sun-Times*, and one described his Sri Lankan visit.

> Clarke's residence is next door to the Iraqi Embassy. I don't know which place is more elaborate – Clarke's or the ambassador's. The Clarke home is like Merlin's castle – spacious, with every convenience, and a beautiful garden.
>
> He has just about every device that can bring the world to him instantaneously. In the space of moments, we watched a television programme going on in Moscow, then other programmes in every part of the world. We observed his communicating with the same dazzling speed with his associates in Hollywood in connection with his new film . . .
>
> Clarke is chancellor of the University of Moratuwa; his life is full of meetings, speeches, technology, all of which he handles effortlessly because he takes such joy in everything.

Elmer and his wife, Mamie, heard about the recent violent uprisings in Sri Lanka during their visit.

> A small group of guerrillas, who called themselves Tamil Tigers and favoured a separate Tamil state within Sri Lanka, had ambushed and killed Sinhalese police officers, soldiers and civilians. The mobs had taken revenge on them.
>
> Fortunately, during our brief stay we were not subject to the sight of such savagery.

Hector Ekanayake's nephew, Rohan, then Arthur's secretary, accompanied him to England and the United States in late April.

In New York Arthur attended the annual meeting of the American Association for the Advancement of Science at the Hilton as well as a Planetary Society meeting at Carnegie Hall. In Washington Fred and Pip Durant gave a cocktail party the day after Arthur arrived. Several of the guests, including Joe Pelton and Naren Chitty, were involved in forming the Arthur C. Clarke Foundation of the US. So too were three students, representing the next generation, who shared Arthur Clarke's vision of the future: Todd Hawley, Bob Richards and Peter Diamandis. These three enthusiasts had founded Students for Exploration and Development of Space (SEDS), and they actively helped Durant, Pelton and McLucas to set up the Foundation, including fund-raising. Out of this association would eventually grow the International Space University. More immediately, however, they had organised the lecture platform scheduled for 30 April at George Washington University to benefit the Arthur C. Clarke Foundation of the US.

When Arthur stood at the podium in Lisner Auditorium he faced an enthusiastic audience of more than six hundred. He spoke for thirty minutes about the telecommunications revolution and the newly established Arthur C. Clarke Centre for Modern Technologies. He also showed slides of the centre, the inauguration ceremonies and the newly donated satellite dishes.

There was a photo session after his talk, and easily a hundred of his fans lined up with books (most were copies of his latest novel, *2010*), for Arthur to autograph. He had dealt with most of the line, but then suddenly felt woozy; he couldn't go on.

'He was physically exhausted,' says Todd Hawley, 'and had stomach pains. He almost fainted, but Fred Durant cut off the line and took him behind the stage curtain. The remaining people were terribly disappointed. One man in particular, a senior NASA person, had an early Clarke novel, *The City and the Stars*, which he had had for almost thirty years. This book, the man claimed, had changed his life and motivated him to a career in the space agency. But Arthur's protectors firmly said no; he was too shaky to sign even one more book. It was a terrible disappointment for the man.'

Arthur recovered after resting, but he knew that he must regularly pace and protect himself or face the consequences.

A big two-book contract was signed at the Durants' home on 9 May between Arthur and Ballantine Books – big in terms of potential if not up-front cash. Arthur received exactly the advance he requested: one dollar and ten cents for both books – *The Songs of Distant Earth* and *20,001: The Final Odyssey*.

'In an extraordinary show of faith in his publisher and in his forthcoming works,' read the publicity release, 'Clarke has asked for an advance of ten cents on *Songs* and, in consideration of probable inflation, an advance of one dollar for *20,001*.

'Clarke further explained that he had originally intended to ask for one cent for the first book, but realised that the sum would not be easily divisible to enable him to pay the ten per cent commission to his agent, Scott Meredith. Clarke upped the advance to ten cents.'

'The token figure was agreed upon,' says Scott, 'because Arthur was reluctant to accept any money for *20,001*, which he wasn't sure he'd ever actually write. I persuaded Arthur that money had to pass hands on any book he might do, so that token initial payment (the total advances were well into seven figures, of course) was agreed to.

'What Arthur then ended up writing wasn't the concluding book to the *2001* saga that Del Rey had been expecting from *20,001*, but rather another intermediate volume in *2061*. Del Rey wanted and wants to have whatever moral suasion results from having *20,001* under contract, and a separate contract was then struck up for *2061* after delivery, so technically the second half of that old two-book deal remains unfulfilled.'

A photograph was taken of the contract signing, with Arthur, Scott and Judy-Lynn sitting at the Durants' dining room table. Judy-Lynn is handing Arthur a dime and Arthur is handing Scott a penny. To celebrate the event a bottle of champagne was uncorked and a toast was made to these yet unborn novels.

'If I don't deliver, of course,' he wrote Stanley Kubrick, 'I'll cheerfully refund the advances; if I do, some slightly larger amounts will be forthcoming. Meanwhile I'm proud to have brought back the dime novel . . .'

Arthur made his own transit across the United States and spent a few days in Los Angeles, seeing friends and visiting the MGM studios, although he was too late to see the main sets.

'The first time I met Arthur face to face was on the set,' says Peter Hyams. 'It was towards the end of shooting the film. I think it was the time when I was actually shooting in one of the MGM buildings used as a location. This was just before we flew east to shoot the Washington sequence . . . When Arthur came to visit the shooting of *2010*, he was wonderful and I was like a great puppy.'

One of the more memorable events while on the west coast was a lunch with several *Apollo* astronauts, Edwin 'Buzz' Aldrin, Alan Bean and Charles 'Pete' Conrad, arranged and hosted by Arthur's friend and one-time deputy administrator of NASA, George Mueller.

A few days later Arthur was back in Washington, and so were

Hyams and the film crew of *2010*. They were going to shoot a scene in front of the White House, and Peter had a surprise gift for Arthur: a cameo part, a Hitchcock!

It was the scene where Roy Scheider, playing Floyd, is sitting on a bench in front of the White House explaining to the head of NASA, played by James McEachin, why they must go on the mission. Arthur was two benches away, feeding the pigeons.

Says Arthur, 'My Method acting, alas, was excised on the video version due to picture-ratio problems.'

Soon Arthur was back in Sri Lanka shooting Yorkshire Television's *Arthur C. Clarke's World of Strange Powers*.

On 12 July, when this was over, he wrote to Stanley Kubrick, giving him news of his recent US trip. But the main reason for the letter was to receive Stanley's blessing for his next Odyssey novel.

'Ever since *Odyssey Two* came out,' he wrote, 'Scott has been bullying me to do *Odyssey Three*, and even sent me two juicy contracts, the first of which I returned unsigned and the second of which I tore up . . .

'I realised that Scott would try again when I came to the US in May, so I launched a pre-emptive strike. I said I'd sign contracts for *both* books – on my terms.'

This was Arthur's tough guise for Stanley's benefit.

Arthur then summarised for Stanley the advance deal for a dollar and ten cents and the circumstances surrounding the signing ceremony. Then he sent his love and signed off, 'As ever, Arthur'.

Stanley eventually did send his blessing. And why not? He had, after all, a percentage interest in all future Odyssey projects.

July was also the month that the Parliament of Sri Lanka officially certified 'AN ACT TO PROVIDE FOR THE ESTABLISHMENT OF THE ARTHUR C. CLARKE CENTRE FOR MODERN TECHNOLOGIES; AND TO PROVIDE FOR THE STUDY OF COMMUNICATION, COMPUTERS, ENERGY, SPACE TECHNOLOGIES AND ROBOTICS . . .' Act No. 30 of 1984 made legal what the boiling milk and flame of the oil lamp had symbolically inaugurated some seven months earlier.

In August Arthur videotaped a presentation that was shown before the Senate Foreign Relations Committee on 17 September 1984. Co-operation between the two superpowers in future space missions has been one of Arthur's important and consistent themes over the years. In the last half of his speech, he advocated a joint American/

Russian mission to Mars (and at the same time got in a good plug for his latest novel, and the movie adapted from it).

'As you doubtless know,' he told the Senators, 'the novel *2010: Odyssey Two* describes a joint US–USSR mission – though to Jupiter, not Mars! – and at this very moment Peter Hyams is filming it at MGM/UA.'

He went on to confess that he was currently in disgrace in the Soviet Union (no doubt an exaggeration) because someone 'has noted the extraordinary coincidence that all seven Russians in *2010* are named after well-known dissidents'.

Before Arthur addressed the subject of co-operative space missions (what he called 'technological decency'), he opened his fifteen-minute video with a discussion of his views on Star Wars weaponry (in one context referred to as 'technological obscenities').

'I have also talked with many of the experts involved – hawks, doves, and those who, like myself, might be classified as anxious falcons,' Arthur said, before telling the Senators that, yes, he believed that ICBMs could be intercepted and destroyed by projectile or beam weapons, but a ninety per cent success rate would be astonishing.

'I doubt if any informed person really believes that such a figure is possible.' But if it were, Arthur went on, if nine out of ten missiles were effectively stopped the remaining ones that got through would unleash a destructive power equivalent to a World War II every ten seconds: 'The result would make *The Day After* look like an optimistic exercise in wishful thinking.'

The cost of a manned Mars mission, hopefully a joint venture between the United States and Russia, would be less than *just* the research into anti-ICBM systems, he told the Senators, and actual deployment costs would be 'orders of magnitude greater'.

'I am not so naive as to imagine that this could be achieved without excruciating difficulty, and major changes in the present political climate. But those changes *have* to be made, sooner or later, and I commend your committee for its courage in recognising this fact.'

Late in September Arthur left for Rome to attend the Study Week on 'The Impact of Space Exploration on Mankind', which was organised by the Pontifical Academy of Science. He delivered his speech, 'Space Communications and the Global Family', before the Academy on 1 October.

This was not his only title for that speech, however. During the conference he became friendly with the Vatican astronomer, an

American by the name of George Coyne, and visited the Vatican Observatory during his six days in Rome.

'Coyne was quite a character,' says Arthur, 'and he's been to Sri Lanka twice now. I told George what my first choice of a title for my speech was when I was asked to lecture at the Vatican – "After Giordano Bruno, Who?" And he said, "If you had used that title, the answer would have been *you*."'

He had his audience with Pope John Paul II and presented him with a copy of *Ascent to Orbit*, his collected scientific articles. A photographer captured Arthur's brief encounter with the pontiff and a few weeks later Father Lee Lubbers, a Jesuit priest and a friend of Arthur's, received some coloured photos of the event mounted and pasted in staggered fashion on a piece of paper, with short humorous balloon captions (supposedly spoken by the Pope) written in by Arthur. In one photo they shake hands, and the caption reads, 'How nice to meet at last!' Next to another photo, as Pope John Paul holds the book just handed him, the caption reads, 'What – *another* book?'

Before leaving Rome Arthur attended the Marconi Award ceremony on 5 October, where he gave a progress report on the Centre for Modern Technologies which bore his name and which had received its initial funding from his award two years earlier. He also attended a reception at the British Ambassador's residence. Then he flew from one ancient capital to another and was back in Sri Lanka in time to meet some visitors from Hollywood.

Bob Swarthe and Susan Marie Phillips, as partners and co-producers, held the film rights to Arthur's novel *The Fountains of Paradise* and wanted to scout the locations where the story takes place – primarily Sigiriya and Adam's Peak. The film adaptation of *Fountains* has been in the gestation stages for several years, but Bob hopes it will reach the screen by the mid-1990s. With all such movie ventures Arthur has learned never to hold his breath, although he does keep his fingers crossed.

Later in October Arthur flew to Hong Kong and joined Lloyd Lewan and his floating university on the SS *Universe*. By the time the ship arrived in Colombo on 31 October, Dr Clarke had taught the college students much about the history and customs of Sri Lanka.

After this there was less than two weeks to catch up on work before he was off to the United States for the preview, premiere and promotion of *2010: Odyssey Two*. Soon Arthur's schedule became hectic. Peter Arthurs, a neighbour and friend since the Hotel Chelsea days and the author of *With Brendan Behan: A Personal Memoir* (1981), was handling the bookings and was running Arthur ragged. He had the authority to say no to agents, but it was difficult.

'When you're in a production line of TV interviews, it's very hard to stop them,' says Arthur. 'These interviews are totally blurred together. I did thirty in one day, and I don't think I can remember a single one.'

The premiere was held on 7 December 1984 at the Village Theater in Westwood. The Ekanayake family – Hector, Valerie, Cherene and Tamara – arrived in time for the event, having been delayed because of Hector's mother's death, and so did Fred and Pip Durant. Because of his frenzied schedule, Arthur doesn't recall much about the premiere. But there is one exception: 'I couldn't believe how bald Sean Connery was,' he said, 'when I saw him in the foyer.' Connery probably showed up out of courtesy to Hyams, because he had starred in Hyams' *Outlander*.

Everyone enjoyed themselves, even the *New York Times* critic, Vincent Canby, who wrote that '*2010* is a perfectly adequate – though not really comparable – sequel to Stanley Kubrick's witty, mind-bending science-fiction classic, *2001: A Space Odyssey*'.

Canby went on to say that the film, unlike most sequels, avoided the tacky, but never quite escaped from the feel of something made by 'clever copyists who . . . do their work well and efficiently though without the excitement of truly original inspiration and lunatic risk . . .

'Mr Hyams and Mr Clarke carefully avoid the sort of poetic and – to some – maddening ambiguities that forever separate the Kubrick film from all that came before and all that have come after.' The reviewer went on to list some of the plot elements of the original film that reappeared in the sequel, including the spaceship *Discovery*, the monoliths, the character of Dave Bowman played by Keir Dullea, and 'the embryonic baby last seen floating toward Earth'. It was a positive and fair review, and no one had cause for serious complaint.

The morning after the premiere, Arthur invited Ray Bradbury and Bob Bloch to breakfast, but Bob couldn't make it that early. He did arrive just before they finished, however, and the threesome left the hotel together and were photographed out front by the doorman.

'Then Ray pedalled away,' recalls Bloch, 'and Arthur said, "Come with me, I've got something to show you." So he popped me into a limo, and we went down to a place in Culver City, about a mile away from MGM. This was where all the special effects had been done for *2010*. He, as always, was fascinated with the technology.

329

We went through the whole place, and he showed me what they had done and how they had done it.

'What he wanted to show me particularly was the space child, the baby, operated by remote control, some kind of wind pressure. It was rubberised, a beautifully done thing, and he was fascinated by it, and he knew I would be too. I looked at it, and I said, "Arthur, it looks just like you!"

'I never saw the original shooting script, so I don't know what happened. But when we saw the premiere, there was only a second or two of that on screen, and I had thought it would play a much larger part.'

On Saturday 8 December a group of approximately forty people met at the home of writer Larry Niven in Tarzana, California. They were all members of the Citizens Advisory Council on National Space Policy, a group organised in 1980 by Jerry Pournelle. The membership consisted of scientists, professors and aerospace and military men who advanced and promoted a space defence posture for the United States. Most of them were politically conservative and were strong proponents of SDI, the military concepts that would become popularly known as 'Star Wars'. Portions of President Reagan's 'Star Wars' speech of March 1983, in fact, originated from a similar meeting of the Council in 1982.

'About fifty of the top experts in the country were in the room,' says Jerry Pournelle. 'They were not just space enthusiasts, but people like Max Hunter, General Daniel O. Graham [author of *High Frontier*], Lowell Wood, Edward Teller's chief deputy and so on.

'Arthur arrived at about eleven o'clock in the morning, when the formal meeting was still going on. He was not a member of the organisation, but he had been invited and was there on his own behalf.

'Well, Arthur had published this article in which he had said that no idea was ever dumber [than SDI] because there were extremely simple ways to destroy this thing. Almost everybody there had read it. So he walked into the room and looked at Max Hunter and said, "I think I'm in trouble." And Max said, "Why?" And Arthur said, "Because I learned all I know about orbital mechanics from you, Max." And Max said, "You didn't learn enough, Arthur."'

The article in question was 'War and Peace in the Space Age', first published in *Analog Science Fiction/Science Fact* in March 1982. Two years later it was reprinted in the collection of essays, *1984: Spring*. The pro-SDI group objected to what Arthur presented as an 'absurdly cheap and simple' means of destroying SDI laser fortresses in orbit.

'Assume that there's an unfriendly object in a two-hour orbit – that's about seventeen hundred kilometres up. To destroy it, you launch your counterweapon into exactly the same orbit – *but in the opposite direction.* And you do it on the other side of the Earth from your target, so you won't be detected.

'Your warhead is rather cheap; it's a bucket of nails.'

Arthur was telling people that any multi-billion-dollar orbiting SDI system could easily be knocked out by launching a bucket of nails in a retrograde orbit to the 'Star Wars' hardware.

Says Jerry Pournelle, 'This doesn't turn out to be true. It doesn't work for the simple reason that space is big, very big. As a matter of fact, if you just take cross-sectional areas of the orbits of the objects and a bucket of nails, you will discover it's not true.'

Several of the people there pointed this position out to Arthur, telling him that his understanding of celestial mechanics was somewhat less than perfect. It was not a heated discussion or debate at this time, although at one point the word 'imbecile' was used against him, but not with any real viciousness.

While there were no doubt other criticisms of the article (Arthur also referred to General Daniel O. Graham's 'High Frontier' study as 'a horrifying description of the next phase of space warfare'), the main criticism was focused on Clarke's proposed method of destroying the orbiting laser stations.

'As far as this technical discussion was concerned,' says Jerry, 'Arthur had no defence. He asked several questions, and at the end of it he admitted, "I clearly was wrong."'

'I certainly have a more open mind [now] about the bucket of nails concept,' Arthur said recently. 'Even if it isn't viable, I'm sure it will scare the hell out of any manned fortresses. But even if these systems can work – and I think the reflecting mirrors and the laser stuff is utter nonsense for decades at any rate – they may be a bad idea because of their destabilising influence.'

Soon after the formal session had ended and everyone had broken for lunch, a confrontation took place between Arthur Clarke and Robert Heinlein.

Heinlein had said nothing during the meeting itself, but he soon made up for it. Arthur had made a lot of sceptical remarks about SDI which he believed upset the group; unfortunately Heinlein had taken the remarks personally. What followed has been variously referred to as the 'bloodbath sequence' or the 'battle of the Titans'.

'Arthur had made some statements about what the United States ought to do about strategic defence, weapons in space, foreign policy and so forth,' recalls G. Harry Stine, who has known both Arthur and Bob since the early 1950s. 'And Robert Heinlein lit into him verbally. He took Arthur apart. And all of us just sat there.

'I've never seen Arthur defensive. He really just sat there too. He made a few rather semi-defensive comments, but he basically almost withered from the scathing verbal attack from Heinlein. And after his blistering attack, Heinlein wouldn't talk to him.

'I think what shocked Arthur as it shocked us was the fact that Robert Heinlein did this in public, among his own peers and Arthur's peers.'

'He accused me of typically British arrogance,' says Arthur, 'and he really was vicious. It really hurt me. I was very sad about it.'

Gregory Benford remembers that when Arthur stated his reservations about the very idea of strategic defence, Heinlein chose not to argue about it as a technical problem but rather to say something like, 'Look, this is a matter of the defence of the United States, and you're not assisting the United States, and therefore you really don't have call to have an opinion about it.' Heinlein continued in that vein, saying that if he were visiting England or Sri Lanka he would not tell those people how to run their country.

At some point Arthur said that he had doubts about it as a moral issue. This outraged Heinlein, who then loudly told Arthur that *he* had no moral right to frame a moral argument about something in which he had no stake. This was a matter of national sovereignty, and Arthur was not a citizen.

'Heinlein was always big on freedom and the balance with responsibility,' says Greg Benford. 'I mean that's what *Starship Troopers* is all about. You don't get to vote unless you fight. And similarly, you don't get an opinion unless your skin is personally risked.'

After the Heinlein blast, people had lunch and conversations continued – at a normal volume. Arthur spoke to several of the group and then spent a lot of time talking to General Graham. When that conversation ended, he said to the general, 'Well, you may be right.' This was hardly a ringing endorsement of the general's SDI advocacy.

Later, when the meeting was breaking up, Arthur approached Heinlein and said, 'I can't help being British, but I'll try to do something about the arrogance.' That was the last time Arthur ever saw Robert Heinlein, who died in May 1988.

Jerry Pournelle walked Arthur out to the car. 'He looked at me and he said, "I know that Robert thinks I am, but I'm really not inflexible, and I don't really believe I'm infallible."' And with those parting words, the chauffeur drove Arthur back to the Beverly Wilshire.

Months later friends said that Arthur and Robert had reconciled their differences. As far as it went, this was a tribute to their long-standing friendship.

'Usually,' says Greg Benford, 'if you violated Heinlein's standards you went into Coventry. That didn't happen to Arthur, and they patched things up. Robert told me the last time I saw him that they had exchanged some letters and had ironed out their positions. Heinlein said to me, "Arthur changed his position; I didn't." Which I would gather is the case,' says Benford.

Bob Heinlein did not change his position – there's no doubt about that in Arthur's or anyone else's mind. 'And I wasn't quite so arrogant about mine after that,' Arthur says. 'I'm prepared to admit that there are certain aspects of SDI that made sense, and in fact that may still do so. What I was attacking was the utter nonsense about putting an umbrella over the United States. That was the version I was attacking. You couldn't even put an umbrella over a missile site. You could put a leaky roof over it, which might be worth doing.'

The reconciliation between Clarke and Heinlein was at arm's length and not complete, it turns out.

'I did send notes to him,' Arthur says, 'and Ginny acknowledged them. I do remember one thing: I came across a photograph of two bull elephants in a Congo scene, sort of butting each other, and I sent it to him and said, "Does this remind you of anything?"' Arthur laughs, then turns serious again. 'I imagine he probably would have responded himself eventually, but it wasn't to be, and of course we never discussed or mentioned SDI again.'

In a short tribute for a Heinlein memorial volume in September 1990, Arthur said that he was not resentful about the verbal attack. 'I realised that Bob was ailing and his behaviour was not typical of one of the most courteous people I have ever known.' He then bid a final farewell to his friend.

'Goodbye, Bob, and thank you for the influence you had on my life and career. And thank you too, Ginny, for looking after him so well and so long.'

CHAPTER 29

A Near and Distant Earth

> It was a song for all exiles, and it spoke as
> clearly to those who were sundered from
> Earth by a dozen generations as to the
> voyagers to whom its fields and cities still
> seemed only weeks away.
> – 'The Songs of Distant Earth' (short story),
> 1958

The first spacecraft launched in 1985, *Sakigake*, was one of two Japanese probes bound for that famous celestial vagabond, Halley's Comet. It reached escape velocity from planet Earth on 7 January and fifteen months later flew past the comet and measured the solar wind in its vicinity.

While this 'Made-in-Japan' spacecraft began its cosmic journey through the solar system, Miss Japan was being filmed underwater in the Indian Ocean with Arthur C. Clarke. The shoot took place at Coral Gardens, Hikkaduwa, about fifty miles due south of Colombo where a new hotel complex had been built a few years earlier. The footage was for a programme that would inaugurate Japanese satellite television.

In early 1985 Arthur was in London to attend the Royal Charity Premiere of *2010*. It was, he told friends, 'only the promise of meeting Princess Di' that brought him back to the United Kingdom so early in the year. 'I did my best,' he deadpanned, 'to put Prince Charles and Princess Diana at their ease.' He was very pleased that his cameo part was noticed. 'Everything went splendidly, and Princess Di made my evening by recognising me in the White House scene.'

Later in the month, across the Atlantic, another famous person referred to the space cadet from Somerset, but Arthur wasn't there to hear him.

President Ronald Reagan gave a speech before the National Space Club on 29 March 1985 at the Shoreham Hotel in Washington, DC. The President was presented with the Goddard Award on this occasion.

'Dr Goddard persevered for decades of intense research and development,' said the President. 'And as so often happens, his genius was not apparent to many until after his success.

'Arthur C. Clarke, distinguished author of science and fiction, says ideas often have three stages of reaction – first, "It's crazy and don't waste my time." Second, "It's possible, but it's not worth doing." And finally, "I've always said it was a good idea."'

It was appropriate to mention Arthur, who had taken Goddard's dream, mixed it with his own and retold it thousands of times, with many variations and new plots, to readers and audiences around the planet. Arthur was, in a real sense, Goddard's protégé, his messenger to the masses. For fifty years, from the time he was a lanky, bespeckled farmboy, Arthur Clarke had been spreading the word about rockets and space travel and our future in space. President Reagan's association of Clarke with Goddard was cosmic justice from a high station.

In May Arthur was invited to face the friendly Washington crowd in person and speak at the MIT Club there, but he wasn't feeling that well (he noticed regularly that he had less energy), and he also had a French television crew in Sri Lanka to keep happy. They were filming a biographical piece: *Star-Glider: Portrait of Arthur Clarke*. As a compromise, he packaged his electronic image and speech in a thirty-minute video cassette, which he titled *Visions of Space*, and sent to Washington to stand in for him.

There he was, wearing a bright blue shirt, sitting at his desk with books and more books filling his office shelves in the background. Script in hand, he spoke of the deep and treacherous gravitational well of Earth and how difficult it was for us to climb out of it into space. He spoke of various propulsion systems, including the recent British single-stage-to-orbit, oxygen-collecting ramjet design 'based on an engine that's still secret'.

He spoke of nuclear propulsion and the cancelled Project Orion; of his electromagnetic slingshot launch concept for the Moon; of colonies in space and multi-generational starships; and of the possibility of communicating with or meeting extra-terrestrial beings.

During the first six months of 1985 almost all Arthur's writing efforts were focused on his interstellar novel *The Songs of Distant Earth*, the early notes of which he had composed some thirty years before. Although he had made several attempts to get on a regular writing schedule in late 1983 and 1984, little progress was made on the novel before 1985.

In his *Visions of Space* video Arthur quoted a person he loved to quote, the British geneticist J. B. S. Haldane, who many years before had told him that 'the human race had obviously been designed for interstellar – yes, interstellar – travel, because by accelerating at a comfortable one g for one year you get to the speed of light. An interesting coincidence!' And in a letter to Arthur dated 8 January 1964, as Haldane lay dying of cancer in London, he raised yet another intriguing possibility: 'I suggest the following hypothesis: interstellar travel occurs on a vast scale. Cosmic rays are merely the exhausts of rockets.'

The interstellar travel of *The Songs of Distant Earth* was predicated on the realities of future science, not on a *Star Trek* propulsion fantasy like 'warp speed'. To bring the human and cosmic time scales into harmony without abusing the universal laws of physics and human life spans, Arthur again relied on a future science of hibernation (as he did in *2001* and *2010*), where the human body was suspended in time during the long voyages between planets or stars. This grand master of hard science fiction did not have to compromise scientific realities to move his characters from star to star.

In his new novel, the interstellar voyage to the planet Oceana, located fifty light years away from Earth, took five hundred years travelling at ten per cent of the speed of light. This was a reasonable propulsion system projected from the technology of the late twentieth century. As a matter of fact, the feasibility of such a starship had already been confirmed in the 1970s by the British Interplanetary Society's detailed report, *Project Daedalus*. (The study was dedicated to the memory of Arthur's dear friend, Val Cleaver, who had given it constructive encouragement until his death.)

Beyond the technology in *The Songs of Distant Earth* is the love affair between a man and a woman put up against the vast impersonal gulfs of space and time and future generations. Thematically, as in much of Arthur's fiction, there is the quest for a purpose and the immortality of the species in contrast to the certain death of the individual. The loneliness of man is intensified by the immensity of cosmic space and the finiteness of human time. Even if the survival of *Homo sapiens* is assured through interstellar travel, are not individuals doomed even as they embrace in love and light to keep the fall of night at bay? Arthur's 'songs of distant earth' are not as joyous and uplifting as we might first expect. Always present in the novel is the feeling of insurmountable separation across the voids of space, time and death.

Back on Earth, global distances continued to be bridged at the speed of light. On 28 June Arthur participated in the first United States Information Agency's Worldnet global link-up. From London, Prime Minister Margaret Thatcher emphasised that communication satellites were a British invention.

'In view of the UK's current deplorable space record, she's now been reminded of this,' Arthur told friends.

By spring 1985 the Arthur C. Clarke Centre for Modern Technologies had appointed its first director, Cyril Ponnamperuma. Dr Ponnamperuma divided his time between the United States, where he was Director of the Laboratory of Chemical Engineering at the University of Maryland, and his native country, Sri Lanka, where he headed (at the request of President J. R. Jayewardene) both the Institute for Fundamental Studies and the Arthur C. Clarke Centre.

'What was important at that time,' says Cyril, 'was the feeling that here was a country in the third world wanting to move into the twenty-first century, wanting to build an awareness of future technology – advanced communications, computers and so on. And during my directorship what I really wanted to do was set the programmes in place and bring the people together.

'One of the first important things we did in 1985 was to set up a programme for bright young people. On a national and competitive basis, we selected twenty-five, and they came to the centre six or seven Saturdays in a row. One Saturday they were exposed to computers; the next weekend to communications; the next Saturday to robotics and so on. Out of that eventually came the Young Astronomers' Association and the Computer Society of Sri Lanka. These were the first important teaching activities at the centre.'

The political situation in Sri Lanka in August was unstable, and the Underwater Safaris business near Trincomalee was closed down because of the conflict.

'All the hotels there have been robbed and some even blown up,' Arthur wrote Michael Craven who was at the helm of his late father's film company. 'Just heard that the terrorists have stolen one of our eighteen-foot boats.'

He also told Michael that he was looking forward to a holiday in England, 'now that I have finished the novel [*The Songs of Distant Earth*] I have been working on for thirty years.'

The Rocket Publishing Company held its annual general meeting on 28 August, and Arthur was at Dene Court in Somerset to attend. Arthur, Fred, Mary and Michael all gathered. After the family business was discussed, they had a portrait taken and then enjoyed dinner together.

'We went to Minehead and saw Aunt Nellie who was then in a nursing home,' says Fred Clarke. 'She had a lot to do with bringing Arthur up, of course. Probably more than mother did who was so tied up with the farm.'

Four months later, on 30 December, Aunt Nellie died in her ninety-fourth year. She was 'the last of her generation,' Arthur says, 'and my strongest remaining tie with England was broken'.

Back in Sri Lanka things had not improved. While there was no violence in and around Colombo, the north-east was a battle zone. Underwater Safaris began to restart business at the Coral Gardens Hotel at Hikkaduwa, fifty miles south of Colombo.

A different sailing rendezvous was on Arthur's autumn agenda, however, and again he flew to Hong Kong for his annual voyage on the SS *Universe*. This renewed his spirits, he told friends, and he hadn't felt so fit for years. He arrived home in Colombo on 28 October and confronted his usual mountain of mail.

One of the letters brought bad news. Two days later he relayed it to Michael Craven in New York.

'My publisher Judy-Lynn del Rey is desperately ill and may well be dead by now (she has had a brain clot and has been in a coma for over a week).'

Judy-Lynn remained unconscious for months and never recovered. She died in early 1986. The following year Arthur dedicated *2061: Odyssey Three* to her: 'To the memory of Judy-Lynn del Rey, editor extraordinary, who bought this book for one dollar – but never knew if she got her money's worth.'

One of the last books Judy-Lynn del Rey ever edited was *The Songs of Distant Earth*, published in May 1986. She was a great editor in the genre and would be deeply missed.

Above Isaac Asimov and Arthur C. Clarke greet one another before sailing off on separate ships to view a total eclipse.

Below Clarke and Asimov trade insults at the Commonwealth Hall, London, June 1974.

Arthur and Fred Clarke in
Colombo.

Left Gentry Lee and his wife
Tracey at Dene Court.

Below In the living room of
'Leslie's House', Barnes Place,
Colombo.

CHAPTER 30

Borrowed Time

After the examination, the doctors told
Arthur he had only fifteen months to
live . . .
— Fred Clarke, speaking of July 1986

My objection to organised religion is the
premature conclusion to ultimate truth it
represents.
— *Playboy* interview, July 1986

In his December 1985 Christmas message Arthur told friends that his
next novel, the one he had 'been tinkering with for a quarter century,
The Songs of Distant Earth', would be published the following May.
In a playful mood (his normal state), he went on talking about himself
in the third person: 'As he's convinced that it will make him famous,
he's decided (again) to do no more writing, and now spends his time
sorting videotapes, reading computer magazines, coping with mail
and visitors. However, if *Galileo* reaches Jupiter according to schedule
on 11 December 1988, he *may* start thinking about *Odyssey Three*.'

All bets were off when the *Challenger* tragedy occurred on 28 January. The future of the entire US space programme, manned and
unmanned, was in doubt, and the mission of spacecraft *Galileo* was
delayed for years.

Scott Meredith knew he'd have to come up with something special
to get Arthur motivated again. As it happened, the well-known film
producer Peter Guber (*The Color Purple, The Deep, Midnight Express*)
wanted to do a Clarke film. Scott called Arthur in early 1986 to tell
him of Guber's interest and to persuade him to listen to the proposal.
Arthur listened, but with a sceptical ear.

'I groaned inwardly when Scott went on to say that Peter had a
friend with a brilliant idea he'd like me to develop into a screenplay,'
Arthur wrote in the late eighties.

Peter Guber wanted to fly to Sri Lanka with his friend and discuss
the project. Arthur began to warm to the possible collaboration when

he learned more about Guber's friend. His name was Gentry Lee, and his credentials impressed even Arthur. He worked at the Jet Propulsion Laboratory and was chief engineer on Project Galileo. Before that he had been director of mission planning for the *Viking* Mars landers. He was also a partner with Carl Sagan in the company that produced the *Cosmos* television series and, in fact, was manager for the entire production.

Peter and Gentry flew to Colombo on 12 February 1986 and went to Barnes Place to meet Arthur.

'The first day we went to see him,' says Gentry, 'Arthur was probably thinking to himself, "What are these people here trying to get me to do?" On top of that, when Arthur's at home he can be easily distracted. Often there are interruptions, and sometimes he has a hard time focusing on anything.

'After the first five or ten minutes of conversation with Peter and me, one of the help walked in and needed to borrow a hundred rupees. Arthur interrupted the conversation to give this guy a hundred rupees – about four bucks or something like that.

'Well, Peter Guber is one of the most focused people you'll ever meet in your life,' says Gentry, 'and he could not believe that Arthur interrupted the conversation for such a trivial matter. He took me aside and said, "He's a lunatic. I fly halfway around the world to talk to this guy, and he's worried about giving some little guy four dollars."

'Peter was going to go home. He was going immediately. I assured Peter that if he would just be patient everything would work out well. And it did. All in all, I thought the meetings went very well. Arthur was willing to do most anything except go through the intensity of another *2001*.'

Thus began the literary collaboration between Arthur C. Clarke and Gentry Lee. For the next several weeks Arthur worked on story elements and eventually produced a four-thousand-word outline which became the foundation for their film script treatment for Guber. Then Gentry Lee again travelled to Sri Lanka to work with Arthur on the treatment, and they began the creative process of working out the plot, characters and backgrounds. It was during this first working session together on the movie script that they realised they were well on their way to a novel. As a result they later agreed to co-authorship and to a division of labour, and that's how their book collaboration started.

Cradle was the first book produced by their joint efforts. No other similar projects were foreseen in the beginning. The novel was written by early 1987. It never got to the silver screen, however. Warner bought the film rights but, says Gentry, 'Their writers wrote an absolutely ghastly screenplay, and eventually the studio abandoned the deal.'

In April 1986 a celestial event spurred Arthur on to a new solo novel. He saw Halley's Comet from his rooftop for the first time. His fourteen-inch Celestron, with its binocular eyepieces, provided the view despite the city lights. Later he saw the comet's feather-like tail spread across the stars.

'I realised that its next appearance, in 2061, would provide a splendid opportunity for a third Space Odyssey.' Halley's Comet thus made its important appearance in Arthur's novel in progress, *2061: Odyssey Three.*

On 26 May, *The Songs of Distant Earth* was published.

'I tried to write a lyrical book; I wanted to make people cry,' Arthur told John Cunningham of the *Guardian*. 'I'm rather tired of critics going on about the lack of characterisation, and my rather flat prose.'

Most reviewers believed he succeeded. 'In his seventieth year, he's written a novel to prove to the critics he cares as much about human beings as scientific concepts,' wrote Cunningham.

This interstellar novel was a blueprint for Utopia, a 'cosmic yet essentially serene tale', wrote another reviewer, which rewarded him the more he thought about it.

Ian Watson believed it could change the way we view reality. '*The Songs of Distant Earth*,' he wrote, 'is certainly a novel to hand to any adolescent sf fan, to make them think and feel differently about the universe, the future and fellow life.' The novel remains a favourite of Arthur's to this day.

In July 1986 *Playboy* published 'a candid conversation about the future of space travel – and about sex, immortality and *2001* – with the witty dean of science fiction writers'.

Ken Kelley, the interviewer, visited Sri Lanka for a week and a half, interviewing Arthur several times and absorbing his unique lifestyle and character.

Even in final printed form, it was a long interview. Arthur's prolific output was discussed and then they talked about the difference between 'extrapolation' and 'prediction'. Arthur had always emphasised that he was extrapolating not predicting, but Kelley got him to admit that sometimes when he extrapolates he is trying to predict.

Then he brought up some of the earlier Clarke predictions that had turned out wrong: that Arthur himself would go to the Moon by 1980; that mankind would have landed on other planets by 1980; that actual colonisation of other planets would take place by the year 2000. All these predictions had been made in 1966.

'You're trying to pin me to the wall,' Arthur protested, 'and believe me, it's a tough job being a prognosticator – for instance, the success of *Apollo* and then trying to recover from the immediate-post-*Apollo* emotions. I remember standing next to Vice-President Spiro Agnew, just after he'd seen the *Apollo 2* leave, and hearing him say, "Now we must go to Mars." It seemed quite reasonable that we'd be on Mars during this century. And we would have if the momentum had continued.'

The Odyssey trilogy was discussed, including the mysterious monolith: 'I like to think of the monolith as a sort of cosmic Swiss army knife – it does whatever it *wants* to do,' Arthur told his interviewer. His slightly changing position on SDI/'Star Wars' came up ('Reagan's Star Wars may turn out to be a stroke of political genius, even if his motivations and political conclusions are quite wrong'), but he was steadfast in his conviction that the long-term solutions were diplomatic ones.

About the *Challenger* accident in early 1986 Arthur answered: 'The [final] shuttle is simply the wrong system. It was designed, then *re*designed by Congress.' He was convinced that budgetary cuts created some of the problems that may have ultimately resulted in the accident. But he still believed, as he had stated before the *Challenger* explosion, that catastrophes were inevitable in such complex systems.

When interviewer Ken Kelley said, 'You don't believe in organised religion, yet a major theme in so many of your works seems to be a quest for God', Arthur agreed.

'Yes, in a way – a quest for ultimate values, whatever they are. My objection to organised religion is the premature conclusion to ultimate truth that it represents,' he said, then went on to describe his unhappy Anglican Sunday school experiences as a boy, when he had to walk several miles to church only to hear 'horribly boring sermons'. The children were given stamps which they had to stick in a book, and when the book was full they were allowed to go on an outing. Young Arthur considered this a form of bribery.

'I remember doing it for a couple of months, and then saying, "This is a bunch of nonsense, and I don't intend to do it any more." Never went again.'

Towards the end of the interview, the topic turned to sex – one which Arthur rarely talks about in public.

Some school boards in the United States banned *Imperial Earth* because of references to a homosexual relationship the protagonist, Duncan Makenzie, had when he was young. When Kelley used the word 'lover' Arthur thought it was too strong.

'They'd just mucked around as boys,' he said, adding that there was 'a whiff of that in *Rendezvous with Rama*, too. I guess I get more and more daring as I get older.'

Kelley then asked Arthur what he meant by that.

'I guess I just don't give a damn any more,' he replied. There was a pause. 'Maybe that isn't true, actually. One of my problems now is that I'm not just a private citizen. I have to keep up certain standards, or at least pretend to, so I don't shock too many people.'

Bisexuality was discussed. 'I think Freud said something to the effect that we're *all* polymorphously perverse, you know. And, of course, we are,' Arthur said, adding (when asked) that he had had bisexual experiences.

'Who hasn't? Good God! If anyone had ever told me that he hadn't, I'd have told him he was lying. But then, of course, people tend to "forget" their encounters. I don't want to go into detail about my own life, but I just want it to be noted that I have a rather relaxed sympathetic attitude about it – and that's something I've not really said out loud before. Let's move on.'

The novel *2010* also briefly alludes to bisexuality, when Heywood Floyd questions his own motivation for talking to one of the crew members about a relationship that was causing some stress in another member of the crew.

So the intervention had been worthwhile, whatever the impulse behind it. Even if, as Floyd sometimes ruefully suspected, it was no more than the secret envy that normal homo- or heterosexuals feel, if completely honest with themselves, toward cheerfully well-adjusted polymorphs.

The Ghost from the Grand Banks (1990) briefly describes a lesbian relationship between Edith Craig and her psychiatrist's nurse, and also a bordello, 'The Villa', near Gatwick Airport, and a somewhat unusual case history of one of its clients, 'OG', a successful engineer who enjoys various forms of bondage. 'He likes my personnel to wrap him up in bandages like an Egyptian mummy,' says the bordello's owner, Dame Eva, 'until he is completely helpless. Only in this way, after considerable stimulation, can he achieve a satisfactory orgasm.'

Alfred C. Kinsey's study, *Sexual Behavior in the Human Male*, first published in 1948, had a tremendous influence on Arthur when he was in his early thirties. This landmark study allowed Arthur to gain an objective perspective on his own sexuality, and it became very important to him.

One friend remembers Arthur coming into the White Horse pub in London one evening with a copy of the Kinsey report, and he was much more effervescent than usual. Apparently the book gave Arthur a new confidence in his own sexuality; he could compare himself with all the people whom Kinsey had interviewed. Had Kinsey included the United Kingdom in his data base, Arthur would have been ready to help.

'At one time I kept a chart of the number of times I masturbated! And when Kinsey published his results, I was astonished at how feeble Americans were,' Arthur says, laughing.

Kinsey's published observations produced change in a great many people which eventually was reflected in larger-scale changes in society.

In July Arthur went to London to attend an H. G. Wells Symposium and then on to Bishops Lydeard to visit his family. During the trip he was not feeling well. He had been walking with difficulty and tiring easily, and because of these symptoms he decided to get a complete check-up at London's National Hospital for Nervous Diseases.

'Hector went with him to the hospital,' says brother Fred. 'After the examination, the doctors told Arthur he had only fifteen months to live. Their diagnosis was that he had Amyotrophic lateral sclerosis, commonly known as Lou Gehrig's disease in the United States. It is a degenerative motor neuron disease of the spinal cord and brain.

'Hector was livid because they had told Arthur. Hector was furious. He believed that you never tell a person that sort of thing, no matter what the situation is. Some people would break up immediately.

'It depends on the doctor, of course, whether a patient is told or not,' says Fred. 'In this case, the doctor thought Arthur was the sort who would really want to know.

'When I saw him he was very subdued and obviously not too happy about things, but after the initial shock he more or less said, damnit, he'd got an enormous amount he wanted to do, and if he'd only got fifteen months to do it he'd better whack into it. And he did. In the next year he produced four books.

'Eighteen months later he was still writing, and all the horrible things they told him might happen to him hadn't happened. Of course, they had told him what he should do to keep it under control – what diets to take and what exercises to do, which he very religiously did. He carried on working intensely, which might have been the saving grace. If he had been the sort to say, "Oh my God, I'm going to die in fifteen months", he probably would have.

'By the end of eighteen months he was able to walk better than he could before and he thought, "Well, I better have a second opinion." With the help of his friends in Washington, a complete and thorough examination was set up for the summer of 1988 at Johns Hopkins.'

Soon after the London diagnosis Arthur updated his friends. 'Saw neuro-specialists who gave gloomy diagnosis. Rather depressed until I reminded myself (a) I'm not a baseball player so my career will be, if anything, assisted (b) my two typing fingers will be the last to go (c) a hi-tech wheelchair might be fun to play with. (Stephen Hawking is now a source of much inspiration.) Started taking intensive physiotherapy in an attempt to prove the experts wrong.'

Not surprisingly, Arthur did prove them wrong. He worked hard on his body. His physiotherapist was first-class and had been trained in England. Arthur received treatment three times a week. He considered himself in better physical and mental shape than he'd been in for years.

'The only problem is my undercarriage – sometimes I can walk perfectly normally, but at other times I limp badly,' he wrote Roger Caras in late October. 'I still don't need to use a stick and may graduate directly to a hi-tech wheelchair (solar powered, computer controlled, video etc.).'

As Fred said, he whacked into it. He completed the creative brainstorming and plotting with Gentry Lee for their novel *Cradle*, and then moved on to several other projects. He put the finishing touches and added his editorial stamp of approval to *Arthur C. Clarke's July 20, 2019*, a book of essays (and slick visuals) about the future by *OMNI* magazine writers, an idea conceived by Robert Weil, then editor at *OMNI*.

'I got very excited about the idea of taking one day in the life of the future – the fiftieth anniversary of the *Apollo* Moon landing – and writing a book about it,' says Weil. Arthur also thought it was a great idea when he saw the proposal and agreed to lend his name to it. This was all Weil needed; he sold it immediately to Macmillan in 1985.

When the book was finally published in late 1986, however, Arthur was disturbed that Macmillan was marketing it as if it were *his* book and not the work of several writers whose chapters he'd overseen and finally approved. In a very short list of acknowledgements various people were thanked for their contributions, but a reader would be hard pressed to know that they were the actual writers of the book. The publisher was trading on the Clarke name, which in itself was not a problem – that's what they had bought, after all. Arthur, however, objected to the way the group authorship was hidden from the reader.

'To add insult to injury (and the many distinguished contributors were undoubtedly injured),' Arthur wrote later, 'I was never sent the final proofs, so didn't know what happened until it was too late. (Almost equally annoying were the stupid sub-sub-editorial mistakes that I never had a chance of correcting.)'

Earlier on he had agreed to promote the book on ABC's 'Good Morning America' via satellite link, but he cancelled when he realised the publisher was promoting *2019* as if it were his book.

When science fiction's own magazine *Locus* reported Arthur as 'frail-looking' in September (from seeing him in London in July), he was mildly miffed and wrote a letter to Charlie Brown, the editor, saying that a more accurate description would be 'clumsy'.

> I'm now glad to say that, since my return to Colombo, daily physiotherapy and massive vitamin inputs have restored my mobility almost to normal. (How many *Locus* readers can walk across the room, *backwards*, balancing the Ray Bradbury omnibus on their head?) My personal physician gives me until 2001; then he'll take an option on 2010. Frankly, I've not felt so well for years and am now involved in about twenty projects, including two movies and a novel. If I *am* eventually incapacitated I'll get wired into a word processor – and then, Isaac, look out!

Throughout the rest of 1986 Arthur continued to play table tennis at the Otters Club for an hour or more each day and was beating all his opponents – at least some of the time.

'Arthur gets a charge out of seeing and talking with people there,' says Gentry Lee. 'He's eccentric, lovable, humorous – *puckish* is a good adjective, and not one that most people would think of – while he challenges and plays table tennis with the young people.'

Fit as he claimed to be, he nonetheless decided to cancel all engagements with one exception: the Nehru Memorial Lecture in the autumn of 1986. His personal physician, Dr Theva Buell, travelled with him to New Delhi, where he delivered the Nineteenth Jawaharlal Nehru Memorial Lecture on 13 November. Before his speech, Arthur had a private meeting with Prime Minister Rajiv Gandhi.

His lecture was 'Space Wars and Space Peace' (the variant title on the printed text itself was 'Star Wars and Star Peace'), which gave an overview of the SDI scenarios and discussed what he believed to be some of the inherent problems of such systems, including their destabilising influence. The last half of his lecture emphasised the peaceful uses of space such as reconnaissance satellites that had no offensive capability ('Peacesats') and helped to build international trust.

Concluding, he spoke of his vision of the Global Family brought together by the telecommunications revolution: 'Its loyalties and interests will transcend all the ancient frontiers,' he said. And speaking of the age of the dinosaurs and their extinction he said, 'Intelligence, not armour, was to inherit the Earth. May it do so once again.'

Arthur enjoyed the applause and the compliments that followed, especially the Prime Minister's brief thank-you speech, which included some wit: 'I can assure Dr Clarke that if *Playboy* is banned in India it is not because of anything he may have written in it.'

Prime Minister Gandhi arranged a special flight to Agra and the Taj Mahal. Arthur taxed his strength with a long walk through the gardens there, but even so he said it was well worth it.

'Incredibly, the Taj Mahal is *not* over-rated,' he told friends later. It was 'a pretty good finale to thirty-five years of globe-trotting'.

The last month of 1986 gave Arthur an opportunity to reflect on the year that soon would be history. It was a year of major setbacks: the space shuttle programme was grounded indefinitely after the worst space disaster in history; and Arthur C. Clarke was diagnosed as having a terminal illness.

But the positive notes were there also. He was still alive and was feeling reasonably healthy as the New Year approached – no matter what the doctors said. It was also natural to think of one's legacy after being diagnosed as terminally ill. Such thoughts no doubt motivated him to establish the Arthur C. Clarke Award in 1986. It would be given each year for the best science fiction novel published in Britain. Margaret Atwood won the award the first year for her novel *The Handmaid's Tale*.

Much of Clarke's good work would remain, even if he didn't last out the decade. But that thought of legacy, perhaps positive from an immense Stapledonian perspective, didn't offer much emotional comfort. Instead, he went to his work. It was always there for him. That is what Arthur Clarke put up against the fall of night.

CHAPTER 31

Threescore and Ten

My great-grandfather Arthur Heal barely
missed the century mark, dying in the year
I was born and passing on his name to me
. . . We farm boys have good genes.
            – *Arthur C. Clarke's July 20, 2019*

Arthur's opus numbers climbed toward the seven hundred mark in
early 1987. The major work in progress was *2061: Odyssey Three* and
he continued to devote most of his time to it, at one point removing
himself and his portable Kaypro 2000 to a hotel near Galle where he
did 'ten thousand words of ODYSSEY III in four days', he wrote
Roger Caras in early May. Roger was worried about Arthur's welfare
because of the violence and political unrest in Sri Lanka. Two mass-
acres in the east and a random killing at a bus station had recently
occurred. He pleaded with Arthur to get out while he could – before
he became a victim of the violence and chaos going on around him.
'You can't live with your head in a bag,' Roger told him.

'The situation is indeed tragic, yet it's amazing how things continue
normally,' Arthur replied, adding that he had been taking some action
by shipping some files and important books back to his brother Fred
for the 'Clarkives'.

Hector's wife Valerie was Australian, the girls half Australian; it
would be a logical place for the family to live if things went from
bad to worse in Sri Lanka. With this in mind an apartment was
purchased in Brisbane, to be leased in the meantime, in case the family
was forced to escape the country.

In February President J. R. Jayewardene opened the new Laboratory Building of the Arthur C. Clarke Centre, and Dr John McLucas,
Chairman of the International Space Year 1992 (and one-time Comsat
vice-president and Secretary of the US Air Force), came to give a
lecture and receive the first Arthur C. Clarke Award for an 'outstanding contribution to communications technology'. This annual award
is presented in Colombo by the Sri Lankan President. McLucas was

also a board member of the Clarke Centre, and a board meeting was called when he was there.

The International Space University held its Founding Conference in April 1987 at MIT in Cambridge, Massachusetts. Arthur couldn't attend, but he air-expressed a special video presentation for the occasion. ISU was founded in large part because of Arthur's inspiration and encouragement of 'the gang of three' (Todd Hawley, Peter Diamandis and Bob Richards) who were involved in the ACC Foundation of the US before founding ISU.

In May Arthur went to Paris to accept one of his highest honours: the Tenth Charles A. Lindbergh Award, given annually to recognise an individual whose lifetime's work has contributed to the balance of technological advancement and preservation of the environment. He was in good company. Past recipients included Jacques Cousteau, General James Doolittle and Thor Heyerdahl, great explorers all.

The trip to Paris would be a good test of his endurance, he knew. Although he felt reasonably fit, his walking was either difficult or normal, depending on what day you asked.

The ceremonies for the Lindbergh Award included a re-enactment of the historic landing.

'I was at Le Bourget Airport,' says Arthur, 'watching a perfect replica of the *Spirit of St Louis* land exactly sixty years later, while a Concorde took off on the next runway!'

During his Paris stay he met composer Jean-Michel Jarré and Opéra de Paris star Eric Vu-An. He enjoyed himself, but was happy to be back in Colombo by 1 June.

The planet's population was projected to reach five billion in July 1987 and the United Nations produced a programme, 'The Day of Five Billion', for global telecast. Arthur was honoured to have some time on the show.

Ted Turner wrote to Arthur a few months later, thanking him for his contribution to the programme. 'I'm looking forward to your participation in "The Day of Six Billion" which should roughly coincide with the year of your first major odyssey.'

2061: Odyssey Three was now completed, Arthur began to itch for a new project – no matter how many people he told he had stopped writing. By the end of July he had begun his rather chatty work on early science fiction and science fiction writers who appeared in the pulp magazines of the late 1920s and thirties. These early stories had stirred Arthur's fantasies and fired his imagination – and they had a tremendous influence on him.

This work was pure nostalgia for Arthur. What his memory couldn't bring forth his personal library could. *Astounding Days: A Science Fictional Autobiography* was first published in Great Britain by Gollancz in May 1989 and was 'Gratefully and affectionately dedicated to the memories of Harry Bates/F. Orlin Tremaine/John W. Campbell'.

While he was writing *Astounding Days* Gentry Lee arrived in Sri Lanka. 'Arthur,' says Gentry, 'gave me his schedule for the next year. One of the things on it was a sequel to *Rendezvous with Rama*, and it said in parentheses "(with collaborator)". And I knew what he was doing. He was playing a game – that was his way of asking me if I wanted to collaborate with him on the sequel.'

Gentry was thrilled, of course, and they discussed how they would approach it. What with Gentry's expertise in the space sciences (he was, after all, chief engineer on Project Galileo), this would be an ideal project on which to collaborate.

'In a remarkably short time Scott had sold a whole package to Bantam's Lou Aronica,' wrote Arthur. It was originally defined as a sequel to *Rendezvous with Rama*, plus two other books, which were not named at that time. Ultimately the two other books turned out to be sequels to *Rama II: The Garden of Rama*, and *Rama Revealed*, written during the 1989–91 period.

So after the film treatment and then novel of *Cradle*, he and Gentry had three more novels on which to collaborate. That they got along and worked well together was more than half the battle. They genuinely enjoyed one another.

Gentry willingly travelled halfway around the world for these working sessions with Arthur and handled all the communications between publisher, editor and agent ('So that Arthur wouldn't be battered.'). All this helped Arthur fulfil his lifelong goal of avoiding the mundane 'mechanics of life', as he said, and gave him more time for creative endeavours and play – Arthur's speciality in childhood and adulthood! And Gentry enjoyed the travel and the different culture of Sri Lanka – at least when things were not out of control. Towards the end of his July 1987 visit, however, things got rough. It was not even safe in the streets of Colombo.

Says Gentry, 'The Sri Lankan government had just signed an agreement with India to allow Indian troops to come into the country and help control the separatist Tamils – the Hindu minority who were trying to secede. Because of this agreement with India, another group of Ceylonese extremists and terrorists, the Sinhalese People's Liberation Front (JVP), had gone wild and burned down the state building in Colombo and a lot of other things. I was at Arthur's house and things got very uncomfortable in the city. I had to get back to the Meridian Hotel in Colombo, where I was staying, and I saw all sorts of terrible things along the way. We were stopped once by a soldier who stuck his machine gun into my chest in the back seat of the car.

'Just as I went in the front door of the hotel, shots rang out. I went up to the second floor where the foreigners who had courage were sitting out by the swimming pool, leaning over and watching some Sri Lankan gunmen shoot down a couple of students who were trying to burn a bus. They slapped a curfew on the whole town, and I had to bribe a taxi driver to get me out of Colombo to the airport to get home.'

On 16 December 1987 Arthur celebrated his seventieth birthday. His new age seemed rather unreal to him. 'I still don't believe it,' he told friends afterwards.

He entertained special visitors for the occasion.

'My old friend, the *Echo* and *Telstar* pioneer Dr John Pierce, arrived with his new wife Brenda to receive the second Arthur Clarke Award. President Jayewardene cut the cake, and we all took part in a Colombo–Washington live panel discussion via USIA's Worldnet with Fred Durant (Arthur Clarke Foundation), Todd Hawley (International Space University), Joseph Pelton (Intelsat).'

John Pierce remembers that the presentation was held at a big building complex given to the Sri Lankan government as a gift by the Chinese.

'We went to the award ceremony in his red Mercedes, with the little flag flying on the left front fender, showing that he was Chancellor of the University of Moratuwa. It was quite a colourful ceremony. We all traipsed in covered with flowers. There was a band of antique instruments, and they lit this huge candle-like lamp.

'My wife and I were there about ten days,' says Pierce. 'We stayed at the residence of the US Ambassador. After we'd been there a couple of days my wife asked Arthur, "Is there a word corresponding to *mañana* in Sinhale?" And he said, "Yes, but it doesn't have the same sense of urgency."'

Dr Cyril Ponnamperuma, first director of the Clarke Centre, was also there and he had a birthday surprise for Arthur: a felicitation volume, with messages from the famous and not-so-famous friends of Arthur C. Clarke.

'It was my privilege to gather this bouquet for you,' Cyril wrote in his birthday letter to Arthur. 'The outpouring of affection, appreciation and admiration from world leaders in the art and technology of communication is a powerful testament. Your pre-eminent position in the "Global Village" which you helped to forge from the babel of sounds on planet Earth is recorded for posterity.'

There were letters from Neil Armstrong, Isaac Asimov, Walter Cronkite, Norman Mailer, Gene Roddenberry, Carl Sagan, Ted Turner and so on. An impressive verbal outpouring for Arthur's seventieth – what he jokingly called 'embarrassingly fulsome messages'.

Back in Great Britain, Fred and Michael Clarke represented their older brother in yet another ceremony. The Mayor of Minehead, Arthur's birthplace, unveiled a plaque at the old house on 13 Blenheim Road. 'All this,' said Arthur, 'gave me a distinctly posthumous sensation.'

The release of *2061: Odyssey Three* came in the autumn of 1987, and its timing was an extra present for Arthur's seventieth birthday. The last of the Odysseys (so far!) was quite an accomplishment for someone who, according to the London doctors, was lucky to be alive. That was the most important outcome of 1987. He was still alive and feeling good. And he had no reason to fear a second childhood. He had never left his first – an advantage to any creative person.

By the beginning of 1988, the contract was in place for the three new co-authored novels, *Rama II* being the first. Gentry Lee arrived in January for another work session with Arthur.

'We holed up in a beach hotel with my Kaypro 2000 portable and produced a 10k word treatment of *Rama II* – as well as the outline of *Rama III*,' Arthur told friends in his newsy Egogram.

When people ask Gentry how he and Arthur work together, he tells them, '"The creative process we do together, and then I do the writing process with Arthur looking over my shoulder." Then they say, "Well, that doesn't sound like he's doing that much." And I say, "You don't understand that the creative process is where the ideas, the great sweeping interactions between character and situation, get developed. You couldn't have two people doing the writing process – it would be disjointed."

'It's not as if there's a left brain mechanism where we follow a structure,' says Gentry. 'It's literally sitting down after the BBC news, staring around at the palm trees in a southern Sri Lankan resort and saying, "Well, what do you think about this?" Then my job is to weave these things together.

'The next day I'd say to him, "Okay, if you put this thing together that you talked about and this thing that we both talked about, and these in the story, then we'll have a first quarter of the novel that looks like this." Then he'll say, "No, no, that won't work for the following reasons. And by the way, last night I had a dream about such and such and that reminded me of such and such." And then he says "Somehow that ought to fit into the story, but I just can't see how." And I get all excited and I'll jump up and I'll say, "That's great! Suppose we put that in this piece," and so on. And now all of a sudden we're working on the back third of the novel, whereas we had thought that morning we were going to work on the first quarter.

'A lot of people misunderstood what we were doing by breaking the chapters into parts and actually thought that Arthur had written some of them and that I had written others. It was amusing to us that people would spend time (particularly the Japanese who like to analyse everything) trying to figure out who contributed what in *Cradle*.

'We both admitted that *Cradle* was on the one hand very good for a first collaboration and on the second not quite as good as we thought it ought to be.'

Several critics agreed with the last part of that statement when *Cradle* was published in August 1988. 'When is an Arthur C. Clarke novel not an Arthur C. Clarke novel? When it's co-written by someone called Gentry Lee and entitled *Cradle*,' wrote one reviewer who referred to the work as a 'ludicrous hybrid'.

Another reviewer wondered in print 'why Arthur C. Clarke, who can write intelligent and suspenseful novels when he wants to (eg, *Rendezvous with Rama*), should have got himself involved with this leaden piece of self-parody'.

While the first collaborative work between Clarke and Lee was not well received in some quarters, this did not damage their friendship or working relationship. One result of the criticism was that they agreed to play down the explicit sex in *Rama II*. Such sexual descriptions were so foreign to Arthur Clarke's fiction that it was another dead giveaway that it was Gentry's apprenticeship prose, not Arthur's.

Their general attitude about the criticism was that some of it was justified; theirs was a new working relationship, after all. Book buyers and reviewers, they assumed, would understand that a co-authored novel by Clarke and Lee was an entirely different entity than an Arthur C. Clarke novel.

The response to *Cradle*, however, told them that their assumption was wrong. They underestimated audience expectations of a novel bearing the name ARTHUR C. CLARKE, even though Gentry Lee's name also appeared (in a lower position and in smaller type) on the book jacket. For readers it became an identity crisis of authorship. This was not what many of them expected, and for some the standards of truth in advertising had been violated.

Such reader and critic responses would continue for their other collaborative efforts to one degree or another, including the *Rama* sequels. Some of the reaction, no doubt, came from established writers who resented the fact that Gentry Lee, who was not a professional writer but a space scientist, hitched his name to Arthur C. Clarke's and received half the large, seven-figure advance for a three-book contract.

'The Clarke–Lee collaboration,' says Arthur, 'is much like thousands of other co-authorships, but during the past few years Scott has got me involved in several more unusual deals. It hasn't been very difficult, because curiosity is my most abiding characteristic, and I tend to agree with the British nobleman who told his son: "Try everything once – except incest and folk-dancing."'

Another project the Scott Meredith Agency handled, a more straightforward use of Arthur's name, was a series of six paperbacks published by Byron Preiss/Avon Books and written by Paul Preuss: *Arthur C. Clarke's Venus Prime V.*

'They are loosely based on short stories of mine, and in each case I have contributed an "Afterword",' says Arthur. 'But the novels themselves, as is clearly stated, are all written by Paul Preuss, and I did not agree to the project until I had read some of his excellent fiction (and non-fiction).

'The use of an author's name on projects with which he is only marginally – or not at all – connected is known as "franchising", and is of course well-known in the fields of sport and entertainment. Literary agent Richard Curtis, biting the hand that feeds him, has wittily termed the practice "strip-mining an author"; perhaps it is better than mind-stripping, a torture much practised in Hollywood's gilded Gulags.'

Before January 1988 was over, two birthdays were celebrated in the Ekanayake family. Hector was forty-eight on 14 January, but Arthur forgot all about it. Cherene was eight on 11 January and Arthur bought her present early: 'A tiny bundle of fluff I've named Dainty, after one of the Cairn terriers Mother had at the farm half a century ago. This Dainty is one of the most engaging puppies I've ever known – and bullies Rikki though he's about fifty times her size.'

In March Arthur and the family boarded the *Queen Elizabeth II* in

Colombo Harbour and sailed to see the total eclipse on the eighteenth. Before departure he wrote friends, 'Barring icebergs – in which case Bob Ballard knows just how to find us – we should fly back from Hong Kong around the twenty-sixth. I look forward to giving a few talks and meeting interesting people on what may very well be my last trip outside Sri Lanka. Although I still think I've a fair chance of seeing 2001, even before my current disability travelling was becoming too time- and energy-consuming, while telecommunications and visitors steadily reduced its importance to me.'

The reference to Robert Ballard and the iceberg was evidence that Arthur had begun thinking about his Titanic novel. The proof came in a 9 May letter to Charles Pellegrino, in which Arthur wrote that he had indeed started work on the novel.

As much as he wanted to remain in Sri Lanka in the summer of 1988, Arthur's physical condition warranted outside medical attention. But it took some real behind-the-scenes manoeuvring by several people to get him to leave home.

'We had a visit by a chap named Michael Snowden,' says Arthur, 'the only one I know of a vanishing species, of which Percival Lowell is a prototype – a gentleman astronomer. Michael travels around the world, living where he pleases. These days, all a professional astronomer needs is a desk and a computer, and he can work anywhere he likes.

'Michael got very friendly with us during his visits to Sri Lanka. When he came to Barnes Place in 1988, he noticed my health and was worried about my mental and physical deterioration.

'Well, it so happens that Michael and Jay Keyworth (President Reagan's science adviser for six years) are best friends. They were college roommates together. In fact, Michael is godfather to Keyworth's son, George Jr. So Michael wrote to Keyworth and told him about my declining health, and then Keyworth wrote to Valerie and Hector behind my back.

'I was quite willing to go, really, but I just didn't have the strength because of some kind of pneumonia which I had for the whole of 1988. It knocked me out. I was getting treatment in Colombo, but there wasn't much improvement. I began to think that it may be the moist environment, some kind of allergy. I'm in a closed air-conditioned room, and the carpets mildew. This was my state when Jay made the necessary arrangements for me to fly to the United States and have a thorough, several-day examination at Johns Hopkins Hospital in Baltimore.'

The examination would confirm or refute the 1986 London diagnosis of Amyotrophic lateral sclerosis (also known as Lou Gehrig's Disease) – the same illness that the world-famous Cambridge physicist, Stephen Hawking, has been afflicted with for many years.

Hector accompanied Arthur on the trip, which took them through England as usual. They were in London for four days. Even though Arthur was in a wheelchair, there was one media event he was eager to participate in – a videotaping session with Dr Stephen Hawking in a London studio and (via satellite link) Carl Sagan at Cornell University in Ithaca, New York.

The discussion, 'God, the Universe and Everything Else', was never broadcast as intended, but there's little question that it will be broadcast (or certainly portions thereof) at some future date. The narrator, Magnus Magnusson, introduced this trinity of intellect.

'Tonight: the time before time began. The universe, black holes, God and the laws of science. Professor Stephen Hawking, Dr Carl Sagan and Arthur C. Clarke, discuss the mysteries man faces as he starts to explore the stars.'

Besides free-wheeling discussions of the universe (its beginning and its ending), unified field theory, extra-terrestrial life and interstellar travel between Clarke, Hawking and Sagan, Magnus Magnusson asked Arthur to do some computer doodling with what mathematicians call a Mandelbrot Set, named in honour of a French scientist working for IBM. It is a mathematical equation which leads toward the infinite, making the universe visual.

'You can use the computer as a microscope,' said Arthur, 'and you can continue that process for ever. Some of the images are incredibly beautiful and are going to have a great impact on artistic design in the next decade or so. I found what looked like black holes and I'd like to show them to you.'

Arthur zoomed in on screen, magnified the image about a thousand times, and came to a so-called black hole. The original picture he had showed the audience was now about five hundred feet across, and the screen was showing a detail from it. After the next magnification the original Mandelbrot Set's image would be about ten million miles wide.

'This is black hole number three,' said Arthur. 'And this one took me twenty-two hours of computing. The day before I left Sri Lanka, I had the computer running all night. I'm rather proud of this one because on this scale that original little picture you saw is the width of the orbit of Mars. So you understand that no human being has ever seen that picture pattern before, simply because of probabilities.

357

'You can go on for ever and ever,' he continued. 'Now I would like to ask Stephen this question: is the real universe also infinite in detail? I mean, we know we have molecules, atoms, electrons, protons, subatomic right down to the quarks so far, but does it continue for ever and ever or is there a limit, is there a basement to the real universe?'

Stephen Hawking's computer-driven voice synthesiser answered to the will of its owner.

'We will discover new structures when we look at the universe on smaller and smaller scales,' Hawking said, 'but in the case of the universe, there seems to be a limiting scale. It is called Planck length, and this is about a million billion billion times smaller than an inch. This means that there is a limit to how complex the universe can be. It also means that a universe could be described by a theory that is fairly simple at least on scales of the Planck length. I just hope that we are smart enough to find it.'

Arthur, of course, was about to embark on a fantastic voyage closer to home – into his own ailing body – and he and Hector flew to Dulles Airport outside Washington, DC, on 13 July. John McLucas, friend and director of the International Space University, was there to meet them.

'He was sitting in a wheelchair,' recalls McLucas, 'which they had ready for him as soon as he got off the plane. I met him in the area where you meet international visitors, and then we managed to get the car as close to the exit as we could. He was quite preoccupied with his malady and about how there seemed to be some difference in the medical views. But he was looking forward to the diagnosis by the Johns Hopkins team.'

The testing began the next day under the direction of Dr Daniel B. Drachman, director of the Neuromuscular Unit at Johns Hopkins.

'I was somewhat unprepared for the sight that originally greeted me when he arrived in our clinic,' recalls Drachman. 'He had come from the front entrance of Johns Hopkins via wheelchair. He was being wheeled by Hector, and was sitting in the chair wearing what I can only describe as a "team jacket" and peaked sort of baseball cap. This unassuming appearance was entirely consistent with his compliant behaviour as a patient.'

The entire evaluation process took about a week, and Dr Drachman knew nothing about the 1986 London diagnosis of Amyotrophic lateral sclerosis until his last meeting with Arthur.

'He was very coy about that,' says Drachman. 'He didn't even tell me about the earlier diagnosis of ALS until after we had done all our tests and electromiography and biopsy. The electromiography in fact showed that he had very long-standing, quite old muscle denervation – the muscle had lost its nerve supply a long time previously.

'I insisted that he hold still for a biopsy, and that really gave it away. It showed very striking features of so-called target fibres. These are characteristic of old denervation – an attempt of the nerves to resupply the muscles. So having seen that and all other test data, I simply put it together and decided he had old polio,' says Drachman.

After the medical tests were completed Arthur rested quietly and recuperated from the biopsy surgery on his leg. He was cheerful enough, and he was eager to hear the full and formal test results from Dr Drachman.

'As I was summarising all the results for him during our last meeting and telling him I thought he had a case of Post-Polio Syndrome, he pulled out the earlier diagnosis and confronted me with the fact that the London doctor had made this other diagnosis which, although it's hard to say, may have been made a bit casually. The diagnosis of ALS, since it carries with it such a dire prognosis, should be made only when you're absolutely sure. It doesn't do anybody any good to know early on. I am very circumspect about making that diagnosis. But with Arthur I felt very fortunate to be able to bring him good news.

'Arthur's immediate reaction to the good news that he did not have ALS was an expression of relief that he would live till the year 2001. The second reaction was a rather mischievous satisfaction regarding the misdiagnosis by my British colleague.'

Dr Drachman judged Arthur a 'terrific patient'. 'People who are well known or celebrated can be terrible patients,' he says. 'They can be very demanding or directing. They can ruin their medical care. Arthur was quite the opposite. He was compliant, but not passive. He went along. He was trusting. He was very modest in a funny way. That really is a characteristic of his – that he has a curious combination of modesty and the opposite.

'He has a very open approach to everything, and he's constantly – I can't quite say astonished – intrigued by new impressions. He's always amused and always quite open to new ideas.'

Later Arthur told friends in a newsy letter, 'The Johns Hopkins specialists diagnosed something much less serious [than ALS] – the recently discovered Post-Polio Syndrome. This was both a relief and a surprise, since my complete paralysis in 1962 had been attributed to a spinal injury. [Sri Lankan doctors decided it was a spinal injury, but British doctors correctly diagnosed his problems as polio back then.] The prognosis now is that instead of having already used up most of an ALS victim's usual two to five years of survival, I have a good chance of seeing 2001, even if from a wheelchair (which, I have discovered, is the secret ingredient required for painless transit through today's over-crowded airports).'

Arthur wasn't completely immobilised during his stay at Johns Hopkins. On 19 July he went to Hughes Network Systems to be taped as part of the twenty-fifth anniversary of the first synchronous satellite, *Syncom 2*, in orbit in July 1963. Hughes had originally planned to do it live via satellite link from Sri Lanka later in the month, but Arthur was close by, had no tests scheduled and so he went and taped the birthday message for Hughes. Before he left the United States he visited the offices of Worldnet, the television network of the United States Information Agency, and spoke on camera with Betty Karwasinski for 'America Today'. Also during this time Fred Durant took Arthur to the National Air and Space Museum to see 'The Dream is Alive' on the huge IMAX screen. This spectacular production could easily have been dedicated to the space cadet from Somerset who was in the audience – the man who had devoted his life to keeping alive the dream of space flight and voyages to the Moon, the planets and, one day, even the stars.

It was gratifying to Arthur to see hundreds of people walking through the great halls of the National Air and Space Museum that housed so many of the rockets and spacecraft of the twentieth century. Besides Fred and Hector, writer Gregory Benford accompanied Arthur in his wheelchair.

'He was much on the up when I saw him at the museum,' says Benford. 'It was just days after his good medical news. Among other things, we talked about contemporary science fiction and both agreed that it doesn't take much of a long perspective, that the recent fashion has been very near future with somewhat repetitive themes. We started talking about *Against the Fall of Night*, and at some point I noted that his early novel had been written before the discovery of DNA – that biology really had been left out of the entire story.

'He then told me he had deliberately fixed on the city in the desert in which biology had no rule, in part because he'd never known anything about biology and was interested in the metaphor machines. And I said it would be fun to look back at that and see if his early novel couldn't be reconciled with the world as we know it, because science had learned so much since he wrote it. He said that, yes, it would be a fun project, and I told him I'd talk to my agent about it. That's how *Beyond the Fall of Night*, published in 1990, got started.'

CHAPTER 32

New Lease on Life

I had a nice chat with the Queen yesterday!!
– October 1989

I sat next to Prince Sultan, who kept piling
food on my plate despite all my feeble references to weight-watching.
– November 1989

Once again Arthur crossed the Atlantic, this time without the heavy
burden of a terminal illness weighing on his mind. He continued his
recuperation in London and at Dene Court with Fred and Babbs for a
week or so in early August. They drove Arthur to Minehead to see the
house where he was born, and the owner's son took them through and
showed them the grounds. When Arthur saw the garden hut he was
flooded with memories of changing into his bathing suit there as a young
boy before following the well-worn path down to Minehead beach.

Also during this stay he and his sister Mary, his brothers Fred and
Mike and their wives Babbs and Joyce, had a family luncheon together
at the County Hotel in Taunton. It was a rare event to have all four
children of Charles and Nora Clarke together for a meal, so this was
a memorable occasion.

Arthur was back in Colombo late in the month, 'full of energy and
feeling about ten years younger', he told friends. 'Which is just as
well, since to my amazement I am involved with fourteen (yes 14)
books and my first TV fiction series – *A Fall of Moondust.*'

Todd Hawley, Peter Diamandis and two other representatives of
the International Space University visited Sri Lanka in October 1988.
Invited by the Arthur C. Clarke Centre, they met centre personnel,
learned about the centre's various projects and investigated the possibility of a future ISU campus in Sri Lanka.

At the end of 1988 Arthur was feeling so young that even the
possibility of a space shuttle ride to an orbiting campus of ISU in the
early twenty-first century didn't seem all that outrageous.

★

The political situation in Sri Lanka was still extremely unstable as the new year began. The terrorist Sinhalese People's Liberation Front (JVP) was indiscriminately killing innocent people. In March Arthur wrote to Willie Mendis, his friend who was serving in Washington as the Minister of Technology Transfer at the Embassy of Sri Lanka. A mutual colleague, the vice-chancellor of the University of Colombo, had recently been murdered in cold blood in his office.

'I'm sorry to say that the situation here is still very gloomy as far as the university is concerned and, of course, you'll have heard about poor Stanley Wijesundara's murder.

'I dropped into the campus two days ago, and had a few words with Patu [Dr Patuwathawithane, Arthur's vice-chancellor at the University of Moratuwa] – he has received threats. For that matter, so have we, but we don't take them seriously.'

The fact that Arthur was playing down such threats greatly concerned many of his friends, including Roger Caras. But before the year was out Arthur's attitude would change.

In March Arthur received visits from two men who represented the major interests in his life: telecommunications and writing. Joe Pelton, then director of policy planning for Intelsat, arrived early in the month for lectures and other business, followed by British writer John Brunner a few weeks later.

When Joe Pelton checked into the Intercontinental Hotel the manager offered him a suite for the price of a regular room. With all the political unrest few tourists were travelling to Sri Lanka. There were suites to spare, said the manager, who then asked for a favour.

Someone in the Sri Lankan government had decided that receive-only satellite dishes would no longer be allowed, probably on the grounds that foreign information was somehow corrupting the citizens and undermining the government. The hotel manager told Pelton that the government ordered the Intercontinental, other hotels, businesses and so forth to take down their Earth stations and re-export them. This was impossible to do, the manager explained, because the dishes were built at the Arthur Clarke Centre in Moratuwa a few miles down the road. How could he re-export something that had never been imported?

Pelton had a meeting scheduled with the man who was in charge of international communications in Sri Lanka, Mr Rodrigo, and he promised to raise this matter with him.

After discussing many other issues at their meeting, Pelton brought up the subject. As it happened Rodrigo had a receiving dish at home and thought they were beneficial technology for Sri Lanka. He didn't even know why such a policy was in place, but he promised to find out.

He did. His own colleagues, he discovered, had come up with the restriction without his knowledge, and after a meeting the government policy was reversed – receive-only Earth stations would be allowed after all, and the Arthur C. Clarke Centre for Modern Technologies could assemble them.

'Arthur was pleased as Punch that this had come out of my visit,' says Pelton. 'He said he was going to inform President Premadasa about it and emphasise how valuable the centre can be to help create new and good government policy. The idea that he could help stimulate a more progressive policy in science and technology really excited him.'

When fellow British writer John Brunner arrived in mid-March, Arthur was playing table tennis again, saying 'It's a good sign that I'll live.' Soon he was once more a fierce competitor.

'I'm very proud,' he said, after winning a small silver cup as runner-up for the table tennis tournament in March. 'It was the national champion I played against, for heaven's sake.'

Besides John Brunner's masterful science fiction, he also publishes mainstream fiction and poetry. He is internationally known for his work, and his fiction has been the subject of a panel discussion of the Modern Language Association. (A writer knows his or her work has reached a new level of recognition once academia embraces it for study.)

During his visit to Sri Lanka, Brunner spent time with Arthur at Barnes Place, peering through Arthur's superb optics at the Moon and southern constellations and talking literature. Brunner admired and was influenced by Arthur's early work.

'I read "Rescue Party" when it first came out in 1946, and I remember going back and reading it again a few days later. It was an inspirational kind of story, very upbeat at a time when the world was in the shadow of the atomic bomb and there were an awful lot of downbeat stories in the magazines. When I first ran across it, it was very inspiring. And of all the novels, I still have to say that *Childhood's End* made the biggest impact on me, and I'm pretty certain that the majority of his fans were turned on to his work by the scope and range of that book.'

As more than one critic has pointed out, *Childhood's End* spoke to the postwar generation in a unique way. It created a positive vision for the evolutionary future of humanity at a time when there was widespread fear of an atomic holocaust that would destroy us all.

By early April Arthur was trying hard to get started again on his new novel. This one was a solo effort he referred to as his Titanic novel and was not a collaboration with Gentry Lee. By 10 April he had completed the outline and synopsis. Eighteen months later, in late 1990, it would be published as *The Ghost from the Grand Banks*, first in England by Gollancz and then in the United States by Bantam.

The novel had been gestating in Arthur's imagination for several years – similar to the incubation period he went through for most of his novels – and he was pleased to be back at it. He often discussed the latest technology and methods for raising the *Titanic* with his friend Charles Pellegrino who had worked with Robert Ballard during the reconnaissance made by the submersible *Alvin* in 1986. In one of his letters to Arthur, Pellegrino admitted that he had very mixed emotions about actually raising the *Titanic*, even though he had been trying to figure out how it could be done for years.

'I told him I just wished the whole thing would go away with an avalanche on the Grand Banks – then no one ever would be able to raise the ship again,' says Pellegrino, whose misgivings about disturbing the gravesite of more than fifteen hundred people are shared by many.

The sinking of the *Titanic*, even though it occurred five years before Arthur Clarke was born, has always haunted him. One of the very first stories he ever wrote, in fact, 'Icebergs in Space', was based on the *Titanic*.

'It must have been written around 1930 when I was at Ballifants and attending Huish's Grammar School in Taunton,' says Arthur. This opus Arthur affectionately refers to as 'a luckily long-lost epic . . . I am happy to say no copy survived.'

He also added the *Titanic* to the plot of his 1975 novel, *Imperial Earth*, before giving the ship a lead role in *The Ghost from the Grand Banks*.

Towards the end of April, Arthur learned that the paperback edition of *2061: Odyssey Three* was on the *New York Times* bestseller list. He mentioned this news to a friend and the friend asked, 'Does the thrill remain for you?'

'Not really,' answered Arthur. 'It didn't give quite as much thrill as my finding out I'd lost two pounds in weight, which is what I'm trying to do.'

May brought forth the British edition of *Astounding Days: A Science Fictional Autobiography*, Clarke's memoirs of early pulp magazine stories and writers.

Isaac Asimov wrote a review for the *Observer* titled 'King Arthur's heavenly nostalgia'. No one expected Isaac to be a harsh critic – and he wasn't. Nor did the work deserve such tough scrutiny. It was, after all, a personal memoir of a young reader's love affair (recollected in septuagenarian tranquillity) with a magazine. While it was a friendly piece, however, it was not a blatant puff.

Wrote Isaac: 'The contents deal almost entirely with the authors and stories of the first fifteen years of that magazine, the period that culminated in what will always be the Golden Age (to science fiction people of my age and Arthur's) under John W. Campbell.'

The review expressed Isaac's genuine appreciation of and love for Arthur.

'Clarke is incapable of nastiness or captiousness,' wrote his friend. 'He discusses stories that in some cases were sub-literary, but does not use his own mastery of the field to sneer at them and reduce them to literary rubble. He remembers them as he enjoyed them at the time. His concern is not with their literary values, but with their ideas . . .

'In his social thinking he is humane, liberal and gently sceptical, a fact entirely admirable in his outlook on the world.' Isaac concluded: 'You will find Clarke in this book as he is – utterly free of any trace of modesty. But he is so artless in his appreciation of himself that you will not be offended. Rather, the book will endear him to you.'

The civil war in Sri Lanka continued unabated, and everything was on strike – buses, hospitals, trains and telephones. But in the midst of the crisis Arthur received some good news from England.

'The word came directly from His Excellency David Gladstone (the British High Commissioner to Sri Lanka), confidentially, as it was not to be announced,' Arthur recalls. 'He delivered the news in person to my house.'

The London *Times* and other newspapers of 17 June 1989 announced the Queen's Birthday Honours. And there, under the rank Commander of the British Empire (CBE), was 'Dr Arthur Charles Clarke, for service to British cultural interests in Sri Lanka'. This honour, which was to be presented by the Queen herself in October, was in recognition of what Arthur had done for his adopted island of Sri Lanka – not for his literary accomplishments.

'I'd been waiting a rather long time,' says Arthur, 'and I was wondering if some of the powers didn't like me because it had been so long.'

He and Hector began to make plans for the autumn trip to the

United Kingdom as the civil war worsened in Colombo. Since Valerie was pregnant they wouldn't be able to pack up and get out before then, which would have been a reassuring option under the dangerous and unpredictable conditions. Their anxiety increased as the situation went from bad to worse. Somehow Arthur managed to write a few short pieces while the chaos raged on around him. He also worked on the script for a Japanese Asahi TV show he had agreed to do, which was scheduled to be broadcast in the New Year. It would be filmed in England.

In mid-July anti-government terrorists stopped three buses in eastern Sri Lanka and gunned down at least thirty-five Muslim passengers in cold blood. During a two-day period of intensive fighting between the Tamil rebels and government troops almost 150 people were killed. It was scary and heart-breaking.

Valerie and Hector Ekanayake's third daughter was born on 6 August 1989, though they (including Arthur) couldn't decide what to name her at first. The name Melinda was soon chosen.

While the birth enabled Arthur and Hector to set a departure date for England, the ever-changing political situation kept things uncertain. It was important that Valerie, the baby and the girls remained safe and well taken care of while they were away. The date of the investiture at Buckingham Palace was 25 October.

By 9 September even the hospitals in Colombo were closed down. 'It's a nightmare,' said Arthur. 'They've been killing the doctors. People are dying. The doctors are being killed for treating patients – while they're treating them. If you're sick, you can't go to the hospital. It's almost like Cambodia.'

Everyone believed that this was really it, that anarchy and the forces of destruction and death had come to Colombo to stay. Arthur and the family began to have serious doubts about continuing to live in Sri Lanka.

'We're making contingency plans to leave the country now,' he said in early September, 'and after thirty years, it's a hell of a job. Everything will have to be abandoned; we can't take it with us.'

The president of Sri Lanka, Ranasinghe Premadasa, brought together all political parties and ethnic groups for talks in mid-September. An agreement between Sri Lanka and India to remove the Indian troops that had been asked to come and disarm the militant Tamils in 1987 was close at hand. Over the two-year period, the JVP terrorists had used the presence of the Indian troops to rally others to their cause. Their actions, and the backlash, had left some five thousand people dead since 1987. Their avowed goal was nothing less than to bring down the government. They did not care how many innocent people were killed in the process.

The first session of the assembly provoked more violence from the radicals, including a bomb exploding and several fires starting in government buildings. More than a dozen bodies were found on the outskirts of Colombo.

It was in this context of violence and anxiety that Arthur seriously began making plans to flee the island he had fallen in love with more than three decades earlier.

He refused to leave the house during this period, but kept busy transferring his computer files on to disks so he could carry them to England. When friends called he would tell them that he couldn't talk and that he would call them when he could. 'I'm in a Salman Rushdie mode,' he would say and then try to give them basic information like his arrival date in London with an elaborate code using various chapter or part titles in books from his library.

'I hope no one listening in understands either,' he would tell them, when the communications of the makeshift code system broke down. 'I'm sure this is totally unnecessary, but you know one gets a little bit paranoiac.'

Arthur and Hector arrived at Gatwick Airport on 23 September and went directly to the home of a friend, Navam Tambayah, in Holland Park in London. This was now Arthur's British base when he wasn't at home in Somerset with his brother Fred.

During his stay he met with dozens of friends, saw his publishers and agents and had a thorough physical examination at the hospital. He even met his Johns Hopkins doctor, Daniel Drachman, who was in London with his wife. Arthur took them out to dinner on 5 October. Drachman was also able to examine him and found him to be recovering.

In early October, also, he saw a special friend and colleague – Stanley Kubrick.

'I had a most interesting day with Stanley and managed to escape by the skin of my teeth,' Arthur said mischievously. 'He wanted me to work on his next movie! No way, of course. And then he said, "Well, you're here for a few weeks with nothing to do. Why don't you come in and work for me?"' Arthur laughs at what he thinks was an absurd (and perhaps frightening?) proposition.

Writer Gregory Benford met Arthur on 11 October to discuss his novella *Beyond the Fall of Night*.

'He was in much better physical condition than when I saw him in

August of 1988,' says Benford. 'He can walk short distances, two hundred metres at a go, which is a vast improvement over the wheelchair he was in a year earlier.

'We spent most of our time discussing *Beyond the Fall of Night*, in which I attempted to follow his grand perspectives of *Against the Fall of Night*, written over forty years before. Throughout Arthur was quick, spontaneous, brimming with news.'

Dick Jenvey, Arthur's friend from the 1930s, came to London to see him. They met for lunch and enjoyed stirring up the memories of summer days on the farm and later meetings in London where they were both working before the war.

The word in London was: 'No interviews or press conferences.' One exception, however, was made and, later, another.

'I had a long interview with Godfrey Smith from the *Sunday Times*,' Arthur said. 'He's a very good writer.'

Writing aside, Mr Smith thought Arthur Clarke's oral tradition was lacking.

'Clarke is a hard man to interview,' wrote Smith. 'Ask him about his recent illness, and he will whip out a bulletin about it. Ask him about his writing, and he will give you a print-out summary of his seventy books, five hundred articles, nine contracts for future books, and film or television options on four more. Then good nature and an unflagging interest in the way the world is going get him talking.'

'Still using his season ticket for tomorrow', the headline read. The interview led off with the news of Arthur being given the CBE by the Queen on the following Wednesday. It went on to relate another forthcoming event: Arthur being honoured by the most exclusive club in the world, the members of which are veteran astronauts and cosmonauts – the Association of Space Explorers.

Godfrey Smith, apparently, was not just a 'very good writer' as Arthur observed; he was also a wise and insightful interviewer. About Arthur he wrote: 'He is seventy-one, an amiable, bespectacled, gangling man, slightly reminiscent of a numerate P. G. Wodehouse. There is, however, nothing remotely goofy about the brain or wit behind those mild glasses.'

Arthur's first few weeks in England were leisurely and not too hard on him physically, but the last two weeks showed no mercy. Besides the audience with the Queen, Arthur and Gentry Lee had the Japanese television show to shoot at Dene Court, and only a few days to do it in. The Japanese crew for Asahi TV was in place and ready to roll on 18 October. The five-part series was *The Future with Arthur*

C. Clarke, which was going to be shown in Japan during the first week of 1990.

After one long work day before the cameras, Arthur searched and found his 'journals in their little iron box'.

'I have about thirty volumes, beginning on 4 December 1938,' Arthur told a friend. 'Right up to now. It's the best part of three or four or five million words, I imagine. Minute detail. There's no way I'm going to do anything about it. And no one looks at them until fifty years after my death.'

The big day at Buckingham Palace finally arrived: Wednesday, 25 October 1989. He was allowed to bring two guests, so brother Fred and Hector accompanied him. Arthur donned his morning dress and top hat for the ceremonies, while Fred and Hector wore suits.

A woman journalist from *Figaro* was still interviewing Arthur when the hired limo arrived to take them to Buckingham Palace. Instead of breaking off the interview Arthur kindly allowed her to accompany them on their ride through London before saying good-bye to her at the palace gates. They arrived at about ten a.m. and were directed into the reception area, at which time Arthur went off to be briefed.

Unknown to him, his early fan and long-time friend Ian Macauley was also at Buckingham Palace that Wednesday.

'I got into the palace with my press credentials,' says Macauley, 'sat down, and watched the whole ceremony. Of course it was very boring because we had 150 people getting awards and it took two and a half hours. There were two people who received the most attention from the Queen. Arthur was one of them, and the other was the British Consul from San Francisco, who received an award for promoting British products in California.'

'I had a nice chat with the Queen,' Arthur told friends later. For her part, after noting that he was from Sri Lanka, the Queen mentioned the problems and turmoil there. Arthur reminded her that they had met during her last visit to Sri Lanka, and expressed how sad the current political situation was.

After the ceremony Ian worked his way over to where Arthur, Fred and Hector were.

'He was totally flabbergasted that I got in,' says Ian, 'because he only had the two tickets for Fred and Hector. He was elated when he saw me. We walked from the Ballroom in Buckingham Palace, down the Grand Staircase until we got to the Palace entrance. He leaned on Fred and me to support him. He was exhausted and weak, but happy that the ceremony went well.'

The next day Arthur fainted. He was complaining of vertigo and had the doctor in and was treated for fatigue.

Ian noticed that Arthur seemed very tired and not too responsive, and sometimes had lapses of memory.

'On the Saturday after the ceremony, 28 October, he had a signing session at the Forbidden Planet bookshop. It was sponsored by Victor Gollancz to promote the British publication of *Rama II*.

'Fred and I were there with Arthur,' says Ian. 'About two hundred fans showed up to have books signed. Two new books, *Rama II* and *Astounding Days* were on sale. One fan showed up with his entire collection – about a hundred books – and Arthur had to refuse to sign them all. Throughout the session he was very tired and would sometimes nod off just like that – probably fatigue more than anything else.'

That evening the two Clarke brothers attended a reunion of Arthur's old RAF group at the St Ermyns Hotel. Arthur enjoyed himself as much as he could, although he was still exhausted.

He and Hector flew back to Sri Lanka on 31 October. Arthur had to work on the speech he would deliver at Riyadh, Saudi Arabia, the following month.

By the time they returned from England, the violence in Sri Lanka had subsided. Government troops had crushed the terrorists and regained control over most of the trouble areas. The contingency plans to move out of the country were put on the back burner – and that was a tremendous relief. Besides his personal safety being more assured, Clarke no longer had to face the anxiety-producing prospect of moving tons of books, furnishings, computers, and other equipment half way around the planet – the accumulated possessions of thirty-five years of living on the tear-shaped island in the Indian Ocean.

Only ten days at home at Barnes Place – that's all Arthur had before he was off to Saudi Arabia for the Fifth Planetary Congress of the Association of Space Explorers, where he would be an honoured guest. (Imaginative space flights of the mind don't count as membership credentials; only veteran real-life rocketmen are eligible.) Arthur's presence there was, of course, high status for someone who hadn't yet flown in orbit.

Hector and Arthur's personal physician, Dr Theva Buell, travelled with him. Upon arrival at the Intercontinental Hotel – 'apparently brand-new, like almost everything else in Riyadh', Arthur observed

Right Dollar and dime contracts for two new novels, *2061* and *The Songs of Distant Earth*, signed at the Durants' home in Washington, DC, 1984, with agent Scott Meredith and editor Judy-Lynn del Rey.

Below Test-riding Arthur's Hovercraft with Russian cosmonaut Vladimir Lyakhov.

Bottom Another toy for Arthur, his solar-powered Sinclair C5 scooter.

Arthur and Bill Temple, his London roommate from the late 1930s, visit the home of H. G. Wells in 1975.

Right Fred and Arthur Clarke with their mother Nora.

Below Nora Clarke with her children and grandchildren.

– Arthur was delighted to meet Alexei Leonov in the lobby. 'My old friend!' Leonov cried, and they embraced.

Arthur continues: 'When I produced the video cassette of *2010: Odyssey Two* which I'd planned to show him, I found it wasn't necessary: "Best film I ever saw!" he declared.' That the spaceship *Leonov* in the book and film was named after him no doubt influenced his opinion!

In all more than fifty astronauts and cosmonauts attended from the United States, the Soviet Union and a dozen other countries. Arthur was one of two guests. The other was Yash Pal, his friend from India. Pal was the Congress's keynote speaker and was honoured for his experimental work in educational TV – the SITE programme in rural India in the 1970s.

The opening ceremony was held in a splendid conference hall next to the hotel. Host astronaut Prince Sultan (payload specialist on the space shuttle *Discovery* flight in June 1985) gave the opening speech. He was followed by Rusty Schweickart and Alexei Leonov, who gave brief speeches, before everyone fell out and socialised.

'Afterwards I was pleased to meet many new and old friends – astronauts Mike Collins, Joe Allen, Charles Walker, space artists Bob McCall and Andrei Sokolov, the International Space University's Peter Diamandis and Bob Richards, and dozens of others.'

That afternoon the group was driven to Tuwaiq Palace. While it looked like a giant fortress from the outside, it was actually a modern art gallery inside with an impressive collection of space art displayed for the Fifth Planetary Congress.

'I toured round in a wheelchair,' says Arthur, 'without which I would not have been able to cope.' Arthur met Prince Sultan for the first time and chatted with many other people as well. He was unable to avoid the press. 'Began to feel I'm a celebrity,' Arthur said, after being filmed and photographed constantly. Hector took some pictures also, and a few showed the Prince holding Arthur's novel, *2010: Odyssey Two*.

Space art from France, Russia, the United States and NASA was displayed. The names of three Russian artists, including Arthur's friend, Alexei Leonov, appeared to dominate the list, but many more individuals from different countries were represented in the NASA-owned collection.

The first session of the Congress, whose theme was 'Space for Earth', was held on Sunday morning, 12 November. Yash Pal spoke about the large number of Indian lives saved during recent devastating cyclones because of satellites in orbit. A similar storm a decade earlier had killed ten thousand people, whereas only twenty-five lost their lives in a more recent but equally violent storm – because of active weather satellites.

Back in his suite, Arthur turned on the television. Lo and behold, the film *2010* was being shown.

'It was weird to hear conversation about the spaceship *Alexei Leonov* when Alexei himself is here in the same hotel,' Arthur wrote in his journal. 'But they've billed the movie as "The Year We Make Contact" starring Helen Mirren! (I was unable to find who was responsible for this absurdity, still less get it corrected.)'

That evening Arthur spoke at the King Feisal Foundation, giving his lecture, 'The Colours of Infinity: Exploring the Fractal Universe', the subject which plays such an important role in his 1990 novel *The Ghost from the Grand Banks*. Arthur thought it was one of the most distinguished audiences he had ever addressed.

'Besides Prince Sultan there were at least thirty astronauts and cosmonauts,' says Arthur. 'I showed slides from the Mandelbrot Set, extracts from "Nothing But Zooms", and my 1988 video-taped discussion with Stephen Hawking when I showed him some black holes I'd found in the M-Set.'

Perhaps the most memorable event of the Fifth Planetary Congress in Riyadh was a desert feast on Monday evening. From the hotel a bus drove everyone for about an hour into the desert twilight.

'Just before nightfall, we reached a huge tent set up in the middle of nowhere. It was an artificial oasis – with carpets, camels, horses – and a beautiful but deadly-looking falcon, which several of us handled rather nervously.'

When a group of Bedouin dancers began to perform, they were soon joined by the astronauts and cosmonauts who were in Arab dress. Arthur was asked to join by Air Force Captain Hussein, which he did, all the while wearing the same flight jacket that Roy Scheider had worn on screen in *2010*, with its *Leonov* spaceship patch and other American and Soviet flight patches. The fact that Arthur joined in no doubt encouraged his friend, Alexei Leonov, to participate.

'The three of us orbited together for five minutes – on the sand (I wouldn't have dared risk it on marble). Great fun.'

What excitement! Arthur couldn't get over the fact that he had danced in the desert with the first man on Earth to walk in space – Alexei Leonov. A glorious full Moon illuminated the scene.

The feast was held in another huge tent. There was whole roasted sheep and a variety of Arab sweetmeats to chose from.

'I sat next to Prince Sultan, who kept piling food on my plate despite all my feeble references to weight-watching.'

The next morning began with an hour-and-a-half international video conference, with two-way video links between Riyadh, New York, Washington, DC, and Atlanta. Moderated by Prince Sultan, the participants were Dr Yash Pal of India; West German astronaut, Ulf Merbold; US astronaut and founding member of the Association of Space Explorers, Rusty Schweickart; Alexei Leonov of the Soviet Union; Georgi Ivanov of Bulgaria and Arthur C. Clarke of Sri Lanka.

After the questions and answers flew back and forth to the satellites in geostationary orbit for more than an hour, Arthur spoke of the tremendous dividends all of us were getting from applications satellites, including those for weather and communications.

'Whether we become a multi-planet species with unlimited horizons,' he concluded, 'or are for ever confined to Earth will be decided in the twenty-first century amid the vast plains, rugged canyons and lofty mountains of Mars.'

Tuesday evening was the Awards ceremony, and Alexei Leonov presented Arthur with the ASE's Special Achievements Award, a massive medal weighing about six pounds. Arthur then delivered his speech of thanks.

'As it was already about eleven p.m., I said I'd make it short – and got a good laugh by releasing a twenty-page printout which snaked across the stage.'

He then spoke about a 1939 controversy between the British Interplanetary Society and the BBC magazine, the *Listener*. The argument was about space travel. Arthur quoted a few choice portions of the text, including one from the sceptics who described in detail 'the horrible things that would happen to any humans foolish enough to attempt space travel'. It was a reminder of the nonsense early space enthusiasts had to put up with, and the audience loved it.

Arthur's last two days in Saudi Arabia included a pleasant mix of experiences: a visit to the recently built Space Research Institute, where he inspected the Landsat/Spot equipment; a farewell dinner during which he conversed with his Indian friend, Yash Pal and his wife, as well as several Soviet cosmonauts; a local TV interview; a visit to the palace and a conversation with Prince Sultan and his beautiful English-born wife; and then dinner with new friend Nasr Al-Sahhaf (a man who earned four college degrees in different subjects before he was twenty-five), and Dr Jim Wise, an ex-NASA psychologist who told Arthur 'that his PhD thesis had been directly inspired by the docking sequence in *2001*'.

This, of course, Arthur loved: 'Must tell Stanley Kubrick,' he said.

Leaving such good times behind was done with reluctance, but the next day Arthur, Hector and Dr Buell boarded the Saudair 747 and flew back to Colombo, landing on 17 November at the Katunayake Airport.

'I want to take things easy for about a month and relax completely,' Clarke told a friend upon his return, adding, 'I'm determined not to budge until I finish the Titanic novel.' So Saudi Arabia would be Arthur's last international hop of the decade. He was more than happy to stay off airplanes for the foreseeable future – with one exception. He and the Ekanayakes wanted to take a family holiday in the Maldives during December.

But Arthur was disheartened by some bad news. Rodney Jonklaas had died when Arthur was out of the country. It was Jonklaas who had first introduced him to Ceylon almost thirty years before, and for a number of years had been an active partner in the diving business Arthur invested in. Rodney and Arthur had remained close friends, but their respective work didn't allow for their spending much time together – 'more so Arthur who is very much a "writerholic"', wrote Rodney early in 1989 before he died.

In late November a memorial programme about Jonklaas was broadcast on Colombo television.

'They showed the film, *Beneath the Seas of Ceylon*, that Mike Wilson and I made with him back in 1960,' says Arthur, 'and they showed some stills of him from some of my books like *The Treasure of the Great Reef* and *The First Five Fathoms*.'

Rodney was not the only friend Arthur lost in 1989. Reginald Ross died in England after a long illness. He was an even earlier friend from the 1930s, whose family had taken summer holidays at Ballifants, and he and Arthur both knew Dick Jenvey.

Marcus Morris, the editor of the comic strip 'Dan Dare', died as well in 1989. In the late 1940s Arthur had been a consultant for this comic strip, occasionally giving some technical and plot advice when they had problems.

At the end of December the *Washington Post* reviewed *Rama II*, which had just been released in the United States. 'Rama Redux', written by novelist Gregory Feeley, was a very negative review. That it was soon balanced out by more positive (although shorter reviews) in the *New York Times* (which praised a few of the characters as being more interesting than those of Clarke's other novels) and elsewhere did not deflect the impact of this hard-hitting piece.

'Readers may welcome Clarke's newfound prolificity, even with the proviso of partnership with his unknown (and previously unpublished) collaborator. They should be warned: There is good reason to hold the gravest doubts as to the extent of Clarke's contribution to this exploitative and amateurishly written book.'

Mr Feeley went on to write that *Rama II* was 'abominably written' and that 'the sensibility of the book is simply not that of Arthur C. Clarke, nor is it one to which he might plausibly have made a major contribution. The handling of religious matters is simply the most obvious: Clarke is a famously secular atheist, while *Rama II* was plainly written by a Roman Catholic.'

The reviewer closed by saying he couldn't imagine 'any lover of Clarke's fiction who would not feel cheated by this subcontracting job . . . If I paid for my copy, I would be in a rage.'

Because this devastating review appeared on 31 December Arthur did not see it until early 1990. This was a blessing in disguise because he was getting up to speed again on his solo effort – a genuine all-Clarke novel, *The Ghost from the Grand Banks*.

CHAPTER 33

Toward 20,001

> As he stared into the blue infinity that had
> swallowed his son, the stars seemed sud-
> denly very close. 'Give us another hundred
> years,' he whispered, 'and we'll face you
> with clean hands and hearts – whatever
> shapes you be.'
>
> – *The Deep Range*

'I'm working hard on the Titanic novel,' Arthur told a friend in early January 1990. 'I've started and it's going quite well. A third has been written for nearly a year, and it's entirely plotted. It's just a question of sitting down and writing it. If I'm left alone, I can complete it in three months.'

Arthur Clarke was never left alone, however. That's why he loved to tell people he was a 'failed recluse'. During intensive writing periods he was only partly successful in avoiding the 'mechanics of life', including the demands of the daily influx of mail, most of which was handled by assistants with form-letter replies. But there were also plenty of letters that required personal (and often lengthy) responses. No matter how much he tried to focus his energies on the project at hand, some of these demands would penetrate the defences and command his attention.

In fact, some unfinished Russian business from 1982 bobbed up to the surface and required correspondence early in 1990. It had to do with the controversy over publication of portions of the novel *2010: Odyssey Two* in Russia.

In 1984 the Russian magazine, *Tekhnika Molodezhi* ('Technology for Youth'), published two excerpts from *2010*, and even these were printed with considerable omissions. But the fact that several charac-ters had the same last names as Russian dissidents had not been noticed by the magazine's editor, Vasili Zacharchenko. Then much of the world press noticed the names, and editor Zacharchenko was in big trouble; he was summarily dismissed after working for the magazine for forty years.

The novel was banned in the Soviet Union. According to the Soviet censors, the publication of those portions in *Tekhnika Molodezhi* was 'a gross blunder which happened due to the loss of vigilance by Zacharchenko V. D., Editor-in-Chief, as well as due to the unprincipled positions of other staff members of the magazine'. Some of the staff members were also severely reprimanded.

Nearly six years later, two Soviet officials from the Russian Embassy in Sri Lanka visited Barnes Place and presented Arthur with a November 1989 copy of *Tekhnika Molodezhi*. The issue contained a complete translation of *2010: Odyssey Two*, along with an honest commentary on what had happened in 1984, which in part stated:

'Today, all these accusations seem to be ridiculous . . . The attitude toward "dissidents" has radically changed.

'The decision on the novel by Arthur Clarke was one of the last "flights" of the stagnation period in our ideology, demonstrating the paradoxical inability of the administrative guidance in literature.'

Arthur's hope, stated in the end-of-book acknowledgements (and apologies) in *2061: Odyssey Three* (1987), that 'the subscribers to *Tekhnika Molodezhi* can read the instalments of *2010* that so mysteriously disappeared . . . had actually come true.'

'The last thing I'd intended,' Arthur wrote Vasili Zacharchenko in January 1990, was for the names of the dissidents to be a "time bomb" – in fact, I regarded it as little more than a mild joke or a gentle criticism (which shows how I had misjudged the situation). Had I dreamed of the consequences, I would have alerted you immediately – as it was, I felt certain that you would recognise the names and either: (1) decide they didn't matter; or (2) change them. In fact, when I received your last letter at the time saying you had "sanitised" the novel, I assumed all these matters had been taken care of.'

Zacharchenko had no qualms about detailing the misfortunes that had befallen him as a result of the incident, and he asked Clarke for help. Arthur replied that he would be more than happy to do some television segments with him in Sri Lanka and also assist him with a book on space art he was compiling.

2010: Odyssey Two's Russian publication was welcomed by everyone. It became a small literary bridge between the West and the East at a time when the USSR was undergoing a revolution – one that might help the world become a global village.

A Catholic priest in Colombo, a friend of Arthur's who was also the president of the local Astronomical Society, helped to arrange an exhibition in Arthur's honour in late January.

The young people organised an exhibition of space models and photographs, which also included most of Arthur's trophies. Cyril Ponnamperuma, director of the Institute for Fundamental Studies in Sri Lanka and past director of the Arthur C. Clarke Centre, gave a short speech and presented a beautifully bound felicitation volume. Local television covered the activities, and Arthur found it all 'rather ego-boosting'.

Later he enjoyed seeing the coverage on television, which showed him looking very thoughtful as they presented the volume to him. With his many friends in the audience, he held it up to the camera and waved. Then there was footage of the exhibition itself, showing the Marconi Award, the *2001* posters and a model spaceship. But it was a surprise at the end of the coverage that really pleased Arthur. Two beautiful butterflies flew around the exhibit for the concluding footage.

By the end of January, with his assistant sick in hospital, Arthur was fighting to get back to the Titanic novel, but too many distractions made it all but impossible.

'I'm being bombed out by visitors and mail. I've received more than thirty books and magazines in a day – and not enough time to physically sort them out, let alone read them.'

He continued fighting for every minute he could get and in late January did manage to write some of chapter ten, 'The Isle of the Dead', named after Arnold Boecklin's famous nineteenth-century painting. It was, Arthur said, a key element in his new novel.

Arthur also loved Sergey Rachmaninoff's symphonic poem, 'The Isle of the Dead', which was based on the Basle painter's work. Rachmaninoff was one of Arthur's favourite composers (along with Sibelius) and he especially enjoyed his piano concertos.

By early February he was in the swim again, 'working night and day on the novel', and hoping to complete it by March. He had polished the first thirty thousand words and had actually written the conclusion.

'I've been writing whatever I've wanted to write – bits of the book that interest me at the moment. Then I'll link them together later. It's like a jigsaw puzzle, but it's going very, very fast. This isn't my usual approach,' he confesses. 'Most of my books have been linear, but this has been like a mosaic.'

Despite his complaints about daily distractions, Arthur met his goal of completing *The Ghost from the Grand Banks* in late February 1990 and sent floppy disks off to Scott Meredith and his brother Fred Clarke in early March.

The political situation in Sri Lanka was still dangerously unstable, especially in the north and the east of the country.

'I'm afraid all the best people are going,' Arthur wrote Willie Mendis in Washington, 'and psychologically it's very depressing.'

Some good news came out of a meeting Arthur attended at the Presidential Secretariat. Ted Turner and CNN had offered Sri Lanka five to ten minutes of free air time each month on their 'World Report' programme. Arthur knew it was a wonderful opportunity, and he persuaded the decision-makers that it would be good for the country. The Arthur Clarke Centre also officially began to act as the distributor for CNN in Sri Lanka in 1990.

Once his manuscript *The Ghost from the Grand Banks* was safely out of the country, he could decide what to write next. He said yes to a few prefaces for worthy projects, one of which was a major volume for MIT, with top computer scientists in the field: *Technology 2001*. When they told Arthur that he was the only person who could write the preface he believed them, enjoyed the flattery and wrote the short piece in early March.

The first half of 1990 was 'spectacularly uneventful', and this suited Arthur very well. Michael Deakin, film producer and president of Griffin Productions, arrived in Colombo in March, and he and Arthur made final revisions to the television script for *A Fall of Moondust*. It was, regretfully, turned down by Universal later in the year. Deakin visited again in the autumn and they worked together on the 'Deplorable Inventions' TV series together. Arthur could do as little or as much as he liked for this project; he wasn't even obliged to introduce the programme, although he thought he probably would do so.

Although there was no contract in place for his Titanic novel Bantam had the option, and in early April Arthur learned of the splendid deal that had been negotiated by the Scott Meredith Literary Agency. In the UK Jacqueline Korn of the David Higham Agency had placed the book with Gollancz.

'Everybody loves it, and some of them say it's the best thing I've ever done,' Arthur told a friend. 'It's my first contemporary novel and is completely different from anything else. It begins in 1977 and goes up to 2012. It starts with Howard Hughes and the *Glomar Explorer*. Bantam is rushing it through to bring it out at Christmas.'

Another volume of Arthur's short pieces, *Tales from Planet Earth*, was published in June. It was produced in a handsome quality paperback edition and illustrated by the artist, Michael Whelan. Arthur also wrote short introductions to each of the fourteen stories, placing them in time and in the context of his other work. Most of them were originally written in the 1950s and 1960s, but the last piece, 'On Golden Seas', was from 1986.

'It was written as a reaction to the mountains of literature I'd read on the Strategic Defense Initiative,' Arthur said, and he summarised how it had made its way into the White House and the inner sanctums of SDI research.

July 1990 brought forth the sequel by Gregory Benford to Arthur's early novel, *Against the Fall of Night* (published by Gollancz in the UK and Putnam in the US). If ever there was a lifelong literary project for Arthur C. Clarke, it was this book which he'd begun to write as an adolescent in the 1930s. After several versions and two rejections by John Campbell, it was first published in 1948 in *Startling Stories*. Publication did not completely satisfy Arthur, however. He continued to work on it from time to time, and it finally evolved into the completely revised version, *The City and the Stars*, published in the mid-1950s.

'It was a voyage of discovery,' said Arthur after reading Benford's sequel. 'It's particularly interesting to see how some of the concepts of this half-century-old story are now in the forefront of modern science: I am especially fond of the "Black Sun", which is an obvious description of the now extremely popular Black Holes.'

Several reviewers concentrated on the differences in style between Clarke's original and Benford's sequel. At least one writer believed that the two halves didn't fit, and that both good works suffered as a result. Of course, science fiction buffs were pleased to have these two authors in the same volume.

The 'global village', especially the eastern European branch, was going through some major changes in the autumn of 1989. Arthur believed, as did many others, that these geopolitical shifts could eventually evolve into a new world order of international co-operation and interdependence. Perhaps his long-standing vision of a global family was in the process of being realised. He hoped this was true.

It was these revolutionary events in the real world that led Arthur to his next major literary project, a non-fiction book on telecommunications – past, present and future – and how they have changed (and would continue to change) the planet. And he chose for it a catchy title: *How the World Was One: Beyond the Global Village*. The book was scheduled to be published by Gollancz in Britain and Bantam in the United States in June 1992.

'This has turned out to be a much bigger project than I planned,' he told friends in September. 'It will also be my longest book (possibly

150,000 words). It may also be one of my most important, since it's covering the whole history of telecommunications, from the invention of the telegraph, up to the fibre optic revolution.'

For the seventieth birthday of Satyajit Ray, the famous Indian film director (who died nearly two years later, in April 1992), Arthur wrote a short piece, 'Stanley and Satyajit', in September, in which he told of Stanley Kubrick's admiration for Ray as a film-maker.

'Though I can't be sure after a quarter of a century, Stanley may even have admitted that Ray was Number One. Or was it Number Two?'

Chancellor Arthur C. Clarke delivered his penultimate convocation address at the University of Moratuwa on 21 September. There would only be one more in late 1991.

'I've now resigned as I feel that ten [years] is enough, and it's becoming too much of a strain, though I hope I can retain a connection with the University, perhaps as "Chancellor Emeritus" or some such title.'

His address, 'The Colours of Infinity: Exploring the Fractal Universe', was the same basic speech he had given in Saudi Arabia in 1988, and the text evolved into the appendix of *The Ghost from the Grand Banks*.

In October Gentry Lee submitted the manuscript of *The Garden of Rama* – the third collaborative novel he and Arthur had written – to Bantam and Gollancz. Gentry worked on the revisions suggested by editor Lou Aronica through to the year's end. The novel was published in the autumn of 1991 in the UK and the US and received a warmer reception than *Rama II*. The *Locus* reviewer wrote, 'It is not often that collaborations produce a work that not only exceeds what each author might achieve on his own, but which must be recognised as a genuine achievement.'

Arthur C. Clarke's Century of Mysteries, co-authored with Simon Welfare and John Fairley, is being published by HarperCollins in 1993.

'I'm still waiting, but have written an introduction and one essay that can be used somewhere in the text.'

The essay, 'The Mona Lisa of Mars', was about the controversial image on the Martian surface which some people believed to be an ancient alien artifact. Arthur's old colleague, Richard Hoagland, who had been a science adviser to CBS during the *Apollo* coverage, was a strong and relentless advocate of this possibility. He persuaded enough people in Washington, including some congressmen who had influence with top NASA brass, to retarget the Mars *Observer* spacecraft so that it would scrutinise the site with its remote sensing instruments. (Arthur gave Hoagland credit for thinking of Jupiter's moon Europa as a possible abode for life, a key plot factor in his *2061: Odyssey Three*.)

The Mars essay was the last piece Arthur Clarke would write in 1990. His views on the subject were consistent with those of a good scientist and similar to those he held on UFOs. He needed some real evidence – not just suggestive shapes seen in images taken from an orbiting spacecraft above the Martian surface.

'The Mona Lisa of Mars' was written some fifty-five years after Arthur had penned his first known story about the Red Planet, 'Mars', in 1935, which was circulated among employees at the 'FB & Co'.

'I have no idea who or what the company was,' recalls Arthur, 'but suspect the contact may have been through my friend (and first collaborator!) Eric Frank Russell.'

In December 1990 *The Ghost from the Grand Banks* was published.

Several reviewers were lukewarm about the novel, pointing out that some of the plot elements were created only to allow Arthur to lecture about number theory. The cast of characters, one writer said, were 'mainly technical wizards with flat personalities – the most interesting character is a fifty-ton-octopus – but then no one reads a Clarke story to find out about human nature'.

Ever since the early 1950s, reviewers and critics have pointed out the weak fictional characters in Clarke's novels and his apparent inability (or unwillingness) to describe in-depth human relationships. At least one Clarke expert suggests that this weakness does not come from any lack of technique but rather from underdeveloped traits in his own personality. Arthur confronted this criticism with his 1986 novel *The Songs of Distant Earth*, in which he had spent more effort developing characters. He was in part successful, especially when compared to earlier fiction. But in *The Ghost from the Grand Banks* Arthur again neglected character development. The characters were lightly sketched, and did not offer readers much with which to identify and empathise. One notable exception was Edith Craig, who was compulsively searching for her dead daughter among the fractal images on her computer screen.

Kirkus Reviews closed its review of *Ghosts*, 'Average Clarke, more emotional than usual, with excellent extrapolation of future technologies.' A reviewer in *Locus* magazine wrote that the novel was a 'fast and pleasant read', but nevertheless was 'a latticework book, a sketch of a larger, deeper work, resonant but not dense'. A British reviewer said it was 'vintage Clarke, with all the virtues and weak-nesses that we have come to expect from this Grandmaster'.

The best came last. Writing for the *New York Times*, Gerald Jonas called the novel 'sunny' and its author 'a happy man'. Clarke, he wrote, 'sees the universe as a marvellous toy, coquettishly begging to be understood yet always mocking our success with some deeper mystery . . . His ability to keep a story moving ahead while teaching us what we must know to follow narrative logic wherever it leads is the very essence of his art. He only makes it look easy.'

On the morning of 16 December Harold Rosen and his wife, Arthur's cousin John Clarke and the Ekanayake family gathered at Barnes Place for a modest party for Arthur's seventy-third birthday.

'Quite a big cake was made,' says John Clarke, 'in the shape of an ocean liner, but it didn't have the right number of funnels for the *Titanic*. When Arthur cut the first slice, he said, "This is where the iceberg went."

'Later in the morning a bunch of people from the Arthur Clarke Centre came with another cake for him before everyone headed off for the award ceremonies in the afternoon.'

The Arthur C. Clarke Award for vision and achievement in global communications was presented to Dr Harold Rosen by Sri Lanka's President Ranasinghe Premadasa. Rosen, a vice-president at Hughes Aircraft Company, developed the comsat hardware that Arthur envi-sioned in his 1945 global geostationary satellite system published in *Wireless World*. The two men have known one another since the pioneering days of communication satellites in the late fifties and early sixties.

In his introductory remarks President Premadasa praised Arthur and the award. 'Our tribute to you is not really for your birthday alone. We salute your achievements. Even more, we esteem your humanity. For us, you have no age. You belong to all ages. The conventional chronology of time has no meaning for men of vision. Arthur is such a visionary.'

The crew of spaceship Earth is co-operating better now as we approach the new millennium than it has in the past, Arthur believes, his lifelong optimism about humanity's future again holding sway.

'I used to say mankind has a fifty-one per cent chance of survival; I'd put the figure now at a solid fifty-five per cent.'

He is also optimistic about his personal future. For more than a decade, Arthur has often stated his genuine hope and intention of seeing the year 2001. When his death sentence of terminal illness was stayed in 1988 with a new diagnosis of post-polio syndrome, his first words of relief were that he would live to see the first year of the new millennium – the year he helped make famous. (It is not, by the way, the year 2000 because our calendar began with 1 January 1 AD and there is no year zero. The twentieth century, in other words, will run through the year 2000, and the centennial (and millennial) celebrations should not really begin until midnight, 31 December 2000, although it will be impossible to restrain people from celebrating a year earlier.)

Arthur will be eighty-three years old when New Year's Day 2001 comes to pass.

'There's been a lot of talk about immortality and the extension of the human lifespan,' Arthur told Roger Caras in the early 1980s. 'I have a feeling that our lifespan is about right, because our brains begin to wear out, let's say around about a hundred years. If we can keep good health for that period of time, I think most people will settle for that. The idea of immortality I find horrifying, even though I've written all about it.' Arthur had then reflected a few seconds.

'I don't feel I am the person who was alive fifty years ago. I feel very little feeling towards that person. I am a different person now. So immortality, in the sense of you, yourself, as you are now, being able to exist for ever is a contradiction, I think.'

Arthur Clarke's first seventy-five orbits around the sun indicate that he enjoys life, ever keeping busy, making no distinction between work and recreation. When asked in the early 1990s what new work, fiction and non-fiction, readers can expect in the future, Arthur paused to consider his reply.

'*The Ghost from the Grand Banks* will almost certainly be my last novel; certainly there won't be one for years,' he said. 'If I'm still fit and the *Galileo* spacecraft does something spectacular in '95, there may be a final odyssey,' he added, covering all the bases and well aware of his literary history of 'last novels'.

When asked how he might view his work from the perspective of a hundred or five hundred years in the future, Arthur hedged and said he hadn't the faintest idea.

'I don't think I'm a sufficiently detached and unbiased observer. I've often said that on occasion I've had delusions of significance,' he responded with a chuckle. About all he will commit to regarding his work a hundred years from now is the likelihood that his 1945 *Wireless World* paper on communications satellites will be referred to as a footnote in the textbooks of the period.

Of course, Arthur is right about his lack of detachment regarding his own work. Remember? Back in early 1938 he wrote to his friend Sam Youd, confessing that he didn't see any reason to believe that he had 'any great literary ability'. He thought he could do better than most of the pulp writers, however, if he spent enough time perfecting his style, adding that he didn't have the time to devote to writing seriously. Science fiction fans, of course, are happy that Arthur was mistaken.

'He is the greatest living science fiction writer,' says Gregory Benford, 'in part because he stands in a tradition that began with Julian Huxley, J. D. Bernal and, of course, Olaf Stapledon, and goes through Freeman Dyson and Clarke himself. The cool, distant, analytical thinking patterns apply to immense perspectives, and that's a discernible, intellectual English tradition.

'Stapledon, whom Clarke idolised, dragged the conflicts of his era into far-future visions, attributing Marxist – indeed, Stalinist – dynamics to even alien, insectoid races. This riddles some of Stapledon's work with anachronisms.

'Clarke never loses his bearings this way, and his work will probably wear well.

'Arthur is also the most read science fiction writer in the world, and his British agent has the numbers to prove it,' says Benford.

Lester del Rey, who ran the leading science fiction and fantasy publishing imprint for Ballantine Books until 1992, has known Arthur for forty years and harks back to his first visits to the United States in the early 1950s.

'I have never heard of anyone,' says del Rey, 'looking at the bulk of Arthur's work, saying they didn't like it. He's had his share of bad reviews, but they never take his total work apart and knock it. There is a humanity, and often an innocence to Arthur's work. And although he doesn't generally draw characters well in his books, he draws the race of man well.'

Science fiction has in part been defined as the last refuge of the morality tale, and writer John Brunner believes that much of Arthur's work, where rationality and intelligence usually prevail, fits well into this definition.

'In the context of a science fiction story, the hero is the man who knows what's going on. And I see this over and over and over in Arthur's books, as well as in Heinlein's and Asimov's. The person who has the knowledge and understands is the person you can rely on, and he appears in all kinds of guises. After all, in *Childhood's End*, he's Karellen, the alien delegate from the stars. He's the only one who knows what's going on.

'"The Star" is the most emotionally charged story Arthur ever wrote,' says Brunner. 'It's the only work of his that I have ever read which I could imagine him crying over when he finished. And it's strictly abstract. But you can feel your way into the person who has just discovered he has got to give up his lifelong faith. Because if he's going to believe in an unjust God, he doesn't want to. That's a terrific piece of work. It's certainly the one that hits – and hurts.'

Fellow writer Frederik Pohl, who also bought some of Arthur's work as an editor in the 1950s, judges Arthur 'a very graceful and dependable writer'.

'Science fiction novels last for ever, and I am confident that Arthur's work will be read in the next century,' says Pohl when asked – a rather safe prediction that even Arthur himself declines to make. 'And Arthur is a significant figure in the twentieth century because of what he has done – the writing and everything else.

'I owe Arthur for a quotation I've used many times for years. A long time ago he was interviewed by some fans who published a symposium of what writers thought about this and that. They asked Arthur why he wrote science fiction, and he said, "Because no other literature concerns itself with reality." I agree. I agree that science fiction is the literature of change and change is the biggest reality we all face.'

Eric S. Rabkin of the University of Michigan, a Clarke scholar, points out that much of his work is not the hard science fiction for which he is so well known.

'Hard sf seems to be a stylistic trope for Clarke,' says Rabkin, 'rather than the heart of the matter. *The Lion of Comarre* is not hard science fiction at all, and the same can be said for the book that runs throughout his career, *Against the Fall of Night*, which in its final version became *The City and the Stars*. And if you look at the end of *Imperial Earth* he has an "Additional Note" in which he points out that several experts found fault with the genetics of his novel. He more or less says in response, "I'm a writer and I can do whatever I want."'

Two fundamental themes occur repeatedly in Clarke's work, Rabkin observes. One is that the world has somehow stagnated and an essentially adolescent character somehow has to reinvigorate it. This story gets told again and again – *Childhood's End*, *The Lion of Comarre*, *The City and the Stars*, *The Deep Range* and *Dolphin Island*.

The other recurrent theme is when the human race has to confront its own relative insignificance.

'This happens in his two greatest books,' says Rabkin, '*2001* and

Rendezvous with Rama. In *2001* we confront our own insignificance, but it turns out that although we are insignificant we don't have to stay insignificant. The monolith has control over human evolution, and its Star-Child is "master of the world".

'With *Rendezvous with Rama* he has us confront the universe, and we stay insignificant. And that's his boldest book. All its technical detail – its hard science fiction – becomes thematically crucial. In a sense, what it leaves you with is a recognition that no matter how complete and accurate our understanding of the physical objects of the world may be, we still don't have the answers to the deepest issues. We explore scientific fact in this novel, but the narrative does not allow us to make a leap of faith from scientific fact to dominance of the universe.

'In the other novels, however, he seems to be saying, "Not only do we know how to calculate orbits, but we're also the soul of the universe."

'It's as if Clarke is of two conflicting minds. There's this conscious mind that appreciates classical mechanics – the old-fashioned kind of science that's entirely deterministic. The early novels such as *Earthlight*, *Prelude to Space*, *The Sands of Mars* and *Islands in the Sky* all have lots of classical mechanics in them. Such science may be complicated to some of his readers but in mathematical terms, conceptual terms, and in ethical terms it's as simple as you can get.

'Then on a lower level, thinking in Freudian and Jungian terms, Clarke seems to want the ability to dissolve himself into something great and powerful that is of the order of importance of the universe as a whole. I think that's what links the sky and the sea for him, which constantly resonates in his work. He never gets on to the ground, physically, in a happy way. It's always in the sky or in the ocean. These are both realms in which he can dissolve himself. Like the Overmind in *Childhood's End*. By joining the Overmind, he can occupy all of space at once. That's what Clarke wants to do. Somehow get to the heart of this huge web of reality that's everything.'

Perhaps it is in this elusive heart of reality that Arthur has been seeking what he lost in his youth, that eclipsed aspect of his own identity, his life's black hole, created by his long-missed father whose death and absence during his adolescence had a powerful, mostly unconscious, effect on him. Indeed, his father's long illness and early death may have been a primary motivation for his endless explorations, be they on the printed page or around the planet. This interpretation may help to explain why Arthur has said more than once that writing is a hole in his life. His creative quest is an attempt, on one level, to fill in that hole deep inside himself.

An insurmountable distance often separates father and son in Clarke novels (*Childhood's End*, *The Deep Range*, *2010*, *Imperial Earth* and *The Songs of Distant Earth* are examples).

'The starship *Magellan* was still no more than a few light hours distant when Kumar Lorenson was born, but his father was already sleeping and did not hear the news until three hundred years later,' Arthur wrote in *The Songs of Distant Earth*.

'He wept to think that his dreamless slumber had spanned the entire lifetime of his first child . . .'

At a crucial time in Arthur's early development (he was thirteen when his father died), he discovered the work of Olaf Stapledon, his most influential literary mentor.

'Stapledon's influence on Clarke was considerable,' continues Rabkin, 'and he's admitted this. In *Last and First Men* the happiest humans of all are those that have a group mind. The whole book is based on the possibility of telepathic intercommunications, and it seems to me that at the age of thirteen Clarke was really bowled over by this. Stapledon's book was published at the beginning of the Depression. The whole world was fragmented. The recovery from the Great War was a false recovery. Political tensions and nationalism were on the rise everywhere.

'So here's this impressionable lad who's feeling what everyone else is feeling in the early thirties [*as well* as the loss of his father], and suddenly he reads this book and says, "Everything has its place in this grand scheme of things and you can lose your individuality if you wish, submerge it into this great whole."

'Clarke has an obvious desire to construct a world in which some kind of higher benign order makes clear the centrality and importance of humanity. He really does seem to want to believe there's something higher and that it cares for us. This desire appears in his work in various ways, but in all of them it can be recognised as a statement of faith, not a statement of scientific fact.'

Such a quest for faith appears throughout much of Arthur Clarke's fiction, and this continuing search, which takes many forms in his work, is one of the foremost reasons that his novels have permanent value.

As the quincentennial of Columbus' discovery of the New World is celebrated in 1992, along with the activities of the International Space Year (*and* Arthur's seventy-fifth birthday), it is fitting to acknowledge that Arthur C. Clarke is one of this century's great explorers in the realm of ideas and possibilities. His life's work – the voluminous literature, the lectures, the Hollywood and documentary films – has been devoted to searching for the future of the human race and its place in the ever-mysterious and boundless universe of space and time. In a real sense Arthur is a Columbus of the future, and his spaceship is his mind.

'In projecting our ideas into the future,' he says, 'much of the technology that exists now is going to be around for the next hundred years. But about every ten years there will come along something completely unexpected, like the transistor and its successors, which will bring in a new dimension.'

It is the future evolution of artificial intelligence and its relationship with the human mind that Arthur believes will have the most profound effect on *Homo sapiens* and our descendants. Arthur has gone on record saying that the development of Artificial Intelligence is the most important breakthrough in the twentieth century. As the third millennium rushes to become present, the potential and actual capability of this revolutionary technology expands explosively. He believes that ultimately – in context of the evolution of *Homo sapiens* to its next level (*Homo electronicus?*) – it may be the most important technology ever.

'One day we may be able to enter into temporary unions with any sufficiently sophisticated machines, thus being able not merely to control but to *become* a spaceship or a submarine or a TV network,' he writes. 'The thrill that can be obtained from driving a racing car or flying an aeroplane may be only a pale ghost of the excitement our great-grandchildren may know, when the individual human consciousness is free to roam at will from machine to machine, through all the reaches of sea and sky and space.' (Readers of *2010* immediately think of David Bowman's superhuman flights in the chapters 'Homecoming' and 'Fires in the Deep'.)

This pure and powerful mentality, free from physical limitations, appears in many of Clarke's novels. It represents transcendence over human limitations, and a more complete knowledge of the universe and ultimate reality. In *The City and the Stars* Callitrax says that the conception of a pure mentality was 'common among many of Earth's ancient religious faiths, and it seems strange that an idea which had no rational origin should finally become one of the greatest goals of science'.

When will the artificial intelligence of computers attain the level of human intelligence?

'Not by 2001,' Arthur believes, 'but certainly by 2100. And their intelligence and insight will, of course, continue to grow and expand after that. This may lead to some very interesting things. I think man is a transitional species, to be supplanted by some new life form that includes computer technology.'

Does Arthur dare extrapolate into the far future? In his fiction, of course, he gives himself more freedom of time and space than in his non-fiction forecasting.

Will humanity or its future evolutionary progeny have made contact (physical or electromagnetic) with other intelligent life in the universe by 20,001? Not even with this eighteen-thousand-year leeway will Arthur C. Clarke make a commitment to when this event (arguably the most important one in the history of our species) might occur – even though his most famous novel puts it at 2001.

When he created his 'Chart of the Future' at the end of *Profiles of the Future*, and revised it in 1984, Arthur put 'First Contact' as occurring sometime *beyond* 2100. He is convinced, after looking at what has happened in the last 150 years, 'that no imagination can hope to look beyond the year 2100'. He therefore limits his credible, 'real world' forecasts to a hundred years to retain any reasonable probability and value. But as the twentieth century has shown, planet Earth can undergo great changes in a mere century.

And while he hesitates to give any forecasting odds as to the likelihood of contact with alien life forms, he is willing to put some numbers on the probability of extra-terrestrials existing in our vast and wondrous universe.

'I think there's a ninety-nine per cent chance of life all over the universe and a ninety per cent chance of intelligent life being all over the place as well. The most likely scenario for contact is reception of a radio signal of some sort. Next most likely would be detection or interception of astro-engineering or physical artifacts. And they might land tomorrow on the White House lawn.

'This is the wild card,' says Arthur. 'This is one future of fate we can do absolutely nothing to control.'

Arthur confesses he *wants* to believe that there is life elsewhere in the universe, 'because it's very lonely if there's nobody else out there. But we haven't the slightest evidence for such existence. There's only statistical argument, and it's very tantalising.

'The fact that we have not yet found the slightest evidence for life – much less intelligence – beyond this Earth does not surprise or disappoint me in the least,' he says. 'Our technology must still be laughably primitive; we may well be like jungle savages listening for the throbbing of tom-toms while the ether around them carries more words per second than they could utter in a lifetime . . .

'One of the great lessons of modern science is that millennia are only moments,' says Arthur, referring to the cosmic scale and the life cycles of stars and galaxies – and perhaps the universe itself. He admits to being sceptical about finding answers to the great questions and problems of existence that humans have debated for thousands of years. And the reason he is sceptical is that such questions will not likely be answered in such short time scales. He doubts that 'we will really know much about the universe while we are still crawling around in the playpen of the Solar System'.

Make no mistake: Arthur has had a lot of fun playing. He's said more than once that he writes because it's fun – adding that he also likes to eat. Having 'great fun' (one of his more common expressions) extends to all his explorations, cerebral and geographical – not just to his writing craft. He's somewhat coy about any deeper driving forces in his life.

'Actually, my motivation and aim in life is very simple,' Arthur lightly confessed in 1990. 'It's been expressed by a famous remark of a British Prime Minister (Stanley Baldwin, I think) who was talking about the newspaper world of Fleet Street in London and comparing its advantages with those of another profession: the privilege of the harlot throughout the ages, which is power without responsibility. I recently told the President of Sri Lanka that this was my goal, and I'd now achieved it.'

Of course Arthur C. Clarke's responsibility has been self-imposed, and when it comes to work and worthy causes he's a tough taskmaster. On the other hand he doesn't really think of himself as having any great amount of power. So while he may want 'power without responsibility', and has casually claimed success, his actual circumstances may be closer to the reverse: responsibility without power. In appraising himself, however, he plays down this all-too-familiar adult dilemma.

'I thought of my epitaph the other day,' he said recently. '"He never grew up, but he never stopped growing." It occurred to me that it was quite appropriate. Not that I thought it was for any imminent use.'

Notes

In the interest of saving space and paper, the sources for this biography have been divided into two sections.

First, there is a selected list of interviews, with alphabetised names and dates, from which came interview quotes that *actually appear* in the text. This format will save many pages of repeated interview notes, but also it will provide specific sources and dates in most cases. The only exceptions will be for those few people who have been interviewed many times. For such serial interviews, inclusive dates covering all conversations are given. In such cases, the reader will know what general period the interviews took place, but not the specific interview dates. This selected interview list contains the names of about one-third of all people interviewed – conservation at work.

Second, a section of complete notes for all print, audio, and video sources; all quotes are listed by chapter and text page. Each note is keyed to quoted words (or a phrase) that appear on a specific page in the text.

The interview list and the endnotes will enable any reader to find the spoken or written source for any quoted material.

SELECTED LIST OF INTERVIEWS

Forrest Ackerman (26 March 1989)
Brian Aldiss (30 March 1989)
Isaac Asimov (5 December 1989)
Ian and Betty Ballantine (22 May 1989)
Joel Banow (6 February 1990)
Gregory Benford (17 and 21 November 1989)
Louis Blau (10 December 1989)
Robert Bloch (8 April 1989)
Ray Bradbury (6 December 1989)
John Brunner (15 January 1990)
Roger Caras (19 September 1989; 31 May 1990); and several other telephone interviews
Arthur Clarke (31 July 1988 to 9 May 1992); probably over 100 interviews, most by telephone and satellite link
Fred Clarke (23 March 1989 to 9 May 1992); also dozens of telephone interviews over this period of time
John Clarke (31 December 1990)
Marilyn Mayfield Clarke (24 July 1989)
Michael Clarke (2 August 1990)
Michael Craven (4 April 1989)
Walter Cronkite (5 April 1990)
Lester del Rey (2 December 1989)
Hugh Downs (15 February 1990)
Daniel Drachman (31 October 1990)
Olga Druce (16 March 1989; 16 May 1989); and several other telephone interviews
Fred Durant (8 July 1989; 1 July 1990)
Bert Fowler (19 March 1989)
David Fowke (28 June 1989)
James Gunn (22 January 1990)
Todd Hawley (13 September 1990)
Dick Hoagland (30 December 1989)
Leonard Hobbs (6 April 1989)
Peter Hyams (19 June 1990)
Dick Jenvey (4 April 1989)
Dot Jones (25 July 1989)

393

Steven Jongeward (26 June 1990); and several other telephone interviews
Kathy Keeton (4 April 1989)
David Kennard (9 August 1990)
Dick Kriegel (15 March 1989)
David Kyle (23 March 1989; 6 June 1989); and several other telephone interviews
Gentry Lee (13 August 1990; 9 October 1990); and other telephone interviews
Lloyd Lewan (18 April 1990)
Ray Lovejoy (21 December 1989)
Lee Lubbers (21 November 1989)
Ian Macauley (6 August 1989; 30 October 1989); and other telephone interviews
John McLucas (27 September 1990)
Marjorie May (17 May 1989)
Scott Meredith (28 March 1989)
Harry Morrin (28 July 1990)
Sam Moskowitz (7 February 1989)
George Mueller (25 March 1989)
Julian Muller (23 January 1990)
Kerry O'Quinn (27 February 1990)
Fred Ordway (1 October 1989)
Thomas Paine (8 September 1989)
Charles Pellegrino (10 November 1990)
Joseph Pelton (25 March 1989; 4 June 1990)
John Pierce (21 February 1989)
Bobby Pleass (31 March 1989)
Frederik Pohl (17 March 1989; 22 April 1989)
Cyril Ponnamperuma (9 September 1990)
Jerry Pournelle (11 September 1990)
Eric Rabkin (7 December 1990)
Gene Roddenberry (22 January 1990)
Carl Sagan (20 February 1990)
Bernie Shir-Cliff (11 July 1989)
Ken Slater (26 January 1990)
Harry Stine (11 March 1989)
Eric Taylor (22 February 1990)
Joan Temple (8 February 1989)
Pat Weaver (7 February 1990)
Robert Weil (1 September 1990)

SOURCE NOTES (PRINT, AUDIO, VIDEO)

(All page numbers refer to the American editions cited.)

Chapter 1

p. 2 'Mother decided . . .' Nora Clarke, *My Four Feet on the Ground* (London: The Rocket Publishing Company, 1978), 56.

p. 3 'The seller had . . .', 'The price . . .' and 'The name was . . .' Ibid., 59, 60.

p. 4 'or better still, hovering . . .' ACC, 'Of Sand and Stars' in *1984: Spring* (New York: Ballantine Books, 1984, 152; London: Granada Publishing, 1984).

p. 4 'Underfoot, the sand . . .' ACC, *The Nine Billion Names of God* (New York: New American Library, 1967), 243.

p. 5 'Beyond the sea wall . . .' and 'but he was a solitary . . .' Ibid., 243, 244.

p. 6 'I can still hear . . .' ACC, 'Astounding Days' (prepublication ms.), 2–3.

p. 6 'The first card . . .' Shirley Thomas, ed., *Men in Space*, Vol. 1 (Philadelphia: Chilton Book Company, 1968), 14.

p. 8 'I was able . . .' *My Four Feet*, 61.

p. 9 'More than his father . . .' ACC, *Glide Path* (New York: New American Library, 1987, 181; London: Sidgwick & Jackson, 1969).

Chapter 2

p. 10 'His first telescope . . .' Letter, Mary Clarke Maclean to NM (4 July 1990), 2.

p. 10 'It came as . . .' Thomas, *Men in Space*, Vol. 1, 14.

p. 11 'Please could you send . . .' Letter, ACC to L. J. Johnson (in unpublished ms., 'No Air to Push Against'), L. J. Johnson, 18.

p. 12 'First there were balsa . . .' Fred Clarke, unpublished ms., 'Foreheads in the Air' (received July 1989), 68.

p. 13 'As the rocket rose . . .' Fred Clarke, 'Foreheads' 68.

p. 13 'When the light . . .' Fred Clarke, 'Foreheads' 72.
p. 14 'I remember listening to music . . .' Fred Clarke, 'Foreheads' 71 ff.

Chapter 3

p. 17 'When any major catastrophe . . .' Letter, Mary Clarke Maclean to NM (4 July 1990), 2.
p. 19 'I read that March 1930 . . .' ACC, *Astounding Days* (New York: Bantam Books, 1990, 12, 11; London: Victor Gollancz, 1989).
p. 19 'I'd save up all my spare . . .' Shirley Thomas, ed., *Men in Space*, Vol. 8 (Philadelphia: Chilton Book Company, 1968), 15.
p. 20 'There were heart-breaking . . .' Ibid.
p. 20 'The stories brimmed . . .' 'Of Sand and Stars' in *1984: Spring* (New York: Ballantine Books, 1984, 154; London: Granada Publishing, 1984).
p. 21 'He was very good . . .' Letter, ACC to Sam Youd (ca 1939).
p. 21 'Nothing had changed . . .' ACC, *Against the Fall of Night* (New York: Harcourt Brace Jovanovich, 1986, 120; London: Victor Gollancz, 1991).
p. 22 'Perhaps the final result . . .' 'Interplanetary Man' in ACC, ed., *The Coming of the Space Age* (New York: Meredith Publishing Co, 1967, 260; London: Victor Gollancz, 1967).
p. 24 'Our houses are built . . .' ACC, 'News from the Torrid Zone' ('Huish Magazine' 22, Christmas, 1933), 34–5.

Chapter 4

p. 28 'The appellation was born . . .' Letter, Bill Temple to NM (23 February 1989), 3.
p. 28 'You BIS Moonatic . . .' Bill Temple, 'The British Fan in his Natural Haunts' (London: *Nova Terrae*, June 1938), 15, 16.
p. 29 'I beheld a tallish . . .' Ibid., 17.
p. 29 'I have four short stories . . .' Letter, ACC to Sam Youd (10 October 1937).
p. 30 'At the moment . . .' Ibid. (17 January 1938).
p. 30 'I don't want . . .' Ibid. (28 January 1938).
p. 31 'I maintain . . .' Ibid. (14 May 1938).
p. 31 'I quickly realised . . .' ACC, 'Astounding Days' (prepublication ms. via Fred Clarke), 167–8.
p. 32 'Today, of course, it is . . .' ACC, *Ascent to Orbit* (New York: John Wiley & Sons, 1984), 207.
p. 32 'I can thank science fiction . . .' ACC, 'Astounding Days' (prepublication ms. via Fred Clarke), 173.
p. 33 'We have plenty of space here . . .' Letter, ACC to Sam Youd (2 July 1938).

p. 33 'The huge Moon photo . . .' Bill Temple, 'The Saga of the Flat' (London: copy of ms., ca 1946).

p. 33 'The British Interplanetary Society is . . .' ACC, Brochure for BIS public relations and membership drive (London: BIS, ca 1938/39).

p. 35 'Maurice came . . .' Bill Temple, 'The Saga of the Flat' 2.

p. 35 'We were a group . . .' Letter, William Temple to NM (23 February 1989), 7.

p. 35 'tall fellow with the quiet . . .' William F. Temple, 'The Flat Truth' in *Gargoyle* (April 1940).

p. 35 'I think we succeeded . . .' Letter, William Temple to NM (22 April 1989).

p. 36 'We note your remarks . . .' Ibid.

p. 36 'The meetings were often . . .' Ibid. (23 February 1989), 8.

p. 36 'One night we returning . . .' William Temple, 'The Saga of the Flat' (London: copy of ms., ca 1946).

p. 37 'The cover of the March . . .' William Temple, 'Publicity Staggers On' *Bulletin of the British Interplanetary Society* (London: March 1939), 10.

p. 37 'I fell to examining . . .' William F. Temple, 'Chingford Chiaroscuro (A Layman's First Experimental Meeting)' (London: *Bulletin of the British Interplanetary Society*, September 1938).

p. 38 'Sometimes when it was . . .' William Temple, *Bulletin of the British Interplanetary Society* (January 1939), 3.

p. 38 'The theory of . . .' ACC, 'Memoirs of an Astronaut (Retired)' in *Voices from the Sky* (New York: Harper & Row, 1965, 171; London: Victor Gollancz, 1966).

p. 38 'Here Messrs Edwards . . .' Temple, 'Chingford Chiaroscuro' (September 1938).

p. 39 'Soon, reported Temple . . .' Ibid.

p. 40 'Excuse me, sir . . .' *Voices from the Sky*, 169, 170.

p. 42 'With present-day materials . . .' ACC, 'Into Space' *Chequer-Board* (October 1937).

p. 42 'I married in haste . . .' Letter, William Temple to NM (23 February 1989), 7.

p. 42 'I still know exactly . . .' ACC, *The Lion of Comarre, Against the Fall of Night* (New York: Harcourt Brace Jovanovich, 1968, vii; London: Victor Gollancz, 1970).

p. 43 'We used to . . .' Letter, Temple to NM (23 February 1989).

p. 43 'When I was demobilised . . .' Ibid.

p. 44 'It still stands . . .' ACC, 'Astounding Days' (prepublication ms. via Fred Clarke), 17.

p. 44 'Early in 1940 . . .' ACC, *The View from Serendip* (New York: Ballantine Books, 1978, 116; London: Victor Gollancz, 1978).

p. 44 'Here I sat out the Blitz . . .' ACC, 'Astounding Days' (prepublication ms. via Fred Clarke), 129.

p. 45 'He really is a beauty . . .' Letter, ACC to Sam Youd (17 September 1940).

p. 46 'I determined to go . . .' ACC, *Ascent to Orbit* (New York: John Wiley & Sons, 1984), 25.

p. 47 'If it moves . . .' ACC, 'Astounding Days' (prepublication ms. via Fred Clarke), 128.

p. 47 'how to behave . . .' ACC, *Glide Path* (New York: New American Library, 1987, 23; London: Sidgwick & Jackson, 1969).

p. 47 'It was near Aldgate . . .' ACC, 'Astounding Days' (prepublication ms. via Fred Clarke), 128, 129.

p. 48 'One day we were . . .' ACC, *Ascent to Orbit*, 26.

p. 48 'When he discovered . . .' Ibid.

p. 48 'Arthur was sent . . .' Letter, Barry King to NM (23 February 1989).

p. 48 'I suspect that . . .' Ibid.

p. 48 'I spent the next . . .' ACC, *Ascent to Orbit*, 26.

p. 50 'on an airfield . . .' ACC, Ibid., 31.

p. 51 'Luis' brainchild . . .' ACC, MIT Speech (March 1976), transcribed from audio.

p. 52 'The idea's extremely simple . . .' ACC, *Glide Path*, 38.

p. 53 'found the American scientists . . .' ACC, *Ascent to Orbit*, 33.

p. 53 'I can still remember . . .' ACC, MIT Speech (March 1976), transcribed from audio.

p. 53 'I soon decided he . . .' Neal Jolley (unpublished ms., Spring 1989), 49.

p. 55 'We were very much . . .' ACC, *Ascent to Orbit*, 33.

p. 56 'The scene might have come . . .' Ibid., 32.

p. 56 'The hissing roar . . .' ACC, *Glide Path*, 205.

p. 56 'The pilot was unable . . .' ACC, *Ascent to Orbit*, 34.

p. 58 'Some time in the winter . . .' *Ascent to Orbit*, 36.

p. 58 '1945. July 2 to 6 . . .' ACC, Private journal entry (July 2–6, 1945).

p. 59 'If I had not . . .' ACC, *1984: Spring* (New York: Ballantine Books, 1984, 31; London: Granada Publishing, 1984).

p. 59 'sixty degrees ahead of Venus . . .' *Ascent to Orbit*, 53, 54, 57, 61.

p. 62 'Once I had got the idea . . .' ACC, 'Introduction' (*The Beginnings of Satellite Communications* by John R. Pierce), vi.

p. 63 'for in my heart of hearts . . .' ACC, *Voices from the Sky* (New York, Harper & Row, 1965, 126; London: Victor Gollancz, 1966).

Chapter 6

p. 65 'I was swiftly rejected . . .' ACC, *Ascent to Orbit* (New York: John Wiley & Sons, 1984), 69.

p. 67 'This, I thought . . .' ACC, *1984: Spring* (New York: Ballantine Books, 1984), 180.

p. 68 'It would only be fair . . .' Letter, ACC to C. S. Lewis, in A. N. Wilson, *C. S. Lewis: A Biography* (New York: W. W. Norton, 1990), 177, 178.

p. 68 'I hope I should not be . . .' Ibid.

p. 69 'Needless to say . . .' ACC, *Voices from the Sky* (New York, Harper & Row, 1965, 175–6; London: Victor Gollancz 1966).

p. 70 'The great radio and telegraph . . .' ACC, *Prelude to Space* (New York: Ballantine Books, 1954, 20; London: Sidgwick & Jackson, 1953).

p. 70 'Good frend . . .' ACC, 'The Curse' in *Reach for Tomorrow* (New York: Ballantine Books, 1987, 111; London: Victor Gollancz, 1962).

p. 71 'I decided to devote . . .' *Ascent to Orbit*, 83.

p. 71 'Unlike most of my . . .' ACC, *The Sentinel* (New York: Berkley Books, 1986, 117; London: Panther Books, 1985).

p. 72 'Luckily I escaped . . .' *Ascent to Orbit*, 83, 'My job was to . . .' Ibid., 117; 'I probably had . . .' Ibid., 118.

p. 73 'My job was interfering . . .' *Roanoke Times* (29 April 1954); also *Ascent to Orbit*, 119.

p. 73 'The article attracted . . .' ACC, *Interplanetary Flight* (New York: Berkley Books, 1985, ix; London: Temple Books, 1960).

p. 74 'When I was in high school . . .' Carl Sagan, 'In Praise of Arthur C. Clarke' (*The Planetary Report*, No. 3, 1983), 3.

p. 74 'Never in my wildest . . .' *Interplanetary Flight*, xi.

p. 75 'As an educational experiment . . .' 13 May 1950, no page.

p. 76 'After terrifying my wife . . .' Fred Clarke, *Fred Clarke's Cameos*, 'Green on the Screen' (17 January 1986).

p. 76 'It is also widely . . .' *Ascent to Orbit*, 175–6.

p. 77 'We were defeated . . .' ACC, *Expedition to Earth* (New York: Ballantine Books, 1953, 83; London: Sidgwick & Jackson, 1954).

p. 77 'You called on me . . .' Letter, Wernher von Braun to ACC (30 August 1951).

p. 77 '*Picture Post* gave . . .' (25 August 1951).

p. 78 'Space flight is . . .' Coverage of Programme for the Second International Congress on Astronautics (London: September 1952).

p. 79 'All these weeks . . .' ACC, *The Sands of Mars* (New York: New American Library, 1974, 71; London: Sidgwick & Jackson, 1951).

p. 79 'I am agreeably surprised . . .' Ibid., v.

Chapter 7

p. 82 'in a moment . . .' Clifton Fadiman, 'Introduction' *Across the Sea of Stars* (New York: Harcourt, Brace & Company, 1959), 151–2.

p. 85 'His hand had gone . . .' ACC, *The Other Side of the Sky* (New York: New American Library, 1959, 98; London: Victor Gollancz, 1961).

p. 86 'watching the performance . . .' ACC, 'Ego Visits America' Fanzine, edited by Ian Macauley (summer 1952).

p. 87 'There are no fundamental . . .' *The Baltimore Sun* (June 1952), no page available.

p. 89 'I have a theory . . .' ACC, 'Ego Visits America' (summer 1952).

Chapter 8

p. 94 'I met Arthur . . .' Bill MacQuitty, 'Clarke of Ceylon' (unpublished ms., received autumn 1989).

p. 94 'I submitted it to . . .' ACC, *The Sentinel* (New York: Berkley Books, 1986, 41; London: Panther Books, 1985).

p. 98 'There was a mist . . .' ACC, *Childhood's End* (New York: Ballantine Books, 1953, 187; London: Sidgwick & Jackson, 1954).

p. 98 'I was carrying . . .' ACC, *The Deep Range* (New York: New American Library, 1958, ix; London: Frederick Muller, 1957).

p. 99 'A fair-sized alligator . . .' Ibid., x.

p. 102 'A boy needs his father . . .' ACC, *2010: Odyssey Two* (New York: Ballantine Books, 1982, 302; London: Granada Publishing, 1982).

p. 105 'In *Childhood's End* . . .' Basil Davenport, *New York Times Book Review* (23 August 1953), 19.

p. 109 'I've learned a lot . . .' Letter, ACC to Val Cleaver (19 April 1954).

p. 110 'There was Dr Wernher von Braun . . .' ACC, *The Making of a Moon* (New York: Harper & Brothers, 1957, 39–40; London: Frederick Muller, 1957).

p. 111 'If you want to continue . . .' ACC, *Christian Science Monitor* (10 February 1972), 10.

p. 111 'I can still remember . . .' ACC, *The View from Serendip* (New York: Ballantine Books, 1978, 116; London: Victor Gollancz, 1978).

Chapter 9

p. 112 'A good deal of . . .' ACC, *The View from Serendip* (New York: Ballantine Books, 1978, 2–3; London: Victor Gollancz, 1978).

p. 113 'I spent the first three . . .' Letter, ACC, 'Report to the Globe (First and Probably Last Report)' (27 December 1954), 2.

p. 113 'In particular certain developments . . .' ACC, *The City and the Stars* (New York: New American Library, 1957, vii; London: Frederick Muller, 1956).

p. 113 'Colombo was my first real . . .' ACC, 'Report to the Globe', 2.

p. 113 'In Colombo I . . .' 'Ceylon: An Adventurer's Retreat' in *True* (April 1972), 39.

p. 114 'Rodney suggested . . .' *The View from Serendip*, 4.

p. 114 'I now realise . . .' 'Ceylon' in *True*, 39.

p. 114 'Saw little of Fremantle . . .' ACC, 'Report to the Globe', 2.

p. 115 'We spent a couple . . .' Ibid.

p. 115 'I had had my first swim . . .' ACC, *The Coast of Coral* (New York: Harper & Row, 1956, 4 ff; London: Frederick Muller, 1956).

p. 115 'I met my first . . .' Letter, ACC to Val Cleaver (1 January 1955).

p. 116 'It now looks . . .' Letter, ACC to Val Cleaver (2 April 1955).

p. 116 'We had planned . . .' *Coast of Coral*, 65.

p. 116 'We are just going . . .' Letter, ACC to Val Cleaver (7 May 1955).

p. 117 'I was to see . . .' *Coast of Coral*, 26.

p. 117 'I did not enjoy . . .' Ibid., 125, 127.

p. 118 'We now have some . . .' Letter, ACC to Val Cleaver (2 August 1955).

p. 118 'Coming in from . . .' ACC, *Voices from the Sky* (New York, Harper & Row, 1965, 178; London: Victor Gollancz, 1966).

p. 119 'Harper's are very . . .' Letter, ACC to Val Cleaver (24 September 1955).

p. 120 'saying that I am . . .' Letter, ACC to Val Cleaver (24 September 1955).

p. 121 'In an age . . .' *Coast of Coral*, 201.

Chapter 10

p. 122 'Both Mike and I . . .' Letter, ACC to Val Cleaver (16 October 1955).

p. 124 'We knew that the earlier . . .' ACC, with Mike Wilson, *The Reefs of Taprobane: Underwater Adventurers Around Ceylon* (New York: Harper & Brothers, 1957, 12; London: Frederick Muller, 1957).

p. 124 'We went ashore . . .' Letter, ACC to Val Cleaver (13 January 1956).

p. 124 'A thin line of fire . . .' *Reefs of Taprobane*, 12.

p. 125 'Arthur came ashore . . .' Letter, Mary Clarke Maclean to NM (4 July 1990)

p. 125 'a small but pleasant apartment . . .' *Reefs of Taprobane*, 15, 16, 18, 21.

p. 126 'Mike also seems happy . . .' Letter, ACC to Val Cleaver (7 February 1956).

p. 127 ff 'We had the satisfaction . . .' *Reefs of Taprobane*, 33, 52, 56, 57, 58, 61, 69.

p. 130 'I've been getting up . . .' Letter, ACC to Val Cleaver (27 May 1956).

p. 131 'Working from 7 a.m. . . .' Letter, ACC to Ian Macauley (25 May 1956).

p. 131 'The contrast between here . . .' Letter, ACC to Val Cleaver (6 April 1956).

p. 131 'Hector was working . . .' Fax, ACC to NM (2 June 1990).

p. 131 'spoilt by silly . . .' Letter, ACC to Val Cleaver (16 June 1956).

Chapter 11

p. 134 'I hope to sit . . .' Letter, ACC to Val Cleaver (16 September 1956).

p. 134 'No other form of literature . . .' ACC, Speech to the 1956 World Science Fiction Convention (2 September 1956), 10, 23, 25, 26.

p. 136 'Lectures are now . . .' Letter, ACC to Val Cleaver (3 December 1956).

p. 139 'For some reason, at . . .' ACC, *The Sentinel* (New York: Berkley Books, 1983, 254; London: Panther Books, 1985).

p. 139 'They stared at each other . . .' ACC, 'The Songs of Distant Earth' in *The Other Side of the Sky* (New York: New American Library, 1987, 224; London: Victor Gollancz, 1961).

Chapter 12

p. 142 'In my 1958 season . . .' ACC, *The Challenge of the Space Ship* (New York: Harper & Brothers, 1959, 160; London: Frederick Muller, 1960).

p. 143 'It is hard to believe . . .' Ibid., 164, 210, 165, 166, 167, 180, 181, 179.

p. 145 'I cannot believe . . .' HRH Prince Philip, quoted, *Daily Mail Reporter* (15 April 1958).

p. 145 'If anyone thinks . . .' ACC quoted, Ibid.

p. 145 'into a brisk argument . . .' Fax, ACC to NM (2 June 1990).

p. 145 'We saw *Sputnik* . . .' Letter, ACC to Sam Youd (23 May 1958).

p. 146 'About two hundred people . . .' Letter, ACC to Sam Youd (10 July 1958).

p. 146 'We are just floating . . .' Letter, ACC to Sam Youd (13 August 1958).

p. 146 'As he was leaving . . .' Ibid. (21 September 1958).

p. 147 'I'm getting quite reactionary . . .' Ibid. (13 August 1958).

p. 147 'I also hope (touch wood) . . .' Letter, ACC to Val Cleaver (1 January 1959).

p. 148 'Should the Soviet Union . . .' Letter, ACC to Val Cleaver (23 February 1959).

p. 148 'Everyone told me later . . .' Elmer Gertz, *Chicago-Sun Times* (15 April 1984).

p. 149 'I seem to be regarded . . .' Letter, ACC to Val Cleaver (23 February 1959).

p. 149 'I was about to switch . . .' ACC, *The Treasure of the Great Reef*, revised ed. (New York: Ballantine Books, 1974, 259; London: Arthur Barker, 1964).

p. 150 'But the struggle . . .' ACC, *Treasure* (Harper & Row, 1964), 18.

p. 150 'We had sharks . . .' Letter, ACC to Val Cleaver (13 May 1959).

p. 151 'Usually Ali Baba . . .' ACC, *Treasure*, 25.
p. 151 'Writing the script . . .' ACC, 'Sri Lanka and Me' (*Millimeter*, March 1977), 41.
p. 151 'Just acquired demolition . . .' Letter, ACC to Roger Caras (21 May 1959).
p. 152 'He hopes to revolutionise . . .' Letter, ACC to Sam Youd (30 June 1959).
p. 152 'The first draft . . .' Letter, ACC to Val Cleaver (17 September 1959).
p. 152 'Our new house . . .' Letter, ACC to Val Cleaver (20 November 1959).
p. 153 'I hope to be . . .' Ibid. (29 September 1959).

Chapter 13

p. 154 'Mixing fact and fiction . . .' Letter, ACC to Val Cleaver (14 April 1960).
p. 155 'We'll be using America's . . .' ACC, 'I Remember Babylon' in *The Nine Billion Names of God* (New York: New American Library, 1987), 33; Ibid., 22.
p. 155 'Only a few years after . . .' Ibid., 22–3.
p. 156 'I seem to have lost . . .' Ibid.
p. 157 'It varies in a way . . .' Letter, ACC to Val Cleaver (14 April 1960) and 'quite a tough piece . . .' Ibid. (13 June 1990).
p. 157 'I spoke to all . . .' Ibid. (24 July 1960).
p. 158 'All hell has broken . . .' Ibid. (24 August 1960).
p. 158 'After Macmillan and Harper . . .' Letter, Scott Meredith to NM (28 June 1990).
p. 158 'That means I've gambled . . .' Letter, ACC to Val Cleaver (24 August 1960); 'If the worst comes to the worst . . .' Ibid. (28 February 1960).
p. 158 'And any moment . . .' Letter, ACC to Val Cleaver (24 August 1960).
p. 159 'I decided to . . .' Ibid. (17 October 1960).
p. 159 'I've had the advance . . .' Letter, ACC to Sam Youd (21 November 1960).
p. 159 'Liz is now . . .' Letter, ACC to Val Cleaver (17 October 1960) and 'He doesn't seem . . .' Ibid. (1 December 1959).
p. 160 'No need for . . .' Letter, ACC to Val Cleaver (5 December 1960).
p. 161 'He decided to spend . . .' Letter, ACC to Val Cleaver (5 December 1960).

p. 163 'I will await . . .' Letter, ACC to Val Cleaver (7 January 1961).

p. 163 'I am pretty firm . . .' Letters, ACC to Val Cleaver (7 January 1961; 14 January 1961; 16 March 1961).

p. 165 'After a very few lessons . . .' ACC, *The Treasure of the Great Reef* (New York: Harper & Row, 1964, 32; London: Arthur Barker, 1964).

p. 165 'They were thinking . . .' ACC, with Mike Wilson, *Indian Ocean Adventure* (New York: Harper & Row, 1961, 100; London: Arthur Barker, 1962).

p. 166 'After we got to . . .' ACC, *Treasure*, 38, 39.

p. 167 ff 'Well, Mike has done . . .' Letter, ACC to Val Cleaver (26 March 1961).

p. 168 'Well, the Russians . . .' Letter, ACC to Val Cleaver (15 June 1961); 'I was pleased that . . .' Ibid. (16 May 1961) and 'Or will the country . . .' Ibid. (3 June 1961).

p. 169 'Mike and Liz got . . .' Letter, ACC to Val Cleaver (ca June 1961).

p. 170 'I'm sorry to say . . .' Letter, ACC to Sam Youd (26 June 1961).

p. 170 'We met at his 14th . . .' Fax, ACC to NM (June 1990).

p. 170 ff '*Horizon* is holding . . .' Letters, ACC to Val Cleaver (29 September 1961; 4 October 1961).

p. 171 'I had spent several weeks . . .' ACC, *Treasure*, 73.

p. 173 'I was walking back . . .' ACC, Opus 729, prepublication ms. for 'Close Encounters with Cosmonauts' (*OMNI* October 1989, Russian edition).

p. 173 'Why doesn't your film . . .' ACC, *Treasure*, 81.

Chapter 15

p. 174 'By this time . . .' ACC, *The Treasure of the Great Reef* (New York: Harper & Row, 1964, 79; London: Arthur Barker, 1964).

p. 174 'The first trials . . .' Letter, ACC to Roger Caras (21 February 1962).

p. 175 'Leaving one store . . .' *Treasure*, 86. Also ACC, *The View from Serendip* (New York: Ballantine Books, 1976, 33; London: Victor Gollancz, 1978).

p. 175 'I was almost completely . . .' *Treasure*, 86–7.

p. 176 ff 'immensely improved . . .' Letters, ACC to Sam Youd (4 May 1962; 23 May 1962).

p. 177 'I wrote a couple . . .' ACC, *Treasure*, 88.

p. 177 'Though he never stopped . . .' ACC, *Dolphin Island* (New York: Ace Books, 1987, 154; London: Victor Gollancz, 1963).

p. 177 'I'm still astonished . . .' Letter, ACC to Sam Youd (4 May 1962).

p. 178 '*Ranmuthu Duwa* turned out . . .' ACC, *Treasure*, 89.

p. 178 'The photography really . . .' Letter, ACC to Roger Caras (26 November 1962).

p. 178 'There is not much . . .' ACC, *Treasure*, 89.

p. 179 'In addition to the pride . . .' ACC, *Voices from the Sky* (New York: Harper & Row, 1965, 161–3; London: Victor Gollancz, 1966).

p. 180 'I am now able . . .' Letter, ACC to Roger Caras (November 1962).

Chapter 16

p. 181 'I exercised and trained . . .' ACC, *The Treasure of the Great Reef* (New York: Harper & Row, 1964, 93; London: Arthur Barker, 1964).

p. 182 'all of us a chance . . .' Isaac Asimov, *The New York Times Book Review* (15 April 1963), 22.

p. 182 'a splendid introduction . . .' Fritz Leiber, *The National Review* (9 April 1963).

p. 184 'Though Mike had pressed me . . .' ACC, *Treasure*, 115.

p. 185 ff 'I very quickly recognised . . .' ACC, *Treasure*, 127, 128, 134–6.

p. 187 'the further we try . . .' ACC, with R. A. Smith, *The Exploration of the Moon* (New York: Harper's & Son, 1954, 112; London: Frederick Muller, 1954).

p. 188 'I was determined . . .' Letter, ACC to Sam Youd (6 January 1964).

p. 189 '*Glide Path* describes . . .' *New York Herald Tribune Book Week* (17 November 1963), 16.

p. 189 'Meanwhile I remain . . .' Letter, ACC to Sam Youd (24 October 1963).

Chapter 17

p. 191 'FRIGHTFULLY INTERESTED IN WORKING . . .' Jerome Agel, editor, *The Making of Kubrick's 2001* (New York: New American Library, 1970), 11.

p. 192 'He wanted to do the proverbial . . .' ACC, *Report on Planet Three and Other Speculations* (New York: Berkley Books, 1985, 234–6; London: Victor Gollancz, 1972).

p. 193 'I am continually annoyed . . .' ACC, *The Sentinel* (New York: Berkley Books, 1986, 117 and 'glittering, roughly pyramidal . . .' Ibid. London: Panther Books, 1985).

p. 193 'I was happy to find . . .' *Report on Planet Three*, 236.

p. 194 'We talked for eight . . .' Ibid.

p. 194 'Stanley was in some danger . . .' ACC, *The Lost Worlds of 2001* (New York: New American Library, 1972, 29; London: Sidgwick & Jackson, 1972).

p. 194 'I was working at Time-Life . . .' Jeremy Bernstein, *Experiencing Science* (New York: Basic Books, 1978), 225; also ACC, *Report on Planet Three*, 237.

p. 195 'six additional stories . . .' and 'He proposed that . . .' ACC, *Report on Planet Three*, 239; ACC, *Lost Worlds*, 31; Bernstein, *Experiencing Science*, 225.

p. 195 'In theory, therefore . . .' *Lost Worlds*, 31.

p. 196 'I felt that when . . .' Ibid., 32.

p. 196 'Stan's a fascinating . . .' Letter, ACC to Sam Youd (19 June 1964).

p. 196 'We shook hands . . .' *Report on Planet Three*, 238.

p. 196 'I can still remember . . .' Ibid., 328.

p. 198 'I argued that . . .' Carl Sagan, *The Cosmic Connection* (New York: Dell Books, 1975), 182.

p. 198 'Just bought a ream of paper . . .' Letter, ACC to Sam Youd (19 June 1964).

p. 198 'Stanley installed me . . .' *Report on Planet Three*, 239–40.

p. 199 'The merging of our streams . . .' *Report on Planet Three*, 240.

p. 199 'Across the gulf of centuries . . .' ACC, *The Challenge of the Space Ship* (New York: Harper & Brothers, 1959, 213; London: Frederick Muller, 1960).

p. 199 'We set out . . .' *Report on Planet Three*, 243; also Jerome Agel, ed., *The Making of Kubrick's 2001* (New York: New American Library, 1970), front matter.

p. 200 'MGM doesn't know . . .' *Report on Planet Three*, 243 and 'This was typical . . .' Ibid., 239; also *Lost Worlds*, 33.

p. 200 'Stanley decided . . .' *Report on Planet Three*, 239.

p. 200 'We've extended the range . . .' ACC, *Lost Worlds*, 34–5.

p. 201 'My primary job . . .' *Lost Worlds*, 36.

p. 203 'equally divided between . . .' *Lost Worlds*, 37.

p. 204 'suddenly realised how the novel . . .' *Lost Worlds*, 38 and 'Bowman will regress . . .' Ibid.

p. 204 'The ending was altered . . .' Agel, ed., *The Making of Kubrick's 2001*, end of photo section.

p. 205 'After all, Odysseus . . .' *Lost Worlds*, 38.

p. 205 'happened to remark . . .' *Lost Worlds*, 39 and 'He called to say . . .' Ibid.

Chapter 18

p. 207 'About a hundred technicians . . .' ACC, *The Lost Worlds of 2001* (New York: New American Library, 1972, 41; London: Sidgwick & Jackson, 1972).

p. 208 'I got quite scared . . .' *Lost Worlds*, 45.

p. 208 'I have never seen . . .' Sarras, *Village Voice* (May 1979).

p. 208 'Stan spliced together . . .' *Lost Worlds*, 45.

p. 209 'make them highly suited . . .' ACC, 'Explorations in Tomorrow' in *Man and the Future*, James Gunn, ed. (Lawrence, Kansas: University Press of Kansas, 1967), 263.

p. 209 'I cabled Stanley . . .' *Lost Worlds*, 46, 47.

p. 210 'I gather that there . . .' Letter, ACC to Sam Youd (12 September 1966).

p. 210 'He keeps promising . . .' Ibid. (1 December 1966).

p. 210 'It was a very sad period . . .' *Lost Worlds*, 46.

p. 211 'The *2001* novel contract . . .' Letter, ACC to Sam Youd (June [no day] 1967).

p. 211 'I had to invent . . .' Jerome Agel, ed., *The Making of Kubrick's 2001* (New York: New American Library, 1970), 351 ff.

p. 213 'Keir Dullea, dressed . . .' Jeremy Bernstein, *A Comprehensible World* (New York: Random House, 1967), 241.

p. 214 'Maybe the company can . . .' Ibid.

p. 215 'It is the year 2001 . . .' *The Making of 2001* (New York: Thomas Craven Film Corp., 1966).

p. 216 'I tried to work things . . .' Agel, *The Making of Kubrick's 2001*, photo section; no page.

p. 216 'banal to the point of extinction . . .' Ibid., 299.

p. 216 'There are certain areas . . .' *The Making of Kubrick's 2001*, photo section, no page.

p. 217 'This is what makes *2001* . . .' Ibid.

p. 217 '*2001: A Space Odyssey* is about man's . . .' Ibid., front matter.

p. 217 'Stan and I used . . .' Letter, ACC to Sam Youd (2 August 1968).

p. 218 'I can still recall . . .' ACC, *Astounding Days* (New York: Bantam Books, 1989, 21; London: Victor Gollancz, 1989).

p. 218 'It's hard to find anything . . .' Agel, *The Making of Kubrick's 2001*, photo section, no page.

p. 218 'the longest flash forward . . .' ACC, *Lost Worlds*, 51–2.

p. 219 'I'm now in a blissful . . .' Letter, ACC to Sam Youd (28 August 1967) and '(ugh!) my 50th!!! . . .' Ibid. (21 October 1967).

p. 220 'I just felt . . .' Agel, *The Making of Kubrick's 2001*, 170; 'I think it just affected . . .' Ibid. and 'Well, that's the end of . . .' Ibid. photo section, no page.

p. 221 'dazzles the eyes and gnaws . . .' *Life* (April 1968).

p. 221 'They were plotting . . .' *Life* (5 April 1965), 34–5.

p. 222 'Whenever the thunder . . .' Agel, *The Making of Kubrick's 2001*, 229, 244–5, 245–6.

p. 222 'If anyone understands . . .' Ibid., 329.

p. 222 'I still stand by . . .' ACC, *Report on Planet Three and Other Speculations* (New York: Berkley Books, 1985, 245; London: Victor Gollancz, 1972).

p. 223 'Now I feel I've been . . .' Agel, *The Making of Kubrick's 2001*, photo section, no page.

p. 223 'It was a particularly . . .' Postcard, Neil Armstrong to NM (May 1989).

p. 223 'I remember thinking . . .' Agel, *The Making of Kubrick's 2001*, photo section, no page.

p. 223 'I always used to tell people . . .' Ibid.

p. 224 'All the parts of the movie . . .' Ibid., 309.

p. 224 'since the motion picture . . .' Agel, *The Making of Kubrick's 2001*, 256.

p. 225 'As an artist . . .' Agel, *The Making of Kubrick's 2001*, photo section, no page.

Chapter 19

p. 226 'When I published . . .' ACC, *The View from Serendip* (New York: Ballantine Books, 1978, 70; London: Victor Gollancz, 1978).

p. 228 'I am sitting glued . . .' Letter, ACC to Tom Craven (24 December 1968).

p. 228 'How many people have powerful . . .' ACC, quoted in the *Ceylon Observer* (27 December 1968).

p. 229 'The sf Symposium was only . . .' Frederik Pohl, *The Way the Future Was* (New York: Ballantine Books, 1978), 301.

Chapter 20

p. 232 'I hadn't cried for twenty years . . .' Jeremy Bernstein, 'Profiles: Out of the Ego Chamber' in *New Yorker* 45 (9 August 1969), 40.

p. 232 'It is one of the most thrilling . . .' *0:56:20PM 7/20/69: The historic conquest of the moon as reported to the American people by CBS News over the CBS Television Network*, 21–2.

p. 233 'Yes, I'm always running . . .' CBS, *7/20/69*, 59–60.

p. 234 'We're going out indefinitely . . .' Ibid., 107.

p. 235 'Now the Moon has yielded . . .' Ibid., 129.

Chapter 21

p. 237 'I had to check . . .' Letter, ACC to Tom Craven (14 January 1970).

p. 238 'I begged him . . .' ACC, 'Ceylon: An Adventurer's Retreat' in *True* (April 1972).

p. 238 'They liked it so much . . .' Letter, ACC to Sam Youd (25 April 1970).

p. 239 'I have a long-standing . . .' Dialogue between ACC and Alan Watts in 'At the Interface' Technology and Mysticism, *Playboy* (19 January 1971), 94–7, 130 ff.

p. 240 'For it may be that . . .' ACC, 'Epilogue: Beyond Apollo' in *First on the Moon* (Boston: Little, Brown and Company, 1970, 419; London: Michael Joseph, 1970).

p. 240 'That's what I *intended* . . .' ACC, *Imperial Earth* (New York: Ballantine Books, 1976, 128, 303; London: Victor Gollancz, 1975).

p. 241 'despite political and economic . . .' Letter, ACC to Sam Youd (21 December 1970).

p. 242 'We were driving down . . .' ACC, *The View from Serendip* (New York: Ballantine Books, 1978, 116; London: Victor Gollancz, 1978).

p. 243 'Over the previous decade . . .' ACC, *The Sentinel* (New York: Berkley Books, 1986, 207; London: Panther Books, 1985).

p. 243 'island of thirteen million . . .' ACC, *The Treasure of the Great Reef*, Rev. ed. (New York: Ballantine Books, 1974, 254–5; London: Arthur Barker, 1964).

p. 244 'When I was a boy . . .' Letter, Joseph Allen to ACC (September 1984).

p. 244 'We are here . . .' (Audio transcript from film coverage of the event), Thomas Craven Films, Inc., August 1971.

p. 245 'Do we have the imagination . . .' ACC, Speech, State Department, August 1971.

p. 246 'It was Edgar Rice Burroughs . . .' ACC et al. *Mars and the Mind of Man* (New York: Harper & Row, 1973), 27–8.

Chapter 22

p. 248 'I was tempted to give . . .' ACC, *The Wind from the Sun* (New York: Harcourt Brace Jovanovich, 1972, vii–viii; London: Victor Gollancz, 1972).

p. 249 'Actually, nineteen . . .' Letter, ACC to Sam Youd (4 January 1972).

p. 249 'I was standing . . .' ACC, 'The Last Revolution', speech given at Goddard Dinner (Washington, DC, 14 March 1972).

p. 249 'I am working flat out . . .' Letter, ACC to Tom Craven (7 September 1972).

p. 250 'It has often been suggested . . .' ACC, *Report on Planet Three and Other Speculations* (New York: Berkley Books, 1985, 133; London: Victor Gollancz, 1972).

p. 251 'This statement by a spokesman . . .' Saul Bellow, 'Literature in the Age of Technology' in *Technology and the Frontiers of Knowledge* (Garden City, New York: Doubleday, 1975), 4.

p. 251 'I count it as noble . . .' ACC, *The View from Serendip* (New York: Ballantine Books, 1978, 187; London: Victor Gollancz, 1978).

p. 251 'enjoyed none more . . .' Letter, Joseph Allen to ACC (ca spring 1973).

p. 252 'We should build them . . .' ACC, *View from Serendip*, 126.

p. 252 'That was very nearly . . .' Fax, ACC to NM (27 February 1990).

p. 253 'IBM invited me . . .' ACC, *View from Serendip*, 166; also Fax, ACC to NM (20 March 1990).

p. 253 'I went up a hundred metres . . .' Fax, ACC to NM (20 March 1990).

p. 253 'People there will be . . .' *Publishers Weekly* (10 September 1973).

p. 254 ff 'I stood in the back . . .' Kerry O'Quinn, 'Rendezvous with Clarke' *Starlog* (December 1983), 4.

p. 255 'Science fiction is often called . . .' Interview, ACC and Alice Turner, *Publishers Weekly* (10 September 1973).

p. 256 'story-telling of the highest order . . .' *New York Times* (22 August 1973), 35.

Chapter 23

p. 258 'It will be hell . . .' Letter, ACC to Tom Craven (3 December 1973).

p. 258 'Fighting to get . . .' Letter, ACC to Tom Craven (21 December 1973).

p. 259 'I have finally started . . .' Letter, ACC to Tom Craven (15 January 1974).

p. 260 'I spent several days . . .' ACC, *The View from Serendip* (New York: Ballantine Books, 1978, 137; London: Victor Gollancz, 1978); 'Well, Isaac . . .' Ibid., 138 and 'It's an awesome output . . .' Ibid., 140, 143.

p. 261 'done *con amore* . . .' Letter, ACC to Tom Craven (29 December 1974).

p. 262 'Many years ago . . .' ACC, 'Goodbye Isaac' (Colombo, Sri Lanka: 7 April 1992), a fax copy of Clarke's tribute to his friend shortly after Asimov's death.

p. 263 'I have been very busy . . .' Letter, ACC to Tom Craven (27 August 1974).

p. 265 'Am delighted . . .' Letter, ACC to Tom Craven (18 February 1975).

p. 265 'I consider it a breakthrough . . .' *Christian Science Monitor* (28 May 1975).

p. 265 'If this is so . . .' Letter, ACC to Sam Youd (20 June 1975).

p. 266 'I am now taking things . . .' Letter, ACC to Tom Craven (21 April 1975).

p. 266 'Since I delivered . . .' Letter, ACC to Sam Youd (20 June 1975).

p. 267 'He [the reviewer] believes . . .' ACC, *View from Serendip*, 161.

p. 267 'Neil Armstrong and I waited . . .' Fax, ACC to NM (20 March 1990).

p. 268 ff 'I was both flattered . . .' ACC, *View from Serendip*, 189, 190, 192, 201, 203, 205, 206, 212, 215.

p. 271 'The best solution for you . . .' Letter, von Braun to ACC (5 August 1974).

p. 271 'Lanka's link with . . .' *Ceylon Daily News* (12 August 1975).

p. 272 'I am now inviting . . .' Letter, ACC to Yash Pal (11 August 1975).

p. 273 'This book has more plot . . .' Joseph McLellan, *Washington Post* (23 January 1976), C-4.

p. 273 'at the height of his . . .' Gerald Jonas, *New York Times Book Review* (18 January 1976), 20.

p. 273 'after twenty years work . . .' Letter, ACC to Roger Caras (23 January 1975).

Chapter 24

p. 274 'Since your remarkable forecast . . .' Letter, Jerome Weisner to ACC (21 October 1975).

p. 275 ff 'one could have face-to-face . . .' ACC, *The View from Serendip* (New York: Ballantine Books, 1978, 217, 219, 221, 239; London: Victor Gollancz, 1978).

p. 277 'easily be regarded as the grandfather . . .' *Publishers Weekly* (14 June 1976).

p. 277 'Our beautiful new Earth station . . .' Letter, ACC to Tom Craven (May 1976).

p. 278 'In a very important . . .' ACC, *Spaceflight*, Vol. 18, No. 12 (British Interplanetary Society, December 1976), 429–31.

p. 278 'I am hard at work . . .' Letters, ACC to Tom Craven (13 August 1976; 9 October 1976; 28 October 1976).

p. 278 'We stayed at the old Raffles . . .' Letter, ACC to Roger Caras (9 October 1976).

p. 279 'Can't you persuade them . . .' Letter, ACC to Tom Craven (28 October 1976).

p. 279 'neo-Somerset Maugham . . .' Ibid., 78.

p. 280 'The Bell System knows . . .' Script, *The Making of 2076* (Thomas Craven Films, 1976).

p. 281 'The big problem is . . .' Letter, ACC to Tom Craven (16 June 1977).

p. 281 'I was going to . . .' Letter, ACC to Roger Caras (13 July 1977).

p. 281 'Leslie was also perhaps . . .' Letter, ACC to Sam Youd (3 December 1978).

p. 282 'For forty years he . . .' Ibid.

p. 283 'Old Arthur C. Clarke . . .' Fax, ACC to NM (Summer 1991).

p. 283 'I'm proud of it . . .' *Christian Science Monitor* (14 December 1977), 29.

p. 284 'I've become more and more . . .' Letter, ACC to Sam Youd (3 December 1978).

p. 285 'I'm thinking of taking . . .' Malcolm Kirk, interviewer *OMNI* (March 1979), 102.

p. 285 'I spend half an hour . . .' Letter, ACC to Tom Craven (20 December 1979).

p. 285 'The January *Playboy* . . .' Letter, ACC to Sam Youd (3 December 1978).

p. 286 'It's the most ambitious . . .' Martin Walker, 'The Man with Space for Development' in *Guardian* (30 August 1978), 8.

p. 286 'A clear case of plagiarism . . .' ACC, *1984: Spring* (New York: Ballantine Books, 1984, 210; London: Granada Publishing, 1984).

p. 287 'Space travel is a technological mutation . . .' *Time* (16 July 1979), 16.

p. 287 'Today's comsats demonstrate . . .' ACC, *1984: Spring*, 98.

Chapter 25

p. 288 'For the last four days . . .' Letter, Fred Clarke to ACC (15 February 1980).

p. 288 'Mother died . . .' Letter, ACC to Tom Craven (10 March 1980).

p. 289 'There's the corona! . . .' ACC, Audio from *Arthur C. Clarke's Mysterious World: The Journey Begins* (Pacific Arts Video, 1989).

p. 290 'Here in the sea . . .' ACC, Soundtrack from *OMNI* TV ad, 1980.

p. 292 'I met Harry . . .' Fax, ACC to NM (20 April 1990).

Chapter 26

p. 294 'As I sat on the bench . . .' ACC, *1984: Spring* (New York: Ballantine Books, 1984, 195; London: Granada Publishing, 1984).

p. 294 'When I made it clear . . .' Letter, ACC to Tom Craven (March 1981).

p. 295 'Last month I had . . .' ACC, *1984: Spring*, 24.

p. 295 'Rather to my surprise . . .' ACC, 'New Communications Technologies and the Developing World,' in *Analog Science Fiction/Science Fact* (December 1983), 36–7.

p. 297 'I realised he was right . . .' Interview with Roger Caras, 'Our Man in the Future' in *Science Digest* (March 1982), 95.

p. 297 'The most extraordinary feature . . .' ACC, *2010: Odyssey Two* (New York: Ballantine Books, 1982, 205; London: Granada Publishing, 1982).

p. 298 'If you are an optimist . . .' Caras, 'Our Man in the Future', 95.

p. 298 ff 'In biological diversity . . .' Caras, ABC News *20/20: Arthur C. Clarke Transcript*, no page available.

p. 299 'Now working night . . .' Letter, ACC to Roger Caras (16 November 1981).

p. 299 'I can honestly say . . .' ACC and Peter Hyams, *The Odyssey File*

(New York: Ballantine Books, 1985, xv; London: Granada Publishing, 1984).

p. 299 'The marvellous thing . . .' ACC, 'Egogram 1' (6 April 1982).

p. 300 'Scott Meredith is entirely . . .' Ibid.

p. 300 'have made a significant . . .' ACC, *Ascent to Orbit* (New York: John Wiley & Sons, 1984), 3.

p. 301 'They had installed . . .' ACC, 'Report on the Hague-Moscow-Leningrad Trip' (Letter to friends, 27 June, 1982).

p. 301 'two orthogonal brass rings . . .' Fax, ACC to NM (5 July 1990).

p. 301 'So communications and astronautics . . .' ACC, *Ascent to Orbit*, 10, 11.

p. 302ff 'Though it was now late . . .' ACC, 'Egogram 2' (27 June 1982).

p. 303 ACC, *1984: Spring*, 38-9.

p. 305 'It was a great thrill . . .' ACC, *2010: Odyssey Two*, 335.

p. 306 'It is hard to believe . . .' ACC, *1984: Spring*, 107, 110, 114.

p. 306 'My Geneva speech . . .' Marcia Gauger, 'Arthur C. Clarke Spins Tales of Outer Space' in *People* (20 December 1982).

p. 306 'The importance of halting . . .' ACC, *1984: Spring*, 53, 56.

p. 307 'I called Stanley . . .' Interview, ACC and the *Washington Post* (November [no day] 1982).

p. 308 'The *2010* book contract . . .' Letter, Scott Meredith to NM (16 March 1990).

Chapter 27

p. 311 'Don't blame me . . .' ACC, *Ascent to Orbit* (New York: John Wiley & Sons, 1984), 213.

p. 312 'Tell Satyajit . . .' Andrew Robinson, *Satyajit Ray: The Inner Eye* (London: André Deutsch, 1990), 295. Also ACC's 'Satyajit and Stanley', unpublished ms., 15 September 1990.

p. 312 'I was invited . . .' ACC, *Ascent to Orbit*, 213.

p. 313 'The Americans . . .' ACC, Ibid., 221.

p. 315 'A number of the top . . .' Press Release, White House (23 June 1983).

p. 315 'At a generous assessment . . .' ACC, John Fairley, Simon Welfare, *Arthur C. Clarke's World of Strange Powers* (New York: Putnam, 1984; London: William Collins, 1984).

p. 316 'Human judgment must . . .' Ibid., 243.

p. 317 'It might be fun . . .' ACC and Peter Hyams, *The Odyssey File* (New York: Ballantine Books, 1985, xvi, xvii; London: Granada Publishing, 1984).

p. 317 'Peter and I started . . .' Ibid.

p. 318 ff 'giving Cherene . . .' ACC, 'Egogram' (1983). Newsy letter to friends.

p. 321 ff 'I feel very happy . . .' ACC and Peter Hyams, *The Odyssey File* (New York: Ballantine Books, 1985, 100; London: Granada Publishing, 1984).

p. 323 'Clarke's residence is next door . . .' Elmer Gertz, *Chicago Sun-Times* (15 April 1984), 6, 7.

p. 324 'In an extraordinary show of faith . . .' Press Release, Press Syndicate, a Media Service of Book Communications Systems, no date.

p. 325 'The token figure . . .' Letter, Scott Meredith to NM (28 June 1990).

p. 325 'If I don't deliver . . .' Letter, ACC to Stanley Kubrick (12 July 1984).

p. 326 'My Method acting, alas . . .' ACC, 'Egogram, 1984.' Letter to friends.

p. 326 'Ever since *Odyssey Two* . . .' Letter, ACC to Stanley Kubrick (12 July 1984).

p. 327 'As you doubtless know . . .' Video presentation, 'A Martian Odyssey'. Audio transcript (17 September 1984).

p. 329 'Mr Hyams and Mr Clarke . . .' Vincent Canby, *New York Times* (7 December 1984).

p. 331 'Assume that there's an unfriendly . . .' ACC, *1984: Spring* (New York: Ballantine Books, 1984, 55; London: Granada Publishing, 1984).

p. 333 'I realised that Bob . . .' ACC, 'Tribute to R.A.H.' (prepublication ms., 5 September 1990).

p. 334 'I did my best . . .' Letter, ACC to Ian Macauley (May 1985).

p. 335 'Dr Goddard persevered . . .' President Ronald Reagan, speech before the National Space Club (29 March 1985).

p. 335 'based on an engine . . .' Roger Caras, 'Our Man in the Future', *Science Digest* (March 1982), 58.

p. 337 'In view of the UK's . . .' ACC, 'Egogram 1985', newsy letter to friends.

p. 337 'All the hotels there . . .' Letter, ACC to Michael Craven (14 July 1985).

p. 338 'My publisher Judy-Lynn . . .' Letter, ACC to Michael Craven (30 October 1985).

p. 339 'As he's convinced . . .' ACC, '85 Update', newsy letter to friends.

p. 339 'I groaned inwardly . . .' ACC and Gentry Lee, *RAMA II* (New York: Bantam Books, 1989, v–vi; London: Victor Gollancz, 1989).

p. 341 'I realised that its next . . .' *Guardian* (9 August 1986).

p. 341 '*The Songs of Distant* . . .' Review, Ian Watson, 'Today', Thursday (3 July 1986).

p. 342 ff 'You're trying to pin me . . .' Interview, Ken Kelley for *Playboy* (August 1986), 57, 66 ff.

p. 343 'So the intervention . . .' ACC, *2010: Odyssey Two* (New York: Ballantine Books, 1982, 164; London: Granada Publishing, 1982).

p. 343 'He likes my personnel . . .' ACC, *The Ghost from the Grand Banks* (New York: Bantam Books, 1990, 126; London: Victor Gollancz, 1990).

p. 345 'Saw neuro-specialists . . .' ACC, 'Egogram '86', newsy letter to friends.

p. 345 'The only problem . . .' Letter, ACC to Roger Caras (20 October 1986).

p. 346 'To add insult . . .' ACC, 'Coauthors and Other Nuisances,' unpublished ms., received autumn 1990.

p. 346 'I'm now glad to say . . .' Letter, ACC to Charles N. Brown (6 October 1986).

p. 347 'Its loyalties and interests will transcend . . .' ACC, Speech, Nehru Memorial Address, New Delhi (13 November 1986).

p. 347 'Incredibly, the Taj Mahal . . .' ACC, 'Egogram 1986'.

Chapter 31

p. 349 'ten thousand words of ODYSSEY III . . .' Letter, ACC to Roger Caras (11 May 1987) and 'The situation is . . .' Ibid.

p. 350 'I'm looking forward . . .' Letter, Ted Turner to ACC (20 November 1987).

p. 351 'gave me his schedule . . .' ACC and Gentry Lee, *RAMA II* (New York: Bantam Books, 1989, viii; London, Victor Gollancz, 1989).

p. 352 'I still don't believe . . .' ACC, 'Egogram 1987', newsy letter to friends.

p. 352 'It was my privilege . . .' Letter, Cyril Ponnamperuma to ACC (16 December 1987), birthday greeting.

p. 353 'a distinctly posthumous sensation . . .' ACC, 'Egogram 1988', newsy letter to friends.

p. 354 'When is an Arthur C. Clarke novel . . .' Review, 'Bookends' (26 October 1988).

p. 354 'why Arthur C. Clarke . . .' Jonathan Coe, *Guardian* (22 July 1988).

p. 355 'The Clarke–Lee collaboration . . .' ACC, 'Coauthors and Other Nuisances,' unpublished ms., received autumn 1990.

p. 355 'A tiny bundle of fluff . . .' ACC, 'Egogram 1988', newsy letter to friends.

p. 357 ff 'Tonight: the time before time . . .' Transcript, 'God, the Universe and Everything Else', 25, 30, 31. Copy of transcript, July 1988.

p. 358 'I was somewhat unprepared . . .' Letter, Daniel Drachman, M.D. to NM (13 November 1990).

p. 359 'Arthur's immediate reaction . . .' Ibid. (13 November 1990).

p. 359 'The Johns Hopkins specialists . . .' ACC, 'Bulletin from Baltimore or: A Medical Odyssey' (August 1988).

Chapter 32

p. 361 'full of energy . . .' 'Bulletin from Baltimore', August 1988.

p. 362 'I'm sorry to say . . .' Letter, ACC to Willie Mendis (22 March 1989).

p. 364 'It must have been written . . .' Fax, ACC to NM (13 December 1990).

p. 365 'The contents deal almost . . .' Review, Isaac Asimov for *The Observer* (7 May 1989).

p. 365 'The word came directly . . .' Fax, ACC to NM (29 November 1990).

p. 368 'Clarke is a hard man . . .' Interview, Godfrey Smith/ACC, *Sunday Times* (22 October 1989).

p. 369 'I had a nice chat . . .' Fax, ACC to Scott Meredith Literary Agency (26 October 1989).

p. 370 ff 'apparently brand new . . .' ACC, 'Arabia Astronautica' (unpublished newsletter to friends), 1 ff.

p. 373 'Whether we become a multi-planet . . .' Transcript, Satellite Video Conference between Riyadh, New York City, Washington, DC, and Atlanta (November 1989), 24.

p. 373 'As it was already . . .' ACC, 'Arabia Astronautica', 1 ff.

p. 374 'more so Arthur who is . . .' Letter, Rodney Jonklaas to NM (6 April 1989).

p. 375 'Readers may welcome Clarke's . . .' Review, Gregory Feeley, 'Rama Redux', *Washington Post* (31 December 1989).

Chapter 33

p. 377 'a gross blunder . . .' *Tekhnika Molodezhy* (November 1989).

p. 377 'The last thing I'd intended . . .' Letter, ACC to Vasili Zacharchenko (January 1990).

p. 379 'I'm afraid all the best . . .' Letter, ACC to Willie Mendis (Summer 1989).

p. 380 'It was written as a reaction . . .' ACC, 'On Golden Seas' in *Tales from Planet Earth* (New York: Bantam, 1990, 299; London: Century Hutchinson, 1989).

p. 380 'It was a voyage of discovery . . .' ACC and Gregory Benford, *Beyond the Fall of Night* (New York: Ace/Putnam, 1990, xi; London: Victor Gollancz, 1991).

p. 381 'Though I can't be sure . . .' ACC, 'Satyajit and Stanley', unpublished ms. (1 September 1990), 1.

p. 382 'I have no idea . . .' Fax, ACC to NM (18 January 1991).

p. 382 'mainly technical wizards . . .' Review, John Sladek for the *Washington Post* (25 November 1990).

p. 382 'A British reviewer . . .' Review, Dan Chow for *Locus* (October 1990), 22.

p. 383 'sees the universe . . .' Jonas, *New York Times Book Review* (3 February 1991), 33.

p. 383 'Our tribute to you . . .' *Colombo Daily News* (17 December 1990), 12.

p. 383 'I used to say mankind . . .' Prepublication interview transcript (received June 1990), Bob Frost and ACC.

p. 384 'There's been a lot of talk . . .' Interview, Roger Caras and ACC for ABC's *20/20*, unpublished transcript (September 1981), 114.

p. 385 'any great literary ability . . .' Letter, ACC to Sam Youd (28 January 1938).

p. 385 'Clarke never loses his bearings . . .' Gregory Benford, 'Arthur C. Clarke: The Prophet Vindicated' in *Lan's Lantern*, No. 28 (1989), 4, 5.

p. 389 'In projecting our ideas . . .' Interview, Roger Caras and ACC for ABC's *20/20*, unpublished transcript (September 1981), 92.

p. 389 'One day we may be able . . .' ACC, *Profiles of the Future* (New York: Holt, Rinehart and Winston, 1984, 242; London: Victor Gollancz, 1962).

p. 390 'Not by 2001 . . .' Prepublication interview transcript (received June 1990), Bob Frost and ACC, last page.

p. 390 'This is the wild card . . .' ACC, *OMNI* (October 1989), 8.

p. 390 'because it's very lonely . . .' ACC, *Los Angeles Times* (1 December 1982), 15.

p. 391 'One of the great lessons . . .' ACC, 'Credo', prepublication ms., Opus 735 (30 July 1989), 4, 5, 10.

p. 391 'Actually, my motivation and aim . . .' Fax, ACC to NM (18 January 1991), 2.

Index

426